A Handbook for
Counseling International Students in the United States

Edited by

Hemla D. Singaravelu
Mark Pope

AMERICAN COUNSELING ASSOCIATION
5999 Stevenson Avenue
Alexandria, VA 22304
www.counseling.org

A Handbook for
Counseling
International Students
in the United States

10 9 8 7 6 5 4 3 2 1

American Counseling Association
5999 Stevenson Avenue
Alexandria, VA 22304
www.counseling.org

Director of Publications • Carolyn C. Baker

Production Manager • Bonny E. Gaston

Editorial Assistant • Catherine A. Brumley

Copy Editor • Elaine Dunn

Cover and text design • Bonny E. Gaston

Library of Congress Cataloging-in-Publication Data

A handbook for counseling international students in the United States / edited by
Hemla Singaravelu, Mark Pope.
    p. cm.
  ISBN-13: 978-1-55620-238-4 (alk. paper)
  ISBN-10: 1-55620-238-5 (alk. paper)
    1. Students, Foreign—Counseling of—United States—Handbooks, manuals, etc. 2.
Counseling in higher education—United States—Handbooks, manuals, etc. I.
Singaravelu, Hemla. II. Pope, Mark, 1952–

LB2376.4.H37 2007
378.1′ 940973—dc22   2006009719

Table of Contents

Part I
Difficulties Experienced by International Students

Part II
Characteristics of International Students From Around the World

Acknowledgments

It has been an honor to work with such a respected and diverse team of contributors. Thank you for your hard work and your passionate contributions. Our heartfelt gratitude goes to our families and many friends for their encouragement and support. We thank Carolyn Baker, Director of ACA Publications, for believing in this project and for her hard work, kindness, and patience.

Finally, we would like to dedicate this book to international students around the world: *May your quest for higher education be greeted with enthusiasm and your dreams fulfilled.*

—*Hemla D. Singaravelu and Mark Pope*

Preface

Hemla D. Singaravelu

For years, international education has flourished throughout the world and has provided individuals the opportunity to attain tertiary education. Individuals desiring to study abroad come from different parts of the world, represent various age groups, and may even sojourn to the new country with their spouses and children. In the United States, international students make up a notable portion of the student population in colleges and universities and are contributing members of U.S. society. In the year 2004, as many as 547,867 international students attended U.S. colleges and universities, bringing in more than $13.3 billion of non-U.S. funds in living expenses, tuition, and fees (Institute of International Education, 2005). Campus data from *Open Doors* (Institute of International Education, 2005) indicate that nearly 72% of all international students reported their primary source of funding coming from personal and family resources or other sources outside of the United States. Further, the Department of Commerce continues to rank U.S. higher education among the five largest service sector exports. Despite the benefits of international education, the United States has witnessed a steady decline in the number of international students. This phenomenon is attributable to the stringent security measures imposed by the U.S. government in reaction to the September 11, 2001, tragedy. This incident has compounded the problems already faced by international students in the United States, as illustrated in several chapters of this book.

Regardless of the decline in numbers, there remains a significant number of international students in the United States experiencing a variety of adjustment difficulties. International students' experiences tend to differ from the experiences of ethnic minorities in the country, in that immigration issues and the temporary nature of their stay in the United States can be a salient force in these students' lives. Labeled as nonresident aliens upon arrival, international students have encountered adjustment issues and alienation amid their excitement and pride in studying in the United States. Many face a multitude of challenges in addition to the high cost of a U.S. education. Some of these challenges include family expectations to succeed, living in unfamiliar surroundings, being immersed in a new culture and educational system (Cheng, Leong, & Geist, 1993; Dillard & Chisolm, 1983; Lin, 2000; Pedersen, 1991; Popadiuk & Arthur, 2004; Sandhu & Asrabadi, 1994; Thomas & Althen, 1989; Yeh & Inose, 2002), and language barriers (Cadieux & Wehrly, 1986; Lin, 2000; Mori, 2000; Rai, 2002; Roysircar, 2004; Yeh & Inose, 2002).

The obstacles faced by international students may have a compounding effect on adjustment and may result in academic failure. Although faced with this harsh reality, some international students tend not to seek out support services readily for fear of being culturally different and not being understood. For others, it is the stigma associated with counseling and the shame it will bring onto the family name (Aubrey, 1991; Brinson & Kottler, 1995; Kim, Atkinson, & Umemoto, 2001; Pederson, 1991; Sandhu, 1994; Uba, 1994; Wehrly, 1988; Zhang & Dixon, 2003). Customary ways of addressing or resolving problems may unexpectedly become unavailable to them in their new environment. These students may be referred to counseling services or may seek help on their own. It is imperative that helping professionals be cognizant of the issues faced by international students and culturally competent to provide services to this unique population.

The American Counseling Association (2005) and the American Psychological Association (2002) have made concerted efforts to promote and implement multicultural competencies in counselor trainees, counselors (Pope-Davis & Coleman, 1996), and psychologists. However, training programs may not have extended these competencies to include working with international students; hence, these counseling professionals and trainees may not be equipped to work with such a diverse student population (Fouad, 1991). Perhaps this lack of focus and knowledge could be due to the scarcity of information and research on the international student population. With the above reasons in mind, counseling professionals and counselor trainees, particularly in university counseling centers, need to increase their knowledge base and repertoire of skills to better serve this population.

Our hope is that this book will provide counseling professionals an image of what it is like to be an international student in unfamiliar surroundings, identify some psychosocial and systemic difficulties they typically encounter, and recommend approaches to attend to their needs. This book can serve as a resource for (a) counselors and psychologists who provide counseling services to international students; (b) counselor trainees who are learning about working with diverse populations; (c) counseling professionals, educators, and psychologists who conduct research on diverse populations, particularly the international students; and (d) international student advisors. Hence, helping professionals and trainees will get a glimpse into the lives of international students from the time they prepare to qualify for a student visa to the time they graduate and seek practical training in the United States or return home. We believe the strength of this book lies in its comprehensiveness and in the unique contributions of the chapter authors, many of whom originate from different parts of the world.

This book is divided into three parts. The first part provides general information about the experiences and some issues encountered by international students. Topics addressed in this first part include the following: immigration; adjustment and acculturation; career development and decision making; students with disabilities; gay, lesbian, bisexual, and questioning students; students with families; and issues related to returning home. The second part of this book addresses unique characteristics of international students from various parts of the world and offers suggestions on how to work with these groups. While describing these characteristics, the authors have emphasized the uniqueness of each individual and within-group differences. The third part of the book focuses on competency and theoretical, practical, and outreach approaches to working with this population.

Readers are cautioned to be aware of variables that seem extraneous affecting international students' levels of adjustment. These variables include students originating from English-speaking countries versus non-English-speaking countries, students from collectivistic versus individualistic countries, and students from countries experiencing civil unrest or governmental changes versus students from politically stable countries. While reading the second part of the book about students from different continents, it is important that readers recognize the complexity and differences inherent in each country within each continent in terms of language, culture, colonialization effect, education systems, and socio-political-economic status and development.

References

American Counseling Association. (2005). *ACA code of ethics*. Alexandria, VA: Author.

American Psychological Association. (2002). Ethical principles of psychologists and code of conduct. *American Psychologist, 57,* 1060–1073.

Aubrey, R. (1991). International students on campus: A challenge for counselors, medical providers, and clinicians. *Smith College Studies in Social Work, 62,* 20–33.

Brinson, J. A., & Kottler, J. (1995). International students in counseling: Some alternative models. *Journal of College Student Psychotherapy, 9,* 57–70.

Cadieux, R. A. J., & Wehrly, B. (1986). Advising and counseling the international student. *New Directions for Student Services, 36,* 51–63.

Cheng, D., Leong, F. L., & Geist, R. (1993). Cultural differences in psychological distress between Asian and Caucasian American college students. *Journal of Multicultural Counseling and Development, 21,* 182–190.

Dillard, J. M., & Chisolm, G. B. (1985). Counseling the international student in a multicultural context. *Journal of College Student Development, 24,* 101–105.

Fouad, N. A. (1991). Training counselors to counsel international students: Are we ready? *The Counseling Psychologist, 19,* 66–71.

Institute of International Education. (2005). *Open doors: 2005, Report on international educational exchange*. New York: Author.

Kim, B. S. K., Atkinson, D. R., & Umemoto, D. (2001). Asian cultural values and counseling process: Current knowledge and directions for future research. *The Counseling Psychologist, 29,* 570–603.

Lin, J. -C. G. (2000). College counseling and international students. In D. C. Davis & K. M. Humphrey (Eds.), *College counseling: Issues and strategies for a new millennium* (pp. 159–183). Alexandria, VA: American Counseling Association.

Mori, S. (2000). Addressing the mental health concerns of international students. *Journal of Counseling & Development, 78*, 137-144.

Pedersen, P. B. (1991). Counseling international students. *The Counseling Psychologist, 19*, 10-58.

Popadiuk, N., & Arthur, N. (2004). Counseling international students in Canadian schools. *International Journal for the Advancement of Counselling, 26*, 125-145.

Pope-Davis, D. B., & Coleman, H. L. K. (Eds.). (1996). *Multicultural counseling competencies: Assessment, education, and training, and supervision.* Thousand Oaks: CA: Sage.

Rai, G. (2002). Meeting the educational needs of international students: A perspective from US schools. *International Social Work, 45*, 21-33.

Roysircar, G. (2004). Counseling and psychotherapy for acculturation and ethnic identity concerns with immigrant and international students. In T. Smith (Ed.), *Practicing multiculturalism* (pp. 255-275). Boston: Allyn & Bacon.

Sandhu, D. S. (1994). An examination of the psychological needs of the international students: Implications for counseling and psychotherapy. *International Journal for the Advancement of Counseling, 17*, 229-239.

Sandhu, D. S., & Asrabadi, B. R. (1994). Development of an acculturative stress scale for international students: Preliminary findings. *Psychological Reports, 75*, 435-448.

Thomas, K., & Althen, G. (1989). Counseling foreign students. In P. B. Pedersen, J. G. Draguns, W. J. Lonner, & J. E. Trimble (Eds.), *Counseling across cultures* (3rd ed., pp. 205-241). Thousand Oaks, CA: Sage.

Uba, L. (1994). Culture shock and adaptation. *Journal of Counseling & Development, 73*, 121-126.

Wehrly, B. (1988). Cultural diversity from an international perspective. *Journal of Multicultural Counseling and Development, 16*, 7-15.

Yeh, C. J., & Inose, M. (2002). Difficulties and coping strategies of Chinese, Japanese, and Korean immigrant students. *Adolescence, 37*, 69-82.

Zhang, N., & Dixon, D. N. (2003). Acculturation and attitudes of Asian international students toward seeking psychological help. *Journal of Multicultural Counseling and Development, 31*, 205-222.

About the Editors

Hemla D. Singaravelu, PhD, is a licensed professional counselor and associate professor in the Department of Counseling and Family Therapy at Saint Louis University (SLU). She was the cochair and director of SLU's master's program. Prior to teaching at SLU, she served as an assistant professor at Southwest Missouri State University and as coordinator of career and mentor programs at Fitchburg State College in Fitchburg, Massachusetts. She received her doctorate in educational psychology–counselor education from Southern Illinois University at Carbondale, specializing in career development and multicultural/diversity counseling. She has published and presented in the areas of multicultural counseling issues, career development of diverse populations, and international students. She is currently on the editorial boards of the *Journal of Counseling & Development* and *The Career Development Quarterly*. She was born and raised in Malaysia and came to the United States as an international student.

Mark Pope, EdD, is a professor and chair of the Division of Counseling and Family Therapy at the University of Missouri—Saint Louis. He is a past president of the American Counseling Association (ACA) and the National Career Development Association and has served as the editor of *The Career Development Quarterly*. He is a fellow of the ACA, National Career Development Association, American Psychological Association, Society of Counseling Psychology, Society for the Psychological Study of Ethnic Minority Issues, and Society for the Psychological Study of Lesbian, Gay, and Bisexual Issues. He has written extensively on career counseling and cross-cultural and multicultural issues in counseling. He chaired the International Network of the Association for Counselor Education and Supervision and has presented at various international counseling conferences, including at the Third International Counseling Conference (Singapore), Fifth International Counseling Conference (Hong Kong), and Sixth International Counseling Conference (Beijing). He has lectured at the University of Hong Kong and National Institute of Education in Singapore and provided consulting services to businesses and schools throughout Asia. He was invited to keynote the International Vocational Technical Conference in China and the National Association of Graduate Careers Advisory

Services Conference in Australia, and he was appointed as a representative of the United States for the International Symposium on Career Development and Public Policy held in Ottawa, Canada; Vancouver, Canada; and Sydney, Australia. He is also the founder and editor of *Global Career Resources,* the international newsletter for career counseling and organization development, and he has been appointed a fellow and research associate at the Center for International Studies at the University of Missouri—Saint Louis.

About the Contributors

Nancy Arthur, PhD, is a professor in the Division of Applied Psychology and a Canada Research Chair in professional education at the University of Calgary, Calgary, Alberta, Canada. Her research and teaching interests focus on multicultural counseling and career development. She authored the book, *Counseling International Students: Clients From Around the World,* and her coedited book, *Culture-Infused Counselling: Celebrating the Canadian Mosaic,* received the Canadian Counselling Association Book Award for 2006. She is currently coediting a book with Paul B. Pedersen about counseling for international transitions, in collaboration with authors from 12 different countries.

Alexander Chang, MS, is the senior international student advisor in the Office of International Programs at San Francisco State University.

Mary M. Chittooran, PhD, is a school psychologist and chair of the Department of Educational Studies at Saint Louis University. She teaches courses in multicultural issues, ethics, assessment, and educational psychology, and her primary research interests include diversity, urban poverty, and ethical decision making. Her degrees are in educational psychology and special education, and she has worked in public schools, hospitals, and clinics with populations ranging in age from birth to adulthood. She is associate editor of *School Psychology Quarterly* and is on the editorial boards of *School Psychology Review* and the *Communiqué.* She is a native of India and completed three degrees and raised two children while an international student in the United States.

Madonna G. Constantine, PhD, is a professor of psychology and education in the Department of Counseling and Clinical Psychology at Teachers College, Columbia University. She received her doctorate in counseling psychology from the University of Memphis and completed bachelor's and master's degrees from Xavier University of New Orleans. She is a highly esteemed researcher in the areas of Black psychology and multicultural counseling. The scope of her work includes exploring the psychological, educational, and vocational issues of African Americans; developing models of cross-cultural competence in counseling, training, and supervision; and examining the intersections of variables such as race and ethnicity in relation to mental health and educational processes and outcomes. She is currently involved on several editorial boards in her field and serves in various leadership capacities in counseling and psychological associations in the United States.

Robert K. Conyne, PhD, is a professor and director of the counseling program at the University of Cincinnati. He is licensed as a clinical counselor and a psychologist and has been elected as a fellow of several professional organizations. He has published extensively in the area of group work with several books and nearly 300 scholarly articles and presentations, and he has delivered and studied the application of group work with Chinese populations.

Carla Coppi, MFA, is the associate director of international programs and services at Southern Illinois University Carbondale (SIUC). She has worked in international education since 1982 when a temporary position as financial clearance officer evolved into a graduate assistantship to fund her master's program in music. Ultimately, the lure of the operatic stage could not pull her from her southern Illinois home, and she decided to remain in Carbondale to further her career in international student services. She is regarded as the regional expert in matters relating to immigration compliance for international students, faculty, and staff. A frequent presenter at NAFSA: Association of International Educators conferences, her sessions have been named "Best of Region" on two occasions, resulting in placement on the national conference schedule in 1994 and 1996. Over the past two decades, she has coauthored numerous grant proposals resulting in professional and financial enrichment for SIUC's international student population. Of particular note are the BEEP/REEP grants of the early 1990s that provided funding to students from former communist countries transitioning to market economies. Other funded projects include programs addressing domestic violence within the international student community and a collaborative effort that partnered SIUC with the Carbondale Rotary Club.

Edward A. Delgado-Romero, PhD, is an associate professor of counseling psychology in the Department of Counseling and Human Development Services at The University of Georgia. He received a BA degree in psychology from Rhodes College in Memphis, Tennessee, in 1988, and an MA (1995) and PhD (1997) in counseling psychology from the University of Notre Dame. He was an intern at Michigan State University during 1996–1997. He was a clinical assistant professor at the University of Florida from 1997 to 2002 before joining the faculty at Indiana University in counseling and counseling psychology from 2002 to 2005. He has held several national professional leadership positions, and his research interests are in multicultural psychology, Latino/Latina psychology, race and ethnicity, faculty-of-color retention, the preparation of international student counselors, and multicultural competence.

Mary Beth Engel, MA, was a graduate assistant in the Department of Counseling and Family Therapy at Saint Louis University.

Nadya A. Fouad, PhD, is a professor in the Department of Educational Psychology at the University of Wisconsin—Milwaukee (UWM) and training director of the counseling psychology program there. She chaired the UWM Task Force on Climate for Women and chaired the American Psychological

Association's (APA) Task Force for Women in Academe. She is the chair of the APA's Board of Educational Affairs. She was recipient in 2003 of the John Holland Award for Outstanding Achievement in Career and Personality Research. She is editor-elect of *The Counseling Psychologist* and was president of APA Division 17 (Counseling Psychology) from 2000 to 2001, and is currently co-vice president for communications. She is chair of the Council of Counseling Psychology Training Programs. She serves on the editorial boards of the *Journal of Counseling Psychology, Journal of Vocational Behavior, The Career Development Quarterly,* and the *Journal of Career Assessment.* She has published articles and chapters on cross-cultural vocational assessment, career development of women and racial/ethnic minorities, interest measurement, cross-cultural counseling, and race and ethnicity. She has served as cochair (with Patricia Arredondo) of the writing team for the Multicultural Guidelines on Education, Training, Practice, Research, and Organizational Change, which were approved by the APA in August 2002 and published in *American Psychologist* in May 2003.

Mary A. Fukuyama received her PhD from Washington State University and has worked at the University of Florida Counseling Center for the past 24 years as a counseling psychologist, supervisor, and trainer. She is a clinical professor and teaches courses on spirituality and multicultural counseling for the Department of Counselor Education and also the counseling psychology program. She coauthored with Todd Sevig a book titled *Integrating Spirituality Into Multicultural Counseling* (New York: Sage). She was recently recognized as a fellow by APA's Division 17 (Counseling Psychology). Her practice specialties include working with university students from a developmental perspective, multicultural counseling, and training. She is an active member of the University of Florida's Center for Spirituality and Health, and her research interests include conducting a qualitative study on "multicultural expressions" of spirituality.

Dale S. Furbish, EdD, is a senior lecturer and program leader for the Master of Career Development and the Graduate Diploma in Career at Auckland University of Technology, Auckland, New Zealand. He is a native of the United States. He worked in U.S. higher education counseling centers for 20 years before immigrating to New Zealand with his wife Joan in 1996. Lifestyle, professional opportunities, and incomparable natural beauty were major influences on his decision to relocate to New Zealand. He is active in the Career Practitioner Association of New Zealand and has served as its president for two terms. He is interested in professional issues for New Zealand career counseling and has written a number of articles on this topic. He is also interested in international standards for career counseling and the impact of sabbaticals on career development.

Caroline G. Henry, MS, is a doctoral candidate in the counseling psychology program at the University of Wisconsin—Milwaukee. Her research interests include career counseling, multicultural issues, and identity development. She is the 2005 recipient of the National Career Development Association

Graduate Student Research Award. She has published articles and chapters on cross-cultural career counseling, career services for college students, and the career counseling process. She has worked in university counseling centers at the University of Wisconsin—Milwaukee, Marquette University, and Northwestern University.

Farah A. Ibrahim, PhD, is a professor in the Division of Counseling Psychology and Counselor Education at the University of Colorado at Denver and Health Sciences Center. She is a fellow of the APA and a licensed psychologist. She is past president of Counselors for Social Justice (2002–2003). She is a nationally and internationally renowned scholar on cultural issues in counseling and psychotherapy. She has published in the areas of culture, counseling, South Asian women's issues, South Asian identity, and curriculum development with cultural competencies, and she is the author of the Scale to Assess World View© (with Harris Kahn) and the Cultural Identity Check List©. She has led workshops and done presentations on empowering women, children, and adults both from underrepresented and mainstream populations.

Michael Anthony Ingram, EdD, is an associate professor in the Department of Teacher and Counselor Education at Oregon State University, Corvallis. He is also a visiting professor in the School of Professional Studies in Business and Education at Johns Hopkins University. His areas of research include clinical supervision, self-efficacy through sociocultural poetry, career counseling, and multicultural counseling.

Gina Insalaco, MA, was a graduate assistant in the Department of Counseling and Family Therapy at Saint Louis University.

Laura R. Johnson, PhD, is an assistant professor of psychology at the University of Mississippi, where she pursues research and clinical interests in multicultural, cross-cultural, and ethnocultural psychology. She is a cofounder of the Intercultural Connections project, a project designed to assess international student concerns at the University of Mississippi and to design culturally competent services to meet their needs. She cosupervises an international student conversation group and international women's support group. She is a former Fulbright scholar, Peace Corps volunteer, and international student.

Kristi Kennon is a graduate assistant in the Department of Counseling and Family Therapy at Saint Louis University.

Supavan Khamphakdy-Brown, MA, is a doctoral candidate in counseling psychology and counselor education at the University of Missouri, Kansas City. She was born in Laos and entered the United States as a refugee in 1980. Her research interests include the mental health of refugees, immigrants, and international students, as well as multicultural supervision. She is currently on internship at Kansas State University Counseling Services.

S. Alvin Leung, PhD, is a professor in the Department of Educational Psychology, The Chinese University of Hong Kong. He received his PhD in counseling psychology from the University of Illinois at Urbana-Champaign in 1988 and served as a faculty member in the counseling psychology programs at the University of Nebraska—Lincoln (1988-1991) and the University of Houston

(1991–1996). He was associate editor of *The Counseling Psychologist* and is currently editor of *Asian Journal of Counselling*. He is a fellow of the APA and Hong Kong Professional Counselling Association. His major areas of research and teaching are career development and assessment across the life span, counseling students with diverse psychological and learning-related concerns, multicultural and cross-cultural issues in counseling, and counselor training and supervision.

Shu-Ping Lin, PhD, is an assistant professor in the Department of Psychology at the University of Alaska, Fairbanks. She received her undergraduate and master's degrees in Taiwan. In summer 2006, she earned her PhD from the Ohio State University after her internship at the University of Maryland. As an individual who is proud of her international background, she is passionate about enhancing the well-being of international students in professional and personal situations. Her dissertation in investigating and declaring the strengths of international students was a recipient of the "Award of Excellence" from the APA Division 52 in 2005. Born in Mazu, a small island between Taiwan and China governed by Taiwan, she is the first female in her hometown who has earned a PhD. With the spirit of pioneering, she is launching her career and is urging for the well-being of people of diversity.

Margaretha S. Lucas, PhD, born and raised in Holland, is a staff psychologist at the Counseling Center and an associate professor in the Department of Counseling and Personnel Services at the University of Maryland. Her research has focused on psychological aspects of university students' career decision making and identity processes, as well as evaluations of services for university counseling center clients.

Stacie Murray, MA, is a graduate assistant and a doctoral student in the Department of Counseling and Family Therapy at Saint Louis University.

Johanna E. Nilsson, PhD, born and raised in Sweden, is an associate professor in the Division of Counseling and Educational Psychology at the University of Missouri—Kansas City. Her research interests focus on mental health and adjustment in international populations (international students, refugees, and immigrants), social advocacy, and supervision.

Barbara J. Palombi earned her PhD in counseling psychology from Michigan State University. She is a licensed psychologist and currently the director of the Counseling and Career Development Center at Grand Valley State University in Michigan. Her research and writing interests include the multicultural aspects of disability, college/university counseling, psychological wellness, and professional development in the fields of psychology and student affairs.

Paul B. Pedersen, PhD, is a visiting professor in the Department of Psychology at the University of Hawaii. He has taught at the University of Minnesota, Syracuse University, University of Alabama at Birmingham, and for 6 years at universities in Taiwan, Malaysia, and Indonesia. He was also on the summer school faculty at Harvard University in 1984–1988 and the University of Pittsburgh–Semester at Sea voyage around the world in spring 1992. His international experience includes numerous consulting experiences in Asia, Australia, Africa, South America, and Europe. He has authored, coauthored, or edited 40 books, 99 articles, and 72 chapters on aspects of multicultural counseling and international communication. He is a fellow in Divisions 9, 17, 45, and 52 of the APA. Research activities include codirecting research for a 10-day intercultural communication laboratory for 60 Japanese and U.S. intercultural communication experts at Nihonmatsu, Japan, funded by the Lily Foundation; reentry research among LASPAU students from Brazil; a National Science Foundation 6-year grant to study the reentry adjustment of engineers returning to Taiwan after study abroad; a National Institute of Education grant to develop a measure of cross-cultural counseling skill; a 2-year Harvard Institute for International Development project in Indonesia to evaluate and upgrade training at Bank Rakyat Training Centers; and an Asian Foundation grant to co-organize a conference in Penang, Malaysia, on constructive conflict management in a cultural context. Professional activities include 3 years' presidency of the Society for Intercultural Education Training and Research; senior editor of the Multicultural Aspects of Counseling (MAC) Series (Sage); advising editor for the Education and the Psychology book series (Greenwood Press); board member of The Micronesian Institute headquartered in Washington, DC; external examiner in psychology for Universiti Putra Malaysia, University Kebangsaan, and Universiti Malaysia Sabah; senior Fulbright scholar teaching at National Taiwan University 1999–2000; and member of the Committee for International Relations in Psychology at the APA 2001–2003.

Tanya I. Razzhavaikina received her MA in psychology from Moscow State University, Moscow, Russia. In 2001 she left her country, Belarus, to study in the United States. She is currently a doctoral candidate in counseling psychology at the University of Nebraska—Lincoln. Her research interests include immigrant and refugee mental health, counseling process, family and couples therapy, and cross-cultural differences.

Samuel Sanabria, PhD, is an assistant professor in the School of Professional Psychology and Behavioral Sciences' Counseling Department at Argosy University, Sarasota, Florida. He received his master's and doctorate degrees in mental health counseling from the University of Florida. He has worked in numerous counseling settings, including private and government-funded agencies. He currently has a private counseling practice in which he works with sexual and ethnic minorities. His teaching and research interests include human sexuality and diversity issues in counseling. He is also an active member of several professional organizations, including the American Counseling Association (ACA), the Association for Counselor Education and Supervision, the Association for Multicultural Counseling and Development (AMCD), and the Association of Gay, Lesbian, and Bisexual Issues in Counseling. He is currently the cochair of ACA's Ethics Committee.

Daya Singh Sandhu, EdD, NCC, NCSC, NCCC, is professor and chair of the Department of Educational and Counseling Psychology at the University of

Louisville in Kentucky. He has authored or edited several books, numerous book chapters, and more than 50 articles in refereed journals. He was honored as one of the 12 pioneers in multicultural counseling. Sage published his autobiographical account in 2001 in the *Handbook of Multicultural Counseling* (2nd ed.). He is the recipient of the President's Distinguished Faculty Award at University of Louisville, Alumnus of the Year Award (2001) at Mississippi State University, Multicultural Teaching Award at the University of Louisville (2000), and AMCD Multicultural Research Award (2000). In 2001, he received the Fulbright Research Award to India to conduct cross-cultural studies on depression. He served as the chair of ACA's Research and Knowledge Committee from 2000 to 2002. He also represented AMCD on the Council for Accreditation of Counseling and Related Educational Programs' executive board of directors from 1996 to 2001.

Anita Sankar-Gomes, PhD, is an assistant professor in the Department of Counseling, School, and Educational Psychology at the State University of New York, Buffalo. She is a native of Singapore and came to the United States as an international student to pursue a master's in school counseling and a doctorate in counselor education from the University of Iowa. She has taught a wide range of counseling courses, including multicultural counseling and practicum in school counseling. Her research interests are cross-cultural differences in adolescent development, diversity issues in schools, and adjustment and acculturation issues of children of immigrant populations in the United States.

Hung-Bin Sheu is a doctoral candidate in the counseling psychology program at the University of Maryland, College Park (UMCP). He received his first master's degree in counseling from the National Taiwan Normal University, Taipei, Taiwan in 1997, and another two master's degrees in related areas from the UMCP in 2005. In Taiwan, he had served as a counselor for 2 years at college settings and 1 year as a project consultant in the business setting. Since 2002, he has worked at the UMCP Counseling Center as a counselor-in-training. His research interests include issues related to multicultural counseling and training, subjective well-being, and career development. He has presented several papers regarding career development, multicultural training, and help-seeking attitudes at national and international conferences.

Christopher Sullivan, MEd, MA, is an assistant director in the Center for International Studies and a doctoral student in the Division of Counseling and Family Therapy, both at the University of Missouri—St. Louis. His areas of interest include the impact of culture on individual and family therapy with a special focus on cultural transitions, accommodations, and adaptations.

Maria Sveinsdottir, MEd, was born and raised in Iceland but has lived in the United States for the past 12 years. She received a BA in Icelandic language and literature from the University of Iceland in 1990 and an MEd in counseling from the University of Missouri—St. Louis in 2001. She is currently a PhD candidate at the University of Missouri—St. Louis, Department of Education, in the division of counseling and family therapy.

Laurie A. Walker, MA, is a licensed professional counselor and National Certified Counselor, as well as a member of several professional organizations. She is a doctoral student in the field of community counseling at the University of Cincinnati and a contract therapist for a local community mental health clinic. She is established as a facilitator of group work and was involved with the application of group work with Chinese populations as the result of a cross-cultural study.

Anika K. Warren, PhD, is a director in research at a New York–based nonprofit organization and a part-time adjunct professor at Teachers College, Columbia University. Dr. Warren specializes in multicultural training and counseling, diversity consulting, people-of-color issues, gender dynamics and issues, work-life effectiveness, career counseling and coaching, inclusive strategies, and performance management issues. Prior to joining the nonprofit organization, Dr. Warren was a full-time adjunct professor at Teachers College, Columbia University, in the Counseling Psychology program. She also was a consultant to telecommunication and financial service companies, provided career coaching, and published research articles and book chapters on issues related to diversity and inclusion. Dr. Warren has given numerous talks, workshops, and lectures and has served as an educator, consultant, and counselor to several Fortune 500 companies, universities, nonprofit organizations, government agencies, and community health organizations. She has also developed two multicultural career counseling training videos, distributed by Microtraining Associates. Prior to graduate school, Dr. Warren worked as a financial analyst at the Gap and Charles Schwab and was involved in recruitment and career development efforts at both companies. She received her BBA in finance from Howard University, earned her MA and MEd in psychological counseling at Columbia University, focusing on organizational and cultural psychology, and completed her PhD in counseling psychology at Boston College.

Oksana Yakushko, PhD, is an assistant professor at the University of Nebraska—Lincoln's counseling psychology program. Her areas of clinical and research interests are immigrant and refugee mental health and well-being, gender and sexuality, and cross-cultural differences. She came to the United States as an international student from Ukraine, and her own experiences have continued to motivate her passion for helping international students adjust to and thrive in their host environments.

Part I

Difficulties Experienced
by International Students

Chapter 1

The Changing Landscape of International Student Advisement: Balancing Bureaucracy With Student Advocacy

Carla Coppi

I have often compared my position of international student advisor to a circus tightrope artist, constantly balancing between adherence to the immigration laws and concern for students' welfare. Leaning too far in one direction encourages me to become a government bureaucrat, while veering too far in the other direction endangers the student's ability to remain legally in the country. This chapter outlines the obstacles international students must overcome to be allowed to further their educational dreams in the United States. It also provides an overview of the immigration rules and regulations that they must follow once they arrive. Finally, I hope the chapter will supply useful suggestions for counseling staff unfamiliar with the nuances of international student advisement. The chapter includes many of my personal anecdotes and opinions that have developed over three decades of serving international students and collaborating with professional colleagues in the field of international education for over 25 years.

The United States is primarily a nation of immigrants, settled by rugged individualists searching for freedom from persecution and improved quality of life. These values have defined the country's youthful existence and shaped government policies for over two centuries. It has not been uncommon, however, for immigration trends to mirror global politics. The encouraged influx of immigrants witnessed at the turn of the 20th century became politically problematic during the economic depression of the 1930s, accelerating plans to closely monitor the number of visitors permitted to remain permanently in the country. The effects of World War II, strained relationships with former allies, concerns for the citizen workforce, and fluctuations within the U.S. economy all became major influences on the development of immigration policy.

The Immigration and Nationality Act (INA) of 1952 revised the immigration laws penned at the turn of the century, creating a quota system based on job skills (Title 8 of the United States Code). The following five decades have included numerous updates to the act. In the late 1990s, technology companies became the major proponents of increasing the number of visas issued to foreign workers, whereas blue-collar America was troubled by the notion of international employees replacing U.S. workers.

In the 2002 edition of *Open Doors*, the annual statistical analysis of international student enrollment prepared by the Institute of International Education, enrollments figures were the highest since 1981 (Koh, 2002). Multiculturalists praised their global counterparts' presence on campus, whereas others worried that classroom quotas and shrinking financial aid dollars were being wasted on foreign visitors. Election campaigns identified the advantages or disadvantages of immigration reform, depending on the politician's platform. It became impossible to watch the evening news or read a daily periodical without encountering an article addressing the issues. The final decade of the century that had been lit by the torch of the Statue of Liberty ended with clearly divergent opinions as to the future direction of immigration in the United States.

Conversely, the new millennium saw modest economic prosperity that embraced international workers and celebrated their intellectual contributions. The anti-immigration rhetoric had not completely disappeared but had declined significantly. Even the most conservative politicians agreed that the United States could once again open its doors to the world. Sadly, no one could imagine the tragedy looming on the horizon that would alter the course of immigration history and, indirectly, international education for many years to come.

Regulations and Obstacles to Studying Abroad

The "post-9/11 years" have proved to be particularly challenging for professionals working in the field of international advisement. In the past, advisors believed that they possessed flexibility to interpret immigration regulations with a modicum of latitude and to make important judgment calls depending on the student's individual situation and the practice advisories issued by the National Association of Foreign Student Affairs (NAFSA) to assist with such interpretations. Today, efforts to thwart terrorist activity have changed the lives of international students as they pursue their academic endeavors in the United States.

It is absolutely essential that counselors consider the current political environment and its effect on international students when providing counseling to those in need. Despite personal politics or cultural bias, the counselor must understand, and be accepting of, governmental restrictions placed on the international student population to refrain from compounding problems as they arise. Being sensitive to the numerous obstacles students have overcome just to be able to embark on the trip to the United States to begin their studies may help university personnel to understand the tenacity international students exhibit once they arrive. It is also important to understand that governmental roadblocks may have influenced international students' impressions of the United States. To understand their emotional psyche upon arrival, a counselor must be aware of the lengthy admission and visa issuance process that students have already encountered.

I often marvel at the courage a young foreign student exhibits when deciding to study abroad, far away from family and friends. The hurdles that they must overcome to be admitted to the university are many. The Code of Federal Regulations is the annual update of the INA and specifies all of the guidelines for admission, in addition to the regulations that will govern the students throughout the duration of their studies ("Aliens and Nationality," 2004). Scholarly excellence is but one requirement. English language proficiency must be proven via standardized testing (Test of English as a Foreign Language) administered at sites that are often thousands of miles away from home. Computerized exams have become more common, but in remote areas of the world it is not out of the ordinary for prospective students to travel for days by train to sit for the test. Financial solvency is also required and must be verified by a sponsor's bank statement or other monetary documentation claiming responsibility for the prospective student. Only after careful review of the scholar's academic record, English proficiency, and monetary stability can a U.S. school offer admission.

Once admitted, the student must visit a U.S. embassy or consulate in their home country to secure a visa. Under the governance of the State Department, the visa issuance criteria are also clearly defined ("Foreign Relations," 2004). The visa interview must be scheduled well in advance of the commencement of study, with a waiting period of 3 months quite common. During the interview, the students must convince a consular officer that they can succeed in a university abroad and that they have no intention of remaining in the United States after they have completed their education. This is a most difficult point to prove, and students are often denied visas if the officer feels that they will not return to their homeland, and therefore, many students' educational dreams end because of the subjective whims of the consulate officer. The heightened level of scrutiny imposed on prospective students during the interview will certainly affect their future perceptions as to just how welcoming the United States will be during their studies.

If granted an F-1 or J-1 visa, students can travel to the United States, present documentation at the airport for one final review by port of entry officials, and be allowed to enter the country for travel to their new university (see the Appendix for description of classifications of visas). Once in the country, new students must adhere to a variety of rules and regulations that do not apply to the domestic population. The U.S. government has placed additional requirements and restrictions on international students for decades, and it is incorrect to assume that the events of recent years were the impetus for these restrictions. Students must enroll for a minimum of 12 hours each semester, limit their on-campus employment to no more than 20 hours per week, and refrain from off-campus employment without special permission (CFR Title 8, update 2003). The Immigration Service, now formally called United States Immigration and Citizenship Services, looms large in the lives of international students, complicating an already stressful existence, thousands of miles away from home, in a culture and language that is not their own.

Student and Exchange Visitor Information System

Though numbering nearly one-half million (Koh, 2002), international students were but a small segment of the total number of visitors who arrived in the United States each year. Regarded important to the economy and cultural diversity, their presence was somewhat unremarkable. However, the 1993 World Trade Center bombing became the flashpoint for the development of the student reform legislation that exists today. The individual who drove the bomb-laden van into the garage at the World Trade Center was said to be an out-of-status foreign student who had remained in the United States beyond the expiration date of his visa. The reaction from the U.S. government was the creation of a tracking program designed to monitor international students' arrival, enrollment, graduation, and departure (Meisner, 2002). Launched in 1997 at 20 different universities throughout the Southeast, a pilot program tested the project's effectiveness and accuracy. After 2 years of experimentation, it was sent back to the drawing board for major revisions, and the entire project seemed destined to quietly fade away until the fateful morning of September 11, 2001.

Within weeks, the program was resurrected bearing the name Student and Exchange Visitor Information System (SEVIS) and earmarked for implementation at every university enrolling international students by January 30, 2003 (8 CFR 214). The system was designed to link several different agencies composing the Department of Homeland Security, giving each access to students' files. Updates would be required on students each semester, including any violation of status that might have occurred. Academic advisors became concerned that their roles would change from confidant to policeman, straining relationships that had been forged despite cultural and language barriers. Policy implementation has posed numerous challenges to universities struggling with budgetary and technological limitations in the face of unfunded government mandates. Most important, SEVIS has created upheaval within student affairs personnel as they grappled with the ethical dilemmas that developed as the result of the new reporting requirements.

SEVIS has been operational for nearly 3 years, and despite initial concerns, it has been surprisingly user-friendly, providing streamlined interviews at embassies and shorter reviews of paperwork at airports (Connell, 2005). Documents can be authenticated by logging onto the Internet, thus reducing the time needed for verification. Numerous features pertaining to a particular student are available in an instant, including enrollment histories and employment authorizations. Those who navigate SEVIS with regularity have reversed their original opinions as to its usefulness. However, the implementation of the tracking system has influenced the global perception that the United States is an inhospitable location for study abroad.

Visa Interviews

Additional obstacles influencing students' decisions to study in the United States stem from problems occurring at embassies and consulates in their homelands.

Visa interviews must be arranged months in advance and are to include face-to-face interviews with visa officers. Prior to August 2003, it was rumored that less than half of all visa interviews were actually conducted at the embassy with a visa officer. Requiring face-to-face interviews initially created huge backlogs and what was once achieved in a few weeks took up to half a year or more; however, improvements have been made in the interview process since 2005, thus speeding up the process. Compounding the delays are extensive background checks imposed on certain individuals from particular countries, especially those in the Middle East. Additional investigations are conducted if a student wishes to study or conduct research in certain sensitive scientific and technological programs, such as nuclear engineering or water treatment management. Finally, after much scrutiny, the student is issued a visa and can begin the journey to the United States. Counselors must have a rudimentary understanding of the entire prearrival process to appreciate the perseverance prospective students must exhibit to study abroad.

Counseling Implications

The most challenging moments of an international student's sojourn to the United States will likely occur during the first hours or days in his or her new surroundings. Confusion and self-doubt may quickly replace the excitement experienced during months of planning for the trip. Culture shock will inevitably occur. Every effort must be made by the host institution and the surrounding community to help the new student feel comfortable, safe, and welcomed during this potentially troubling period of adjustment. Institutions hosting large numbers of international students will often staff a central office of international student affairs to foster their academic, cultural, and social development. In addition, this office will be the official liaison with the immigration authorities and the informational clearinghouse for the enforcement of the numerous regulations stated earlier. As student difficulties often stem from financial duress, the international student office provides advice regarding campus employment, work permits, and other forms of financial aid that might be available to the students. It is essential for counseling centers to build a solid and supportive relationship with personnel at the international student offices on their respective campuses, as employees at both become important colleagues throughout the duration of international students' academic careers.

If given sufficient time to prepare for a counseling session with an international student, the counselor might want to read as much as possible about the social mores of the student's culture. While it would be impossible to become an expert on a particular part of the world in such a short period of time, the counselor might be able to glean small insights that will be helpful during the interview. Even general information could be important, as was illustrated during one of Southern Illinois University Carbondale's (SIUC) darkest hours (Bean, 1997). In December 1992, a fire swept through an off-campus residence hall, killing five students, four of them international scholars. As the blaze was deemed arson, the deaths were considered homicides. Illinois state law required autopsies for deaths ruled as homicide. One of the victims was Muslim, and mutilation of the body at death is considered a religious sacrilege. SIUC officials were able to intervene just before the coroner was to begin the procedure, convincing him to wait until a local judge ruled that the autopsy requirement could be waived.

In addition to the vast amount of culturally informative literature on the Internet, wonderful publications are available through Intercultural Press and the National Association of Foreign Student Affairs. For decades, Brigham Young University has published small flyers known as *CultureGrams,* overviews of numerous aspects of individual countries including traditions, economics, and governmental structures, to name a few. While more appropriate for those who provide hospitality to international students, they do contain snippets that a counselor will find useful during an interview, including greetings and short phrases. A warm welcome spoken in a student's language might evoke a chuckle and ease the tension of the unfamiliar. Counselors are also urged to make use of a valuable human resource, the student population, when preparing for an interview. It is common for universities to have international student organizations representing different parts of the world. The presidents of these organizations are usually happy to share aspects of their culture.

Summary

The future of international education in the United States is uncertain. For the first time in nearly three decades, the 2004 edition of *Open Doors* noted a decline in international enrollment (Koh, 2004). The decline continued and was noted in the 2005 edition as well. Despite marked improvements in SEVIS (Connell, 2005) and visa processing, the global perception that international students are no longer welcome in the United States will certainly continue to affect these numbers. Marlene Johnson, CEO of NAFSA, addressed this situation and numerous other problems facing international education in her July 28, 2006, editorial in the *Chronicle of Higher Education* (Johnson, 2006). At a time when cultural sensitivity is pivotal to world peace, the loss of the contributions these students provide to U.S. campuses and communities will be devastating. In an article published in the March 31, 2004, edition of the *New York Times*, Robert M. Gates, secretary of defense remarked that "no policy has proved more successful in making friends for the United States, during the cold war and since, than educating students from abroad at our colleges and universities" (Gates, 2004, p. A23). As college student personnel, we must facilitate the retention and persistence of these global resources in every way possible and follow our personal compasses as we navigate the ever-blurring lines between bureaucracy and compassion.

References

Aliens and nationality. (2004). *Code of federal regulations* (Title 8). Washington, DC: Office of the Federal Register.

Bean, S. (1997). Students remember tragedy. *Daily Egyptian, 83,* 67.

Connell, C. (2005). Reactions vary. *International Educator, 14*(5), 35.

Foreign relations. (2004). *Code of federal regulations* (Title 22). Washington, DC: Office of the Federal Register.

Gates, R. M. (2004, March 31). International relations 101. *New York Times,* p. A23.

Johnson, M. (2006, July 28). Toward a new foreign-student strategy. *The Chronicle of Higher Education, 52,* p. B16.

Koh, C. H. K. (Ed.). (2002). *Open Doors 2002: Report on international education exchange.* New York: Institute of International Education.

Koh, C. H. K. (Ed.). (2004). *Open Doors 2004: Report on international educational exchange.* New York: Institute of International Education.

Meisner, D. (2002). After the attacks: Protecting borders and liberties. *International Educator, XI*(1), 6.

Appendix

Classification of Visas

Visa Class	*Description*
F-1	*Student:* Individual in the U.S. engaging in a full course of academic or language study in an accredited educational program.
F-2	*Dependent of F-1 Visa Holder:* Spouse and/or children of an F-1 student. May engage in part-time study that is recreational or vocational in nature. No employment is allowed.
G-1 G-2 G-3 G-4	*Representative of International Organization:* Individuals in the U.S. as representatives of an international organization (e.g., the United Nations) and their dependents. Dependents may engage in part- or full-time study. All work (on- or off-campus) for dependents must be first approved by the Department of State by using Form I-566. An Employment Authorization Document (EAD) card from the CIS is required.
H-1B	*Temporary Worker in a Specialty Occupation:* Individuals in the U.S. to perform professional services in a specific position for a fixed period of time. Employment authorization is granted for an initial period of up to 3 years. Extensions for an additional 3 years are possible. May engage in part-time study while maintaining H visa status.
H-2B	*Skilled or Unskilled Worker:* Individuals in the U.S. in a temporary position for which a shortage of U.S. workers exists, working for a specific employer for a fixed period of time. May engage in part-time study while maintaining H visa status.
H-3	*Trainee:* Individuals in the U.S. for a temporary period to participate in a training program provided by a specific employer. May engage in part-time study while maintaining H visa status.

(Continued on next page)

Appendix *(Continued)*
Classification of Visas

Visa Class	*Description*
H-4	*Dependent of H Visa Holder:* May engage in full- or part-time study. No employment allowed.
J-1	*Exchange Visitor (Student):* Individuals in the U.S. as exchange visitors for the primary purpose of studying at an academic institution under the auspices of the United States Information Agency and a Designated Program Sponsor. *Must maintain full-time study unless authorized by Responsible Officer (RO) of Designated Program Sponsor.* May be employed on the campus of the school in which they are enrolled to a maximum of 20 hours per week with prior written authorization from the RO of their Designated Program. May work off-campus under limited circumstances provided they have obtained prior written authorization from the RO. Employment does not require additional permission from CIS or an EAD. Eligible for 18 months of academic training following completion of their program (36 months for postdoctoral training).
	Exchange Visitor (Short-Term Scholar, Professor, Researcher, or Specialist): Individuals in the U.S. as visiting researchers or professors under the auspices of the United States Information Agency and a Designated Program Sponsor. Eligible to receive payment from the organization listed on Form IAP-66 as the source of funds and/or the Designated Program Sponsor for a period of validity as stated on the IAP-66. Under limited circumstances, may receive compensation from other institutions provided prior written authorization from the RO of their Designated Program has been secured. The IAP-66 authorizes the above stated employment. An Employment Authorization Document (EAD) card is not required.
J-1	*Au Pair:* Individuals in the U.S. under the auspices of the United States Information Agency and a Designated Program Sponsor to serve as a live-in child-care provider for a host family.
J-2	*Dependent of J-1 Visa Holder:* May engage in part- or full-time study. Eligible to apply to CIS for work authorization. Once the EAD is issued by CIS, the J-2 may work for any employer. Employer must re-verify employment authorization after expiration date on EAD. Employment cannot be needed for the financial support of J-1 visa holder. It must be for purposes unrelated to basic support.
M-1	*Vocational Student:* Individuals in the U.S. enrolled in a vocational school or program in the U.S. Must study full-time unless authorized by Designated School Official (DSO). May be employed for practical training in field related to major following completion of studies for a maximum of 6 months. EAD card from CIS required.

(Continued on next page)

Appendix *(Continued)*
Classification of Visas

Visa Class	*Description*
M-2	*Dependent of M-1 Visa Holder:* May engage in part- or full-time studies. No employment allowed.

Note. This chart lists the visa classifications that are potentially applicable to international students and their families. It is available at http://www.txstate.edu/International/visa_classifications_chart.htm. For a complete chart of visa classifications, see NAFSA: Association of International Educators at www.nafsa.org. CIS = U.S. Citizenship and Immigration Services.

Chapter 2

Isolation, Adjustment, and Acculturation Issues of International Students: Intervention Strategies for Counselors

Laura R. Johnson and Daya Singh Sandhu

The adjustment experiences of international students are often characterized by a decline in social and economic status, separation from family and social supports, a lack of English proficiency, and isolation from one's cultural background (Pedersen, 1991; Sandhu, 1995; Sandhu & Asrabadi, 1998). Immediately upon arrival in the United States, international students face considerable pressure to assimilate. They must rapidly learn to negotiate the demands of daily living and adjust to new systems of communication and behavior. Given these pressures, it is not surprising that a number of international students will experience psychological problems (Berry, 1997; Popadiuk & Arthur, 2004). Although international students suffer more psychological distress than U.S. students, the psychological aspects of their adjustment are often ignored (Mori, 2000).

This chapter focuses on the cross-cultural adjustment process and how it can cause conflicts, acculturative stress, and psychological distress in international students. We discuss acculturation and acculturative stress as a framework for understanding the adjustment process in international students. The psychological impact of acculturation is explained in terms of common symptoms such as homesickness, loss, and social isolation. Moderators of this impact are discussed and the concept of integration/biculturalism is introduced as a strategy for ameliorating the negative effects of acculturation. We conclude the chapter by describing the implications for developing programs and counseling services to address the psychological needs of international students and offering some specific strategies.

Acculturation: A Framework for Understanding International Student Adjustment

The concepts of acculturation and acculturative stress provide a sophisticated and practical framework for understanding the processes and outcomes of cross-cultural adjustment (Berry, 1998; Roysircar, 2004). *Acculturation* refers to changes in values, beliefs, and behaviors that result from sustained contact with a second culture. International students, classified as sojourners, represent a category of people undergoing acculturation (Berry, 1998). Although refugees, immigrants, and indigenous groups also experience acculturation, international students face unique stressors and concerns. They must quickly adjust to U.S. society and succeed in the U.S. academic system (Misra & Castillo, 2004; Mori, 2000). Moreover, international students have the added stress of reacculturating to their native countries upon return (Lin & Yi, 1997; see also chapter 7).

Whereas acculturation refers to changes resulting from group-level encounters between two or more cultures, the term *psychological acculturation* refers to psychological changes occurring at the individual level (Berry, 1997). Psychological acculturation involves changes across a number of domains, including language, cognitive style, attitudes, style of relating, and identity (Berry & Kim, 1988). Upon arrival, international students experience implicit and explicit pressure to accommodate to U.S. cultural norms (Sandhu & Asrabadi, 1994). There are a variety of ways that international students respond to these stressors (Lazarus, 1997). The demand to change may be viewed as an opportunity or challenge, and it may be easy for some to make the necessary behavioral shifts. However, others will be unable or unwilling to quickly accommodate to the host culture demands. When old patterns of coping are no longer effective and new ones are not available, acculturative stress may result (Berry, 1998; Popadiuk & Arthur, 2004).

Acculturative Stress

Acculturative stress is a particular type of stress resulting from the process of acculturation (Berry, Kim, Minde, & Mok, 1987). It refers to mildly pathological and disruptive behaviors and experiences that are commonly generated during acculturation. Symptoms may include depression, anxiety, physical complaints, anger, identity confusion, substance abuse, and family conflict (Berry & Kim, 1988; Sandhu & Asrabadi, 1998). Acculturative stress is presented as an alternative to and extension of earlier notions of *culture shock* (Furnham & Bochner, 1986). Although the symptoms are similar, culture shock implies a sudden, acute, and negative experience, whereas acculturative stress is thought to arise from the chronic stressors associated with the more gradual and long-term process of adjusting to another culture (Berry, 1998; Lazarus, 1997; Ward, 1997). Experiencing a certain amount of acculturative stress is considered a normal reaction to, and an integral part of, the cross-cultural adjustment process, resulting in positive adaptation (Sandhu, Portes, & McPhee, 1996).

Psychological Impact of Acculturative Stress

How does acculturative stress affect the daily lives and socioemotional functioning of international students? In their development of the Acculturative Stress Scale for International Students (ASSIS), Sandhu and Asrabadi (1994) identified several key manifestations of acculturative stress that contribute to international students' adjustment problems. These included perceived discrimination, homesickness, perceived hate and rejection, fear, culture shock and stress due to change, guilt related to being away from home, and miscellaneous other factors. A profound sense of loss, confusion, identity conflicts, anxiety, somatic complaints, and sadness are also common sources of concern for international students (Constantine, Kindaichi, & Okazaki, 2005; Mori, 2000; Sandhu, 1995). High levels of acculturative stress on the ASSIS have been negatively correlated with overall life satisfaction among international students in the United States (Ye, 2005).

Sense of Loss and Homesickness

Upon moving to another country, international students experience a number of losses—their homes, familiar foods and daily life, culture and customs, family and social supports, and their sense of belonging. As they realize the enormity of what they have left behind, their initial excitement and happiness about being in the United States may turn into feelings of disappointment, sadness, and a deep sense of loss (Hayes & Lin, 1994; Sandhu, 1995). Homesickness, an intense longing for one's family and home, is one of the most common complaints among international students (Sandhu & Asrabadi, 1994). Without the familiar surroundings and supports of their home countries, many international students also experience a loss of social identity, the shared identity and feeling of connectedness that comes from being around family, friends, and the community. This can result in a loss of self-confidence among international students, which can further interfere with social interactions.

Loneliness and Social Isolation

Loneliness, isolation, difficulty making friends, and dissatisfaction with American friendships are central concerns of international students (Mori, 2000; Ying, 2005). Research has clearly demonstrated that having a social support system is particularly important for the positive adaptation of international students (Hayes & Lin, 1994, Maundeni, 2001; Yeh & Inose, 2003). However, many international students report difficulties establishing and maintaining adequate social support networks, and it follows that relational stress is one of their major complaints (Jou & Fukada, 1996). While most international students report a desire for more host national (American) relationships, serious language barriers, including different accents, present a major obstacle (Redmond & Bunyi, 1993; Roysircar, 2004; Ying, 2005). Having to constantly ask for repetitions or explanations can be tiresome, frustrating, and embarrassing for international students and U.S. students alike. The result may be withdrawal from intercultural communications on the part of the international student, the host national student, or both. Negative intercultural communication experiences such as these may reduce social self-efficacy in international students. Add to this ambivalence or rejection on the part of Americans, and it is easy to imagine just how difficult it can be for international students to meet and make friends (Leung, 2001).

Even after initial contacts are made, problems developing and maintaining intercultural relationships abound. Cultural differences between social relationships

15

in the United States and those of an international student's home county also contribute to the problem and result in a high potential for miscommunication, misunderstandings, and dissatisfaction in cross-cultural relationships (Lacina, 2002; Mori, 2000). For example, international students report that Americans are very friendly and sociable, but they complain that their relationships with Americans are transitory in nature and are more like acquaintances, when compared with the deep, meaningful, and long-term friendships they have with people from their own background (Mori, 2000). This type of dissatisfaction and a lack of social connectedness have been identified as a significant predictor of acculturative stress among international students (Yeh & Inose, 2003).

Identity and Values Confusion

International students face a number of experiences that may threaten their sense of self and their feelings of cultural and group identity (Sandhu & Asrabadi, 1994, 1998). Because their sense of self is not endorsed by familiar others, their ideas about who they are and how they fit into society may erode or become confused (Hayes & Lin, 1994; Pedersen, 1991). Students coming from strong religious backgrounds may find themselves without the community supports or structures needed to practice their beliefs. Frustration, guilt about not practicing their religion, and questions about one's religious identity may follow. Additionally, international students may begin to question their personal values, customs, and traditions, seeing negative aspects of their previously held beliefs while being attracted to U.S. values and customs. For example, exposure to new gender roles for women and the importance of privacy and autonomy may be appealing to some students but could result in feelings of dissonance and confusion about cultural norms at home.

Discrimination and Prejudice

Negative experiences related to prejudice, discrimination, and racism can be unsettling and unexpected for international students (Constantine, Okazaki, & Utsey, 2004). For many international students, coming to the United States will be their first experience as a member of a minority group. Moreover, the emphasis on race in the United States is unfamiliar and bewildering to international students who come from countries where social groups are defined in terms of their religious, geographical, ethnic, or cultural group membership as opposed to skin color. The realization that one is a minority and the feeling of being different can lead to a heightened sense of anxiety and an increased tendency to perceive prejudice, discrimination, and rejection by Americans as a harsh reality. In their analysis of factors contributing to acculturative stress, Sandhu and Asrabadi (1994, 1998) found that perceived discrimination accounted for more variance than any other factor. Unfortunately, a state of hypervigilance is reinforced and maintained by real acts of discrimination and racism occurring in the United States (Chepesiuk, n.d.). These experiences may be direct or indirect and range from relatively benign to more serious threats and attacks. Negative stereotyping and inaccurate portrayals of one's country, culture, or religion are some other frequent complaints of international students. International students may be criticized for speaking in their native language or made fun of because of their accent and because they are from a developing country. In many instances they may bear the brunt of anti-immigrant and xenophobic ideologies and actions of Americans. They report teasing, name-calling, threats, verbal harassment (e.g., a Malaysian student had beer cans thrown at him and was told "go back to China"), and even physical attacks.

Some suggest that post–September 11, 2001, international students are viewed with increased distrust and suspicion by people from the United States (Chepesiuk, n.d.). New government policies, such as more aggressive background checks, delays in visa processing, and a database tracking system for international students, have been implemented, raising new concerns, especially among students from Middle-Eastern and Asian countries. It has also been suggested that African international students experience more acculturative stress and depression than students from Asian and Latin American countries because they experience more racial discrimination than other groups (Constantine et al., 2004).

Uncertainty, Fear, and Anxiety

International students are forced to live in a state of uncertainty about a number of different domains in their lives: uncertainty in terms of who they are, how they should behave, whether or not they will succeed in their academic goals, and how and where they fit into the academic environment and U.S. society (Sandhu, 1995; Yi, Lin, & Kishimoto, 2003). Academic success is of primary importance to international students. While they may have been among the most successful in their home institutions, the struggles they face adjusting to the U.S. classroom and educational system can contribute to a good deal of anxiety and a fear of failure (Mori, 2000; Pedersen, 1991; Roysircar, 2004). They also face uncertainty related to their legal status in the United States, and since 9/11, these worries have grown for a number of students because of more difficult clearance procedures and delays (see chapter 1).

Because international students are in a period of transition, they experience significant amounts of worry about their future. Among these concerns are how long they will be in the United States, when they will be able to return home, and how they will fit back into their home culture and surroundings. Those from developing countries have especially high expectations about going home to assist their families and native countries with an array of problems (Sandhu, 1995). As thoughts of going home arise, so do anxieties about the current state of things at home and of barriers to their success there, such as a lack of infrastructure and economic and political instability. Facing so many uncertainties, anxiety is a common concern. Symptoms may be acute or chronic and often include overthinking, rumination, constant and uncontrollable worry, test anxiety, social anxiety, fear and avoidance, panic attacks, and a range of somatic complaints.

Somatic Complaints

International students suffer from a number of physiological conditions related to excessive stress and a heightened level of fear and anxiety. An overactive parasympathetic nervous system may compromise the immune systems of international students, leaving them with an increased susceptibility to illness (Winkelman, 1994). Excessive muscle tension, sweating, blushing, and increased blood pressure and body temperature may be among the physical symptoms experienced. Additionally, international students may complain of vague and chronic somatic symptoms such as headaches, stomach upset, ulcers, low energy, loss of appetite, sleep disturbance, and sexual dysfunction (Ebbin & Balkenship, 1986; Winkelman, 1994). It is further suggested that many international students, because of their cultural backgrounds, may be more apt to express emotional or psychological symptoms somatically and seek out medical help for these problems (Ebbin & Balkenship, 1986; Lin & Yi, 1997; Mori, 2000).

Cognitive Distress

International students face a barrage of new information and experiences on a daily basis and are said to suffer from information overload. The sheer amount of cognitive effort required to process information, communicate in a new language, and behave appropriately in a new academic, physical, and cultural context can result in cognitive fatigue, mental exhaustion, burnout, confusion, and disorientation (Constantine et al., 2005; Mori, 2000; Sandhu & Asrabadi, 1998). Some international students may be affected by negative appraisals and cognitions about themselves, Americans, and/or their home culture. Highly successful individuals in their home countries, international students may set unreasonably high expectations for themselves and their success in the United States (Sandhu, 1995). Indeed the stakes are high, as many students' families have made incredible financial and emotional sacrifices so that they could study in the United States. When the (often unrealistic) expectations are not met, negative thoughts about themselves and a sense of inferiority may begin to dominate their thinking and have unfortunate repercussions for their social interactions, academic performance, and mood states.

Sadness and Depression

It is not surprising that a number of international students suffer from significant levels of emotional pain (Sandhu, 1995; Sandhu et al., 1996). They may feel intensely homesick, longing for familiar surroundings, social supports, and the competent sense of self that they enjoyed prior to coming to the United States. Feelings of powerlessness, resentment, and even hostility may set in as international students struggle to come to terms with their circumstances and shaken self-esteem (Mori, 2000; Sandhu & Asrabadi, 1998). An overwhelming sense of responsibility and feelings of guilt about being away from home are common. The intense sense of loss, loneliness, and unmet expectations can result in sadness, despondence, withdrawal, increased passivity, and, in some cases, clinical depression (Ward & Searle, 1991). Depression has been cited as one of the most common complaints among international students seeking health and counseling services (Pedersen, 1991; Yi et al., 2003).

Symptom Severity

While the psychological impact of acculturation is significant, the seriousness of symptoms and the degree of difficulty will vary considerably among international students. Psychological distress will occur along a continuum, but Berry's (1997) breakdown of symptom severity into three levels of distress may be helpful in planning interventions. Three levels of difficulty are described as (a) mild-to-moderate cultural conflict, (b) acculturative stress, and (c) psychopathology. The first degree of difficulty, mild-to-moderate cultural conflict, is explained by the process of culture learning and social skills acquisition (Ward, 1997). These conflicts arise as certain behaviors, no longer appropriate in the American environment, are unlearned or "shed" while being replaced with a new behavioral repertoire. If serious conflicts occur and behavioral shifts are not readily made, the second level of difficulty, acculturative stress, will occur, resulting in moderate difficulties in psychological functioning. Usually, only moderate difficulties result from acculturation (Berry, 1997). However, when major conflicts are experienced and the degree or rate of change exceeds one's capacity to cope, the third level, serious psychological disturbances and impairment, may result. At this level, a psychopathology perspective is helpful, as individuals may suffer from incapacitating levels of depression, anxiety, or other diagnosable mental disorders needing prompt and serious attention (Berry, 1997, 1998).

Moderators of the Impact of Acculturative Stress

Despite the demands placed on international students during acculturation, psychological problems are not inevitable (Berry, 1997, 1998). In fact, international students have been found to be quite robust in making successful transitions to their host culture and institutions, with most reaching some level of positive adaptation over time (Berry, 1997, 1998; Parr, Bradley, & Bingi, 1991). A number of group and individual factors will interact to moderate the amount of psychological distress experienced by international students and the manner in which they cope with it. These include the following: (a) *macrosocial influences* of the host culture and environment, such as legal constraints, discrimination, degree of tolerance for cultural diversity, and extent of academic pressure; (b) factors associated with the *background* of the acculturating student, such as worldview, social/familial network structure, and cultural distance from U.S. society; and (c) *individual factors* associated with the international student, such as age, gender, marital status, language proficiency, personality, coping skills, cultural knowledge, and intercultural communication competence (Aponte & Johnson, 2000; Babiker, Cox, & Miller, 1980; Berry, 1997). Two additional variables affecting acculturative stress are (d) *phase of acculturation* and (e) *acculturation strategy* (Berry, 1997, 1998; Berry & Kim, 1988).

Phase of acculturation refers to the pattern of adjustment over time (Berry & Kim, 1988). The four phases of acculturation include precontact, contact, crisis, and adaptation. It is during the second (contact) stage when cultural differences are first observed and during the third (crisis) phase that cultural differences are fully realized, resulting in acculturative stress. In terms of a time frame for experiencing acculturative stress, there is little evidence to support a fixed time of maximum risk (e.g., in months) or a specific pattern of adjustment (e.g., a U-curve).

What can be concluded is that psychological problems tend to increase soon after contact, followed by a general (but highly variable) decrease over time (Berry, 1997; Pedersen, 1991).

Acculturation Strategies

Different patterns of responding to the demands of acculturation have been referred to as acculturation attitudes, strategies, or modes, and the strategy is a key factor affecting the amount of acculturative stress the international student will experience (Berry, 1997; Berry & Kim, 1988). Evidence suggests that one's approach to acculturation will have a greater impact on psychological adjustment than any of the aforementioned factors (Aponte & Johnson, 2000; Berry, 1997; Ward & Kennedy, 1994). Four different acculturation attitudes represent four different strategies used by acculturating individuals in adapting to their new environment.

The strategy used will depend on how international students respond to two major issues: cultural maintenance and their contact and participation with the host culture (Berry, 1997). Berry and Kim (1988) posed two questions: "Is there value placed on and a desire to retain my culture of origin?" (cultural maintenance) and "Is there a desire or need for positive relations and interaction with mainstream American society?" (contact and participation). Four different acculturation strategies may be arrived at based on combinations of dichotomous yes or no answers to these questions. Thus, the acculturation strategy affects the nature, extent, and manner of an international student's interactions with his or her own culture and with mainstream U.S. culture. The strategies include (a) assimilation (derived from a no/yes response), (b) separation (derived from a yes/no response), (c) marginalization (derived from a no/no response), and (d) integration or biculturalism (derived from a yes/yes response). There is evidence that most individuals will explore different acculturation strategies in an effort to find one that is both useful and personally satisfying (Berry, 1997). While the strategy used will tend to vary on the basis of the phase of adjustment and the particular context, one strategy is usually used, providing a coherent theme to the student's approach toward acculturation. This is of key importance, as the various strategies are thought to be differentially adaptive (Berry, 1997, 1998; Ward & Kennedy, 1994).

International students adopting the *assimilation* strategy try to disengage completely from their culture of origin in hopes of being completely absorbed and accepted into the dominant host culture (LaFromboise, Coleman, & Gerton, 1993). While assimilation strategies have shown some benefits for the social adaptation of international students and immigrants, negative effects have been seen with regard to psychological adaptation (Kagan & Cohen, 1990; Searle & Ward, 1990). For example, although the assimilationist may operate effectively within the new social, cultural, and academic environment, they may sacrifice their sense of identity, their conational (those from one's own country or culture) supports, and groundedness in their culture of origin (Aponte & Johnson, 2000;

LaFromboise et al., 1993). Not only will complete assimilation be unattainable for most, but these students will also face greater difficulty readjusting to their home countries. Assimilation is considered a risky strategy and likely to result in high levels of stress and anxiety, low self-esteem, difficulties in work or school, and low mood ratings (Ward & Kennedy, 1994; Ward & Searle, 1991).

International students adopting a *separation* strategy, on the other hand, will segregate themselves from U.S. students and establish relationships primarily with others from their own cultural group. While these students may garner much needed social support from their conationals and remain grounded in their cultural identity, they will be socially ineffective within the university community and larger society. As these students face demands to speak English, perform academically, access resources, and negotiate school, legal, or health care systems, they are likely to experience high levels of acculturative stress (LaFromboise et al., 1993). Ward (1997), for example, found that greater social difficulty was found among international students with separation attitudes.

International students who are *marginalized* will experience the highest levels of acculturative stress. They will lack the behavioral repertoire needed to interact with members of their own culture and with people from the United States and thus face the highest levels of acculturative stress and greatest risk of psychological maladjustment (Berry, 1997; Ward & Kennedy, 1994).

The *integration* or *bicultural strategy* is associated with reduced risk and is increasingly recognized as the most adaptive strategy (Berry, 1997, 1998; Roysircar, 2004; Sodowsky & Lai, 1997; Ward & Kennedy, 1994, 1996). Although early notions of cultural adaptation suggested that acculturating individuals would have to choose between either a host or a native country identification (a native extinction–host association model; e.g., Kagan & Cohen, 1990), current views support the concept of orthogonal cultural identification (Oetting & Beauvais, 1990). That is, the degree of affiliation and rejection of one culture is independent of the degree of affiliation and rejection of the other. Therefore, it is possible for international students to have high levels of contact, involvement, loyalty, acceptance, and affiliation with both their culture of origin and U.S. culture (LaFromboise et al., 1993). The bicultural strategy suggests that individuals can acquire the skills and psychological flexibility to function effectively in both their culture of origin and U.S. culture.

Improving Adjustment Outcomes

What constitutes improved adjustment for international students? A distinction has been made between psychological and sociocultural adaptation, with the former referring to a clear personal and cultural identity, good mental health, and personal satisfaction in the new context, and the latter referring to social skills, culture learning, and other external outcomes that link individuals to their context, such as handling daily problems related to school or work (Berry, 1997; Ward, 1996; Ward & Kennedy, 1993). Although there is certainly a relationship between the two types of adaptation, with correlations in the .4 to .5 range, they are predicted by different factors, have distinct processes, and have different implications for program and service development (Berry, 1997).

Sociocultural adaptation is considered to follow a linear process with a gradual increase in learned skills over time. Positive sociocultural adaptation is predicted by cultural knowledge, degree of contact with the host culture, positive intergroup attitudes, and minimal cultural distance between the student's culture of origin and U.S. culture (Ward, 1997; Ward & Kennedy, 1993). On the other hand, psychological adaptation follows a more variable course, and while a "U-curve" has been widely declared, there is little evidence to support this pattern (Berry, 1997). Psychological adaptation is predicted by personality variables (those that make for a good fit with the host culture, e.g., internal locus of control and flexibility in the United States), life change events, social support, and minimal cultural distance (Berry, 1997; Ward, 1997). Both positive sociocultural adaptation and psychological adaptation are predicted by an integration or bicultural acculturation strategy.

Integration, Biculturalism, and Multiculturalism

A bicultural identification, combined with the cognitive, affective, and behavioral competencies needed for social effectiveness in both cultures, can enable international students to be effective and benefit maximally in a range of situations. In practice, bicultural effectiveness may involve the techniques of *code switching*, which involves completely shifting behavior depending on the context, and *culture blending,* which involves merging aspects of two or more cultures (Garcia Coll & Magnuson, 1997). These techniques may be used alone or in combination, and to varying degrees across different affective and behavioral domains. For example, individuals may adopt a code-switching strategy for language usage and a culture-blending approach when it comes to identity or values (Garcia Coll & Magnuson, 1997). Attaining a certain degree of bicultural effectiveness could be especially important for international students given their transitory status. Not only will it be important for them to have successful academic and social experiences while in the United States, but it will also be important for them to readjust to their native countries. Maintaining one's cultural identity and ties to home could aid in this process (Lin & Yi, 1997).

It is important to note that "being an international student" represents a common minority identity that is shared among international students (Schmitt, Spears, & Branscombe, 2003). Despite language and cultural background differences, international students share with each other the challenges of acculturation and can provide a natural and sensitive multicultural support network. In fact, many international students report positive affiliations and interactions with other international students (Schmitt et al., 2003). A multicultural approach to adjustment may be of particular benefit to international students who are alone in coming from their particular country or culture of origin. Therefore, although bicultural identity and effectiveness are important, a multicultural approach may be even more adaptable, allowing for the greatest

22

psychological and behavioral flexibility and multiple sources of social support (Maundeni, 2001).

Achievement of this type of flexibility serves as both a coping strategy for and a protective factor against symptoms of acculturative stress (Berry, 1997, 1998; LaFromboise et al., 1993; Lazarus, 1997). Moreover, there is consistent evidence that integration is the best strategy for achieving both short- and long-term positive health and well-being (Berry, 1997; LaFromboise et al., 1993; Roysircar, 2004; Ward, 1996; Ward & Kennedy, 1993). Ward and Kennedy (1994), for example, found that integration attitudes among international students were associated with fewer depressive symptoms.

Strategies for Program Planners and Counselors

A comprehensive effort to address the psychological needs of international students will need to be continuous, culturally responsive, and collaborative in nature (Lin & Yi, 1997; Mori, 2000). Programs need to address the full range of psychological difficulties from mild cultural conflict to more severe cases of clinical pathology. A wide variety of approaches and different venues and modes of service delivery could be helpful in reaching and appealing to the largest numbers of international students. Additionally, programs should move beyond a sole focus on international students by targeting American staff, professors, fellow students, and the organizations and institutions in which they interact.

Continuous, Culturally Responsive, and Coordinated Programs

International students must deal with the challenges of adjustment on a daily basis, from before their arrival in the United States until after they return to their native countries (Lin & Yi, 1997; Pedersen, 1991; Sandhu & Asrabadi, 1998). Keeping acculturative stress in check and creating a satisfying experience will necessarily involve ongoing efforts. Support services, such as education and outreach, should be available throughout a student's stay. Staff at international offices and faculty should be made aware that student adjustment concerns are ongoing and that their needs change over time. For example, helpful prearrival information might include print or Web-based materials about U.S. culture and pedagogical practices, having realistic expectations, and basic information about cultural adjustment. Upon arrival (and during the initial contact and adjustment period), practical information, resource linkage, problem solving, and skills training may be helpful. Education, outreach, and support for understanding and managing acculturative stress and resolving conflicts should be available throughout the international student's sojourn. Toward the end of their tenure, international students will need assistance preparing for their return home and help handling reentry stress (Arthur, 2003; Lin & Yi, 1997). Cultural responsiveness is also a primary concern in addressing the psychological needs of international students (Mori, 2000). Educational and counseling services should be designed and implemented with an awareness of and sensitivity to the diverse cultural backgrounds of international students (Sodowsky & Plake, 1992). This is particularly true when addressing emotional and psychological needs, as there are numerous culture-based sensitivities about psychological problems, such as stigmas and negative attitudes about help seeking. Culturally responsive programs will use primary and secondary prevention approaches, as well as new and innovative strategies, to reach out to international students in ways that are accessible and acceptable. Additionally, culturally responsive programs and counselors will seek to build their own cultural competence by enhancing their awareness, knowledge, and skills for interacting with international students (Arredondo et al., 1996; see also chapter 18).

Coordination of services and collaboration among stakeholders will be key to ensuring awareness of services and for facilitating access to services. Moreover, linkage of programs and services can strengthen the overall network of support and increase feelings of safety and connectedness among international students (Komiya & Eells, 2001). Offices of international programs remain the major point of contact for most international students, representing a place of support and help at many universities (Abe, Talbot, & Geelhoed, 1998; Yoon & Portman, 2004). These offices should collaborate with other departments and organizations to develop a coordinated system of service provision and establish a formal resource and referral network between departments and potential providers. Linkage should be considered with departments of counseling, educational, or clinical psychology. One creative approach paired counselors in training with international students in a mutually beneficial effort to improve international student adjustment and enhance counselor trainees' multicultural awareness (Jacob & Greggo, 2001). Similar partnerships or collaborations could be organized with departments of international studies, international communications, or international relations; offices of multicultural affairs; campus diversity initiatives; English as a Second Language (ESL) and Teaching English as a Second Language (TESL) programs; cultural associations; and other campus organizations and host-national groups, such as fraternities and sororities. Community-based civic clubs and faith-based organizations are other potential resources for students, offering social support, recreation, and opportunities to practice English.

Preventive Approaches

Because of cultural differences and stigmas, proactive approaches aimed at preventing or ameliorating acculturative stress may be particularly well suited to international students (Berry, 1997, 1998; Lin & Yi, 1997). Moreover, educational and outreach programs can do much to promote the students' overall adjustment and satisfaction (Sandhu, 1995; Sandhu & Asrabadi, 1998; Ward, 1997). For example, education and training about the adjustment process has been shown to boost psychological well-being and emotional satisfaction, enhance interpersonal functioning, improve work performance, and assist cross-cultural sojourners in meeting their goals (Deshpande & Viswesvaran, 1992; Ward, 1997).

24

Preventive efforts can and should use a range of modalities, such as providing information in print and on the Internet, conducting orientations, providing workshops, organizing discussion and support groups, providing support services, organizing social activities, and facilitating individual exchanges with international office staff, professors, and classmates.

Prearrival
Many international students do not receive adequate prearrival information about the life-changing adjustment process they are about to undergo. Information about the U.S. academic system and pedagogical style, social and cultural norms, and common adjustment experiences could help bring initial student expectations more in line with reality (Lin & Yi, 1997).

Contact and Initial Adjustment
Immediately after arrival, most students receive a general orientation that emphasizes practical concerns such as visas and housing, class registration, and rapid sociocultural assimilation. Students may be exposed to the idea of culture shock at this time, but usually in a limited fashion and without any discussion of the complexities of the psychological acculturation process. This may be appropriate at this early contact stage, as students must be equipped to take care of basic needs, and they are being bombarded with information and may not be receptive to details about psychological adjustment. However, they may be more responsive to such topics sometime after the initial orientation, when homesickness, cultural conflicts, and psychological concerns are realized.

Adaptation
Education and discussion of acculturative stress and strategies for coping could be particularly beneficial as a prevention tool if offered relatively soon after arrival in the first few months. After the necessary knowledge and skills are imparted, ongoing activities and support in handling acculturative stress will be needed and should be offered on a regular basis. This could be by holding a series of discussion groups with topics such as dealing with culture conflict, how to engage in class discussions, how to talk to professors, and how to manage stress. Students may need encouragement to talk to faculty members, and offering student support, conversational, or skills-building groups could build self-efficacy in this regard. Maintaining contact and communication could help international students (and those working with them) identify when they are experiencing significant psychological distress or are otherwise in need of additional individual support, counseling, or therapy services. Readily available self-access materials with information and helpful hints can be made available for broad access; increasingly, special pages are being designed and posted for international students. For example, the National Honor Society in Psychology (Psi Chi) offered the following tips through their newsletter: Speak and do not worry about making mistakes, join a student club, ask questions, visit professors, trust yourself, and visit the counseling center to prepare for challenges (Poyrazli, 2005).

Counseling and Therapy

Despite their psychological distress, international students are unlikely to seek out counseling or psychological services (Pedersen, 1991; Yi et al., 2003; Zhang & Dixon, 2001). Several factors may account for this, including a lack of familiarity with mental health services or counseling, stigma associated with psychological symptoms, cultural beliefs regarding the nature of symptoms and what constitutes appropriate help seeking, and a misbelief that counseling services are only for U.S. students. Many international students will not seek services because they believe that psychological difficulties are a result of personal or moral weakness. They may consider the disclosure of personal problems to be a sign of weakness or irresponsibility, and they may fear being seen as a failure or, worse yet, being sent back to their country. Admitting to psychological problems or seeking psychological counseling could have serious implications for oneself and one's family, for example, shaming the family or reducing marriageability. Other international students may not seek mental health services because they view their difficulties as related to the environment (e.g., academic demands, transportation, or financial problems) and do not see how counseling or therapy might be of benefit because it will not change the source of the problem (Mori, 2000).

There may also be a lack of familiarity with the concept and practice of Western counseling and psychotherapy (Wohl, 2000). It will be important to familiarize students with counseling services and providers. Offices of international programs can assist in identifying students in need of help, making referrals, facilitating initial appointment, and/or making personal introductions to counseling center staff. Identifying and working with counselors and supervisors who have experience and knowledge of international student concerns may also be helpful, as multicultural sensitivity and cultural competence have been shown to increase positive perceptions of counseling by international students (Zhang & Dixon, 2001).

When counseling is sought, international students may harbor mistrust and apprehension (Mori, 2000). They tend to have a higher no-show rate after the first session compared with their U.S. counterparts (Anderson & Myers, 1985). Certain routine intake procedures, such as signing consents and confidentiality forms, may further compound these feelings, if not explained properly and in a sensitive way. Additionally, typical counseling sessions use a direct style of communication to identify and address personal problems with a professional who is a stranger. This format may be very foreign to international students coming from cultures with more indirect styles or those that rely on familiar social and religious supports, such as community leaders, family members, priests, Imams, or shamans, for addressing such problems. Therefore, a certain amount of education and "pretherapy" aimed at explaining and demystifying the counseling process and letting students know what to expect may be helpful.

Demonstrating cultural competence throughout counseling will be important in assessment and treatment planning, as a lack of culturally knowledgeable and competent counselors can exacerbate the problems and feelings of unease.

Assessing identity concerns, cultural affiliations, adjustment concerns, and student-held beliefs about their problems will be key to effective treatment process and outcomes. The differences between international students and their counselors in their beliefs about the nature of the problem, its cause, severity, presumed course, and goals for treatment, *and* to the extent that these differences are not explored and negotiated by the counselor, will cause treatment to flounder (Kleinman, 1980; Wohl, 2000). Failing to elicit the student's view and ignoring key factors, such as cultural identity and acculturative stress, can lead to misdiagnosis, inappropriate treatment, early attrition, or reduced treatment benefits.

Although there will be great diversity among international students, group therapy approaches may be particularly helpful (Carr, Koyama, & Thiagarajan, 2003; Yau, 2004; see chapter 17). Some studies suggest that Asian international students may prefer a directive approach to counseling (Seo, 2005). Novel approaches to meeting international students' psychological needs, such as through computer-based services, are being examined. Preliminary findings suggest that international students are actually less receptive to computer-based versus face-to-face counseling (Chang & Chang, 2004). Gender differences in symptom expression and treatment preference should also be explored (Constantine et al., 2004). In planning individual treatment, a cultural formulation can guide the process of selecting and adapting specific treatment objectives and intervention methods (see Appendix I of the *Diagnostic and Statistical Manual of Mental Disorders* by the American Psychiatric Association, 1994, for a cultural formulation outline).

Awareness, Knowledge, and Skills for Integration

The following core content areas, derived from the literature on positive socio-cultural and psychological adaptation, can provide international students with the awareness, knowledge, and skills needed to facilitate healthy adjustment and prevent or reduce acculturative stress (Berry, 1997, 1998; Constantine et al., 2004; Leung, 2001; Lin & Yi, 1997; Poyrazli, Arbona, Nora, Mcpherson, & Pisecco, 2002; Roysircar, 2004; Szapocznik, Santisteban, Kurtines, Perez-Vidal, & Hervis, 1984; Ward, 1996). This information may be incorporated into prevention approaches via printed materials, Web site postings, links and Web-based chat rooms, and group educational approaches using discussion, activities, games, and skits to illustrate concepts. In addition, counselors and therapists should assess these areas in their individual international student–clients and facilitate the students' development of integration or multicultural competencies as part of the overall approach to case conceptualization and treatment (Roysircar, 2004).

Awareness and Knowledge Content

- Students' own worldviews, cultural values, and norms
- American cultural values and norms; differences between own cultural systems and those in the United States

- Positive and negative aspects of host culture and the culture of origin (e.g., nuclear and extended family structures; individualism vs. collectivism, direct vs. indirect communication styles) and how to emphasize the strengths of both
- Importance of support from one's own and other cultural backgrounds
- Acculturation process and factors involved
- Process of acculturation and how acculturative stress may affect academic, social, cognitive, biological, and psychological functioning
- Benefits of an integrated approach to adjustment; strategies used to work toward biculturalism/multiculturalism

Core Skills

Not only will it be important for international students to gain awareness and knowledge, but they would also need to develop skills for implementing the bicultural approach. Skills training for effectiveness in the following areas may be incorporated into preventive, outreach, and counseling services:

- How to cope with prejudice, discrimination, or racism
- How to reconcile cultural differences and handle cultural conflicts
- How to succeed in the classroom (U.S. pedagogical system, asking questions)
- How to negotiate U.S. universities and access resources from other institutions (e.g., health care, legal, employment, etc.) as needed
- How to interact with other Americans in informal social and recreational activities
- How to develop and maintain own group cultural ties and international (multicultural) social supports
- How to respond effectively to acculturative stress, including a discussion of the many positive aspects of the acculturation experience

Strategies

Depending on the international students' particular needs and wishes, a wide repertoire of techniques and strategies may be used in imparting knowledge and skills. Strategies should be selected in collaboration with students and should be consistent with their values and cultural orientation.

- Problem-solving skills
- Social skills or social effectiveness training
- Conflict resolution
- Assertiveness skills
- Time management
- Stress management (relaxation skills and practice; mindfulness approaches)
- Cognitive and behavioral skills (cognitive reframing, activity scheduling, exposure therapy)

- Academic skills (study skills, managing test anxiety)
- Professional or vocational guidance
- Social support
- Values exploration and clarification (working with life purpose, existential, cultural, or religious issues)

Educational approaches may include direct teaching and practicing skills, with use of coaching, modeling, and behavioral rehearsal. Role-plays and discussions of critical incidents may help international students prepare for challenges and transitions and help them develop anticipatory coping strategies (Arthur, 2003). Socratic questioning, thought monitoring, and cognitive reframing may be useful with students who react cognitively to stress (Misra & Castillo, 2004). Drama, storytelling, and other forms of expressive or creative arts may be considered for their potential as culturally appropriate and nonstigmatizing approaches. Some students may need assistance across several areas, others may require a targeted approach, and others may need supportive counseling alone. Most of the approaches described here can be provided in an individual or group format, although groups have obvious benefits of building social support, improving language skills, benefiting more students, and being cost-effective.

Broad-Based Approaches

Beyond the above-mentioned specific strategies, additional tools for enhancing international students' psychological adjustment are suggested and described below. These approaches are more naturalistic and are focused on the larger context in which adjustment occurs.

Encourage Personal Coping

International students should be encouraged to use personal strategies for well-being and coping (Tseng & Newton, 2002). These may include maintaining religious beliefs and practices; being involved with extracurricular activities of interest, such as physical exercise and campus- or community-based clubs; learning to understand oneself, others, and U.S. culture; establishing and maintaining cultural and social contacts; building relationships with advisors and instructors; and becoming proficient in English (Toyokawa & Toyokawa, 2002; Tseng & Newton, 2002).

Build Social and Emotional Supports

At the programmatic level, a variety of efforts have been used to reach out to international students and help them build social supports and connections (Maundeni, 2001; Smith, Chin, Inman, & Findling, 1999; Toyokawa & Toyokawa, 2002). Many such programs focus on building social networks by providing opportunities for recreation and socialization, such as outings and events with other international students. Some offer organized programs to build relationships with U.S. students by matching international students with a partner from the United States. A comprehensive approach to building social support and establishing connections among international students should consider the importance of multicultural supports. For example, it has been suggested that relationships with host nationals, conationals, and other international students serve different social support functions (Toyokawa & Toyokawa, 2002). Host nationals (people from the United States) may provide assistance with language, academics, or other help in negotiating systems and services, whereas other international students may provide opportunities for recreation through cultural events, picnics, and other outings. Conationals are relied on to reaffirm one's cultural identity and assist with personal problems. Programs and counselors should thus emphasize and facilitate the establishment of connections with people from the United States, other conationals, and other international students.

Promote Empowerment

Empowering international students can help them cope with problems and achieve their academic and personal goals (Yoon & Portman, 2004). The literature suggests that finding contributory roles for international students should be a goal of proactive approaches (Sandhu, 1995). International students can be cultural ambassadors, sharing correct and up-to-date information about their culture and country within the university and local community. They can also be engaged in programs designed to prepare U.S. students for study-abroad experiences (e.g., "predeparture workshops") and in courses offered through study-abroad offices or international studies departments. International students can become involved in these and similar programs by sharing their acculturation experiences, their observations about the United States or Americans, and specific information about their country or region to students who may be headed there. In some innovative programs, international students play a role in the multicultural training of counselors (Jacob, 2001). Avenues for such creative approaches should continue to be explored within counseling and psychology training programs. In sum, empowering international students by giving them unique and creative roles in the academic and social environment can do much to promote their overall health, adjustment, and satisfaction.

Involve Host Nationals

Many international students desire more contact with students from the United States but do not feel that Americans are interested in them. Moreover, as Berry (1997) asserted, "integration can only be freely chosen and successfully pursued by international students when the dominate society is open and inclusive in its orientation toward diversity" (p. 10). This call for a "mutual accommodation" suggests that targeting U.S. students, faculty, and other staff will ultimately contribute to improved adjustment outcomes for international students by creating a multicultural, open, and tolerant university environment. Efforts could be made to increase awareness and sensitivity to some of the challenges faced by international students. Faculty could do much to create a safe and supportive atmosphere and classroom environment by encouraging student attendance at multicultural events, incorporating cultural and international issues into class discussion, adding diversity statements to their syllabi, and checking in with their international students.

Summary

International students studying in the United States face a number of challenges and stressors associated with their unique circumstances and unfamiliar surroundings. While there is great strength, courage, and resilience among international students in general, the specific and serious challenges of psychological acculturation remain a reality. The extreme changes in physical, social, cultural, language, and academic environments that occur for international students, combined with the extreme pressures to quickly adapt to these new environments, can easily outpace or overwhelm even the most robust international students. This chapter suggested that a common goal of programs and services for international students should be to alleviate the stress of acculturation and to strengthen the individual's capacity to cope with stressors associated with the adjustment process. It further suggested that the best way of meeting this goal is through culturally competent outreach, support, and counseling services that include information about cross-cultural adjustment, acculturative stress, and the benefits of an integration strategy. Knowledge of the sociocultural and psychological aspects of acculturation can help international students make sense of what they are experiencing, let them know that they are not alone, and provide them with resources and tools to address their difficulties.

References

Abe, J., Talbot, D. M., & Geelhoed, R. J. (1998). Effects of a peer program on international student adjustment. *Journal of College Student Development, 39,* 539-547.

American Psychiatric Association. (1994). *Diagnostic and statistical manual of mental disorders* (4th ed.). Washington, DC: Author.

Anderson, T., & Myers, T. (1985). Presenting problems, counselor contacts, and "no-shows": International and American college students. *Journal of College Student Personnel, 26,* 500-503.

Aponte, J. F., & Johnson, L. R. (2000). Role of culture in the intervention and treatment of ethnic populations. In J. F. Aponte & J. Wohl (Eds.), *Psychological interventions and cultural diversity* (2nd ed., pp. 18-39). Needham Heights, MA: Allyn & Bacon.

Arredondo, P., Toporek, R., Brown, S. P., Jones, J., Locke, D. C., Sanchez, J., & Stadler, H. (1996). Operationalization of multicultural competencies. *Journal of Multicultural Counseling and Development, 24,* 42-79.

Arthur, N. (2003). Preparing international students for the re-entry transition. *Canadian Journal of Counselling, 37,* 173–185.

Babiker, I. E., Cox, J. L., & Miller, P. (1980). The measurement of cultural distance and its relationship to medical consultation, symptomatology and examination performance of overseas students at Edinburgh University. *Social Psychiatry, 15,* 109–116.

Berry, J. W. (1997). Immigration, acculturation, and adaptation. *Applied Psychology: An International Review, 46,* 5–68.

Berry, J. W. (1998). Acculturation and health: Theory and research. In S. Kazarian & D. Evans (Eds.), *Cultural clinical psychology: Theory, research, and practice* (pp. 39–57). New York: Oxford University Press.

Berry, J. W., & Kim, U. (1988). Acculturation and mental health. In P. R. Dasen, J. W. Berry, & N. Sartorius (Eds.), *Health and cross-cultural psychology* (pp. 207–236). Newbury Park, CA: Sage.

Berry, J. W., Kim, U., Minde, T., & Mok, D. (1987). Comparative studies of acculturative stress. *International Migration Review, 21,* 490–511.

Carr, J. L., Koyama, M., & Thiagarajan, M. (2003). A women's support group for Asian international students. *Journal of American College Health, 52,* 131–134.

Chang, T., & Chang, R. (2004). Counseling and the Internet: Asian American and Asian international college students' attitudes toward seeking online professional psychological help. *Journal of College Counseling, 7,* 140–149.

Chepesiuk, R. (n.d.). *International insights: Dealing with discrimination.* Retrieved July 1, 2004, from http://www.graduatingengineer.com/intl_insights/nov2002.html

Constantine, M. G., Kindaichi, M., & Okazaki, S. (2005). A qualitative investigation of the cultural adjustment experiences of Asian international college women. *Cultural Diversity and Ethnic Minority Psychology, 11,* 162–175.

Constantine, M. G., Okazaki, S., & Utsey, S. (2004). Self-concealment, social self-efficacy, acculturative stress, and depression in African, Asian, and Latin American international college students. *American Journal of Orthopsychiatry, 74,* 230–241.

Deshpande, S. P., & Viswesvaran, C. (1992). Is cross-cultural training of expatriate managers effective? A meta-analysis. *International Journal of Intercultural relations, 16,* 295–310.

Ebbin, A. J., & Balkenship, E. S. (1986). A longitudinal health care study: International versus domestic students. *Journal of American College Health, 34,* 179–181.

Furnham, A., & Bochner, S. (1986). *Culture shock: Psychological reactions to unfamiliar environments.* London: Methuen.

Garcia Coll, C., & Magnuson, K. (1997). The psychological experience of immigration: A developmental perspective. In A. Booth, A. C. Crouter, & A. Landale (Eds.), *Immigration and the family: Research and policy on U.S. immigrants* (pp. 91–132). Mahwah, NJ: Erlbaum.

Hayes, R. L., & Lin, H. R. (1994). Coming to America: Developing social support system for international students. *Journal of Multicultural Counseling and Development, 22,* 7–16.

Jacob, E. J., & Greggo, J. W. (2001). Using counselor training and collaborative programming strategies in working with international students. *Journal of Multicultural Counseling and Development, 29,* 73-88.

Jou, Y. H., & Fukada, H. (1996). The causes and influence of transitional stress among Chinese students in Japan. *Journal of Social Psychology, 136,* 501-509.

Kagan, H., & Cohen, J. (1990). Cultural adjustment of international students. *Psychological Science, 1,* 133-137.

Kleinman, A. (1980). *Patients and healers in the context of culture.* Berkeley: University of California Press.

Komiya, N., & Eells, G. T. (2001). Predictors of attitudes toward seeking counseling among international students. *Journal of College Counseling, 4,* 153-161.

Lacina, J. G. (2002). Preparing international students for a successful social experience in higher education. *New Directions for Higher Education, 117,* 21-27.

LaFromboise, T., Coleman, H. L., & Gerton, J. (1993). Psychological impact of biculturalism: Evidence and theory. *Psychological Bulletin, 114,* 395-412.

Lazarus, R. S. (1997). Acculturation isn't everything. *Applied Psychology: An International Review, 46,* 39-43.

Leung, C. (2001). The psychological adaptation of overseas and migrant students in Australia. *International Journal of Psychology, 36,* 251-259.

Lin, J. C. G., & Yi, J. K. (1997). Asian international students' adjustment: Issues and program suggestions. *College Student Journal, 31,* 473-480.

Maundeni, T. (2001). The role of social networks in the adjustment of African students to British society: Students' perceptions. *Race Ethnicity and Education, 4,* 253-276.

Misra, R., & Castillo, L. G. (2004). Academic stress among college students: Comparison of American and international students. *International Journal of Stress Management, 11,* 132-148.

Mori, S. (2000). Addressing the mental health concerns of international students. *Journal of Counseling & Development, 78,* 137-145.

Oetting, E. R., & Beauvais, F. (1990). Orthogonal cultural identification theory: The cultural identification of minority adolescents. *International Journal of the Addictions, 25,* 655-685.

Parr, G., Bradley, L., & Bingi, R. (1991). Directors' perceptions of the concerns and feelings of international students. *College Student Journal, 25,* 370-376.

Pedersen, P. B. (1991). Counseling international students. *The Counseling Psychologist, 19,* 10-58.

Popadiuk, N., & Arthur, N. (2004). Counseling international students in Canadian schools. *International Journal for the Advancement of Counseling, 26,* 125-145.

Poyrazli, S. (2005). International students at U.S. universities. *Eye on Psi Chi, 9,* 18-19.

Poyrazli, S., Arbona, C., Nora, A., Mcpherson, R., & Pisecco, S. (2002). The relation between assertiveness, academic self-efficacy, and psychosocial adjustment among international graduate students. *Journal of College Student Development, 43,* 632-642.

Redmond, M. R., & Bunyi, J. M. (1993). The relationship of intercultural communication competence with stress and the handling of stress as reported by international students. *International Journal of Intercultural Relations, 17,* 235-254.

Roysircar, G. (2004). Counseling and psychotherapy for acculturation and ethnic identity concerns with immigrant and international students. In T. Smith (Ed.), *Practicing multiculturalism* (pp. 255-275). Boston: Allyn & Bacon.

Sandhu, D. S. (1995). An examination of the psychological needs of the international students: Implications for counseling and psychotherapy. *International Journal for the Advancement of Counselling, 17,* 229-239.

Sandhu, D. S., & Asrabadi, B. R. (1994). Development of an acculturative stress scale for international students: Preliminary findings. *Psychological Reports, 75,* 435-448.

Sandhu, D. S., & Asrabadi, B. R. (1998). An acculturative stress scale for international students: A practical approach to stress measurement. In C. P. Zalaquett & R. J. Wood (Eds.), *Evaluating stress: A book of resources* (Vol. 2, pp. 1-33). Lanham, MD: Scarecrow Press.

Sandhu, D. S., Portes, P. R., & McPhee, S. (1996). Assessing cultural adaptation: Psychometric properties of the Cultural Adaptation Pain Scale. *Journal of Multicultural Counseling and Development, 24,* 15-25.

Schmitt, M. T., Spears, R., & Branscombe, N. R. (2003). Constructing a minority group identity out of shared rejection: The case of international students. *European Journal of Social Psychology, 33,* 1-12.

Searle, W., & Ward, C. (1990). The prediction of psychological and sociocultural adjustment during cross-cultural transitions. *International Journal of Intercultural Relations, 14,* 449-464.

Seo, Y. S. (2005). Characteristics of Korean international students and their perceived preferences for counseling style. *International Journal for the Advancement of Counselling, 27,* 359-369.

Smith, T. B., Chin, L. C., Inman, A. G., & Findling, J. H. (1999). An outreach support group for international students. *Journal of College Counseling, 22,* 188-191.

Sodowsky, G. R., & Lai, E. W. (1997). Asian immigrant variables and structural models of cross-cultural distress. In A. Booth, A. C. Crouter, & A. Landale (Eds.), *Immigration and the family: Research and policy on U.S. immigrants* (pp. 221-234). Mahwah, NJ: Erlbaum.

Sodowsky, G. R., & Plake, B. S. (1992). A study of acculturation differences among international people and suggestions for sensitivity to within-group differences. *Journal of Counseling & Development, 71,* 53-60.

Szapocznik, J., Santisteban, D., Kurtines, W., Perez-Vidal, A., & Hervis, O. (1984). Bicultural effectiveness training: A treatment intervention for enhancing intercultural adjustment in Cuban American families. *Hispanic Journal of Behavioral Sciences, 6,* 317-344.

Toyokawa, T., & Toyokawa, N. (2002). Extracurricular activities and the adjustment of Asian international students: A study of Japanese students. *International Journal of Intercultural Relations, 26,* 363-379.

Tseng, W. C., & Newton, F. B. (2002). International students' strategies for well-being. *College Student Journal, 3,* 592-598.

Ward, C. (1996). Acculturation. In D. Landis & R. Bhagat (Eds.), *Handbook of intercultural training* (2nd ed., pp. 124-127). Thousand Oaks, CA: Sage.

Ward, C. (1997). Culture learning, acculturative stress, and psychopathology: Three perspectives on acculturation. *Applied Psychology: An International Review, 46,* 58-62.

Ward, C., & Kennedy, A. (1993). Where's the "culture" in cross-cultural transition? Comparative studies of sojourner adjustment. *Journal of Cross-Cultural Psychology, 2,* 221-249.

Ward, C., & Kennedy, A. (1994). Acculturation strategies, psychological adjustment and sociocultural competence during cross-cultural transitions. *International Journal of Intercultural Relations, 1,* 329-343.

Ward, C., & Kennedy, A. (1996). Crossing cultures: The relationship between psychological and sociocultural dimensions of cross-cultural adjustment. In J. Pandey, D. Sinha, & D. Bhawuk (Eds.), *Asian contributions to cross-cultural psychology* (pp. 289-306). Thousand Oaks, CA: Sage.

Ward, C., & Searle, W. (1991). The impact of value discrepancies and cultural identity on psychological and sociocultural adjustment of sojourners. *International Journal of Intercultural Relations, 15,* 209-225.

Winkelman, M. (1994). Cultural shock and adaptation. *Journal of Counseling & Development, 73,* 121-126.

Wohl, J. (2000). Psychotherapy and cultural diversity. In J. F. Aponte & J. Wohl (Eds.), *Psychological interventions and cultural diversity* (2nd ed., pp. 75-91). Needham Heights, MA: Allyn & Bacon.

Yau, T. Y. (2004). Guidelines for facilitating groups with international college students. In J. L. DeLucia-Waack, D. Gerrity, C. Kalodner, & M. Riva (Eds.), *Handbook of group counseling and psychotherapy* (pp. 253-264). Thousand Oaks, CA: Sage.

Ye, J. (2005). Acculturative stress and use of the Internet among East Asian international students in the United States. *CyberPsychology and Behavior, 8,* 154-161.

Yeh, C. J., & Inose, M. (2003). International students' reported English fluency, social support satisfaction, and social connectedness as predictors of acculturative stress. *Counseling Psychology Quarterly, 16,* 15-28.

Yi, J. K., Lin, J. G., & Kishimoto, Y. (2003). Utilization of counseling services by international students. *Journal of Instructional Psychology, 30,* 333-343.

Ying, Y. (2005). Variation in acculturative stressors over time: A study of Taiwanese students in the United States. *International Journal of Intercultural Relations, 29,* 59-71.

Yoon, E., & Portman, A. A. (2004). Critical issues of literature on counseling international students. *Journal of Multicultural Counseling and Development, 32,* 33-44.

Zhang, N., & Dixon, D. N. (2001). Multiculturally responsive counseling: Effects on Asian students' ratings of counselors. *Journal of Multicultural Counseling and Development, 29,* 253-263.

Chapter 3

International Students' Career Development and Decisions

Nancy Arthur

The lack of literature on the career development of international students is surprising, given recent emphasis on recruitment of greater numbers of students in secondary and higher education (Aigner, Nelson, & Stimpfl, 1992; Bohm, Davis, Meares, & Pearce, 2002; Kuo & Roysircar, 2006). The choice of studying in another country is an important career decision, and many students are seeking ways to enhance career opportunities (Shih & Brown, 2000). Career counseling is an important intervention to help international students develop skills to manage the myriad influences on their current and future career choices (Leong & Sedlacek, 1986; Shen & Herr, 2004; Shih & Brown, 2000; Yi, Lin, & Kishimoto, 2003).

In this chapter, the concept of career is explored to examine a range of lifestyle and life role choices that are relevant for counseling international students. Although the focus is on academic and occupational planning and decision making, readers are reminded that the career issues facing international students are connected to their experience of cross-cultural transition (Arthur, in press). The position taken in this chapter is that career counseling involves personal counseling (Krumboltz, 1993) and supporting students with culturally relevant interventions. Career counseling needs to incorporate programs and services to assist international students during three key phases of cross-cultural transition: (a) managing the initial demands faced during the cross-cultural transition of entering a new culture, (b) learning in a new cultural context, and (c) transferring international expertise to work settings in either the host or home country. The purpose of this chapter is to highlight issues in each of these three phases of cross-cultural transition that are influential for international students' career development and decisions. Case scenarios are presented to illustrate some of the dilemmas faced by international students as they live and learn in a new culture and prepare for the transition home.

Career and Transition Needs

The recent attention paid to the recruitment of international students has not been matched by infrastructure support and services to meet their needs (Arthur,

2003a). There is also a lag in the professional literature from a focus on their concerns and problems to outlining viable directions for counseling international students (Popadiuk & Arthur, 2004). Similar to other student populations, international students require career and life planning skills (Mori, 2000). The experience of living and learning in another country often leads to dissonance about career aspirations and changes in achievement levels (Arthur, 2003a). Acculturation to the host culture affects key career domains such as vocational identity, that is, the development of a stable understanding of aspirations, interests, and abilities (Shih & Brown, 2000). There is a need for more research to ascertain factors that influence international students' career decisions, the stability of their career choices, and what factors help them to persist in attaining their academic and career goals (Singaravelu, White, & Bringaze, 2005).

The majority of literature on the career issues faced by international students emphasizes job search and placement. For example, in one needs assessment of career issues, international students prioritized work experience, interviewing strategies, and job search skills as their main concerns (Spencer-Rodgers, 2000). Job search clubs for international students have been shown to influence competencies such as career self-efficacy and career decision making and also help to consolidate vocational identity (Bikos & Furry, 1999). However, the career placement concerns of international students are diverse, given that students may consider many plans ranging from options for further education, moving to other countries, remaining in the United States after their education, or returning to their home countries (Shen & Herr, 2004; Yang, Wong, Hwang, & Heppner, 2002). Although career services focused on job search and placement are important, counselors need to consider a broader perspective about international students' career issues (Singaravelu et al., 2005), incorporating personal issues associated with the experience of living and learning in a foreign culture (Arthur, in press).

The career development and decision making of international students need to be viewed as a parallel process with the experience of cross-cultural transition (Arthur, 2003a). There are many factors related to the decision to study abroad, many influences on academic choices and achievement in the host country, changing circumstances that lead students to pursue employment in the United States, and career factors related to preparation for returning home. Consequently, counselors need to offer a fuller range of counseling services that address career and transition needs.

The Career Choice to Study in Another Country

Individual, family, political, or economic factors in the home country may be factors influencing the decision to become an international student. These factors are important for understanding students' academic preparation and motivations for academic success (Arthur, 2003a; Thomas & Althen, 1989). Family members, community groups, or sponsorship agencies, such as government and employers, often invest both personally and financially to support international students.

Whereas some students may represent the "best and brightest" of their country in terms of academic potential, other students may be less motivated and less prepared for the demands of studying in a foreign environment (Leong & Chou, 1996). Even when students are used to being the top achievers in their home countries, adjustments to living in a new culture, pressures from family, and exposure to a new curriculum are disruptive for academic performance (Pedersen, 1991; Sandhu & Asrabadi, 1994). However, it should not be assumed that all international students struggle with academic achievement. Prior expertise may result in frustration about a lack of academic challenge, or students may feel disappointed about their educational experiences and feel stalled in pursuing their career goals. These examples illustrate how background preparation and expectations of international students are critical factors for influencing their academic performance and achievement of career goals (Arthur, 2003a). The first case scenario presented in this chapter illustrates how academic issues may be confounded with family expectations, leading to debilitating culture shock (Ward, Bochner, & Furnham, 2001).

Case Scenario 1

Mai was a 23-year-old student from Taiwan who was studying in a business administration program. On the counseling intake card, she listed "study skills" as the main reason for seeking help. When she met with the counselor, they began talking about her academic program, and the counselor noted that Mai appeared to be very anxious. When the counselor asked Mai to tell her a little bit about her experience of studying at the college, Mai's level of anxiety seemed to increase.

> It is like walking around in the dark—I am not sure what it is I am supposed to do here. The ways of teaching are very different than what I am used to at home. The teachers tell us things are important, I study those things, but these are not always the questions on the exam. I can't seem to figure it out. I try to participate in class but feel that I am asking too many questions and the instructor seems impatient. It is hard for me to do everything to get ready for class so I am always trying to catch up.

After exploring Mai's feelings of anxiety about her academic program, the counselor asked Mai what it was like for her to seek help and to come see a counselor. Mai averted eye contact and said,

> I am ashamed to have to be here. My parents don't understand what I am going through here. They keep saying that this is my future in front of me. They would be upset to know that I needed extra help. I remembered you from our student orientation and what you said about services on campus. That is why I came to you for help.

The counselor complimented Mai for seeking resources to help with her program success. The next three sessions were spent exploring Mai's motives and expectations for studying abroad, and the counselor helped Mai to access workshops on strategies for student success.

In this counseling scenario, it was important to acknowledge the strong family values that Mai held as a priority in her career planning and decision making. Counselors who have been trained in Western models of career counseling may be challenged to suspend their beliefs about individual choices to honor the importance of family influences and collectivist decision making (Williams, 2003). An overemphasis on the individual can add to the distress experienced by international students who are trying to live up to perceived family expectations while managing new academic demands.

Typically, international students are expected to identify an academic major and hence a career path prior to their arrival in the United States. This has led to the assumption that international students have well-defined career plans when, in actuality, these plans may not be consolidated by the individual or be realistic (Singaravelu et al., 2005). It is not uncommon for international students to consider changing their majors, while in the middle of an academic program because of an inability to perform well in their chosen fields. Alternatively, with exposure to new curriculum and lifestyles in the host country, students may wish to pursue new career options as they discover new interests or abilities (Singaravelu et al., 2005). Regardless of the circumstances leading students to reassess their academic majors or career choices, counselors need to be aware that international students often experience extreme stress associated with academic concerns (Wan, Chapman, & Biggs, 1992). Academic issues are often linked to concerns about financial sponsorship, family pressures, immigration status, and individual expectations, making the perceived threat of failure an intense pressure. Students' experience of academic difficulties may be connected to culture shock and the loss of usual support systems (Chen, 1999). Early intervention is critical to prevent the devastating consequences of returning home before completing an academic program (Arthur, 2003b; Sandhu, 1994).

Some international students may find themselves on career paths that do not reflect their interests and abilities. Alternatively, with exposure to local curriculum, other students may recognize new academic opportunities and career choices that they wish to pursue. Regardless of the reasons that prompt a review of career direction, the uncertainty of "what next?" is often experienced as a major stressor. Engaging in a career decision-making process can be helpful for students to consider the implications that changing majors may have for their immediate and long-term career goals. Many international students feel conflicted about making choices that are more compatible with personal needs in light of expectations from family and sponsors. When sponsorship is tied to a particular academic program, students may feel "locked into" a path that has not met their personal expectations and is no longer desirable. Even when choices appear to be more flexible, international students may feel considerable pressure about explaining changes that might be perceived by others as personal failure. The second case scenario introduces a situation in which there appeared to be few options for changing an academic program.

Case Scenario 2

Abir was a 28-year-old male from a country in the Middle East and one of 20 students sponsored to study in an engineering technology program. He was referred to the counseling center by the international student advisor who called the counselor to say that Abir was very unhappy with the quality of his academic program. Program quality issues disclosed in counseling are complex because of relationships with academic faculty in the educational institution and pressure to appease program sponsors of international education partnerships. For example, students who are unhappy with the quality of academic instruction or supervisory relationships may feel powerless to complain. In turn, when the quality of academic instruction is challenged, managers in academic institutions need to be prepared to take immediate action to hear students' concerns and mediate a suitable resolution with academic faculty. In this case, the international student advisor emphasized confidentiality and noted that it was very important that nobody else discover Abir's true feelings about his academic program. With this background information, the counselor met with Abir and asked him to describe his situation. Abir's opening statement was that he felt his academic program was "a waste of time." When the counselor responded with probes about the quality of the program, Abir interrupted and said, "That is not it. I don't want to work as a technologist in this field. I want to work at something that is more interesting to me." The counselor immediately sought clarification about the terms of his academic sponsorship. Abir was aware that the terms of his international education were tied to this particular academic program and that if he discontinued his studies, he would be forced to return to his country immediately. The counselor attempted to explore the pressure that Abir must be under to satisfy the terms of his sponsorship by completing the technology program. Abir looked puzzled and said, "I was told by the international student advisor that I could get help here to change careers. What help can you give me?" The counselor felt in quite a dilemma about how to proceed when changing majors was not an immediate option. She offered Abir the opportunity to explore what his current career path might mean for him and his family, how he might incorporate different interests in his life outside of work, and how he might examine other academic options from his home country.

This scenario highlights the importance of orienting international students to the purpose and functions of counseling. It is likely that this student left the counseling appointment with the feeling that it was not helpful. Two things about this career counseling scenario are linked to this outcome. First, the client seemed to have the expectation that he could change academic programs with the support of the counselor. Second, he was also expecting a directive approach from the counselor in which concrete suggestions and solutions would be given. It is important for counseling services to provide an orientation to students about counseling, which may be provided in a written description to be handed out with an intake card and reviewed during the first session. The counselor subsequently met with the international student advisor to discuss how counseling could be described to international students to set realistic expectancies.

Counseling across cultures also requires additional flexibility on behalf of counselors to strengthen the working alliance (Collins & Arthur, 2005). In Abir's case, a better match between the communication style of the client and the counselor may have helped the client to feel that the counselor was more responsive to his concerns. Although it may not have been possible for Abir to change his academic program and maintain sponsorship, exploration of how he could cope with constraints on his career may have helped to build rapport with him. Again, counselors need to check their cultural assumptions regarding freedom of choice to make career decisions. In this case, sponsorship was contingent on community service, which was highly valued in the student's culture of origin.

Many times, international students who seek counseling are looking for immediate solutions for crisis management and problem solving (Hayes & Lin, 1994). Counseling style has been identified as an influential factor with clients, although caution is given about stereotyping international students as preferring one particular style (e.g., directive or nondirective). Cultural norms about hierarchical relationships are an important influence, and students may feel more comfortable working with the counselor as an expert or authority figure (Mori, 2000). However, counselors are cautioned against assuming that students from a particular culture prefer one style of communication over another as research has shown contrasting results (D'Rozario & Romano, 2000; Yau, Sue, & Hayden, 1992). Additionally, when students become more familiar with the counseling process, they may also increase their comfort level for working in more collaborative ways.

The Decision to Pursue Career Options in the United States

There is an assumption in the literature that international students primarily require career counseling services connected to preparation for returning home (Arthur, 2003b; Pedersen, 1991). Yet, the majority of international students consider plans to reside permanently in the United States, and far fewer students plan to return to their homeland (Parr, Bradley, & Bingi, 1992). This possibility raises questions about the direction of career counseling services as student needs will inevitably vary according to whether they are focused on staying in the United States or on returning home (Spencer-Rogers, 2000). Career decision making may be an important intervention to help students explore the implications of staying in the United States and pursuing permanent immigration. Counselors are cautioned that decisions made in one cultural context may have unexpected and profound impacts on an international student's life in another cultural context (Arthur, 2003a). The cultural values of the host culture and the student's level of acculturation to the host culture need to be carefully considered in light of both the process of making important career decisions and how career decisions are related to a student's support system in both home and host cultures.

Students may also need additional support to pursue part-time employment to secure income, to obtain employment experience, or to acquire the skill sets that are preferred by U.S. employers (Spencer-Rogers, 2000). International students are more likely to require specialized services to help them to develop appropriate job search strategies and contacts with local employers. However, career counselors must be informed about policies related to local employment so that false expectations are not set. Although some countries are considering policy changes to attract more international students as permanent residents, stringent U.S. immigration policies mean that most international students will have to deal with returning home. Career counselors can help students to pursue multiple options in their career planning, to access local job placement resources, and to cope with the uncertainty about returning home (Shen & Herr, 2004; Spencer-Rogers, 2000; Yang et al., 2002). These examples illustrate how students' career directions following graduation may have a strong bearing on types of career planning and decision-making services that are required. The third case scenario illustrates how the decision to pursue employment in the United States is connected to a variety of personal considerations within the home and host cultures.

Case Scenario 3

Manuel was in his early 20s when his parents decided to send him from Jamaica to the United States to pursue a degree in science. He said that the decision was "more theirs than mine," and he was living under close scrutiny from an uncle in the house where he was living. Manuel originally sought career counseling because he was not sure if the science program was what he wanted to pursue as a major. However, during the first session, he quickly turned the conversation over to issues of missing his homeland, friends, and his girlfriend. After four sessions focusing on a career-choice assessment process, Manuel decided to remain in his academic program for 1 year and then review his situation. With his outgoing nature, he soon made friends and became involved with the university student association. He made an appointment with the counselor every month to "chat about how things are going." As the year progressed, he felt more integrated into his life in the United States and found that he was enjoying the challenge of his academic program. As he was completing his degree, Manuel sought counseling again to discuss his career options. He said that he never imagined that he would face the dilemma of choosing between his home country and staying in the United States. However, with the encouragement and support of his uncle, he requested help to pursue employment opportunities after graduation. His positive experience during a work-term placement with an engineering firm resulted in a job offer from an employer. Career counseling then focused on the decision making to stay in the United States, the implications for his family relationships, and his perceived career opportunities. The counselor connected Manuel with the appropriate campus resources to pursue an employment visa. Manuel's success with adapting to the social, academic, and employment demands in the local culture was highly influential in his changing perspective about career opportunities after graduation.

Preparing for Reentry

From the point of arriving in the host country, students should be preparing for their eventual return home, including future academic and occupational plans (NAFSA: Association of International Educators, 1996). International students have reported a wide range of reentry concerns that are relevant for their career development. These include loss of contact with the host culture, values conflicts, transferability of educational and language expertise, the impact of economic and political conditions in their home country, resuming prior relationships and/or employment roles, pressure to find employment in the chosen field, and occupational mobility (Arthur, 2003a; Brabant, Palmer, & Gramling, 1990; MacDonald & Arthur, 2004; Pedersen, 1990).

Some students may prolong their international experience by traveling or continuing studies in another country. However, most international students must face the inevitable return to their home country. Reentry transitions involve the ending of their academic program and a physical relocation home; they also involve the psychological process of adapting to the home culture (Arthur, 2003b; Martin & Harrell, 1996). Students may have mixed feelings about reuniting with family, friends, and aspects of their home environment, while at the same time experience a sense of loss about leaving the United States and returning home. Lifestyle changes and personal learning while studying abroad can result in new ways of viewing self, others, and the world (Arthur, 2003a; Ishiyama, 1989; Wang, 1997). Career interventions help students to gain a better understanding of internal and external changes that affect cultural identity.

There is typically more attention paid to preparing international students for entering into the host culture than preparing students for returning home. However, reverse culture shock is a common experience, particularly when international students have studied in a country with different cultural practices from their home culture (Arthur, 2003b; Gaw, 2000; Martin & Harrell, 1996; see also chapter 7). There are several reasons to extend programming on career development and decisions to include the reentry transition. First, international students may be better prepared to face adjustment issues upon entering a new cultural context and to not expect any difficulties in returning home. Second, students are often not aware of how much they have changed through international education and may be surprised by the feedback that they receive from family and friends. In turn, the people involved in international students' support systems may not be prepared for how to interact with and react to the "new person" who returns home. Third, international students may perceive the expectations to have their careers all figured out and to move on with life at home as a lack of support (MacDonald & Arthur, 2004). Fourth, either dramatic change or lack of change in their home environment can trigger doubts about a sense of belonging or about their personal and career goals (Martin & Harrell, 1996). Career counselors can educate international students regarding common issues in reentry transitions to normalize the adjustment process, to help to identify concerns, and to free energy to engage in career planning and decision making. Career workshops in a group format offer a forum for international students to learn from the facilitator and from each other (Arthur, 2003b; Singaravelu et al., 2005; Westwood, Lawrence, & Paul, 1986).

Dissonance about returning home is often based on career concerns, such as pressure to obtain employment in a chosen field, the perceived status of a new job, and how well the curriculum from studying in the United States and academic credentials will transfer to local employment conditions. Finding suitable job placements may be a challenge because of differences in resources available between the United States and students' home countries (Pedersen, 1990), for example, equipment, technology, and workplace systems. A major concern is how well theoretical knowledge attained in a foreign academic program will transfer to practical applications in local contexts. Students who have been away from their home countries for several years may be lacking occupational information from their home countries. Although international education is supposed to provide students with an employment advantage, some employers are reluctant to hire graduates who lack local experience (MacDonald & Arthur, 2004). These examples illustrate how career concerns can be paramount during the reentry transition. Specialized career services are needed to meet the job search and placement needs of international students returning home, pursuing work in the United States, or other educational opportunities (Yang et al., 2002). As the fourth case scenario illustrates, career counseling for returning home involves exploration of the personal meanings associated with living and learning across cultures, and how students have integrated their international experiences into their identity.

Case Scenario 4

Elena was a 32-year-old graduate student from Russia who was finishing a master's degree in environmental studies at the end of the school year. She was referred to counseling services by an academic supervisor who was concerned when Elena mentioned that she had been experiencing insomnia and was feeling depressed. Along with exploring the severity of these symptoms, the counselor invited Elena to talk about her experience as an international student. Elena spoke very positively about her time in the United States and how great it was for her to focus on her graduate studies. She noted that the program had offered her an opportunity to become involved in a prestigious research project that would have very positive influences for her job search at home. When the counselor asked about her experiences outside of her academic role, again Elena noted she was very happy, had made "friends for life" here, and had enjoyed the opportunity to travel to different states. The counselor noted the discrepancy between how she was describing her international education experience and how her symptoms were suggesting that "all is not well." Elena noted that since she began to focus on her graduation, she was having trouble sleeping.

> I stay up night after night wondering about my life. School here has been the best part of my life. I do not yet see my future. Some days I think that I should pursue

opportunities here, as there are many avenues that are not open for me at home. Then, I begin to think about my family at home and how much they have sacrificed for me to be here. It is not easy. I am less certain about the kind of job that I will have when I go home, as many employers are traditional. I really want to use my international experience and keep learning. There are also things about life here that I have come to enjoy and do not want to give up. I wish it were possible to combine my two worlds into one.

Elena was describing essential conflicts that she was experiencing in the process of preparing for reentry home. Many international students have thoughts about immigrating to the United States, and these need to be taken seriously in light of limited opportunities at home and in light of the implications of not returning home. In Elena's case, she seemed to be treating life in the United States as dichotomously opposed to her life at home. This created an opportunity to explore her shift in values and appreciations about each cultural context. The counselor also noted her uncertainty about employment at home. She referred Elena to a workshop about international job search and offered to help her to work on her career portfolio. This plan helped Elena feel like the issues were more concrete, helping her to minimize the ruminations that were fueling her sleeplessness and her negative affect.

Linking International Experience With Career Development

Supporting students to integrate their international experience is a key direction in the delivery of career counseling services (Arthur, in press). Several considerations are given for counselors in designing and delivering career counseling services for international students.

Cultural Relevance of Career Concepts

First, the terms *career* and *career development* need to be examined for their meanings and transferability across cultures. Young and Collin (2000) noted that "career has been and is enmeshed in notions of work, employment, occupations, and jobs" (p. 5). It is not surprising that international students might experience confusion about the meaning of career as it is used in local contexts. In turn, there is considerable variability in the extent to which career development services are made available in countries around the world (Watts, 1996). Counselors must remember that the term *career development* is culturally constructed. For members of diverse cultural groups such as international students, the term *career* may mean different things, if it holds significance at all. Consequently, one of the biggest barriers for international students may be lack of information about what career counseling may offer (Arthur, 2003a). International students who are unfamiliar with career counseling may be reluctant to seek professional assistance (Leong & Chou, 1996; Shen & Herr, 2004). If international students are more familiar with equating career issues with work experience and job placement, this may explain a preference for job search and placement services.

Applying Career Development Theories and Models of Counseling

Counselors need to examine the cultural validity of career development theories and career counseling models (Arthur & McMahon, 2005; Leong & Brown, 1995). Western norms about planning and decision making may be foreign ideas or antithetical to values held by international students. There is a growing amount of literature that challenges the cultural assumptions embedded in Western perspectives on career development theories, such as an emphasis on individualism and autonomy, the centrality of the work role, affluence and the structure of career opportunities, and the linearity or progressive nature of career development (Constantine & Erickson, 1998; Gysbers, Heppner, & Johnston, 2003). As illustrated in the chapter vignettes, international students from collectivist cultures may have strong family and community ties that are inextricably linked to their career decisions. Students may not have the freedom or resources to make decisions independent of the roles and responsibilities that they hold in their home cultures.

In turn, models of career decision making and problem solving (e.g., Miller-Tiedeman & Tiedeman, 1990; Peterson, Sampson, Reardon, & Lenz, 1996) are expanding beyond linear and cognitive frameworks to consider cultural beliefs about intuition, chance, fate, emotional reasoning, and spirituality (Amundson, 1998; Heppner et al., 2004; Sharf, 2002). As illustrated in the case scenarios, some international students may view their situation in light of career paths chosen for them and feel conflicted about how to reconcile their personal preferences with roles assigned to them. In turn, these students may be less motivated to actively pursue individual interests if they are operating from a fundamental belief in fate or spiritual beliefs that a pathway in life has been chosen for them. Again, these examples illustrate the importance of counselors working to establish a strong therapeutic alliance in which the cultural meanings of career issues are explored (Arthur, 2006).

Counselors are invited to consider ways in which theories of career development can be adapted for counseling international students. For example, Super's (1984, 1990) developmental theory has been supported by research in many countries throughout the world. This theory is particularly suited for counseling international students through the exploration of self-identity, values, and life roles. His work also provides the foundation for exploring clients' career adaptability (Savickas, 1997, 2000). A flexible application of the stages of career development outlined in Super's theory can be used to help international students examine aspects of their cross-cultural transition that are related to exploration, consolidation, or maintenance. This is particularly useful as students gain mastery over certain tasks and other aspects of their international transitions surface in challenging ways (Arthur, 2003a). When individuals become international students, there is often a shift in the salience of life roles. Counseling techniques exploring life roles are relevant for diverse populations (Brott, 2005) and can be used to help international students explore influences on their career planning and decision making. Counselors can support international students to explore changes in life roles between home and host cultures and how students perceive changes in current and future responsibilities.

The experience of cross-cultural transitions can result in profound personal learning that prompts an examination of values (Mitchell & Krumboltz, 1996). Exposure to cultural contrasts may lead to a clearer grasp of personal values or lead to a sense of dissonance in which students feel conflicted about their values. Values clarification is an important consideration in career development services for international students. Career counseling can help students to (a) identify salient cultural values in home and host cultures, (b) explore which values related to career are now most salient, and (c) incorporate values into future academic and employment directions (MacDonald & Arthur, 2004). Values clarification helps students to explore their career options and whether their original plans continue to be the most suitable option or whether new career goals have emerged that require exploration. Working with a values-based approach to career counseling can help students to consolidate their sense of cultural identity and to choose career paths that are congruent for job satisfaction (Brown, 2002).

Systems theories (e.g., the ecological approach; Conyne & Cook, 2004; Cook, Heppner, & O'Brien, 2002) and Systems Theory Framework (STF; Patton & McMahon, 1997, 2006) are particularly well suited for career counseling with international students, because they support a broader contextual examination of factors both within the individual and surrounding the individual that are influential for career development. For example, the STF has been recommended for use in multicultural career counseling (Arthur & McMahon, 2005). Keeping the individual central, the STF can be used flexibly to accommodate clients whose career development occurs within either individualistic or collectivist cultures. The STF incorporates aspects of culture that are relevant for each client, including salient cultural dimensions and the intersections of cultural identities that are related to each client's life roles. The individual system, the social system, and the environmental/system account for the content influences of the STF (Patton & McMahon, 2006). At the center of the STF is the individual system, comprising a range of intrapersonal influences such as gender, interests, age, abilities, personality, and sexual orientation. The STF also incorporates the individual's social system and influences on career planning and decision making, such as family, educational institutions, and peers. Other environmental/societal influences such as globalization and changing workplaces seem particularly relevant for understanding many of the career issues presented by international students. Along with the content influences of the individual system, the social system, and the environmental/system, career counseling using the STF takes into consideration process influences, including the interactions between systems, change over time, and chance (Arthur & McMahon, 2005). Therefore, the STF offers counselors a way to frame contextual and cultural influences on the client's unique experiences, while acknowledging that their career issues are likely to change as a result of learning during cross-cultural transitions and also as a result of unexpected events. Essentially, the STF provides a map to guide career counselors while clients are encouraged to fill in the details and reality of the map through telling their career stories.

Constructivist approaches that emphasize narrative approaches and learning with the client are helpful to explore the meanings of individual experiences within cultural contexts (Brott, 2005; Peavy, 1997; Singaravelu et al., 2005). International students are encouraged to tell their stories and to illuminate the challenges and successes they have experienced. Counselors can support students to examine the cultural meanings of their experiences and help students to understand possible new interpretations of their stories in light of their current career issues. Together, counselors and clients can narrate new possibilities for career planning and decision making. Using constructivist approaches can help both counselors and clients to enter into the roles of learners to gain better understanding of cultural influences on career issues and to incorporate culturally relevant perspectives into career counseling interventions (Arthur, 2006).

Enhancing Employability

Another key direction for career counseling is helping students to represent their international experience in meaningful ways to employers. For example, career interventions can be designed to help students identify the competencies they have gained through international experience. Several strategies have been suggested to enhance this planning process (Arthur, 2004; MacDonald & Arthur, 2004):

- Students need to be able to identify their employment competencies. General experiences and general statements, such as "I have studied in the United States" and "I have traveled," need to be translated into concrete examples and specific competencies that are relevant for employers, for example, "During my practicum placement, I had to learn how to use a new management system, and I have specific ideas about how that system could be used in this organization." Career counselors are in an ideal position to deliver group workshops to educate students about how to translate their experience into marketable skills. A bottom line is that the responsibility lies with students to show how their international experience is relevant for employment contexts.
- Career practitioners can provide clients with handouts that define and describe competencies that are valued by employers. For example, in Canada, the Conference Board of Canada has published a list of employment competencies. This can be supplemented by taxonomies of international employment competencies that are typically detailed in three domains: intercultural competencies, technical/professional competencies, and personal competencies (e.g., Wilson, 1998). Literature is

49

also available on competencies for managing cross-cultural transitions to provide international students with anchors for representing their international experience (Arthur, 2002).

- Career counselors can provide feedback to clients about the competencies that are represented in descriptions of international experience. During individual interviews or role-plays during career workshops, this process models to international students ways of identifying specific competencies gained from international experience.
- Documentation pertaining to academic and employment experience is recommended to supplement information that is provided to employers in general applications and interviews. Career counselors can show international students how to create employment portfolios that demonstrate how they have acquired international employment competencies and proof that they can enact those competencies. Portfolios provide evidence for employers about the nature of learning acquired in the United States and provide concrete examples about the benefits of international experience.

Career Planning Resources

Career counselors need to become familiar with resources for gaining additional international experience in either academic or employment settings. Students who wish to keep their international career track going often need help to research opportunities in the United States and in other countries. Studying abroad may lead some students to gain a firmer grasp on their career paths and feel more committed to pursuing academic and career goals. New ideas about adding international dimensions to career planning may help students to increase their career options.

Checking Attitudes Toward International Students

Career counselors are cautioned about the tendency to treat international students as a homogeneous group. As a general principle, the greater the difference between home and host cultures, the greater the adjustment demands faced by international students (Pedersen, 1991). However, services designed to support international students may inadvertently pose as barriers through misunderstandings about their cultural backgrounds and lack of understanding about their academic and occupational needs (Popadiuk & Arthur, 2004). Given the number of countries and cultures represented in this student population, counselors benefit from general knowledge about students' common issues, but they must be prepared to assess and address the unique experiences of individual international students (Arthur, 2003a; Singaravelu et al., 2005). Cultural differences necessitate that career counselors spend more time on educational processes to help international students navigate local expectations for academic performance, job search, and workplace behavior. The career-related needs of undergraduate and graduate students differ because of the stage of specialization and focus in their career preparation (Mallinckrodt & Leong, 1992; Shen & Herr, 2004). These examples underscore the importance of offering a variety of career development programming that meets common needs while addressing the unique career issues faced by individual international students.

Overcoming Barriers for Accessing Counseling

The underutilization of counseling services by international students is an issue that deserves to be highlighted. Barriers for access may be related to lack of information and marketing about counseling services, internal beliefs about help seeking, the stigma associated with counseling, or systemic barriers that impede the cultural appropriateness and perceived effectiveness of services (Anderson & Myer, 1985; Arthur, 2003a; Mori, 2000; Pedersen, 1991; Sandhu, 1994). Counselors are challenged to be proactive about developing creative and culturally appropriate services that are connected to the needs of students, that are publicized to international students and the larger campus community, and that are regarded by international students as useful (Brinson & Kottler, 1995; Sandhu, 1994; Yi et al., 2003). This inevitably means outreach services to engage the international student community in program planning.

Summary

One of the best ways to prepare students for the global workforce is through participation in international education. Studying in another country offers students the opportunity for rich learning about new cultures and prompts learning about their home cultures. The expertise gained by international students is framed by the experience of cross-cultural transition as they enter a new culture and ultimately prepare to stay in that culture or prepare for returning to life at home. As part of comprehensive student support services, programs need to be designed to address the career development issues and decisions that parallel students' experience with cross-cultural transitions. Counselors have an educational role in helping international students to understand the meaning of career development and the relevance of career counseling services. Counselors also need to be willing to adapt their career counseling practices to incorporate the cultural perspectives of international students and some of the unique pressures that they face in their career development. The discussion in this chapter is intended to better position career counselors to support international students with career issues that surface initially as part of adjusting to new academic curriculum, as part of examining new lifestyles and values, and in preparation for returning home. Although the emphasis of this chapter is on academic and occupational issues, counselors are reminded that these issues are inextricably linked to the personal relationships, cultural values, and circumstances of individual international students. A key goal of counseling services is directed at helping students integrate international experience into their career development to foster a positive experience while studying in the United States and to prepare for future career plans.

References

Aigner, J. S., Nelson, P., & Stimpfl, J. (1992). *Internationalizing the university: Making it work.* Springfield, VA: CBIS Federal.

Amundson, N. (1998). *Active engagement.* Richmond, British Columbia, Canada: Ergon Communications.

Anderson, T., & Myer, T. (1985). Presenting problems, counselor contacts, and "no shows": International and American college students. *Journal of College Student Personnel, 26,* 500-503.

Arthur, N. (2002). Preparing students for a world of work in cross-cultural transition. *Australian Journal of Career Development, 11,* 9-13.

Arthur, N. (2003a). *Counseling international students: Clients from around the world.* New York: Kluwer/Plenum Academic Press.

Arthur, N. (2003b). Preparing international students for the re-entry transition. *Canadian Journal of Counselling, 37,* 173-185.

Arthur, N. (2004). Show off your international experience. In *Proceedings of the National Consultation on Career Development—NATCON 2004.* Retrieved July 31, 2006, from http://www.canadacareerweek.com/natcon/papers/natcon_papers_2004_arthur.pdf

Arthur, N. (2006). Infusing culture in constructivist approaches to career counselling. In M. McMahon & W. Patton (Eds.), *Career counselling: Constructivist approaches* (pp. 57-68). London, UK: Routledge.

Arthur, N. (in press). Counseling international students. In P. Pedersen, J. Draguns, W. Lonner, & J. Trimble (Eds.), *Counseling across cultures* (6th ed.). Thousand Oaks, CA: Sage.

Arthur, N., & McMahon, M. (2005). Multicultural career counseling: Theoretical applications of the Systems Theory Framework. *The Career Development Quarterly, 53,* 208-222.

Bikos, L. H., & Furry, T. S. (1999). The job search club for international students: An evaluation. *Career Development Quarterly, 48,* 31-44.

Bohm, A., Davis, D., Meares, D., & Pearce, D. (2002). *Global student mobility 2025: Forecasts of the global demand for international higher education.* Sydney, New South Wales, Australia: IDP Education Australia.

Brabant, S., Palmer, C. E., & Gramling, R. (1990). Returning home: An empirical investigation of cross-cultural reentry. *International Journal of Intercultural Relations, 14,* 387-404.

Brinson, J. A., & Kottler, J. (1995). International students in counseling: Some alternative models. *Journal of College Student Psychotherapy, 9*(3), 57-70.

Brott, P. E. (2005). A constructivist look at life roles. *The Career Development Quarterly, 54,* 138-149.

Brown, D. (2002). The role of work and cultural values in occupational choice, satisfaction, and success: A theoretical statement. *Journal of Counseling & Development, 80,* 48-56.

Chen, C. P. (1999). Common stressors among international college students: Research and counseling implications. *Journal of College Counseling, 2,* 49-65.

Collins, S., & Arthur, N. (2005). Enhancing the therapeutic alliance in culture-infused counselling. In N. Arthur & S. Collins (Ed.), *Culture-infused counselling: Celebrating the Canadian mosaic* (pp. 113-160). Calgary, Alberta, Canada: Counselling Concepts.

Constantine, M. G., & Erickson, C. D. (1998). Examining social constructions in vocational counseling: Implications for multicultural counseling competency. *Counseling Psychology Quarterly, 11,* 189-199.

Conyne, R., & Cook, E. (Eds.). (2004). *Ecological counseling:An innovative approach to conceptualizing person-environment interaction.* Alexandria, VA: American Counseling Association.

Cook, E. P., Heppner, M. J., & O'Brien, K. M. (2002). Career development of women of color and White women: Assumptions, conceptualization, and interventions from an ecological perspective. *The Career Development Quarterly, 50,* 291-305.

D'Rozario, V., & Romano J. L. (2000). Perceptions of counselor effectiveness: A study of two country groups. *Counseling Psychology Quarterly, 13,* 51-63.

Gaw, K. F. (2000). Reverse culture shock in students returning from overseas. *International Journal of Intercultural Relations, 24,* 83-104.

Gysbers, N., Heppner, M. J., & Johnston, J. A. (2003). *Career counseling:Process, issues, and techniques* (2nd ed.). New York: Allyn & Bacon.

Hayes, R. L., & Lin, H. (1994). Coming to America: Developing social support systems for international students. *Journal of Multicultural Counseling and Development, 22,* 7-16.

Heppner, M. J., Lee, C., Heppner, P., McKinnon, L. C., Multon, K. D., & Gysbers, N. C. (2004). The role of problem-solving appraisal in the process and outcome of career counseling. *Journal of Vocational Behavior, 65,* 217-238.

Ishiyama, F. I. (1989). Understanding foreign adolescents' difficulties in cross-cultural adjustment: A self-validation model. *Canadian Journal of School Psychology, 5*(1), 41-56.

Krumboltz, J. (1993). Integrating career counseling and personal counseling. *The Career Development Quarterly, 42,* 143-148.

Kuo, B. C. H., & Roysircar, G. (2006). An exploratory study of cross-cultural adaptation of adolescent Taiwanese unaccompanied sojourners in Canada. *International Journal of Intercultural Relations, 30,* 159-183.

Leong, F. T. L., & Brown, M. T. (1995). Theoretical issues in cross-cultural career development: Cultural validity and cultural specificity. In W. B. Walsh & S. H. Osipow (Eds.), *Handbook of vocational psychology:Theory research, and practice* (2nd ed., pp. 143-180). Mahwah, NJ: Erlbaum.

Leong, F. T., & Chou, E. L. (1996). Counseling international students. In P. B. Pedersen, J. G. Draguns, W. J. Lonner, & J. E. Trimble (Eds.), *Counseling across cultures* (4th ed., pp. 210-242). Thousand Oaks, CA: Sage.

Leong, F. T., & Sedlacek, W. E. (1986). A comparison of international and U.S. student preferences for help sources. *Journal of College Student Personnel, 27,* 426-430.

MacDonald, S., & Arthur, N. (2004). When international experience throws a career curve. In *Proceedings of the National Consultation on Career Development—NATCON 2004.* Retrieved July 31, 2006, from http://www.canadacareerweek.com/natcon/papers/natcon_papers_2004_arthur_macdonald.pdf

Mallinckrodt, B., & Leong, F. T. (1992). International graduate students, stress, and social support. *Journal of College Student Development, 33,* 71-78.

Martin, J. N., & Harrell, T. (1996). Reentry training for intercultural sojourners. In D. Landis & R. S. Bhagat (Eds.), *Handbook of intercultural training* (2nd ed., pp. 307-326). Thousand Oaks, CA: Sage.

Miller-Tiedeman, A. L., & Tiedeman, D. V. (1990). Career decision making: An individualistic perspective. In D. Brown, L. Brooks, & Associates (Eds.), *Career choice and development: Applying contemporary theories to practice* (2nd ed., pp. 308-337). San Francisco: Jossey-Bass.

Mitchell, L. K., & Krumboltz, J. D. (1996). Krumboltz's learning theory of career choice and counseling. In D. Brown, L. Brooks, & Associates (Eds.), *Career choice and development* (3rd ed., pp. 223-280). San Francisco: Jossey-Bass.

Mori, S. (2000). Addressing the mental health concerns of international students. *Journal of Counseling & Development, 78,* 137-144.

NAFSA: Association of International Educators. (1996). *NAFSA's international student handbook.* Washington, DC: Author.

Parr, G., Bradley, L., & Bingi, R. (1992). Concerns and feelings of international students. *Journal of College Student Development, 33,* 20-25.

Patton, W., & McMahon, M. (1997). *Career development in practice: A systems theory perspective.* Sydney, New South Wales, Australia: New Hobsons Press.

Patton, W., & McMahon, M. (2006). *Career development and systems theory: Connecting theory and practice.* Rotterdam, the Netherlands: Sense Publishers.

Peavy, R. V. (1997). A constructive framework for career counseling. In T. L. Sexton & B. L. Griffin (Eds.), *Constructivist thinking in counseling practice, research, and training* (pp. 122-140). New York: Teachers College Press.

Pedersen, P. (1990). Social and psychological factors of brain drain and reentry among international students: A survey of this topic. *McGill Journal of Education, 25,* 229-243.

Pedersen, P. (1991). Counseling international students. *The Counseling Psychologist, 19,* 10-58.

Peterson, G. W., Sampson, J. P., Reardon, R. C., & Lenz, J. G. (1996). A cognitive information processing approach to career problem solving and decision making. In D. Brown, L. Brooks, & Associates (Eds.), *Career choice and development* (3rd ed., pp. 423-467). San Francisco: Jossey-Bass.

Popadiuk, N., & Arthur, N. (2004). Counselling international students in Canada. *International Journal for the Advancement of Counselling, 26,* 125-145.

Sandhu, D. S. (1994). An examination of the psychological needs of students: Implications for counseling and psychotherapy. *International Journal for the Advancement of Counselling, 17,* 229-239.

Sandhu, D. S., & Asrabadi, B.R. (1994). Development of an acculturative stress scale for international students: Preliminary findings. *Psychological Reports, 75,* 435-448.

Savickas, M. (1997). Career adaptability: An integrative construct for life-span, life-space theory. *The Career Development Quarterly, 45,* 247-259.

Savickas, M. (2000). Renovating the psychology of careers for the twenty-first century. In A. Collin & R. Young (Eds.), *The future of career* (pp. 53-68). Cambridge, UK: Cambridge University Press.

Sharf, R. S. (2002). *Applying career development theory to counseling.* Pacific Grove, CA: Brooks/Cole.

Shen, Y., & Herr, E. L. (2004). Career placement concerns of international graduate students: A qualitative study. *Journal of Career Development, 31,* 15-29.

Shih, S., & Brown, C. (2000). Taiwanese international students: Acculturation level and vocational identity. *Journal of Career Development, 27,* 35-47.

Singaravelu, H., White, L., & Bringaze, T. (2005). Factors influencing international students' career choice: A comparative study. *Journal of Career Development, 32,* 46-59.

Spencer-Rogers, J. (2000). The vocational situation and country of orientation of international students. *Journal of Multicultural Counseling and Development, 28,* 32-49.

Super, D. (1984). Career and life development. In D. Brown & L. Brooks (Eds.), *Career choice and development: Applying contemporary approaches to practice* (pp. 192-239). San Francisco: Jossey-Bass.

Super, D. (1990). A life-span, life-space approach to career development. In D. Brown & L. Brooks (Eds.), *Career choice and development: Applying contemporary theories to practice* (pp. 197-261). San Francisco: Jossey-Bass.

Thomas, K., & Althen, G. (1989). Counseling foreign students. In P. B. Pedersen, J. G. Draguns, W. J. Lonner, & J. E. Trimble (Eds.), *Counseling across cultures* (3rd ed., pp. 205-241). Honolulu: University of Hawaii Press.

Wan, T., Chapman, D. W., & Biggs, D. A. (1992). Academic stress of international students attending U.S. universities. *Research in Higher Education, 33,* 607-623.

Wang, M. M. (1997). Reentry and reverse culture shock. In K. Cushner & R. W. Brislin (Eds.), *Improving intercultural interactions: Vol. 2. Modules for cross-cultural training programs* (pp. 109-128). Thousand Oaks, CA: Sage.

Ward, C., Bochner, S., & Furnham, A. (2001). *The psychology of culture shock* (2nd ed.). East Sussex, England: Routledge.

Watts, A. (1996). A framework for comparing careers guidance systems in different countries. *Educational and Vocational Guidance, 58,* 53-62.

Westwood, M. J., Lawrence, W. S., & Paul, D. (1986). Preparing for reentry: A program for the sojourning student. *International Journal for the Advancement of Counseling, 9,* 221-230.

Williams, B. (2003). The worldview dimensions of individualism and collectivism: Implications for counseling. *Journal of Counseling & Development, 81,* 370-374.

Wilson, D. N. (1998). *Defining international competencies for the new millennium* (CBIE Research, No. 12). Ottawa, Ontario, Canada: Canadian Bureau of International Education.

Yang, E., Wong, S. C., Hwang, M., & Heppner, M. J. (2002). Widening our global view: The development of career counseling services for international students. *Journal of Career Development, 28,* 203-213.

Yau, T. Y., Sue, D., & Hayden, D. (1992). Counseling style preference of international students. *Journal of Counseling Psychology, 39,* 100-104.

Yi, J., Lin, G., & Kishimoto, Y. (2003). Utilization of counseling services by international students. *Journal of Instructional Psychology, 30,* 333-342.

Young, R., & Collin, A. (Eds.). (2000). *The future of career.* Cambridge, UK: Cambridge University Press.

Chapter 4

Counseling Gay, Lesbian, Bisexual, and Questioning International Students

Mark Pope, Hemla D. Singaravelu, Alexander Chang,
Christopher Sullivan, and Stacie Murray

Gay, lesbian, bisexual, and questioning (GLBQ) international students may have a number of unique issues to confront during their stay in the United States. Every year in the United States, almost 500,000 students from other countries enroll in U.S. colleges and universities (National Center for Education Statistics, 2003). Even if only 5% of these students identified or eventually identified as GLBQ, that would be 25,000 students attending U.S. colleges and universities who have issues common to all international students as well as having some unique issues. These special issues may include coming out to self and others, dating and relationship formation, obtaining information about sexually transmitted diseases and other health issues, career development and how this may be affected by coming out, rejection by family and friends, special immigration concerns, communication, differences in cultural taboos, isolation, and lack of a reference group.

Sexual minorities may include individuals who identify as gay, lesbian, bisexual, transgender, queer, questioning, or intersex. This chapter is limited, however, to issues of sexual orientation, not gender identity, and only addresses international students who specifically identify as lesbian, gay, or bisexual or those who are questioning their sexual orientation. Although issues are similar for those who identify as transgender and intersex, there are also special concerns regarding this population that are beyond the scope of this chapter.

Informed counselors, psychologists, social workers, university faculty, international student advisers, and anyone who works with or comes into contact with international students in the United States are in an excellent position to provide support for these students and help them during their journey into and through U.S. culture. Providing a safe place for these GLBQ students to discuss their concerns is critical to helping them be successful in achieving their academic, career, and personal goals as such issues may provide potential barriers to their successfully navigating their entry into, transition through, and exit from this new environment.

In this chapter, we identify some of the unique issues that GLBQ international students may confront and offer some guidelines for those who are helping these students. We begin by providing a number of definitions. Then we address the issues that are particularly relevant to the people who are providing counseling, such as recognizing their own biases and providing resource referrals. Furthermore, we identify issues that are relevant to international students, such as identity development, the coming-out process, personal relationships, health issues, career development, family and friends, immigration concerns, cultural differences, isolation, and the need for reference groups. Finally, we address the institutional issues, such as having a GLBQ international student brochure.

Definitions

In the United States, the following definitions are common and particularly useful. As international students become more knowledgeable and acculturated into the country, the more these definitions will become relevant. It is important to note that different cultures around the world may regard same-sex attraction differently. Becoming familiar with specific cultural contexts is paramount for professionals who desire to assist in augmenting the experiences of international students.

The definition of *culture* that we use in our practice as international student advisors, faculty who work with international students, and counselors/psychologists who assist such students is broad and inclusive; it includes race, ethnicity, gender, (dis)ability, socioeconomic status, spiritual nature, *and* sexual orientation (Pope, 1995b). We find that this facilitates our understanding, approach, and work with GLBQ international students. By showing respect for all of our students, we gain their trust and their willingness to approach us with their problems rather than hide them and suffer in silence.

The terms *gay, lesbian, bisexual, transgender, queer, questioning,* and *intersex* (GLBTQQI) are socially constructed identities; meanings can be fluid depending on cultural contexts. There are many cultures in the world that do not equate a social identity to same-sex sexual behavior. Cultures—both within and outside of the United States—create and construct sexuality and gender differently based on their own unique sets of values and practices. Developing an understanding of how these constructs may differ from one's own conception of them is important if professionals are to prepare themselves to interact effectively and appropriately in an intercultural situation. To be most effective, they should be aware of how the following concepts can be barriers to intercultural understanding depending on specific cultural contexts of students (Morrison, 2004; Ogden, 2005).

> *Sexual orientation:* a person's emotional, physical, affectional, and/or sexual attraction and the expression of that attraction. Most people become aware of their sexual orientation during adolescence.
> *Heterosexual:* a person who is emotionally, physically, affectionally, and/or sexually attracted or committed to members of the other sex.

Homosexually-oriented: describes a person who is emotionally, physically, affectionally, and/or sexually attracted or committed to members of the same sex.

Coming out: the process by which a person discovers and accepts his or her own individual sexual orientation or gender identity (coming out to self, generally a single event) or discloses his or her sexual orientation or gender identity to others (coming out to others, ongoing and continuous).

Gender identity: a person's sense of being masculine, feminine, in-between, or androgynous. It is important to recognize that this is independent from a person's biological or physiological sex.

Gender identity versus sexual orientation: Gender identity is distinct from sexual orientation. Gender identity, the sense that one is a boy or a girl, is usually manifested by the age of 3 or 4 years. Sexual orientation, the sense of which gender one is emotionally, physically, affectionally, and/or sexually attracted to, does not manifest itself until later in life, usually after puberty or not until full adulthood.

GLBTQQIA: an abbreviation for gay, lesbian, bisexual, transgender, queer, questioning, intersex, and allies. While not exhaustive, this abbreviation is often used to represent the community as a whole.

Gay: a common and acceptable term for a homosexually oriented person, including those who identify as male and are emotionally, physically, and/or sexually attracted to or committed to others who identify as male.

Lesbian: a common and acceptable term for a homosexually oriented person, including those who identify as female and are emotionally, physically, and/or sexually attracted to or committed to others who identify as female.

Bisexual: a common and acceptable term for a person who may be emotionally, physically, and/or sexually attracted or committed to members of both the male and female sexes.

Transgender: a broad term for all gender-variant people, including transsexuals, transvestites, drag kings, drag queens, and intersexed people, and is meant to include anyone who does not identify with the traditional roles of male/female that are imposed by biological sex.

Queer: a historically negative term meaning homosexually oriented person that members of the queer community have reclaimed to mean simply "different"; often, the term has a positive and political connotation.

Questioning: those who are questioning their sexual or gender orientation.

Intersex: a person born with mixed sexual physiology.

Ally: a member of the dominant majority, in this case heterosexual, culture who works to end oppression in his or her professional and personal life through support of, and as an advocate for, the oppressed population, in this case GLBTQQI people.

Heterosexism: refers to seeing and interpreting things in the gay culture by using the values and perceptions of the culturally dominant heterosexual community. This prejudice assumes that all people are or should be heterosexual, and therefore excludes the needs, concerns, and life experiences of lesbians, gay men, and bisexuals. It is equivalent to ethnocentrism.

Homophobia: refers to the fear and hatred of those who love and sexually desire others of the same sex. Homophobia, which has its roots in sexism, includes prejudice, discrimination, harassment, and acts of violence brought on by such fear and hatred. There are four interrelated types of homophobia:

1. *Personal homophobia* is prejudice based on a personal belief that lesbian, gay, and bisexual people are sinful, immoral, sick, or inferior to heterosexuals.
2. *Interpersonal homophobia* is individual behavior based on personal homophobia. This hatred or dislike may be expressed by name-calling, telling jokes, or verbal or physical harassment.
3. *Institutional homophobia* refers to the many ways in which governments, businesses, and churches discriminate against people on the basis of sexual orientation.
4. *Cultural homophobia* refers to social standards that dictate being heterosexual is better or morally superior to being lesbian, gay, or bisexual.

Desensitization: the process by which an individual's fears, myths, and preconceptions about the gay culture are lessened. By getting to know gay, lesbian, and bisexual people as individuals, much of the prejudice or preconceptions are decreased. The individual is able to put aside preconceived ideas and is open to see the members of this culture as individuals and as people beyond their cultural label. Oppression oppresses, however, and those who are raised in heterosexist societies (including GLBTQQIA people) will find it difficult to fully eliminate all personal homophobia; therefore, this process is a lifelong process that requires constant diligence.

The Counselor

For individuals who are providing counseling to GLBQ international students, there are several issues to consider, such as understanding one's own biases and being knowledgeable about campus and local community GLBQ resources.

The First Step: Understanding Your Own Biases

The first step for those who work with GLBQ international students is to examine their own biases regarding sexual minorities (Dunlap, 2002; Ogden, 2005; Pope, 1995a). Such self-assessments begin with an examination of personal values and beliefs to understand where they stand on specific issues and to explore their willingness to be open and fair. Many people have been socialized to be uncomfortable with homosexuality and, by extension, with gay, lesbian, and bisexual people. The first step toward recognizing discomfort is to assess personal attitudes toward homosexuality. It is important for counselors to know how willing they are to deal with gay, lesbian, and bisexual issues, and at what level they are willing to get involved with GLBQ students. For example, are they best able to present a booklet of GLBQ resource information in orientation packets and refer students to those resources, or are they willing to work with the GLBQ resource center and with students to create educational programs and international GLBQ support groups? It is important to remember that lesbian, gay, and bisexual students are individuals who have had unique experiences and exist in varying stages of identity development.

It is also important to be aware of personal struggles with homophobia and heterosexism, both at the conscious and nonconscious levels. If counselors discover that they have heterosexist biases or internalized homophobia that are proving difficult to overcome, referral may become necessary. Referral is an act that will benefit students by providing access to professionals who are better prepared to assist GLBQ individuals. Referring students does not relieve counselors of their professional responsibility to address their own issues with regard to heterosexism or homophobia. Homophobia and heterosexism can present themselves in subtle ways. If counselors find themselves compulsively talking about their opposite-sex spouse while meeting with GLBQ students, they must seek consultation with other professionals or participate in supervision to uncover and deal with these issues.

Furthermore, to enhance their ability to serve this population, counselors need to increase knowledge about GLBQ resources in their respective locales and in broader society. It is through this self-assessment and knowledge that counselors can begin to aid in the establishment of a college and university environment that is inclusive and accepting of students with diverse sexual orientations (Alexander, Morotani, & Sullivan, 2000; Pope, Prince, & Mitchell, 2000; Sherrill, 1994).

Knowledge of Community Resources

After assessing their own biases, the next step for counselors is to learn about GLBQ issues, both in the United States and around the world. GLBQ sensitivity training, GLBQ resource centers, conferences, books, and some Web sites are excellent sources of information. For example, one outstanding Web site found at http://www.indiana.edu/~overseas/lesbigay/index.html features lists of GLBQ resources, including books, videos, and relevant links that may be of interest to professionals who have a desire to educate themselves about GLBQ students.

Those who come in contact with international students are in the best place to help such students establish contacts in the local community. For those GLBQ students seeking outside support, the counseling professional should be familiar with the following (Ogden, 2005):

1. *GLBQ support services and networks both on and off campus.* Almost every college in the United States has some student or community association for GLBQ people. Larger cities may also have such services as bars, clubs, coffee houses, restaurants, shows, bookshops, video shops, specialty stores, cinemas, religious groups, health services, radio

and television stations, and publications that cater to the GLBQ community. Counselors can serve as the bridge between these resources and GLBQ international students.

2. *Culture-specific attitudes/laws.* It is important for the counseling professional to be familiar with regional, state, and national laws regarding sexuality as well as local attitudes.

3. *GLB home-stays.* International student advisors frequently arrange home-stays for international students. Gay or lesbian couples (host families) could also provide home-stays and a different and special look at U.S. culture.

Visit the Web site of the Rainbow Special Interest Group of NAFSA: Association of International Educators (www.indiana.edu/~overseas/lesbigay). Included among the resources are the following:

- Country and culture-specific information for international students.
- List of over 65 useful resource books for information regarding cultural, lifestyle, and legal information for gay, lesbian, bisexual, and transgender (GLBT) students.
- Information on including GLBT issues as part of predeparture or international student orientation.
- Information on integrating GLBT and international programming on campus.
- First-person experiences of GLBT study abroad and international students.
- List of links to national and international GLBT organizations and resources, many with country and culture-specific information.

Guidelines for Positive Interactions

The following are some guidelines for having positive interactions with GLBQ international students (Morrison, 2004):

1. Be aware of feelings, values, beliefs, and thinking about GLBQ issues and people.
2. Educate yourself about homosexuality, bisexuality, and transgender issues.
3. Talk with GLBQ people and those who support them.
4. Identify community resources to serve as places for referral if needed.
5. Provide a supportive atmosphere for those who are or think they may be GLBQ.
6. Avoid language that implies that all people are heterosexual, "male or female," and either "single, married, or divorced."
7. Advocate and participate in educational programs for your staff, so that GLBQ people receive service without prejudice and with the empathy and warmth deserved by all.

8. Remember that people do not "choose" to have "gay" feelings; people "choose" whether to act on their feelings.

9. Do not presume that all GLBQ people regret their orientation or gender identity.

10. Remember that societal oppression and discrimination create much of the unhappiness of many GLBQ people.

11. Remember that the oppression experienced by lesbians differs in many ways from the oppression experienced by gay men. Non-White lesbians and gay men suffer in unique ways as well.

12. Remember that stereotypical "gay" behavior or appearance does not mean that a person evidencing that behavior or appearance is necessarily "gay."

13. Help people to help themselves by increasing their sense of self-worth, self-acceptance, and self-reliance so they can take charge of their own lives and integrate their feeling, thinking, and behavior in a positive way.

14. Know when your skills and your knowledge reach their limit. Refer people elsewhere when they need help that you cannot effectively supply.

15. Know when and how negative feelings you may have toward GLBQ people may prevent you from offering unprejudiced help. If you cannot change your feelings, refer elsewhere.

Guidelines for Individual Response to GLBQ International Students

There are many ways of letting GLBQ international students know that you are supportive of their struggle. The following are some guidelines:

1. Provide counseling for GLBQ students. The international educator will need to be prepared to counsel GLBQ students who are planning to go abroad and who fear, among other things, ostracism and alienation in the host culture. For many gay, lesbian, and bisexual international students, a return to their native country may mean returning to a place where they can be disowned, imprisoned, or even killed for their sexual behavior. The international educator may be the only person with whom the student may share these feelings of returning to the home country. The international education office staff will need to be familiar with gay and lesbian youth groups, gay community centers, telephone hotlines, and local organizations in their area.

2. Provide career counseling with GLBQ students. Quite often the international educator will counsel students on issues of life planning and career counseling. The international educator will need to be familiar with identity development models, negative stereotypes, AIDS, minority group status, employment discrimination, transition from school to work, and job search information.

3. Play an active role with GLBQ student organizations. It is crucial that the international educator be visibly supportive of campus GLBQ student organizations. Such organizations have many roles, from social, political, and support to service, education, and development. Specifically, some of the services may include speakers' bureaus, discussion groups, workshops, resource libraries, referral services, hotlines, disease testing, peer counseling, and job boards. Furthermore, programs may include film series, lectures, social events, awareness weeks, homophobia workshops, AIDS awareness education, newsletters, trips, conferences, and alumni groups. It is vital that the international educator be aware of what is happening with these groups to make informed referrals.

4. Have a "safe zone" sticker at the entrance to your office or classroom (available from the Bridges Project of the National Youth Advocacy Coalition or at www.glsen.org).

5. Have available in your school guidance office and library literature on sexual minority youth concerns (see www.umsl.edu/~pope for a bibliography).

6. Post online resources for sexual minority students, such as International Lesbian and Gay Youth Association (www.ilgya.org); Parents, Family, and Friends of Lesbians and Gays (www.pflag.org); Gay, Lesbian, and Straight Educators Network (www.glsen.org); Gay and Lesbian Teen Pen Pals (www.chanton.com/gayteens.html); National Resources for GLBT Youth (www.yale.edu/glb/youth.html); *Oasis,* a teen magazine (www.oasismag.com); Outright (www.outright.com); Out Proud, National Coalition for GLBT Youth (www.cyberspaces.com/outproud); The Cool Page for Queer Teens (www.pe.net/~bidstrup/cool.html); and National Gay and Lesbian Task Force (www.ngltf.org).

7. Offer free family counseling services on campus to deal with the issues of same-sex orientation.

8. Use positive gay and lesbian examples in your presentations, teaching, or counseling.

9. Use inclusive, stigma-free language in the classroom or office and in all communication, such as "partners" instead of "husbands and wives."

10. Post pictures of famous sexual minority people (see list at www. umsl.edu/~pope).

By demonstrating an accepting attitude, you can send a strong message to all international students and create a tolerant and welcoming environment.

The Student

There are many issues especially important to GLBQ international students. They include navigating identity development, having questions related to coming out, forming intimate relationships, obtaining health information, coming to terms with family and friends' attitudes regarding their sexual orientation, responding to immigration concerns, and developing a career as GLBQ individuals. In this section, we address the issue of how to understand the international student who has questions concerning his or her sexual orientation.

The Preeminent Issue: Identity Development or "Coming Out"

Since the early 1970s, researchers in multicultural and cross-cultural counseling have noted a predictable set of stages that individuals seem to go through who are discovering and acknowledging their membership in any cultural group while developing a firm sense of self-identity (Cass, 1979; E. Coleman, 1982b; Cross, 1971, 1978, 1991, 1995; Downing & Roush, 1985; Gramick, 1984; Helms, 1990; Ivey, D'Andrea, Ivey, & Simek-Morgan, 2002; Jackson, 1975, 1990; Myers et al., 1991; Parham, 1989; Parham & Helms, 1985; Ponse, 1980; Ponterotto, 1988; Smith, 1991; Sue & Sue, 1990; Zinik, 1985). Common themes emerge from many of these models. Many of them describe the same stages but use different terminology. These stages are as follows: having no idea that one is different from the dominant culture, identifying a difference within oneself, gaining information about this difference, exploring the reality of this difference as it exists outside of oneself, internalizing these explorations, privileging these experiences, and finally, integrating one's race, ethnicity, sexual orientation, and so forth into one's fuller identity.

Cass (1979) and Troiden (1988) presented similar models observing specific stages that lesbians and gay men move through as they develop a healthy sense of self-identity. Cass identified the following developmental stages for gays and lesbians: (1) identity confusion, (2) identity comparison, (3) identity tolerance, (4) identity acceptance, (5) identity pride, and (6) identity synthesis. These stages are part of what is termed the *coming-out process*.

Students who come to the United States from another country are at various levels in their own cultural identity development, which includes their ethnicity, race, gender, ability/disability, sexual orientation, and religious beliefs. They may even be moving from a dominant culture status to a target or minority culture status in the United States. Any of these transitions in cultural identity or status can be difficult. Together they can seem insurmountable. A key strategy for helping international students is to find which cultures are most salient and most important at that specific time, in that specific context, for that specific issue. Being attuned to students' language will enable counselors to understand the multiplicity of issues they have and which are most significant to their immediate situation. We suggest that counselors engage the students and attempt to understand their world through their eyes to more readily facilitate their problem solving and their growth.

Furthermore, knowledge of identity development models can help professionals recognize the developmental tasks being pursued by such students, providing them with tools for analysis and understanding of these unique students. Possessing tools for analysis and understanding of GLBQ students will enable counselors to identify an approach in designing orientation/training programs that address the specific concerns these students face in each stage.

For example, international students come to the United States at different stages in their GLBQ development. They are likely to be concerned with numerous issues while progressing through these identity phases, and counselors need to be knowledgeable of the many variables that are possible in GLBQ development. Some students may present with only a preconscious awareness of their sexual orientation while others are beginning to tentatively explore the possibility of being same-sex attracted. A number of students will be aware of their sexual orientation but are closeted in their own country. Some arrive in the United States having already fully integrated their sexual orientation by being aware and out in their own countries. Furthermore, they may not be in relationships but are seeking long-term partners or may desire to explore sexually as single GLBQ individuals in the United States. Others may be aware, out, and partnered, but their significant others have remained behind, while some individuals' partners have accompanied them to the United States. The myriad of relational configurations challenge counselors to carefully consider individuals' issues in context and relative to the respective identity stages of each student.

Individuals who are in the latter stages of their identity development may manage their transition into a new culture easier than those who are just beginning to realize their sexual orientation. This may be due to their having assumed the role of cultural outsider before they entered the United States. Further easing the transition for GLBQ international students may be an established GLBQ culture to which they can identify with in their new college campuses or cities.

GLBQ international students in early stages of their cultural identity development can have a parallel experience to going away to college for the first time. Studying in a place where no one knows them gives them the freedom to decide if it is time to break from old expectations of family and friends. For some students, studying abroad can be a time to experiment with coming out. Some students might make important first steps toward developing a positive GLBQ academic identity while abroad. They might explore social opportunities or do research that they would not consider doing at home. They might even experiment with sexual or romantic relationships (Dunlap, 2002).

It is important for anyone who works with international students to understand these developmental tasks and to facilitate them where possible, as coming out is an important developmental task for gays or lesbians. J. C. Coleman, Butcher, and Carson (1984) gave a good explanation of general developmental stages and the tasks associated with each stage:

> If developmental tasks are not mastered at the appropriate stage, the individual suffers from immaturities and incompetencies and is placed at a serious disadvantage in adjusting at later developmental levels—that is, the individual becomes increasingly vulnerable through accumulated failures to master psychosocial requirements. . . . Some developmental tasks are set by the individual's own needs, some by the physical and social environment. Members of different socioeconomic and sociocultural groups face somewhat different developmental tasks. (p. 111)

Generally, adolescence is the proper stage for the exploration and discovery of one's sexual orientation in almost all cultures. This is, however, also the time when there is a high probability that many gay males and lesbians will deny most of their differences within their peer group. Unfortunately, if the developmental tasks of sexual orientation identification are not accomplished during this critical time and are denied and delayed, then other tasks are also delayed, causing an identification "chain reaction" and thereby hindering other tasks such as relationship formation. For example, it is common for gay men who came out well after adolescence to have all the problems associated with those of teenagers who have just begun dating. It is important to note that once the critical period has passed in the developmental task, it may be very difficult or impossible to correct the psychological difficulties that have occurred as a result of this (Pope, 1992).

Any approach to helping GLBQ international students must first include the development of a trusting relationship, the basis of all effective counseling. Once rapport is established, counselors must understand in what identity development stage individual students are in as well as understanding attitudes of the culture of origin toward homosexuality. Once this is ascertained, it is important to determine the students' families' and their own views of sexual orientation, including the families' religious beliefs. Also, determining how long the students have been out to themselves and to others (including to whom they are out) is important, as well as learning about their sexual behavior and relationship history. After openly discussing these issues, counselors can begin to understand the very real needs of these students (Morrow, 1997; Pope, Bunch, Szymanski, & Rankins, 2004).

Dating and Relationship Formation

Same-sex dating and relationships are different from opposite-sex dating and relationships. First, there are few role models in any culture about how two individuals of the same gender are supposed to behave either in dating or in relationships. Generally, as people begin to date or form relationships, they rely on role models from their native cultures. For example, if individuals come from very traditional cultures, they expect there are strict do's and don'ts for each gender concerning such rituals. Likewise, if they come from a more modern culture, they may have more fluid expectations. Also, there are many different styles of dating around the world, and new international students who come to the United States may find these issues daunting depending on their dating and relationship history in their native country.

If GLBQ international students are dating or forming relationships with individuals who are from the United States, they may find that these culture-of-origin attitudes hinder or help in forming relationships, depending on the personality traits and characteristics of their partners. The inevitable culture clashes between such couples can be an obstacle to such relationships, but if the couple persists and overcomes such barriers, they can emerge with a stronger relationship. The qualities of the U.S. partner in such instances are critical. Such a partner may be open to new experiences, may even have traveled in the country of the international student and, therefore, be more knowledgeable of that culture, and may have a physical attraction to differences or opposites and others. There are many reasons why such relationships occur and whether they either succeed or fail.

Special Immigration Concerns

It is important to understand that the United States has a love-hate relationship with immigration. Although the country was formed as a result of immigration, it now struggles against matters of immigration. Immigration has been and continues to be an economic issue for the United States with a veneer of compassion—the rich, the educated, the talented, and those who will work for less than minimum wage are welcomed, whereas the poor, those with HIV, and Latin Americans continue to face barriers.

GLBQ international students from countries where they are punished by imprisonment or death for their sexual orientation may want to come to the United States to reside permanently. They have a sense of escaping from a country where they are not allowed to be themselves and arriving at a country where more individual freedoms are allowed. Their task from the beginning may be to find a way to stay in the United States. Identifying resources and helping them plan accordingly are critical to their mental health and survival.

It is, however, important to remember that citizens of other countries who are seeking to come to the United States on most nonimmigrant (temporary) visas (including a student visa) must overcome a presumption of "immigrant intent." This means that the U.S. government begins with the assumption that their plans are really to live in the United States permanently. These individuals must then convince officials that their ties to their country are so strong that they would not possibly want to leave their countries permanently. The more reasons they might have for wanting to leave their country or stay in the United States, the harder it is to get a temporary visa. They will need to show very strong ties to their country of citizenship, such as owning real estate, having a good job, and strong family ties. Likewise, any strong ties that they have to the United States can count against them for receiving such a visa (for more on immigration issues, see chapter 1).

GLBQ international students who come from countries where sexual orientation is a protected category may find the United States less supportive. It all depends on the culture of the college, the community, or even the region of the United States where they are studying. Even GLBQ international students who attend colleges in nonsupportive regions of the country may be able to find or develop their own supportive environment. Safe places can be determined by supportive faculty and staff advisors, GLBT college programs and organizations, and GLBT community centers.

An issue that remains unresolved in the United States is same-sex couples who love each other and want to reside in the same country. This issue is being resolved positively in many other countries such as Australia, Belgium, Brazil,

Canada, Denmark, Finland, France, Germany, Iceland, Israel, the Netherlands, New Zealand, Norway, South Africa, Sweden, and the United Kingdom, among others. As of 2005, the United States is the only industrialized English-speaking country that does not grant same-sex partners immigration preferences. Legalizing same-sex marriages in the United States would eliminate the immigration hurdle facing binational same-sex couples, but there are other mechanisms through which this goal could be achieved. The alternative route in the United States to long-term residency has been opposite-sex marriage, refugee status, or occupations. Consult the Web site of Immigration Equality (http://www.immigration equality.org/) and an immigration attorney for the most up-to-date information on immigration support for international GLBQs.

Almost all students who complete advanced degrees in the United States are eligible for residency through occupational status; that is, if they can find an employer who is willing to go through a very difficult and bureaucratic process. However, few employers are willing to endure this process.

International GLBQ students from countries with draconian laws against sexual minorities may seek asylum in the United States. Each asylum application is reviewed individually and will depend on the particular facts of each case and the conditions in that country. This is an arduous process, and many times persecution based on sexual orientation has been difficult to prove for the asylee.

Some GLBQ international students, in desperation to remain in the United States, have been involved in heterosexual marriages. However, this route is fraught with difficulties, including discovery of a marriage fraud and permanent disbarment from reentry into the United States.

There are no viable alternatives yet, but there is a solution that is slowly working its way through the U.S. Congress. Originally called the "Permanent Partners Immigration Act" and sponsored by only a handful of members of the House of Representatives, this measure is annually gaining momentum; as of 2005, with a new title ("Uniting American Families Act"), it now has over 79 cosponsors in the House and has a companion bill in the U.S. Senate sponsored by 9 members of that body. With passage of this bill, such immigration issues will be resolved, and GLBQ couples can be reunited to live openly with each other. More information can be accessed through the Immigration Equality Web site listed above.

Sexually Transmitted Diseases and Other Health Issues

GLBQ international students are often unfamiliar with the U.S. health care system, and their lack of knowledge can present difficulties. For example, individuals may contract a sexually transmitted disease (STD) such as herpes, chlamydia gonorrhea, or syphilis. How such students' native cultures view STDs will strongly influence how they resolve this important health issue. Their views of contracting an STD and the resolution of it will become a reference point that can affect their future academic work, immigration status, sexual and romantic relationships, and long-term health. GLBQ international students may be less likely to come and talk to their advisors, their classmates, their family back home, and even trusted friends or their partner about such health issues. The fears about discussing such issues can overwhelm students, making them less likely to seek treatment. HIV and AIDS are worldwide phenomena, yet discussing such issues can be complicated by attitudes of the individual students, their families, their classmates, and their native cultures regarding such diseases. Providing readily available information on anonymous HIV and STD testing services as well as on-campus medical services or health insurance is critical to the physical and mental health of such students. Talking openly about such issues may be difficult for students from more traditional cultures, but finding ways to break this barrier may be a life or death issue.

Communication

Communicating in English is difficult for any person who is not a native English speaker. Even in countries where English is the predominant secondary language, individuals generally prefer to speak in their native language. Discussing complex emotional and relationship issues in language other than the primary one can be difficult even for the most confident of individuals whose second language is English. Discussing issues of sexual orientation and STDs in a language that one formally learned is daunting. It is understandable then that GLBQ international students are unlikely to discuss these issues with their advisors, faculty, staff, or counselors. Creating an open, caring, safe environment in which such students can begin to discuss these issues is critical for them to be successful in their academic goals.

Rejection by Family and Friends

International students from collectivist or more traditional cultures are more likely to have the most difficulty in adjusting to the more individualist or more modern culture of countries like the United States. According to Pedersen (1991), for international students who are coming to the United States to attend school, "the greater the cultural difference, the more complicated the international student's adjustment is likely to be" (p. 14). Similarly, the more traditional the family culture of GLBQ international students, the more likely they are to face rejection by their family and friends at home or their friends who have accompanied them to the United States on their educational quest. Coming out to parents, siblings, and extended family back home while the student remains in the United States can be difficult. Some students may feel the need to share this new information as soon as they come out to themselves, whereas others may choose never to share such information with those at home.

There are reasons to be cautious in such a situation. Rarely do parents want to receive such information through the mail or via a telephone call. A face-to-face talk is usually best, but there is always the fear that parents, who may be contributing the bulk of monies to pay for such an overseas education, may not react well, resulting perhaps in their decision to discontinue financial support for education, thereby forcing the student either to return home or to find other funding sources.

Differences in Cultural Taboos

International students come from a variety of national and ethnic cultures that have their distinct taboos. A *taboo* is defined as "a ban or an inhibition resulting from social custom or emotional aversion" (http://www.thefreedictionary. com/taboo). The way that same-sex relationships are viewed varies differently from culture to culture. For example, same-sex relationships have not been taboo for all societies—currently or historically. It is important to understand how an international student's particular culture and family may react to the disclosure of the student's sexual orientation. In addition, it is important to assist the GLBQ student to understand the cultural "rules" of a college and community, so that, if they choose to violate these rules, they can do it properly and understanding that there may be consequences for such violations.

Isolation and Lack of a Reference Group

Many international students will face isolation as one of their hurdles in coming to the United States to study. Such isolation may be lessened through attendance at a college where other students from their native country are also studying. Having others nearby who speak their language and who understand some of the issues they are going through will help international students transition from their home country into the United States. It is important to note that because of their sexual orientation, GLBQ students may not only face isolation from all of the sources that other students do but also face isolation from students from their own country. At one level, they are able to be less isolated from their native culture, but at another level, they may be divided from their peers by their different sexual orientation. Students who have strong cultural identities based on their country or religion, for example, may have more feelings of isolation as they are discovering their sexual orientation.

The Questioning Student

International students who are unsure of their sexual orientation are an important concern for counselors, advisors, faculty, and staff. Most important is for students to accurately discover their true sexual orientation as soon as possible so that they can move to other development tasks that are part of securing their happiness and success in the world.

The topic of sexual orientation is complex, evocative, and confusing (Pope & Barret, 2002). No one really knows yet how sexual orientation is determined, and because conservative religious and political groups around the world tend to view homosexuality as a moral issue, and others see it as a civil rights issue, it cannot be easily separated from either context: Being gay has both political and religious implications. Finally, given the lack of definitive answers from scientific research, confusion and uncertainty tend to dominate the often-intense discussions about the sexual behavior and mental health needs of GLBQs individuals (B. Barret & Logan, 2001; R. L. Barret & Robinson, 1990/2000).

The lack of strong scientific evidence about the etiology of homosexuality allows those on either side of the "nature versus nurture" discussion to claim that their view is the right one. Research in human sexuality is complex and riddled with many challenges (R. L. Barret & Robinson, 1990/2000). Most studies draw their findings from self-reports as opposed to objective observations or measurements, sample sizes are often small and not representative of the populations being studied, and many research participants volunteer for studies because they want to prove a particular point. It is only fairly recently that genetic studies have appeared in research on homosexuality. LeVay (1991, 1999) reviewed the growing scientific data on the causes of sexual orientation and found a few medical studies that clearly show a relationship between genetics or hormones and sexual orientation. He surmised from this evidence that sexual orientation is determined rather than chosen. These studies point to differences in sizes of particular parts of the brain, ear lobes, and even thumbs when comparing gay participants with those who identify as heterosexual.

In contrast, the "nurture" argument is advanced by practitioners who believe that homosexuality is caused by environmental factors. In fact, the view that homosexuality is inherently pathological has its roots in the psychoanalytic community (Bieber, 1965; Socarides, 1968, 1973). Using studies drawn from their own patients who have sought treatment for homosexuality, those in this camp promote the notion that homosexuality emerges after birth in particular family structures. Their neo-Freudian analysis assumes that gay males were "feminized men" because they grew up in households that had strong, dominant mothers and weak, ineffective fathers. If they had grown up in families that had a "normal" constellation of strong, dominant fathers and weak, ineffective mothers, then the children would be heterosexually oriented. Freedman (1971), Lewes (1988), and Isay (1989), respected members of the psychoanalytic community, have refuted this approach by showing that both gay men and nongay men come from families that meet both descriptions.

Social attitudes toward homosexuality have also undergone many changes. From the acceptance and integration of same-sex persons into the Native American tribes of North America (Roscoe, 1988), to the acceptance of same-sex unions by the European Christian church in the Middle Ages (Boswell, 1980, 1995), to the persecution of homosexually oriented persons under the English Victorians (Rowse, 1977), to the enlightened approaches of pre-Nazi Germany (Hirschfeld, 1935), pre-Stalinist Russia (Thorstad, 1974), and imperial China (Ruan, 1991), and finally to the removal of homosexuality from the psychiatric manual of mental disorders (Bayer, 1981), history has seen an ebb and flow in the social acceptance of same-sex orientations.

Still another issue that makes research on homosexuality complex is the rapidly changing nature of the GLBQ experience. Studies conducted prior to 1990 reflect the GLBQ experience in a culture that no longer exists. Today GLBQ individuals appear in virtually every aspect of daily life. They are more out to their families and coworkers, visible in their neighborhoods, assertive in demanding equal rights, and have moved beyond the fear and shame that used to keep most of them invisible. This change can be seen in all aspects of the media, GLB-positive statements from national and local political candidates, and in the debates within virtually all Christian denominations about the role of GLB persons within the church (B. Barret & Logan, 2001).

Another public debate about the ability to change sexual orientation concerns research conducted by Nicolosi (1991), in which he described an approach called reparative therapy (RT). RT aims to change sexual orientation (always from gay to straight rather than the opposite) that parallels another "treatment," conversion therapy (CT), hailed by conservative Christian groups as proof that prayer and meditation can "drive the sin out" and bring the "sick" homosexual back to health. As to queries regarding whether sexual orientation is open to change, Money (1990) stated:

> The concept of voluntary choice is as much in error (as applied to sexual orientation) as in its application to handedness or to native language. You do not choose your native language as a preference, even though you are born without it. You assimilate it into a brain pre-natally made ready to receive a native language from those who constitute your primate troop and who speak that language to you and listen to you when you speak it. Once assimilated through the ears into the brain, a native language becomes securely locked in—as securely as if it has been phylogenetically preordained to be locked in pre-natally by a process of genetic pre-determinism or by the determinism of fetal hormonal or other brain chemistries. So also with sexual status or orientation, which, whatever its genesis, also may become assimilated and locked into the brain as mono sexually homosexual or heterosexual or as bisexually a mixture of both. (pp. 43-44)

Furthermore, according to E. Coleman (1982a),

> It is unethical and morally questionable to offer a 'cure' to homosexuals who request a change in their sexual orientation. While there have been reports that changes in behavior have occurred for individuals seeking treatment, it is questionable whether it is beneficial to change their behavior to something that is incongruent with their sexual orientation. (p. 87)

Both RT and CT have received abundant attention, and both have been soundly condemned by the American Counseling Association, the American Psychiatric Association, the American Psychological Association, the National Association of Social Workers, the National Association of School Psychologists, the American School Health Association, the American Federation of Teachers, the National Education Association, and the American Academy of Pediatrics. Mental health workers are warned that research indicates both of these "treatments" are more likely to be harmful than helpful. Many believe it is unethical for mental health professionals to practice CT or RT (B. Barret, 1999; Just the Facts Coalition, 2000).

Rather than explore each side of this debate in an effort to present overwhelming evidence for either point of view, this chapter makes the assumption that the causes of sexual orientation are not definitive but that sexual orientation is not mutable. As a counselor helping international students struggling with their sexual orientation, conveying the message that the students are welcome to discuss personal issues with you and that you are also willing to refer them to other reliable resources when appropriate is paramount.

The Institution

The institution can play a major role in addressing its GLBQ international students.

New Student Orientation

As we would not send a student to study in another country without some cross-cultural orientation, we should not throw international students into a socially diverse and complex campus without providing the necessary guidance, education, and support (Ogden, 2005). With almost half a million international students coming to the United States each year, it has become standard practice for those who work with international students to help these students adjust to their new environment and to let them know of resources that may be of use to them. Common goals of orientation training are to help students become aware of the host culture's expectations and to become sensitive to their own behavior within that context, to become aware of stages in cultural entry and adjustment, to understand the notion of a multicultural world, and to enjoy their experience to the fullest.

Addressing GLBQ issues as part of that orientation process normalizes sexual orientation issues and provides a sense of safety for GLBQ international students. International student orientation leaders need to be trained in basic counseling skills, both listening and responding. However, it is important to use GLBQ-inclusive language that does not assume the heterosexuality of students during presentations or when preparing orientation materials. The orientation should provide handouts documenting services available to students. It is also important to have representatives of the various campus organizations and student support services to describe available resources for students.

Furthermore, GLBQ issues should be brought up and discussed as part of adjustment to U.S. culture. Using senior and upper-class international students (who have made their own adjustment to and acceptance of GLBQ issues) to introduce and discuss GLBQ issues may encourage participants to keep an open mind and take time to break down stereotypes and misperceptions of GLBQ people. It should be conveyed that this process often takes time and requires that students interact with others and learn to appreciate GLBQ people as individuals first.

As discussed earlier, universities often offer host family programs in which students are placed in home-stay situations, thus allowing international students to immerse themselves in the U.S. culture. It is important that all students are aware of the implications of being identified as GLBQ in the host culture and how coming out might affect the host family relations.

Reentry Orientation

On-campus reentry orientations for international students typically include such sessions as a program evaluation, postreturn counseling, and career counseling. The program must also strive to reintegrate the student into degree studies and campus life. Making a break from unsupportive family or friends can mean that reentry adjustment for the GLBT international student is particularly difficult as the student tries to reestablish these relationships upon return. The new sense of freedom found during study abroad may force the student to find a more supportive community upon return. This can be both an exciting and a lonely process (Ogden, 2005).

For GLBT international students who might have begun to come out while studying abroad, it is particularly important that they be aware of the ways in which they have changed before they return to their native country. The implications of coming out when back home will need to be explored. Often the family and friends may blame the study-abroad experience for the changes in the student rather than acknowledge a lifelong identity. The reentry program should include, therefore, a discussion prompting these students to think about these changes when considering the reentry process. Materials provided to students before they return or during in-country meetings can be useful.

Upon returning home, these students may actually experience a painful recloseting, returning to a life that they had all but left behind, with limited or no support for the important growth that they have experienced overseas. These students are perhaps most at risk, and it is difficult to identify these students unless you have already established your office as a resource for GLBT students (Dunlap, 2002).

In contrast, students who were already in the later stages of coming out who have integrated a higher degree of acceptance prior to coming to the United States are likely to have fewer problems upon returning to their home country. They are more likely to have thoroughly researched the changes in their country in living arrangements or cultural expectations with sexual orientation diversity in mind. Similar to their heterosexual peers, reintegration issues for them may be more straightforward, revolving around returning to an environment that seems to have changed little while they have grown immensely (Dunlap, 2002).

Finally, collecting information about homosexuality in international students' home countries may be very useful, especially for GLBQ students who only came out during their attendance at college. One possibility is to do a survey of colleges' returnees from studying abroad, asking students to describe the reaction of their host country to homosexuality and the availability of support groups and resources. Counselors may also wish to guide these students to reference books that have a country-by-country listing of laws, guidelines, and other information for GLBQ individuals.

Conduct an Institutional Evaluation

It is also important to evaluate the university's commitment to support GLBQ people, including students, faculty, and staff (Kato, 1999). As a whole, does the university acknowledge and support the existence of GLBQ people on campus? The following questions, adapted from a list prepared by Evans and Wall (1991), are helpful:

- Does the campus have GLBQ student organizations supported by student government funds?
- Does the campus counseling center have GLBQ support groups?
- Does the campus have a GLBQ faculty/staff association?
- Does the curriculum include courses on GLBQ history and culture?
- Does the institution's affirmative action statement include sexual orientation?
- Does the campus minority affairs office deal with sexual orientation issues?
- Does the student handbook or conduct code include a clear statement prohibiting harassment and discrimination of minorities and GLBQ people?
- Does the housing office grant room changes on the basis of sexual orientation or must danger to the resident be demonstrated?
- Does the professional or student staff include openly GLBQ people?
- Does the office have a strong commitment to treat all people equally? Is this as evident with the GLBQ populations as it is with other minorities?
- Are GLBQ colleagues encouraged to bring their significant others or partners to office or campus social events?

If you do not know the answers to some of these questions, do some investigation. If the answers are negative, explore the idea of making a few changes on campus.

What More Can We Do?

International students often come to higher education from relatively monocultural home and school environments that leave them unprepared for multicultural and international norms and experiences (Ogden, 2005). They may come from environments in which racial and ethnic conflict, sexual harassment, and homophobia are prevalent and unchallenged. Similarly, some educational institutions in the United States currently have an unfriendly environment for GLBQ students. It is crucial that those who work with international students expand the focus on enrichment and adjustment efforts to issues of inclusion and exclusion.

Here are some recommendations as to how institutions can be more supportive of GLBQ international students.

1. Work to establish a nondiscrimination clause to protect the rights of GLBQ students. An institutional commitment to protect these students

(just as we protect other cultural minorities) is vital for affirming the presence of GLBQ people on campuses. Have an inclusive diversity statement in your promotional materials so that GLBQ students know that your college is a safe and inclusive place, and send those materials to all prospective international students.

2. Develop a supportive residence hall environment. Residence life staff should seek to attract job applicants who understand the concerns faced by GLBQ students living in a residence hall environment. Some of the specific issues include coming out in a rigid heterosexist residence hall, lack of privacy, homophobic roommates, lack of inclusive activities, and dealing with harassment.

3. Increase GLBQ library resources. People should have the chance to learn as much as possible and read literature that speaks to the gay and lesbian experience. Students need to have publications available that address their sexuality and resulting issues. Library exhibits can highlight publications, authors, and pictures of renown individuals to create awareness of contributions of GLB people.

4. Develop a supportive health services staff. Supportive health personnel are crucial to the international student who may be sexually active and need understandable guidance. The use and importance of condoms, for example, will need to be addressed. Those who work with international students can also work with health services in many ways, including providing translated documents to suggesting safe-sex information for the international student. Homosexuality should be included in every discussion of sexuality, from dating to relationships to parenting concerns.

5. Create a GLBQ-friendly environment in the International Studies office. The International Studies office should have available resources for GLBQ students, such as travel guides, safe-sex information, and brochures designed for GLBQ students listing campus and community-based resources. This is also a good place to display a poster acknowledging that gay and lesbian people exist and that they are okay. It may also be useful to keep personal accounts by people who have studied abroad. These resources can help students to connect with the gay community. If you have a GLB center on campus, make their flyers visibly available in your office as a subtle message that your office is gay-friendly. Other types of material work as well (e.g., a safe-zone sticker, a rainbow flag or sticker, and NAMES Project poster). Acquire and make available bibliography and other materials (guidebooks, articles, etc.) about GLBQ students overseas. Provide lists of appropriate GLBQ Web resource sites and also provide links to GLBQ sites on office Web pages. Support GLBQ events and programming on your campus. This can be done through attendance, cooperation, cosponsorship, and so on. Encourage open and honest discussion of issues related to

sexuality and gender identity. Such student programming might include the following:

- Incorporate international and GLBT themes into preexisting programming.
- Develop a human rights letter-writing campaign (provide paper, envelopes, and stamps for students to write about a cause). The Amnesty International GBLT network has a Web site with plenty of resources, including background information and sample letters for taking action. For more information, visit their Web site at http://www.ai-GLBT.org/.
- Host a panel discussion with a combined international and GLBTQQI theme in which you invite international students, international faculty, or students and faculty who have lived or spent significant time abroad to discuss a common topic of GLBTQQI interest (some possibilities include differing cultural attitudes toward sexuality and gender identity, political changes affecting GLBT people in different countries, international GLBT human rights issues, and discussion of GLBT visibility in different cultures).
- Incorporate international or GLBT films into existing movie nights or film series.
- Invite speakers to campus who can address international and GLBTQQI issues.
- Establish good working relations with your GLBQ Support Services Office (or other office that is responsible for GLBQ support, such as Multicultural Affairs) to work collaboratively with international students on GLBQ issues. Let students know it is okay to have questions and to be uncertain and uncomfortable while they engage in the learning process.

6. Enhance staff development. All schools have some diversity in their staff and student populations. Differences may include race, ethnicity, age, gender, socioeconomic status, (dis)ability, sexual orientation, religion, language, and national origin. All staff and students need to be aware of this diversity and have knowledge and understanding about that diversity. Those who work with GLBQ international students will want to combine efforts with campus multiculturalists to encourage staff to become aware of and sensitive to these issues. Those who work with international students should present a positive role model for colleagues in dealing with diverse populations. If there is a professional development committee, the international educator may want to address international and multicultural issues.

7. Offer support and advice on immigration for GLB people whose partners are U.S. citizens. Provide support and referrals to students from home countries where homosexuality is illegal or the environment is

dangerous for GLB people. Political asylum is sometimes granted by the United States, Canada, and some European countries on this basis (Kato, 1999).

8. If you have international program handbooks, include a reference regarding diversity issues, including sexual orientation. This could be something as brief as recommending that the students discuss with the offices here or abroad their questions or concerns regarding local resources, support groups, and so on.

9. When orienting staff members, be sure to mention the probability of GLBQ international students so that they are prepared if they are consulted either by those students or others on the program who may have questions about the GLBQ students who have come out to them.

10. While orienting students, provide some information regarding sexual orientation (see Appendix for brochure sample). Some institutions even have an orientation specifically for GLBQ students, including GLBQ returnees, but that, by design, requires that the student self-disclose. If you are more comfortable with universal orientations, mention GLBQ issues in some capacity so that those students feel included (e.g., "While we're not here to tell you how to handle your personal relationships while you are here, we want to be sure that you are somewhat informed about various mores of the United States and our local community regarding opposite-sex or same-sex relationships"). Some institutions do a special women's issues orientation; if this is done, issues related to lesbians should be included.

11. If there are student-written newsletters, be sure that "Diversity" is one of the categories so that students on-site can address this topic for future program participants.

12. Always include information on STDs, HIV, and AIDS for all students. Although AIDS does not discriminate among populations, it may still be considered a predominantly gay disease in certain countries. The young population that is sexually active, GLB or straight, is now the highest risk group. Students who come to study in the United States may not have access to information on these topics. Students may find AIDS prevention has not been addressed or of little concern in their country. It is important for the health of all students that they get information on AIDS.

Summary

GLBQ international students who are attending U.S. colleges have a number of unique issues that make them different from their peers. These issues may include coming out to self, coming out to others, dating and relationship formation, STDs and other health issues, career development and how this may be affected by coming out, rejection by family and friends, special immigration concerns, communication, differences in cultural taboos, isolation, and lack of a reference group.

This chapter attempted to address the above issues and presented guidelines to help counselors, psychologists, social workers, university faculty, international student advisers, and anyone who works with or comes into contact with international students in the United States have positive interactions with GLBQ international students.

References

Alexander, J., Morotani, M., & Sullivan, C. (2000, November 18). *When a student comes out to you: Help for advisers working with gay, lesbian, bisexual, transgender international students.* Paper presented at NAFSA: Association of International Educators Region IV Annual Conference, Iowa City, IA.

Barret, B. (1999, March). Conversion therapy. *Counseling Today,* 12.

Barret, B., & Logan, C. (2001). *Counseling gay men and lesbians: A practice primer.* Belmont, CA: Brooks/Cole.

Barret, R. L., & Robinson, B. E. (2000). *Gay fathers.* San Francisco: Jossey-Bass. (Original work published 1990)

Bayer, R. (1981). *Homosexuality and American psychiatry: The politics of diagnosis.* New York: Basic Books.

Bieber, I. (1965). Clinical aspects of male homosexuality. In J. Marmor (Ed.), *Sexual inversion: The multiple roots of homosexuality* (pp. 248-267). New York: Basic Books.

Boswell, J. (1980). *Christianity, social tolerance, and homosexuality.* Chicago: University of Chicago Press.

Boswell, J. (1995). *Same-sex unions in premodern Europe.* New York: Vintage Books.

Cass, V. (1979). Homosexual identity formation: A theoretical model. *Journal of Homosexuality, 4,* 219-235.

Coleman, E. (1982a). Changing approaches to the treatment of homosexuality: A review. In W. Paul, J. D. Weinrich, J. C. Gonsiorek, & M. E. Hotvedt (Eds.), *Homosexuality: Social, psychological, and biological issues* (pp. 81-88). Beverly Hills, CA: Sage.

Coleman, E. (1982b). Developmental stages of the coming out process. *Journal of Homosexuality, 7,* 31-43.

Coleman, J. C., Butcher, J. N., & Carson, R. C. (1984). *Abnormal psychology and modern life* (7th ed.). Glenview, IL: Scott, Foresman.

Cross, W. E. (1971). The Negro-to-Black conversion experience: Towards a psychology of Black liberation. *Black World, 20,* 13-27.

Cross, W. E. (1978). The Cross and Thomas models of psychological nigrescence. *Journal of Black Psychology, 5,* 13-31.

Cross, W. E. (1991). *Shades of Black: Diversity in African-American identity.* Philadelphia: Temple University Press.

Cross, W. E. (1995). The psychology of nigrescence: Revising the Cross model. In J. G. Ponterotto, J. M. Casas, L. A. Suzuki, & C. M. Alexander (Eds.), *Handbook of multicultural counseling* (pp. 93-122). Thousand Oaks, CA: Sage.

Downing, N. E., & Roush, K. L. (1985). From passive acceptance to active commitment: A model of feminist identity development for women. *The Counseling Psychologist, 13,* 695-709.

Dunlap, A. (2002, November). *Coming out and coming back: Re-entry issues for GLBT college students who study abroad.* Paper presented at the Council on International Educational Exchange Conference, Atlanta, GA.

Evans, N., & Wall, V. (1991). *Beyond tolerance: Gays, lesbians, and bisexuals on campus.* Alexandria, VA: ACPA Media.

Freedman, M. (1971). *Homosexuality and psychological functioning.* Belmont, CA: Brooks/Cole.

Gramick, J. (1984). Developing a lesbian identity. In T. Darty & S. Potter (Eds.), *Women-identified women* (pp. 31-44). Palo Alto, CA: Mayfield.

Helms, J. E. (Ed.). (1990). *Black and White racial identity theory, research, and practice.* Westport, CT: Greenwood Press.

Hirschfeld, M. (1935). *Men and women: The world journey of a sexologist.* New York: Putnam.

Isay, R. A. (1989). *Being homosexual: Gay men and their development.* New York: Farrar, Straus & Giroux.

Ivey, A. E., D'Andrea, M., Ivey, M. B., & Simek-Morgan, L. (2002). *Theories of counseling and psychotherapy: A multicultural perspective.* Boston: Allyn & Bacon.

Jackson, B. (1975). Black identity development. *Journal of Education Diversity, 2,* 19-25.

Jackson, B. (1990). *Building a multicultural school.* Paper presented at the meeting of the Amherst Regional School System, Amherst, MA.

Just the Facts Coalition. (2000). *Just the facts about sexual orientation and youth: A primer for principals, educators & school personnel.* Washington, DC: Author.

Kato, N. (1999). Working with gay, lesbian, and bisexual international students in the United States. *International Educator, 8,* 29-34.

LeVay, S. (1991, August 30). A difference in hypothalamic structure between heterosexual and homosexual men. *Science, 253,* 1034-1037.

LeVay, S. (1999). *Queer science.* New York: McGraw-Hill.

Lewes, K. (1988). *The psychoanalytic theory of male homosexuality.* New York: Meridian.

Money, J. (1990). Agenda and credenda of the Kinsey scale. In D. P. McWhirter, S. A. Sanders, & J. M. Reinisch (Eds.), *Homosexuality/heterosexuality: Concepts of sexual orientation* (pp. 41-60). New York: Oxford University Press.

Morrison, K. (2004, November). *We don't have those where I come from: GLBT issues in an intercultural context.* Paper presented at NAFSA: Association of International Educators Region VI Annual Conference, Evansville, IN.

Morrow, S. (1997). Career development of lesbian and gay youth: Effects of sexual orientation, coming out, and homophobia. In M. B. Harris (Ed.), *School experiences of gay and lesbian youth* (pp. 1-15). New York: Harrington Park Press.

Myers, L. J., Speight, S. L., Highlen, P. S., Cox, C. I., Reynolds, A. L., Adams, E. M., & Hanley, C. P. (1991). Identity development and worldview: Toward an optimal conceptualization. *Journal of Counseling & Development, 70,* 54-63.

National Center for Education Statistics. (2003). *Digest of educational statistics, tables and figures.* Retrieved August 16, 2005, from http://nces.ed.gov/programs/digest/d03/tables/dt417.asp

Nicolosi, J. (1991). *Reparative therapy of male homosexuals.* Northvale, NJ: Aronson.

Ogden, A. C. (2005). *Welcoming gay culture: Preparing international educators for a new clientele.* Retrieved August 11, 2005, from http://www.indiana.edu/~overseas/lesbigay/index.html

Parham, T. A. (1989). Cycles of psychological nigrescence. *The Counseling Psychologist, 17,* 187-226.

Parham, T. A., & Helms, J. E. (1985). Attitudes of racial identity and self-esteem. *Journal of College Student Personnel, 26,* 43-147.

Pedersen, P. B. (1991). Counseling international students. *The Counseling Psychologist, 19,* 10-58.

Ponse, B. (1980). Lesbians and their worlds. In J. Marmor (Ed.), *Homosexual behavior: A modern reappraisal* (pp. 157-175). New York: Basic Books.

Ponterotto, J. G. (1988). Racial consciousness development among White counselor trainees: A stage model. *Journal of Multicultural Counseling and Development, 16,* 146-156.

Pope, M. (1992). Bias in the interpretation of psychological tests. In S. Dworkin & F. Gutierrez (Eds.), *Counseling gay men and lesbians: Journey to the end of the rainbow* (pp. 277-291). Alexandria, VA: American Counseling Association.

Pope, M. (1995a). Career interventions for gay and lesbian clients: A synopsis of practice knowledge and research needs. *The Career Development Quarterly, 44,* 191-203.

Pope, M. (1995b). The "salad bowl" is big enough for us all: An argument for the inclusion of lesbians and gays in any definition of multiculturalism. *Journal of Counseling & Development, 73,* 301-304.

Pope, M., & Barret, B. (2002). Counseling gay men toward an integrated sexuality. In L. D. Burlew & D. Capuzzi (Eds.), *Sexuality counseling* (pp. 149-176). Hauppauge, NY: Nova Science.

Pope, M., Bunch, L. K., Szymanski, D. S., & Rankins, M. (2004). Counseling sexual minority students in the schools. In B. T. Erford (Ed.), *Professional school counseling: A handbook of theories, programs & practices* (pp. 699-718). Austin, TX: CAPS Press.

Pope, M., Prince, J. P., & Mitchell, K. (2000). Responsible career counseling with lesbian and gay students. In D. A. Luzzo (Ed.), *Career counseling of college students: An empirical guide to strategies that work* (pp. 267-284). Washington, DC: American Psychological Association.

Roscoe, W. (1988). Strange country this: Images of berdaches and warrior women. In W. Roscoe (Ed.), *Living the spirit: A gay American Indian anthology* (pp. 48-76). New York: St. Martin's Press.

Rowse, A. L. (1977). *Homosexuals in history: A study in ambivalence in society, literature and the arts.* New York: Carroll & Graf.

Ruan, F. -F. (1991). *Sex in China: Studies in sexology in Chinese culture.* New York: Plenum.

Sherrill, J. (1994). *The gay, lesbian, and bisexual students' guide to colleges, universities, and graduate schools.* New York: New York University Press.

Smith, E. J. (1991). Ethnic identity development: Toward the development of a theory within the context of a majority/minority status. *Journal of Counseling & Development, 70,* 181-188.

Socarides, C. (1968). *The overt homosexual.* New York: Grune & Stratton.

Socarides, C. (1973). Findings derived from 15 years of clinical research. *American Journal of Psychiatry, 130,* 1212-1213.

Sue, D. W., & Sue, S. (1990). *Counseling the culturally different* (2nd ed.). New York: Wiley.

Thorstad, D. (1974). *The Bolsheviks and the early homosexual rights movement.* New York: Times Change Press.

Troiden, R. R. (1988). Homosexual identity development. *Journal of Adolescent Health Care, 9,* 105-113.

Zinik, G. (1985). Identity conflict or adaptive flexibility? Bisexuality reconsidered. In F. Klien & T. J. Wolf (Eds.), *Bisexualities: Theory and research* (pp. 7-19). New York: Haworth.

Appendix

A Sample Brochure for Gay, Lesbian, and Bisexual (GLB) International Students Advising Resources

Homosexuality: A U.S. Perspective for International Students

Produced with support from the Office of the Dean of Students and the Counseling Center, University of Oregon

Introduction

Every culture has its own attitudes and beliefs about homosexuality. Now that you are attending school in the United States, you may find it useful to have a better understanding of how Americans view homosexuality.

One of the strongest values in U.S. culture is individualism. In the U.S., a dominant belief is that each person has the right to live as he or she wants, as long as it does not interfere with the rights of others. In addition, often Americans think that it is best to speak openly about disagreements, and that this is a good way to find a solution to a conflict. These and other cultural values contribute to U.S. views on homosexuality.

The purpose of this brochure is to provide factual answers to questions which are often asked about homosexuality in the United States. In addition, the brochure gives resources for students who want more information.

What Is a Homosexual?

A: A homosexual" is a woman or man who has a sexual and/or romantic interest in a person of the same gender. The word "lesbian" refers to women, and the word "gay" refers to men.

What Is a Heterosexual?

A: A "heterosexual" is a woman or man who has a sexual and/or romantic interest in a person of the opposite gender.

What Is a Bisexual?

A: A "bisexual" is a person who has a sexual and/or romantic interest in people of both genders. However, a bisexual woman or man does not necessarily have lovers of both genders at the same time.

Can You Tell If Someone Is Gay, Lesbian or Bisexual?

A: It is impossible to tell people's sexual orientation by their appearance. Stereotypes can be misleading.

How Many Lesbians and Gay Men Are There in the United States?

A: No one knows how many lesbians and gay men there are in the U.S. It is estimated that 2% to 10% of the U.S. population is lesbian or gay.

What Causes Homosexuality?

A: This is a common question. Different cultures have different theories and beliefs. In the U.S., there is no agreement on the answer to this question.

Is Being Gay, Lesbian or Bisexual Normal?

A: Homosexuality has existed throughout history and around the world. Some famous lesbians and gay men include Aristotle, Michelangelo, Virginia Woolf, Rudolf Nureyev, Yukio Mishima, and Martina Navratilova. There are lesbians, gays, and bisexuals of every age, race, educational level, and socioeconomic class.

Is Being Gay, Lesbian or Bisexual Healthy?

A: All people who are sexually active risk being exposed to sexually transmitted diseases (STDs), including AIDS, regardless of their sexual orientation. Information on safer sex is available at the Student Health Center. In addition, the American Psychological Association does not consider homosexuality to be a mental illness.

Are Homosexuals Discriminated Against?

A: In the U.S., some organizations and individuals discriminate against homosexuals. For example, school teachers can lose their jobs if someone thinks they are homosexual. Homosexuals can be refused housing or be evicted from their homes. In addition, they are sometimes physically attacked. Homophobia and discrimination against homosexuals exist everywhere in the U.S., including Eugene and the University of Oregon. Lesbian, gay, and bisexual people are often harassed on campus.

What Is Homophobia?

A: "Homophobia" is the irrational fear and hatred of homosexuals. People who are homophobic are often afraid to get to know lesbians and gays. They are sometimes afraid that other people will think they are gay or lesbian. Or, they worry that a gay or lesbian person may be attracted to them. If they do not know gays or lesbians, they don't realize that these fears are not necessary. Homophobia can lead to physical or emotional violence against homosexuals.

Why Are Gays, Lesbians and Bisexuals So Public About Their Sexuality? Isn't This a Private Matter?

A: Some people in the U.S. think that homosexuals and bisexuals talk too much about their lives. In the U.S., heterosexual couples often hold hands and even kiss in public. They commonly talk about boyfriends, girlfriends, husbands and wives. However, lesbians and gays cannot talk about their social lives without revealing their homosexuality and risking discrimination. Therefore, gays, lesbians and bisexuals only want the same freedom of expression that heterosexuals enjoy.

Why Does the Issue of Homosexuality Get So Much Attention in the U.S.?

A: Historically, there have been many social movements for equal rights in the U.S. For example, there have been movements to gain civil rights for women, black people and people of different religions. The homosexual rights movement is another example of people in the U.S. working together for civil rights. Homosexual rights laws would help protect lesbians and gays from discrimination.

Not everyone agrees that homosexuals and bisexuals need legal protection from discrimination. There are some organizations in the U.S. and in Oregon that are working to pass laws against homosexual rights.

Movements for civil rights require legal reform. This process creates a lot of debate and gets media attention. Therefore, the homosexual rights movement is now getting a lot of attention.

How Do Issues of Homosexual Rights and Discrimination Affect Me If I'm Heterosexual?

A: As a university student in the U.S., you may meet lesbians, gays, and bisexuals. They may be your classmates, your instructors, and possibly your friends. You will often read or hear about the issues of homosexual rights and discrimination against homosexuals. If you know about these issues, you will be better able to understand the lesbian, gay, and bisexual people you meet.

What If I Am Homosexual or Bisexual?

A: Maybe you would like to talk with someone, read a book, or make a friend. Check the resource below.

"Many international students who come to the U.S. seem amazed by how many homosexuals there are here. Rather than making a quick judgment, try getting to know someone who's gay, lesbian or bisexual."

—Douglas

"I'm a French major, currently writing my thesis on street art. Having lived in other countries—the Soviet Union, France, and Israel—I think that you can enrich your experiences by trying to see things as natives see them."

—Davina

"I was born in Korea. The gay community here has not judged me by my race. I have found the support I need as a gay minority."

—Amy

"I'm president of my dorm, and I enjoy swimming, poetry and piano. As a Mexican, I have felt comfortable coming out as a gay man in the U.S., even though there's still a lot of homophobia here."

—Enrique

Resources

Campus:

- Lesbian, Gay, Bisexual Alliance (LGBA) (541) 346-3360
- Women's Center (downstairs EMU [Erb Memorial Union]) (541) 346-4095
- Student Health Center (541) 346-4441
- Counseling Center (541) 346-3227
- Educational/Support Services (541) 346-1142
- GLB Coffee Hour
- GLB Youth Group

Community Newspapers:

- *The Lavender Network*
- *Just Out*
- *The Alternative Connection*

For more information, check *The Lavender Network*, available at these bookstores:

- Mother Kali's, 2001 Franklin Blvd.
- Hungry Heat, 1241 Willamette
- Peralandra, 1016 Willamette

University of Oregon Policy Statement on Affirmative Action & Equal Opportunity
The University of Oregon affirms and actively promotes the rights of all individuals to equal opportunity in education and employment at this institution without regard to race, color, sex, national origin, age, religion, marital status, handicap, veteran status, sexual orientation, or any other extraneous consideration not directly and substantively related to effective performance.

Chapter 5

International Students With Disabilities

Barbara J. Palombi

International students have actively sought educational opportunities in the United States. According to the Institute of International Education (2005), 565,039 international students were enrolled in institutions of higher education during the 2004–2005 academic year. International students represent 12% of all master's degrees and 26.7% of doctoral degrees earned in the United States. The Institute of International Education reported that Asian students constituted over half, or 58%, of international students enrolled; European students, 13%; Latin American students, 12%; Middle Eastern students, 6%; African students, 6%; and Northern American and Oceanian students, 5%. Although there are a large number of international students who study in the United States, this chapter explores the issues and challenges faced by international students with disabilities.

International Students With Disabilities

The World Health Organization (WHO) estimates that 600 million people—10% of the world's population—live in the world with a disability; that 80% of the world's people with disabilities live in the developing regions of Africa, Asia, Latin American, and the Caribbean; and that disability affects 25% of the communities in most countries (WHO, n.d.). Using the WHO statistics that 10% of the world's population has a disability, it could then be extrapolated that 10% of the international students attending institutions in the United States may have a disability. Yet in reviewing the literature, it is apparent that international students with disabilities are either overlooked or absent. A possible reason for this absence is that individuals with disabilities have limited opportunities for education and therefore may not attain the level of education needed to be an international student (Alur, 2002). This is especially true for children with obvious physical, visual, hearing, or mental impairments. The focus of this chapter is on cultural and attitudinal perceptions of disability, educational opportunities for those with obvious disabilities, mental health impairments, academic stress and mental illness, international students with learning disabilities, international students with HIV/AIDS, overlooked international students, the Americans With Disabilities

Act, recommendations for university officials, treatment suggestions for mental health providers, and future directions and conclusion.

Cultural and Attitudinal Perceptions of Disability

For those with obvious physical, visual, hearing, and/or mental impairment, the attitude toward people with disabilities in their countries affects educational opportunities (Alur, 2002). A society's response and treatment of people with disabilities are influenced by its social, cultural, moral, and economic values (Alur, 2002; Chan, Lee, Yuen, & Chan, 2002; Chen, Brodwin, Cardoso, & Chan, 2002; Wilhite, 1995). These values shape the attitudes and behaviors toward its disabled members (Lam, 1993). The way disability is regarded within a culture has a direct impact on the opportunities available to people with disabilities (Alur, 2002; Wilhite, 1995). People with disabilities in developing nations have fewer opportunities and resources available to them compared with those living in developed areas of the world (Alur, 2002; Driedger, 1991; WHO, n.d.). In many countries and cultures, having a child with a disability is regarded as a "personal tragedy" (Alur, 2002; Argyrakouli & Zafiropoulou, 2003; Cho, Singer, & Brenner, 2003; Liu, 2001).

In Pakistan, people with disabilities are regarded as "the poorest of the poor" (Hassan, 1991), as objects of charity (Hassan, 1991), and as assisting others in "building credit towards an afterlife" (Alur, 2002; Miles, 1997). A study of Korean mothers (Cho et al., 2003) found that 50% of the participants reported having suicidal ideation when they learned that their child had a disability. Similar feelings returned when their children exhibited problem behaviors. The majority of Korean mothers reported that they frequently encountered negative reactions from strangers on buses and subways, such as passengers being generally intolerant of children who exhibited unusual behavior and keeping a distance from individuals of atypical appearance. The Korean mothers also reported feeling shame and embarrassment because of the public reactions to their children's behavior (Cho et al., 2003).

In a study of Greek mothers of children with intellectual disabilities, researchers identified similar findings as those for Korean mothers of children with disabilities. The researchers found that raising a child with an intellectual disability caused additional stress and lowered the self-esteem of the mothers (Argyrakouli & Zafiropoulou, 2003).

Another important value in many families, especially of Asian parents, is achievement (Chng, Ding, & Perez, 1998; Kwon, 2005; Lam, 1993). The value of achievement affects attitudes toward children with disabilities. Often the person with a disability is viewed as "less capable . . . and as destroying the hope of the family for a bright future" (Lam, 1993, p. 27). Because most parents are ashamed of their disabled children, they seldom advocate for services or benefits (Chan et al., 2002; Kwon, 2005; Lam, 1993; Liu, 2001). As a result of these strong cultural attitudes, families do not regard education of children with disabilities as a necessity.

Educational Opportunities for People With Obvious Disabilities

There are few educational opportunities for people with disabilities, especially in developing countries (Alur, 2002). A survey conducted by UNICEF reports that only 1% of children with disabilities attend school in developing countries (Mittler, 1995). Some schools refuse to accept disabled children in the belief that they will have a bad influence on the nondisabled students (Hassan, 1991; Kwon, 2005). Other reasons for the lack of school attendance are (a) inability to walk to school, (b) lack of accessible transportation, (c) architectural barriers that prohibit attendance of mobility-impaired children, (d) lack of teachers trained in sign language for the deaf child, and (e) lack of teachers trained in Braille for the visually impaired child (Hassan, 1991; Mittler, 1995). The educational opportunities that are available for children with disabilities are frequently provided through special church or charity-run schools. Many of these schools are not regarded as being academically rigorous, and students who attend these facilities are not seen as viable candidates for advanced education (Driedger & D'Aubin, 1991).

Students with disabilities experience poor attachment to the education system because of these attitudinal and architectural barriers in the education systems (Alur, 2002). Researchers found that 21% of their disabled respondents who were disabled while in school reported lengthy interruptions in their education. Twenty percent of students with disabilities reported that they changed schools because of their disability, and 20% of that group attended segregated classes (Driedger & D'Aubin, 1991).

Another issue that plagues many countries concerning the education of students with disabilities is the lack of qualified teachers (Miles, 1997). In many countries the position of special education teacher is viewed as a less-than-desirable position socially and economically. Because of these societal prejudices, many low-achieving students are urged to enter the field of special education (Ghobrial & Vance, 1988; Miles, 1997).

Within many countries there is a gender bias concerning education. When there are few opportunities for basic education or training, disabled boys, not girls, usually receive them (Driedger, 1991; Rajah, 1991). Because of their disadvantaged position in society, women often become disabled (Driedger, 1991). Women in developing countries are weaker and more susceptible to disease. Because resources are limited, they tend to receive less food than their male counterparts. Society tends to view women with disabilities as less important to educate (Driedger & D'Aubin, 1991) and as a burden dependent on the charity of parents or relatives (Shah, 1991). A woman is usually hidden from visitors and strangers because the family is ashamed of her (Alur, 2002; Driedger, 1991; Shah, 1991). When members of the outside community become aware that a member of the family includes a person with a disability, this information may prove to be an obstacle in arranging the marriage of the siblings (Shah, 1991).

Similar attitudes and perceptions of women with disabilities are also found in Latin American countries (Driedger & D'Aubin, 1991). Families do not view education for disabled women as a priority. Families continue to be very protective of women with disabilities and do not allow them to go outside the home unaccompanied. Consequently, it can be very difficult for Latin American women with disabilities to receive educational or vocational training of any type.

Mental Health Impairments

Those individuals with mental health disabilities are also frequently slighted by the educational system (Gannon & MacLean, 1997). Many cultures believe that good mental health is achieved through self-discipline, the avoidance of morbid thoughts, and dietary taboos (Alur, 2002; Liu, 2001). Emotional problems are understood to be associated with weak character (Liu, 2001). In some cases, mental illness is blamed on evil spirits or punishment from god(s). In China, mental illness is viewed as being caused by deeds from past lives or acts against the nature of the universe (Liu, 2001). In many countries, those who have been identified as having mental health disabilities are also denied the opportunity to obtain an education; few of these individuals know how to read or write as a result of being institutionalized (Liu, 2001).

These architectural and attitudinal barriers are also found within the educational systems of many industrial nations, including Australia (Gannon & MacLean, 1997; Ryan & Struhs, 2004; Van Kraayenoord, Elkins, Palmer, & Richards, 2001), Canada (Persinger & Tiller, 1999; Weiner, 1999), Russia (Perfilyeva, 2003), Scotland (Riddell, 1998), South Africa (Losinsky, Levi, Saffrey, & Jelsma, 2003), and the United Kingdom (Riddell, 1998). Unless the education of children with disabilities is supported by legislative initiatives and pressure by advocate groups, children in the industrial nations will struggle with similar prejudice and discriminations. Because individuals with obvious physical, visual, hearing, and mental impairments encounter difficulty being educated, the likelihood of students with these types of disabilities seeking advanced education in the United States may be limited. The majority of international students with disabilities who study in the United States will likely be students who are struggling with mental impairments, learning disabilities, and HIV infections or who are international refugees.

Academic Stress and Mental Illness

Being a university student is stressful for all students, especially international students (Cox & Walsh, 1998; Misra & Castillo, 2004; Misra, Crist, & Burant, 2003). International students have the additional strain of learning different cultural values and language, leaving their support systems, and academic preparation (Carr, Koyama, & Thiagarajan, 2003; Chng et al., 1998; Lee, Koeske, & Sales, 2004; Misra & Castillo, 2004). As stressors accumulate, the ability to cope or readjust can be overtaxed, depleting their physical or psychological resources (Misra & Castillo, 2004). In turn, there is an increased probability that physical illness or psychological distress will follow (Cox & Walsh, 1998; Misra & Castillo, 2004; Misra et al., 2003; Yang & Clum, 1994).

Excessive stress induces physical impairments, and it is not uncommon to find international students afflicted with lack of energy, loss of appetite, headaches, or gastrointestinal problems (Misra & Castillo, 2004; Mori, 2000). In addition, some international students may somaticize their feelings of stress to avoid the stigma of seeking psychological assistance (Cox & Walsh, 1998; Misra & Castillo, 2004). International students' experiences of headaches, loss of appetite, or sleep problems may be attributed to a physical illness even though the complaints have no clear organic basis (Cox & Walsh, 1998; Misra & Castillo, 2004; Mori, 2000). Although American students experience stress reactions such as anxiety or depression, many international students do not distinguish emotional distress from somatic complaints (Misra & Castillo, 2004). As such, they use college health centers more frequently than American students do for stress-related problems (Carr et al., 2003; Mori, 2000). Even when physicians recognize that these symptoms are related to psychological distress and make a referral to a mental health clinician, many international students resist the physician's suggestion and do not seek psychological assistance (Carr et al., 2003).

Psychological distress is reported especially among those who fail to succeed academically (Misra & Castillo, 2004; Misra et al., 2003). Many international students have high expectations about their academic performance in a new educational environment. In their native country schools, these students were recognized as high achievers (Mori, 2000). High grade expectations originate not only from the students themselves but also from their families and culture that value hard work (Chng et al., 1998; Lam, 1993).

An additional pressure for international students is obtaining financial support. There are often limited resources available for international students, as well as immigration regulations limiting international students' opportunity to seek employment outside of the academic institution (Lee et al., 2004; Mori, 2000). Therefore, international students are unable to lessen their financial pressures.

Language deficits have also been found to be a significant source of stress among international students (Carr et al., 2003; Chng et al., 1998; Kher, Juneau, & Molstad, 2003; Misra & Castillo, 2004; Misra et al., 2003; Mori, 2000). This stress is amplified among students from China, Japan, and Korea due to the fact that the only official languages in those countries are the native languages (Chng et al., 1991; Oropeza, Fitzgibbon, & Baron, 1998). In contrast, English is one of the official languages in some South Asian countries such as India and Pakistan. (Dion & Toner, 1988). International students find that the difficulty in communication permeates every aspect of their lives (Kher et al., 2003; Mori, 2000). Because of the language impairment, students may experience social alienation. The lack of language skills also affects the student's daily living activities, including understanding housing procedures, organizing paperwork, and becoming familiar with registration and enrollment schedules (Kher et al., 2003).

According to the National Alliance for the Mentally Ill (n.d.), one in five people will experience mental illness in their lifetime. Many individuals first develop symptoms between the ages of 15–25 (Houston, 2002a). Empirical evidence has linked life stress and cultural adjustment to the development of mental illness

(Yang & Clum, 1994). International students may feel comfortable sharing these concerns with fellow international students (Mori, 2000). Serious problems arise when well-intentioned friends become overly protective of people who are depressed, paranoid, or schizophrenic. Without the support of their families and communities, international students who may have underlying mental health concerns may not be able to handle the academic and social pressures and therefore are more vulnerable to mental illness (Lee et al., 2004; Mori, 2000). In summary, a lack of traditional social support, high academic achievement pressure, financial aid restrictions, and language deficits are a few of the critical stressors international students encounter (Carr et al., 2003; Mori, 2000). Without proper mental health care, some international students may not be able to handle the academic and personal pressures associated with studying in the United States.

International Students With Learning Disabilities

In many countries, students with learning disabilities (LD) are considered to be functionally illiterate (Cottrell, 2000). Because of this assumption, many students with LD fear that they would be unfit for higher education if their learning disabilities were revealed and may not disclose their disability. As a result, students with LD experience increased problems with stress, social life, and family life (Cottrell, 2000; Kwon, 2005).

It is easy for students with LD to become overwhelmed as they transition from their home countries to institutions of higher education in the United States. In countries that provide educational opportunities for students with LD, these students may not be prepared to transition from learning experiences within small groups to group sizes of a few hundred students. Many students with LD have survived by "tagging along" with their peers, depending on them to find rooms, explain assignments, proofread, and provide informal assistance with course work. However, in higher education, students change classes each semester, which makes it difficult for students with LD to have a consistent group of peers from whom to receive academic assistance (Cottrell, 2000).

Another frequent issue is that many international students with LD arrive in the United States without the proper documentation needed by the university to coordinate services (Cottrell, 2000). To receive academic accommodations, an international student must have an LD assessment to document the need for services (Stodden & Conway, 2003). Because of the lack of proper documentation, international students with LD may not obtain the support services that are needed for academic success. Securing proper documentation may seem overwhelming for many international students with LD.

Assessment instruments are available to diagnosis learning difficulties. Yet, the majority of these tests or assessment batteries have been standardized using students from the United States or Western Europe (Kachirskaia, 2002). Many international students with LD are taking these tests in English, which may not be their native language (Niu & Luo, 1999). Also, diagnostic criteria of learning disabilities may vary within countries and may not fit the standards established by the

Diagnostic and Statistical Manual of Mental Disorders (4th ed., Text Revision (*DSM-IV-TR*; American Psychiatric Association, 2000) for a learning disability in the United States (Kachirskaia, 2002; Niu & Luo, 1999). To obtain an accurate assessment for learning difficulties, an international student would need to locate a mental health professional who could provide the testing and was familiar with the cultural biases found in the assessment instruments (Kachirskaia, 2002). For example, in a study of Chinese students with limited English proficiency who were classified as learning disabled, several characteristics were recognized that would inhibit their academic progress. Researchers found that their primary weakness was in reading skills, especially phonetic skills (Niu & Luo, 1999). The deficits in phonetic skills may be the root of reading difficulties because "in order to understand written text, the reader must be able to derive meaning from the strings of printed symbols on the page" (Adams & Bruck, 1995, p. 7). Transferring from Chinese to English is a difficult task as Chinese is a nonalphabetical language (Niu & Luo, 1999). Chinese written language is essentially a self-contained, pictorial-based language that uses ideographs. Because Chinese ideographs are not sound-oriented, the learning style has to emphasize external form and rote memorization (Niu & Luo, 1999). A psychologist who is testing a Chinese student would need to be aware of these language differences and how they may influence the test results to make an accurate diagnosis and recommend educational accommodations.

International students are reluctant to seek assistance that may affect their academic progress. Often, international students with LD fail to inform faculty members that they are struggling or fail to seek accommodations for their learning disability (Kachirskaia, 2002). Because of their hesitancy to self-identify either to university personnel or to faculty members, their academics may suffer.

In addition, the financial costs for the assessment may prohibit an international student from seeking an assessment for learning difficulties. The cost for a learning disability assessment may range from $300 to $1,200. With limited financial resources, the international student with LD may perceive the cost of testing as an unnecessary luxury.

International Students With HIV/AIDS

AIDS cases have been reported in over 150 nations. The Global AIDS Policy Coalition states that 38 million individuals worldwide will have been infected with the HIV virus by December 2003 (Centers for Disease Control and Prevention, 2004). With the increase in HIV comes an increase in the number of college students living with HIV and AIDS (Bower & Collins, 2000). For example, in Nigeria, researchers estimated that by 2004, 4.9 million individuals are HIV-positive. The group that is most vulnerable to HIV infections are college and university students because of "unsafe sexual behaviors, experimentation with alcohol and drugs, and failure to see themselves as at risk for infection" (Chng, Eke-Hueber, Eaddy, & Collins, 2005, p. 61). In Hong Kong, again the most vulnerable age group is college and university students, because they tend to engage in risky sexual behaviors

(Wong & Tang, 2001). Many international students may also engage in risky sexual behaviors for economic reasons, for example, commercial sex work to supplement their income to help pay for college and care for family (Chng et al., 2005). Youths in many countries are poorly informed about reproductive health and HIV/AIDS. Many young people engage in sexual behaviors without using condoms, therefore placing themselves more at risk (Chng et al., 2005; Gurman & Borzekowski, 2004; Kenya, Brodsky, Divale, Allegrante, & Fullilove, 2003; Maswanya et al., 2000; Wong & Tang, 2001).

Each country has different requirements for HIV antibody testing for the purpose of residency. Some countries require testing for any visa or for an extended visa, whereas in other countries actual testing requirements may differ from the official stated policy of the country. International students who are interested in seeking permanent resident status in the United States need to be aware that the United States requires HIV antibody testing of all applicants. Those applicants testing positive are denied status (NAFSA: Association of International Educators, n.d. [under "International Student Issues"]). The fear surrounding AIDS may prohibit individuals infected with HIV from entering specific countries. Similarly, international students coming to the United States from AIDS-infected countries may be subject to these fears and prejudices (NAFSA: Association of International Educators, n.d.).

In recent years the introduction of newer medications has helped to slow the progression of HIV and prevent the onset of AIDS (Beaudin & Chambre, 1996). These medications have also allowed treatment to be given at much earlier stages in the course of the illness. Early intervention reduces the disability associated with compromised immunity and the high risk of infections (Beaudin & Chambre, 1996; Dworkin & Pincu, 1993). Yet the cost of these medications may be prohibitive to international students with limited financial resources. In 1993 the estimates of annual medical care costs for HIV were $119,000 per person; $69,000 was expended after a diagnosis of AIDS (Beaudin & Chambre, 1996).

Every international student is required to have health insurance (NAFSA: Association of International Educators, n.d. [under "Education"]). AIDS and HIV infection have increased the complexity of insurance coverage and benefits. International students may enroll in the group policies offered for students by colleges and universities. The majority of these policies exclude preexisting conditions from coverage. The definitions of preexisting conditions vary. For example, some policies exclude preexisting conditions only if they were diagnosed prior to the date of enrollment, but in others, preexisting conditions are excluded even if they were not diagnosed. If a student is HIV-negative prior to insurance enrollment, this may exclude him or her from benefits should an illness related to HIV infection develop. International students need to be informed by the institution's representatives about insurance procedures and benefits regarding coverage of HIV-infected individuals (NAFSA: Association of International Educators, n.d.).

When working with international students who have HIV infections, it is important to be cognizant of the potentially devastating consequences of an unauthorized disclosure of an HIV infection (Duffin, 2001). This information may affect the students' academic progress and relationships in their home country. International students with HIV/AIDS are concerned about the reaction of peers and their attitudes toward AIDS (Maswanya et al., 2000). HIV-related illness may force an international student's withdrawal from the institution, loss of visa status, or possible deportation. University staff who has access to information about HIV antibody status of an international student should be reminded of the confidential nature of this information (Duffin, 2001).

International students are hesitant to seek HIV testing because of fear about confidentiality, the stress of waiting for the test result, and fear that a positive test result may mean the end of their academic career. Research examining college students and HIV antibody testing indicated that the students were unlikely to visit community clinics or hospitals for HIV antibody testing. International students who are concerned about HIV need to be informed that many campus health centers offer confidential HIV antibody testing and counseling at minimum cost to students at convenient locations (Anastasi, Sawyer, & Pinciaro, 1999).

International students are also fearful about the reaction of family members to a positive HIV test (Beaudin, & Chambre, 1996; Chin & Kroesen, 1999). In a study of Asian Pacific Islander women, being diagnosed with HIV was devastating to the participants because of its association with death, illness, drugs, and homosexuality. These topics are viewed as taboo (Chin & Kroesen, 1999). For Asian Pacific Islander women infected with HIV, the cultural and gender expectations that emphasize sexual modesty also make them feel additional shame concerning an AIDS diagnosis. These women were concerned about discrimination, disappointing or burdening others, stigma in disclosing the HIV diagnosis to family members, and changes in the degree of social support (Chin & Kroesen, 1999).

International students also worry about the reaction and judgment of peers concerning an HIV diagnosis (Bower & Collins, 2000; Maswanya et al., 2000). Johnson and Baer (1996) studied 189 undergraduate students in universities concerning their judgments and perceptions of people with AIDS. The researchers found that participants viewed AIDS as a "gay disease" and that an AIDS diagnosis affects the evaluation of a person with AIDS (Johnson & Baer, 1996). Bower and Collins (2000) reviewed the research on college students and HIV and found that college students do not interact in a positive manner with students who are HIV-positive; rather, they discriminate against and stigmatize these students. In some cultures, international students may have a good understanding of AIDS, yet refuse to interact or live with those who are infected (Maswanya et al., 2000). Students with HIV must cope with feelings of loneliness, isolation, anger, anxiety, and fear (Bower & Collins, 2000).

Bower and Collins (2000) identified the various services needed by students with HIV or AIDS: (a) individuals who are educated regarding HIV/AIDS issues and are "safe to talk to," (b) specific policies and strategies designed to address the concerns of these students, (c) appointment of an HIV/AIDS counselor/advocate, (d) special training for student health center personnel, and

(e) HIV/AIDS education for all college/university personnel. These resources and services are not always readily available. The lack of these resources and services may prohibit international students from successfully completing their academic careers. Many students may be forced to return to their home countries where less resources and services are available.

International students may have fears about studying or traveling in a country with a perceived high prevalence of HIV infection. Institutions in the United States need to be aware that the United States is considered a country with a high prevalence of HIV and AIDS. The students' fears may be based on misconceptions about transmission or exposure through sexual contact or contaminated blood (NAFSA: Association of International Educators, n.d.). International students also need to be educated about AIDS to prevent unwarranted fear of infections and to provide accurate information about prevention (NAFSA: Association of International Educators, n.d.).

The Overlooked Refugee International Students

Within the university community, there is a group of international students frequently overlooked. These are international students who have become refugees and have been exposed to various traumas of wartime or natural disasters in their home countries (Chung & Bemak, 2002; Jamil et al., 2002; Williams & Berry, 1991). Since 1945, more than 3.5 million refugees have entered the United States, with 1.1 million of them arriving in the past 11 years (U.S. Immigration and Naturalization Service, 2003). Many of these individuals have experienced multiple relocations, have been given temporary settlements in unsanitary refugee camps, and have been traumatized by witnessing the death or torture of family members or friends (Gonsalves, 1992; Knipscheer & Kleber, 2006; Lustig et al., 2004; Miller, Worthington, Muzurovic, Tipping, & Goldman, 2002). According to Jamil et al. (2002), "the impact of the trauma is not limited to a single event but instead includes a complex series of both direct and indirect traumatic events involving multiple separations and losses over a long period of the person's past" (p. 335).

Many refugees have been overwhelmed by political events that forced them to leave their homes (Gonsalves, 1992; Knipscheer & Kleber, 2006; Lustig et al., 2004; Miller et al., 2002). Refugees have reported feeling a range of emotional responses, from abandonment and despair to relief and excitement (Engstrom & Okamura, 2004). Though they many feel relieved that their lives are no longer endangered (Hyman, Yu, & Beiser, 2000), they may also feel a profound loss associated with having to leave their homelands (Berliner, Mikkelsen, Bovbjerg, & Wiking, 2004). Chung and Bemak (2002) found that refugees who were forced to leave their homeland without prior preparation may have more struggles with adjustment difficulties. Some refugees may experience guilt for surviving while others did not, or, in the process of being in exile, they have had to betray others in order to survive (Berliner et al., 2004; Engstrom & Okamura, 2004; Gorman, 2001). These types of personal experiences increase the risk of these individuals being vulnerable to emotional distress (Chung & Bemak, 2002; Gonsalves, 1992; Jamil et al., 2002; Lustig el al., 2004; Miller et al., 2002).

Upon being relocated to the United States, refugees may be faced with additional obstacles (Gon-Guy, Cravens, & Patterson, 1991). Many students and their families who have been refugees may struggle with financial concerns (Hyman et al., 2000). Refugee location services may only provide economic support for 3 to 6 months, after which families are expected to be financially solvent. Some refugees may experience difficulty in acquiring work because of lack of language proficiencies and because they are still adjusting to the new culture. These factors may interfere with refugees finding appropriate employment (Chung & Bemak, 2002; Gonsalves, 1992; Jamil et al., 2002; Lustig et al., 2004; Miller et al., 2002).

When international students have experienced trauma, they may arrive on the university campus with symptoms of depression, anxiety, posttraumatic stress disorder, and other health-related problems (Berliner et al., 2004; Farrag, 1999; Gorman, 2001; Gorst-Unsworth & Goldenberg, 1998; Hyman et al., 2000; Knipscheer & Kleber, 2006; Lustig et al., 2004; Takeda, 2000; Williams & Berry, 1991). These patterns of psychological concerns and overall health problems have been found in refugees from Europe, the Middle East, and Southeast Asia (Jamil et al., 2002; Knipscheer & Kleber, 2006; Lustig et al., 2004; Miller et al., 2002). Many refugees are unfamiliar with mental health services in the United States (Gon-Guy et al., 1991). Cultural perceptions also cloud how these mental health services are perceived, for example: (a) Mental illness is passed on to other family members and affects the marriageability of other family members, (b) illness in a family member is related to punishment for past-life sins and therefore damages the family reputation, (c) identification of mental illness may lead to deportation or discontinuation of government benefits, or (d) information will not remain confidential and will be spread through government agencies or within the ethnic community (Gon-Guy et al., 1991). An additional concern of some refugees seeking mental health services is that physicians and mental health care providers in their home countries were frequently involved in acts of torture; these health care providers who were to ease the pain of community members violated the trust of those seeking assistance (Engstrom & Okamura, 2004). The stigma and shame attached with admitting to a mental health problem or other impairments coupled with mistrust of mental health care providers forces the individual to somatize symptoms and ignore the need for assistance (Enstrom & Okamura, 2004; Jamil et al., 2002).

To deliver effective treatment for these students, mental health providers need to (a) have an understanding of the past and present political and human rights conditions of the countries from which these students originate, (b) communicate to these students that they are aware of their country's conditions and use this information to encourage students to share their experiences, (c) assist students in understanding that the violence and trauma experienced are beyond the norms of acceptable behaviors, and (d) assure students that their stories are believable and want to be heard (Engstrom & Okamura, 2004).

Many mental health centers on college campuses have adopted a treatment model of time-limited therapy focused on the elimination of symptoms and advocate the use of medication (Engstrom & Okamura, 2004). For students who are refugees and have been exposed to acts of violence and torture, these models of service delivery may not allow time to build strong therapeutic relationships and trust (Berliner et al., 2004; Gorman, 2001). Service providers may need to consider alternative treatment models to assist these students, for example, additional number of therapy sessions, group treatment, stress reduction, and self-care interventions (Berliner et al., 2004; Gorman, 2001). In their work with refugees and torture survivors, Engstrom and Okamura (2004) identified skills and resources needed to provide effective services for these students: (a) training in the signs and symptoms of mental health problems, (b) understanding the effects of trauma, and (c) identifying appropriate referrals to specialist and treatment centers familiar with issues presented by these students.

Mental health professionals who work with these students may be vulnerable to vicarious or secondary trauma and burnout because of the toxic effect created by listening and responding to the students' experiences (Engstrom & Okamura, 2004). Sometimes clinicians may develop feelings of hopelessness, helplessness, despair, cynicism, and disbelief. It is important that service providers find colleague support and participate in stress-reduction exercises and other self-care measures to keep themselves healthy (Engstrom & Okamura, 2004).

The Americans With Disabilities Act and Institutions of Higher Education

Feelings of shame and embarrassment are consistent themes that emerge when exploring issues associated with disability and being an international student. Because of these feelings, international students are hesitant to seek assistance or to disclose that assistance might be needed. In many countries there may be laws that outline resources and services to people with disabilities. Many international students are knowledgeable of these laws and services for people with disabilities in their home countries, but these laws and services may not be as broad or supportive as those in United States (Stodden, Whelley, & Chang, 2001).

Many international students have little information about the Americans With Disabilities Act (ADA). The provisions of the ADA mandate that institutions of higher education make "reasonable accommodations" for qualified students with disabilities (Stodden & Conway, 2003). The provisions outlined in the ADA allow students with disabilities to compete academically and minimize the effect of the disability on academic performance. To receive accommodations, the student has to self-identify and request special accommodations. In higher education, students with disabilities are responsible for initiating, designing, and ensuring their educational accommodations. Students are also responsible for informing university officials of their disabilities, providing documentation, and suggesting options for meeting their unique accommodations (Stodden & Conway, 2003).

International students from developing nations may also not be aware of the technology and assisted devices that are available to help them be successful in their academics and pursue a career of their choice (Fichten, Barile, Asuncion, & Fossey, 2000; Stodden & Conway, 2003). Many universities in the United States have the technology and assisted devices available to meet the needs of these students. If an international student with a disability has no awareness of technology or assisted devices, it is difficult to request them for assistance.

Recommendations for University Officials

The focus of offices that service international students is to assist with visa concerns, adjustment issues, orientation to the university campus, and available university and community resources. Many university administrators in these offices may have had little experience and knowledge to handle the concerns of international students with disabilities and may also be uncomfortable asking entering international students if they have a disability (Houston, 2002b). If the student does have a disability, international student advisors may not be aware of available campus resources for students with disabilities. With the passage of Section 504 of the Rehabilitation Act of 1977, every institution of higher education has a designated person or office that handles accommodations for students with disabilities. These individuals are trained to assess the needs of the international students and determine what services and resources may be required (Stodden & Conway, 2003). Because of the unique differences associated with each disability, international student advisors need to be aware that accommodation preferences will vary (Houston, 2002b). To better advise international students with disabilities about campus resources and academic accommodations, international program staffs are encouraged to research the services that are available on their university campus.

Because of the special needs of international students with disabilities, university personnel may feel overwhelmed in meeting the needs of these students. Mobility International USA (MIUSA) operates the National Clearinghouse on Disability and Exchange (NCDE). MIUSA also consults with international exchange organizations and provides practical training and information on how to include students with disabilities in academic programs (Houston, 2002b). The following tips have been modified for university personnel based on the MIUSA Web site to assist in the transitions from home country to the host institution concerning disability-related needs (http://www.iienetwork.org/?p=29260):

- Include an accommodation assessment questionnaire along with the acceptance packet sent to each international student. This procedure allows international students the opportunity to disclose any disability information. If international students are aware of what accommodations they may require, arrangements can be made for these services prior to their arrival on campus.

- Encourage disclosure by including disability statements and pictures of international students with disabilities in brochures, handbooks, and other materials.
- Arrange for international students to become familiar with the personnel and facilities of the counseling center, student health center, or other services for international students.
- Provide information about community organizations that focus on issues related to disabilities, as well as local crisis telephone hotlines and other community resources.
- For international students who choose to use counseling or medical services outside of the university, encourage them to check their insurance policy to determine whether coverage is available for these expenses.
- Ask the university's coordinator of services for disabled students to provide information to international students on possible discrimination and prejudice.
- If international students use medications, recommend that they bring an adequate supply until other sources can be secured.

Even with the MIUSA and the NCDE providing resources and information, students with disabilities still do not participate to the same extent as their nondisabled peers in educational exchange programs (Houston, 2002b). MIUSA brought together more than 50 alumni from 11 countries to examine the impact of international exchange on the career, education, and personal paths of people with disabilities. Alumni of MIUSA and other exchange programs recorded that these experiences were life-changing, including (a) careers enhancement, (b) languages learned, (c) friendships formed across cultures, (d) personal benefits of self-discovery, (e) discovering new interests, (f) becoming more adaptable, and (g) being able to embrace a broader worldview (Houston, 2002b). The staff of MIUSA recognize that individuals who become involved in international careers—ambassadors, diplomats, development workers, exchange professionals—began their careers by first participating in international exchange programs.

Treatment Suggestions for Mental Health Providers

Mental health providers have a crucial role in assisting international students with disabilities to achieve a positive academic experience. Mental health providers not only provide direct clinical services but also serve as consultants to the university community concerning the mental health needs of international students. To achieve this goal, mental health providers need to be aware of the unique issues that international students with disabilities have when seeking therapy.

International students with disabilities experience many difficulties both upon arrival and as they adjust to the university experience (Boyer & Sedlacek, 1989). Some of the difficulties they struggle with include language difficulties, adjustment to unfamiliar social norms, eating habits, adapting to new customs and values, differences in education systems, and a loss of established social networks

(Cox & Walsh, 2003; Heggins & Jackson, 2003; Misra et al., 2003; Toyokawa & Toyokawa, 2002). International students may not be able to articulate these concerns to mental health providers and may feel more comfortable sharing feelings of homesickness and loneliness (Heggins & Jackson, 2003).

Another issue that is sometimes overlooked by mental health providers is dealing with prejudice and the perception of prejudice. These are important concerns of international students and may predict symptoms of depression (Rahman & Rollock, 2004). International students with disabilities may vary in their degree of competency to handle these issues. Assessment of specific areas of competency can assist mental health providers in recognizing the students' self-perception of skills and needs. Taking into account the students' perceptions, Rahman and Rollock (2004) identified three different strategies for intervention: (a) When environmental demands are viewed unrealistically or the students see their own skills negatively, cognitive reappraisal strategies may be indicated; (b) when the students lack the skills needed to negotiate their way in the new culture, skill acquisition may be the most appropriate intervention; and (c) when the student is unable to reduce demands or to acquire desirable skills, they may benefit most from coping techniques. Competence-based assessments assist clinicians in providing more specific and useful interventions.

International students may be uncomfortable using psychological services, may rarely endorse emotional or social issues, and may be more concerned with academic and career issues (Boyer & Sedlacek, 1989). Because of this, international students are more likely to overutilize educational and vocational counseling (Heggins & Jackson, 2003). Assisting international students who are struggling with acculturation difficulties by focusing on academic and career issues may make seeking help less intimidating and more comfortable for the student (Boyer & Sedlacek, 1989). It may be beneficial for counselors to help international students to focus on campus activities and connection to campus organizations that can contribute to their successful adjustment and a more positive experience in the host country (Boyer & Sedlacek, 1989; Misra et al., 2003; Toyokawa & Toyokawa, 2003).

A study by Toyokawa and Toyokawa (2003) on the adjustment of Asian international students found that those students who engaged in extracurricular activities reported higher satisfaction with life in the host country as compared with students who were not as engaged in these activities. Being involved in extracurricular activities also had a positive effect on international students' academic involvement; they gained social competence that enhanced their levels of self-esteem and confidence in the classroom. Counselors need to encourage international students with disabilities to become involved in campus activities, residence halls programs, and campus organizations (Misra et al., 2003).

Lee et al. (2004) identified a relationship between acculturation stress and mental health symptoms, with social support as a moderator. Students with high levels of social support reported fewer symptoms when faced with increasing acculturation stress. Successful completion of their academic careers may be dependent on colleges and universities providing programs that enhance the social support systems of international students (Lee et al., 2004). Counselors need to encourage students to develop social networks that are supportive.

Li and Gasser (2005) studied the cross-cultural self-efficacy of international students from 17 Asian countries and found that increased interaction with other American students facilitated international students' sociocultural adjustment process by assisting international students to develop local networks, understand the local culture, and acquire social skills necessary for adjustment to the new culture. Lee and Gasser recommended that international students engage in cross-cultural social interactions, watch their peers' performances in social contexts, solicit feedback and encouragement for their own performance, and focus on their own performance instead of their emotional arousal in social interactions to enhance their self-efficacy.

Specific issues related to the experiences of international students with disabilities have not been studied. Counseling international students with disabilities may require counselors to develop a new area of clinical expertise. Counseling professionals reflect the attitudes and prejudices of the culture and may not be aware of how these beliefs manifest themselves in therapy (Leigh, Powers, Vash, & Nettles, 2004). Kemp and Mallinckrodt (1996) studied counselors' attitudes toward clients with disabilities. They found that counselors may (a) encourage dependency, (b) expect a client to hold an inferior societal status and accept a sick role, (c) maintain low expectations of client capability, (d) impose their own personal values that may not match client values, and (e) fail to address the disability at all. It is crucial for counselors to assess for the possible effects of "social stigma, culturally inferior status, pejorative treatment, feelings of belongingness, and discrimination experiences" (Kemp & Mallinckrodt, 1996, p. 382; see also Leigh et al., 2004). In providing clinical services, counselors need to recognize that international students with disabilities now reside in a culture that values physical beauty, work productivity, and financial success. The lack of awareness about these issues may leave a client who has a disability feeling further marginalized and invalidated (Kemp & Mallinckrodt, 1996; Leigh et al., 2004).

It may be possible that another paradigm concerning mental health needs to be used that integrates culture and disability, such as a wellness model. Prilleltensky and Prilleltensky (2003) suggested that counselors have two roles—as healers and as social change agents. Because of these two roles, the values of social justice, caring and compassion, and cultural diversity are interconnected and support wellness and personal liberation.

Dunn (1961) defined wellness "as an integrated method functioning oriented towards maximizing the potential of the individual" (p. 3). This is an underlying goal of mental health care. Using a wellness model allows the counselor to incorporate many of the research findings associated with successful acculturation, encourages the individual to define for him- or herself what is an optimal level of health, uses the student's culture as a way of enhancing health and well-being, broadens the definition of health to minimize the stigma attached to mental health counseling, normalizes the fact that international students may somatize their mental health complaints, and presses individuals to develop a customized wellness action plan with concrete steps for implementation. Overall, the wellness model incorporates cultural values and differences as a means to increase one's personal well-being.

A new wellness model that focuses on counseling and treatment planning is Myers, Sweeney, and Witmer's (2000) holistic Wheel of Wellness model. This model differs from other wellness models in that it has a multidisciplinary focus and is grounded in theories of human growth and behavior. The model stresses prevention, early intervention, and alternative methods of remediation, all strategies that are familiar to mental health professionals. An underlying belief of this model is that "healthy functioning occurs on a developmental continuum, and health behaviors at one point in life affect subsequent development and functioning as well" (Myers et al., 2000, p. 3).

Myers et al. (2000) identified five major life tasks: spirituality, self, work and leisure, friendship, and love. An important component of the Wheel of Wellness model is that the counselor and student create a wellness plan of action. Students are encouraged to select task areas in which they have a low wellness score as a place to begin the development of their wellness plan and to select one or two tasks to focus on. The next step is for the counselor and student to develop a written behavioral plan with objectives for change, methods to be used, and resources that may be used and/or needed. The student also identifies methods for self-evaluation that will note the progress that is being made and if any changes in the plan need to be made.

Using a wellness model allows both the student and the counselor to create a plan to enhance well-being. This plan does not have to focus on the areas in which international students may struggle with, such as labeling and using emotions, and incorporates research findings that enhance the adjustment and acculturation process. Because each plan is made specifically for the individual, this keeps the wellness processes focused on the person rather than having to meet the expectations of family members, peers, or society as a whole. Wellness also encourages international students to use their personal cultural experiences as ways to enhance their well-being. In using a wellness model, both the student and counselor work together to develop new possibilities to handle current situations and personal struggles and to create an outlook that emphasizes the student's attributes, circumstances, and resources.

Mental health providers working with international students with disabilities are faced with the challenge of incorporating the unique issues that confront students who are both multicultural and disabled. Currently, counselors are encouraged to gain additional training and expertise to be effective multicultural counselors (Arredondo & Perez, 2006; Cokley & Rosales, 2005; Engels, 2004; Sue & Sue, 2003). Yet, many counselors may not have received training on specific issues related to disability (Leigh et al., 2004; Olkin, 1999). Training on disability-related issues should include (a) education on the cultural history of people with disabilities; (b) discussion of ongoing stereotypes and biases; (c) education on related potential mental health issues, such as alienation, discrimination experiences, and relationship issues; and (d) training in effective counseling strategies (Kemp & Mallinckrodt, 1996). Receiving training in issues related to disability will allow counselors to feel more at ease and competent in meeting the mental health needs of international students with disabilities.

Future Directions and Conclusion

Throughout the world, countries are adapting policies that mandate that children with disabilities be educated (Alur, 2002; Riddell, 1998). For example, in the late 1960s and the 1970s the Federal Republic of Germany expanded the educational system to include students with disabilities in higher education (Meister, 1998). In the United Kingdom, access to postsecondary education for students with disabilities or learning difficulties was added to the national agenda in 1986 (Parker, 1998). During the past two decades in Canada, there have been legislative changes, designated campus officers for students with disabilities, and pressure from organizations representing people with disabilities to increase the number of students with disabilities who participate in higher education (Cox & Walsh, 1998).

In 1994, the United Nations Standard Rules on the Equalization of Opportunities for Persons With Disabilities and the Salamanca Statement and Framework for Action on Special Needs Education reaffirmed the rights of people with disabilities to have equal opportunity, be full participants in society, and have an equal role partnership in the planning and implementation of policies that affect their lives (Mittler, 1995). The United Nations has also initiated a campaign to include all disabled children in education through its Education for All programs (UNESCO, 1995). The focus of Education for All is to include all children who are excluded from "the benefits of school" and children with disabilities who have never attended school or who have been excluded as unsuitable (Mittler, 1995).

In 1995, UNESCO surveyed countries to determine whether international support is making a difference in the education of children with disabilities. They found that more countries are accepting responsibility or enacting new legislation for the education of children with disabilities, and 92% of countries had policies on integration of students with disabilities into the educational system (Mittler, 1995). The researchers also noted that a number of innovative reforms have been introduced in many countries. Parents and family members have begun to take a more active role in seeking to provide community-based education for children and family members with disabilities (Mittler, 1995).

In 1997, many Pacific Rim countries including Taiwan were reviewing the ADA (Wang, Chan, Thomas, Lin, & Larson, 1997). Countries were interested in the ADA to determine whether possible legislation could be written that would promote societal support for people with disabilities and that would reflect their cultural values. These types of legislative changes will begin to alter the pool of the educated in both developing and industrial countries.

In today's body of international students, few students with disabilities may be represented. However, within 5 to 10 years, the composition of international students may look different in terms of the number of international students with a disability seeking advanced education. For example, in China, 5% of the population, or over 50 million individuals, have some type of disability. Previously, over 66% of those with disabilities could neither read nor write. In 1995, the leaders of China established as a goal to have 40,000 students with disabilities graduate from their educational institutions (Stratford & Ng, 2000). Upon graduation, these 40,000 students have the potential to become international students. Because of the high degree of services provided to students with disabilities in American universities, it is likely that many of these students will be seeking an education from a university in the United States.

This hiatus of 5 to 10 years provides an opportunity for university administrators, international student advisors, mental health providers, and other campus personnel to begin developing models of service delivery for international students with disabilities. Providing educational opportunities for international students with disabilities may be viewed as a new problem to handle, or as part of the process of changing the world and ensuring that all individuals are acknowledged and provided opportunities to empower their lives with advanced educational opportunities.

References

Adams, M., & Bruck, M. (1995). Resolving the "great debate." *American Educator, 19*(2), 10-20.

Alur, M. (2002). Status of disabled people in India: Policy and inclusion. *Exceptional Education Canada, 12,* 137-167.

American Psychiatric Association. (2000). *Diagnostic and statistical manual of mental disorders* (4th ed., text rev.). Washington, DC: Author.

Anastasi, M. C., Sawyer, R. G., & Pinciaro, P. J. (1999). A descriptive analysis of students seeking HIV antibody testing at a university health service. *Journal of American College Health, 48,* 13-19.

Argyrakouli, E., & Zafiropoulou, M. (2003). Self-esteem of Greek mothers of children with intellectual disabilities. *International Journal of Disability, Development and Education, 50,* 181-195.

Arredondo, P., & Perez, P. (2006). Historical perspective on the multicultural guidelines and contemporary applications. *Professional Psychology: Research and Practice, 37,* 1-5.

Beaudin, C. L., & Chambre, S. M. (1996). HIV/AIDS as a chronic disease: Emergence from the plague model. *American Behavioral Scientist, 39,* 684-705.

Berliner, P., Mikkelsen, E. N., Bovbjerg, A., & Wiking, M. (2004). Psychotherapy treatment of torture survivors. *International Journal of Psychosocial Rehabilitation, 8,* 85-96.

Bower, B. L., & Collins, K. (2000). Students living with HIV/AIDS: Exploring their psychosocial and moral development. *NASPA Journal, 37,* 428-443.

Boyer, S. P., & Sedlacek, W. E. (1989). Noncognitive predictors of counseling center use by international students. *Journal of Counseling & Development, 67,* 404-407.

Carr, J. L., Koyama, M., & Thiagarajan, M. (2003). A women's support group for Asian international students. *Journal of American College Health, 52,* 131-135.

Centers for Disease Control and Prevention. (2004). *CDC annual HIV/AIDS surveillance report.* Retrieved June, 20, 2006, from http://www.cdc.gov/hiv/stats.htm#international

Chan, C., Lee, T., Yuen, H., & Chan, F. (2002). Attitudes toward people with disabilities between Chinese rehabilitation and business students: An implication for practice. *Rehabilitation Psychology, 47,* 324-338.

Chen, R. K., Brodwin, M. G., Cardoso, E., & Chan, F. (2002). Attitudes toward people with disabilities in the social context of dating and marriage: A comparison of American, Taiwanese, and Singaporean college students. *Journal of Rehabilitation, 68*(4), 5-12.

Chin, D., & Kroesen, K. (1999). Disclosure of HIV infection among Asian/Pacific Islander American women: Cultural stigma and support. *Cultural Diversity and Ethnic Minority Psychology, 5,* 222-235.

Chng, C. L., Ding, J., & Perez, M. A. (1998). Validation of the East Asian Student Stress Inventory (EASSI). *American Journal of Health Studies, 14,* 153-161.

Chng, C. L., Eke-Hueber, E., Eaddy, S., & Collins, J. R. (2005). Nigerian college students: HIV knowledge, perceived susceptibility for HIV and sexual behaviors. *College Student Journal, 39,* 60-71.

Cho, S., Singer, G. H. S., & Brenner, B. (2003, Spring). A comparison of adaptation to childhood disability in Korean immigrant and Korean mothers. *Focus on Autism and Other Developmental Disabilities,* 9-20.

Chung, R. C., & Bemak, F. (2002). Revisiting the California Southeast Asian mental health needs assessment data: An examination of refugee ethnic and gender differences. *Journal of Counseling & Development, 80,* 111-119.

Cokley, K., & Rosales, R. (2005). Handbook of multicultural competencies in counseling and psychology. *Measurement and Evaluation in Counseling and Development, 38,* 176-182.

Cottrell, S. (2000, July). *Dyslexia into the universities.* Paper presented at the International Special Education Congress, University of Manchester, Manchester, England.

Cox, D., & Walsh, R. M. (1998). Questions to consider in policy development for postsecondary students with disabilities. *Journal of Postsecondary Education and Disability, 13*(2), 51-66.

Dion, K. L., & Toner, B. B. (1988). Ethnic difference in text anxiety. *Journal of Social Psychology, 128,* 165-172.

Driedger, D. (1991). Introduction. In D. Driedger (Ed.), *Disabled people in international development.* Winnipeg, Manitoba, Canada: Coalition of Provincial Organizations of the Handicapped. Retrieved July 1, 2004, from http://www.independentliving.org/docs1/dispopleintldevl.html

Driedger, D., & D'Aubin, A. (1991). Literacy for whom: Women with disabilities marginalized. In D. Driedger (Ed.), *Disabled people in international development.* Winnipeg, Manitoba, Canada: Coalition of Provincial Organizations of the Handicapped. Retrieved June 20, 2006, from http://www. independentliving.org/docs1/dispopleintldevl.html

Duffin, C. (2001). Students' HIV status leaks are being investigated. *Nursing Standard, 15*(21), 5.

Dunn, H. L. (1961). *High-level wellness.* Arlington, VA: R. W. Beatty.

Dworkin, S. H., & Pincu, L. (1993). Counseling in the era of AIDS. *Journal of Counseling & Development, 71,* 275–281.

Engels, D. W. (2004). *The professional counselor: Portfolio, competencies, performance guidelines, and assessment* (3rd ed.). Alexandria, VA: American Counseling Association.

Engstrom, D. W., & Okamura, A. (2004). A plague of our time: Torture, human rights, and social work. *Families in Society, 85,* 291–300.

Farrag, M. F. (1999, April). *Mental health issues in the Arab American community.* Paper presented at the First National Conference on Health Issues in the Arab American Community, Southfield, MI.

Fichten, C. S., Barile, M., Asuncion, J. V., & Fossey, M. E. (2000). What government, agencies, and organizations can do to improve access to computers for postsecondary students with disabilities: Recommendations based on Canadian empirical data. *International Journal of Rehabilitation Research, 23,* 191–199.

Gannon, P. M., & MacLean, D. (1997). The emotionally affected university student: Support from the university community. *International Journal of Disability, Development and Education, 44,* 217–228.

Ghobrial, T. M., & Vance, H. R. (1988). *Special education in Egypt: An overview.* (ERIC Document Reproduction Service No. ED299721)

Gon-Guy, E., Cravens, R. B., & Patterson, T. E. (1991). Clinical issues in mental health service delivery to refugees. *American Psychologist, 46,* 642–648.

Gonsalves, C. J. (1992). Psychological stages of the refugee process: A model for therapeutic interventions. *Professional Psychology: Research and Practice, 23,* 382–389.

Gorman, W. (2001). Refugee survivors of torture: Trauma and treatment. *Professional Psychology: Research and Practice, 32,* 443–451.

Gorst-Unsworth, C., & Goldenberg, E. (1998). Psychological sequelae of torture and organized violence suffered by refugees from Iraq: Trauma-related factors compared with social factors in exile. *British Journal of Psychiatry, 172,* 90–94.

Gurman, T., & Borzekowski, D. (2004). Condom use among Latino college students. *Journal of American College Health, 52,* 169–178.

Hassan, J. (1991). Disabled people and attitudinal barriers. In D. Driedger (Ed.), *Disabled people in international development.* Winnipeg, Manitoba, Canada: Coalition of Provincial Organizations of the Handicapped. Retrieved June 20, 2006, from http://www.independentliving.org/docs1/dispopleintldevl.html

Heggins, W. J., & Jackson, J. F. L. (2003). Understanding the collegiate experience for Asian international students at a midwestern research university. *College Student Journal, 37,* 379–391.

Houston, P. (2002a). *Accommodation for individuals with psychiatric disabilities*. Eugene, OR: National Clearinghouse on Disability Exchange Mobility International USA. Retrieved June 20, 2006, from http://www.iienetwork.org/?p=29260

Houston, P. (2002b). *International exchange makes a difference:A disability perspective*. Eugene, OR: National Clearinghouse on Disability and Exchange Mobility International USA. Retrieved June 20, 2006, from http://www.iienetwork.org/?p=29260

Hyman, I.,Yu, N., & Beiser, M. (2000). Post-migration stresses among Southeast Asian refugee youth in Canada: A research note. *Journal of Comparative Family Studies, 31,* 281-294.

Institute of International Education. (2005). *Open Doors 2005.* Retrieved June 20, 2006, from http://opendoors.iienetwork.org/?p=69692

Jamil, H., Hakim-Larson, J., Farrag, M., Kafaji,T., Duqum, I., & Jamil, L. H. (2002). A retrospective study of Arab American mental health clients:Trauma and the Iraqi refugees. *American Journal of Orthopsychiatry, 72,* 355-361.

Johnson, M. E., & Baer, A. J. (1996). College students' judgments and perceptions of persons with AIDS from different risk groups. *Journal of Psychology, 130,* 527-537.

Kachirskaia, E. (2002). Special needs provision in international schools. *International Schools Journal, 21*(2), 69-74.

Kemp, N. T., & Mallinckrodt, B. (1996). Impact of professional training on case conceptualization of clients with a disability. *Professional Psychology: Research and Practice, 27,* 378-385.

Kenya, S., Brodsky, M., Divale,W.,Allegrante, J. P., & Fullilove, R. E. (2003). Effects of immigration on selected health risk behaviors of Black college students. *Journal of American College Health, 52,* 113-120.

Kher, N., Juneau, G., & Molstad, S. (2003). From the southern hemisphere to the rural south: A Mauritian student's version of "Coming to America." *College Student Journal, 37,* 564-568.

Knipscheer, J.W., & Kleber, R. J. (2006).The relative contribution of posttraumatic and acculturative stress to subjective mental health among Bosnian refugees. *Journal of Clinical Psychology, 62,* 339-353.

Kwon, H. (2005). Inclusion in South Korea: The current situation and future directions. *International Journal of Disability, Development and Education, 52*(1), 59-68.

Lam, C. S. (1993). Cross-cultural rehabilitation:What Americans can learn from their foreign peers. *Journal of Applied Rehabilitation Counseling, 24*(3), 26-30.

Lee, J. S., Koeske, G. F., & Sales, E. (2004). Social support buffering of acculturative stress: A study of mental health symptoms among Korean international students. *International Journal of Intercultural Relations, 28,* 399-414.

Leigh, I. W., Powers, L. V.,Vash, C., & Nettles, R. (2004). Survey of psychological services to clients with disabilities: The need for awareness. *Rehabilitation Psychology, 49*(1), 48-54.

Li, A., & Gasser, M. (2005). Predicting Asian international students' sociocultural adjustment: A test of two medication models. *International Journal of Intercultural Relations, 29,* 561-576.

Liu, G. Z. (2001). *Chinese culture and disability: Information for U.S. service providers* (CIRRIE Monograph Series, China). Buffalo, NY: Center for International Rehabilitation Research Information and Exchange.

Losinsky, L. O., Levi, T., Saffrey, K., & Jelsma, J. (2003). An investigation into the physical accessibility to wheelchair bound students of an institution of higher education in South Africa. *Disability Rehabilitation 25,* 305-308.

Lustig, S. L., Kia-Keating, M., Knight, W. G., Geltman, P., Ellis, H., Kinzie, D., et al. (2004). Review of child and adolescent refugee mental health. *Journal of American Academy of Child Adolescent Psychiatry, 43,* 24-36.

Maswanya, E., Moji, K., Aoyagi, K., Yahata, Y., Kusano, Y., Nagata, K., et al. (2000). Knowledge and attitudes toward AIDS among female college students in Nagasaki, Japan. *Health Education Research, 15*(1), 5-11.

Meister, J. J. (1998). Study conditions and behavioral patterns of students with disabilities in German universities. *Journal of Postsecondary Education and Disability, 13*(2), 37-50.

Miles, M. (1997). Disabled learners in South Asia: Lessons from the past for educational exporters. *International Journal of Disability, Development and Education, 44,* 97-104.

Miller, K. E., Worthington, G. J., Muzurovic, J., Tipping, S., & Goldman, A. (2002). Bosnian refugees and the stressors of exile: A narrative study. *American Journal of Orthopsychiatry, 72,* 341-354.

Misra, R., & Castillo, L. G. (2004). Academic stress among college students comparison of American and international students. *International Journal of Stress Management, 11,* 132-148.

Misra, R., Crist, J., & Burant, C. J. (2003). Relationships among life stress, social support, academic stressors, and reactions to stressors of international students in the United States. *International Journal of Stress Management, 10,* 137-157.

Mittler, P. (1995). Special needs education: An international perspective. *British Journal of Special Education, 22,* 105-108.

Mori, S. (2000). Addressing the mental health concerns of international students. *Journal of Counseling & Development, 78,* 137-145.

Myers, J. E., Sweeney, T. J., & Witmer, J. M. (2000). The wheel of wellness counseling for wellness: A holistic model for treatment planning. *Journal of Counseling & Development, 78,* 251-266.

NAFSA: Association of International Educators. (n.d.). *NAFSA's statement on AIDS and international educational issues.* Retrieved June 20, 2006, from http://www.nafsa.org/about.sec/governance_leadership/ethics_standards/ nafsa_s_statement_on

National Alliance for the Mentally Ill. (n.d.). *What is mental illness: Mental illness facts.* Retrieved December 6, 2006, from http://www.nami.org/template. cfm?section=About_Mental_Illness

Niu, X., & Luo, W. (1999). Patterns of performance of Chinese-American students with learning disabilities: A pilot study. *International Journal of Disability, Development, and Education, 46,* 117-129.

Olkin, R. (1999). *What psychotherapists should know about disability.* New York: Guilford Press.

Oropeza, B. C., Fitzgibbon, M., & Baron, A. (1991). Managing mental health crises of foreign college students. *Journal of Counseling & Development, 69,* 280-284.

Parker, V. (1998). Promoting inclusive learning in higher education for students with disabilities in the United Kingdom. *Journal of Postsecondary Education and Disability, 13*(2), 19-28.

Perfilyeva, M. (2003). Russia: Education is not yet a universal right for disabled students. *Disability World, 20.* Retrieved from http://www.disabilityworld.org/09-0_03/children/russia.shtml

Persinger, M. A., & Tiller, S. G. (1999). Personality not intelligence or educational achievement differentiate university students who access special needs for "learning disabilities." *Social Behavior and Personality, 27*(1), 1-10.

Prilleltensky, I., & Prilleltensky, O. (2003). Synergies for wellness and liberation in counseling psychology. *The Counseling Psychologist, 31,* 273-281.

Rahman, O., & Rollock, D. (2004). Acculturation, competence, and mental health among South Asian students in the United States. *Journal of Multicultural Counseling and Development, 32,* 130-143.

Rajah, Z. (1991). Thoughts on women and disability. In D. Driedger (Ed.), *Disabled people in international development.* Winnipeg, Manitoba, Canada: Coalition of Provincial Organizations of the Handicapped. Retrieved June 20, 2006, from http://www.independentliving.org/docs1/dispopleintldevl.html

Riddell, S. (1998). Chipping away at the mountain: Disabled students' experience of higher education. *International Studies in Sociology of Education, 8,* 203-222.

Ryan, J., & Struhs, J. (2004). University education for all? Barriers to full inclusion of students with disabilities in Australian universities. *International Journal of Inclusive Education, 8,* 73-90.

Shah, F. (1991). Women and disability. In D. Driedger (Ed.), *Disabled people in international development.* Winnipeg, Manitoba, Canada: Coalition of Provincial Organizations of the Handicapped. Retrieved June 20, 2006, from http://www.independentliving.org/docs1/dispopleintldev1.html

Stodden, R. A., & Conway, M. A. (2003). Supporting individuals with disabilities in postsecondary education. *American Rehabilitation, 27*(1), 24-32.

Stodden, R. A., Whelley, T., & Chang, C. (2001). Current status of educational support provision to students with disabilities in postsecondary education. *Journal of Vocational Rehabilitation, 16,* 189-198.

Stratford, B., & Ng, H. (2000). People with disabilities in China: Changing outlook, new solutions, growing problems. *International Journal of Disability, Development and Education, 47*(1), 7-14.

Sue, D. W., & Sue, D. (2003). *Counseling the culturally diverse: Theory and practice* (4th ed.). New York: Wiley.

Takeda, J. (2000). Psychological and economic adaptation of Iraqi male refugees: Implications for social work practice. *Journal of Social Work Practice, 26,* 1–21.

Toyokawa, T., & Toyokawa, N. (2003). Extracurricular activities and the adjustment of Asian international students: A study of Japanese students. *International Journal of Intercultural Relations, 26,* 363–379.

UNESCO. (1995). *World conference on special needs education: Access and quality.* Paris: Author.

U.S. Immigration and Naturalization Service. (2003). *US immigration.* Retrieved December 6, 2006, from http://www.uscis.gov/portal/site/uscis

Van Kraayenoord, E. D., Elkins, J., Palmer, C., & Richards, F. W. (2001). Literacy for all: Findings from an Australian study. *International Journal of Disability, Development and Education, 48,* 445–456.

Wang, M., Chan, F., Thomas, K. R., Lin, S., & Larson, P. (1997). Coping style and personal responsibility as factors in the perception of individuals with physical disabilities by Chinese international students. *Rehabilitation Psychology, 42,* 303–316.

Weiner, E. (1999). The meaning of education for university students with a psychiatric disability: A grounded theory analysis. *Psychiatric Rehabilitation Journal, 22,* 403–409.

Wilhite, B. C. (1995). Daily life experiences of Japanese adults with physical disabilities. *International Journal of Rehabilitation Research, 18,* 146–150.

Williams, C. L., & Berry, J. W. (1991). Primary prevention of acculturative stress among refugees application of psychological theory and practice. *American Psychologist, 46,* 632–641.

Wong, C., & Tang, C. S. (2001). Understanding heterosexual Chinese college students' intention to adopt safer sex behaviors. *Journal of Sex Research, 38,* 118–126.

World Health Organization. (n.d.). *WHO is guiding and supporting countries to scale up public health programs that promote rehabilitation and make assistive devices available to persons with disabilities.* Retrieved June 20, 2006, from http://www.who.int/disabilities/introduction/en/index.html

Yang, B., & Clum, G. A. (1994). Life stress, social support, and problem-solving skills predictive of depressive symptoms, hopelessness, and suicide ideation in an Asian student population: A test of a model. *Suicide and Life-Threatening Behavior, 24,* 127–139.

Chapter 6

The Families of International Students in U.S. Universities: Adjustment Issues and Implications for Counselors

Mary M. Chittooran and Anita Sankar-Gomes

The number of international students in U.S. universities who are accompanied by their families has increased over the past few decades (Institute of International Education, 2005). About a third of international students bring their families with them (Chittooran & Singaravelu, 2004; Institute of International Education, 2005), which results in their having to manage not only their own adjustment but also the concurrent adjustment of their spouses and children. Given the increasing number of international students and their families in the United States and the fact that the school-age children of these students are enrolled in U.S. schools, it becomes particularly important that counselors and other helping professionals understand and address the needs of this population (Andrade, 2006; Lin & Yi, 1997). This chapter addresses the developmental challenges and adjustment issues faced by the spouses and children of international students studying in U.S. universities, applies useful frameworks for exploring and conceptualizing these issues, provides recommendations to counselors and other helping professionals who work with this population, and offers a brief case scenario that illustrates practical applications of these recommendations.

Definition

The term *families of international students* as it is used in this chapter refers to spouses and children of international students who are enrolled in an undergraduate, graduate, or technical course of study at a college or university in the United States. Because most international students who are accompanied by their families bring only their spouses and children with them, this definition does not include other family configurations like elderly parents, same-sex partners, and extended families.

113

Characteristics of Families of International Students

While there is limited demographic information on the families of international students (Chittooran & Singaravelu, 2004; Mori, 2000; National Center for Education Statistics, 2002), the following profile may be a useful first step toward understanding the complex and unique needs of this population. Although international students have traditionally been male and single (Lin & Yi, 1997), there has been a recent increase in the number of female students and families, particularly from Asia (Institute of International Education, 2005). The *Open Doors Report,* which is issued annually by the Institute of International Education, stated that more than half of all international students and their families reside in California, New York, Texas, and Massachusetts. Most such families also subsist on a limited income, because approximately 60% to 67% of international students pay for their own university education and most are not eligible for state or government benefits or permitted to hold full-time, salaried positions off campus (Institute of International Education, 2005; Lin & Yi, 1997). According to the Bureau of Citizenship and Immigration, families of international students enter the United States as their dependents and remain in the country in legal but temporary status that expires once the course of study is completed.

Adjustment of Families of International Students: General Issues

According to Larson and Ovando (2001), the adjustment of foreign-born individuals to the United States often follows a predictable path, with stress being particularly acute during the initial phase. It is during this phase, referred to as *arrival survival* (Larson & Ovando, 2001), that international student families are confronted with the immediate, practical realities of living in a new country and have to learn basic survival skills related to language usage, dressing, eating, and transportation. Hechanova-Alampay, Beehr, Christiansen, and Van Horn (2002), in an analysis of 294 international and domestic student sojourners at a midwestern U.S. university, found that international students experienced more stress adjusting to college than did domestic students, with a curvilinear pattern of strain that peaked 3 months after the beginning of the semester. Similar findings have been reported by other researchers, including Sandhu (1994) and Poyrazli, Arbona, Bullington, and Pisecco (2001). Given that the degree to which international students adjust to life in the United States often determines the adjustment of their spouses and children (Chittooran & Singaravelu, 2004), we can extrapolate that families of these students are also likely to experience intense stress during this initial phase of adjustment.

Although most families of international students deal with economic challenges while they are in the United States, it is important to remember that many of them have enjoyed a relatively high degree of social status and affluence in their home country (Chittooran, 2006). Their rather bleak financial situation in the United States may be compounded by the fact that spouses and adult children of international students who enter the country as legal dependents, and are therefore not permitted to work, often have to compromise their own careers, professional growth, and studies. The change in occupational status and financial circumstances and the adjustment to living on a graduate student stipend or limited family savings may therefore be associated with considerable distress among the families of these students (Juntunen, Atkinson, & Tierney, 2003).

Adjustment of Families of International Students: Useful Theoretical Frameworks

Given the preceding contextual information about the families of international students, we can begin to examine their adjustment to multiple facets of life in the host country. Larson and Ovando (2001) and others (e.g., Chittooran & Singaravelu, 2004; Lin & Yi, 1997; Mori, 2000; Sam, 2001; Sandhu, 1994; Tseng & Newton, 2002) have delineated four categories of adjustment experienced by international students that we have adapted for use with the families of these students. They are (a) general environmental and physical adjustment to differences in living conditions, food, and transportation; (b) academic and school adjustment, including having to deal with language issues, unfamiliar academic environments, and varying approaches to pedagogy; (c) sociocultural adjustment such as culture shock, learning new customs, experiencing discrimination, loss of familiar social support networks and creating new ones, and reconciling conflicts between native and American values; and (d) intrapersonal, psychological adjustment such as dealing with homesickness, loneliness, depression, alienation, isolation, and loss of status or identity.

Larson and Ovando's (2001) model provides a useful framework to broadly examine adjustment issues of the families of international students and is incorporated throughout the chapter. However, it must be remembered that families vary along a number of dimensions and that responses of family members to relocation are mediated by several variables, including their gender, ethnicity, cultural distance between host and native country, and level of social support (Mori, 2000; Tseng & Newton, 2002; Zhang & Rentz, 1996).

There is a paucity of studies that examine the factors that influence the adjustment of families of international students (Chittooran & Singaravelu, 2004; Mori, 2000). What little research there is seems to suggest that international students and family members who are likely to adjust most easily to the United States tend to be younger rather than older and male rather than female (Sam, 2001). International students and their families who have an easier adjustment are more likely to have had prior cross-cultural experiences (Heggins & Jackson, 2003) and tend to be Caucasian (Sam, 2001). In addition, they tend to engage in more social interactions with the local community (Zhang & Rentz, 1996) and have strong social networks that include friends, teachers (Sam, 2001; Ying, 2003), and, often, a mentor or advocate. They are also more likely to be psychologically stable, with higher self-concepts and lower levels of susceptibility to stress (Sandhu, 1994). Financial stability and knowledge about the host country have both been positively associated with successful adjustment, although, surprisingly, familiarity with the language has not consistently been associated with such adjustment (Andrade, 2006; Poyrazli et al., 2001; Sam, 2001; Ying, 2003). The available literature also suggests that duration of stay in the United States has a variable impact on ease of adjustment (Chittooran & Singaravelu, 2004; Klomegah, 2006; Sam, 2001; Wilton & Constantine, 2003).

This rather frustrating inconsistency in findings may be attributable to the failure of researchers to develop technically adequate measures or to differences across studies that have to do with variables, populations, and methodology (Crano & Crano, 1993). Indeed, several scholars, including Pederson (1991), have bemoaned the lack of a "grand theory" to tie the research in this area together as well as the fact that the existing research consists of "isolated, uncoordinated and fragmentary studies on specialized variables with no clear implications of results to comprehensive theory building" (p. 50). Fifteen years after Pederson first made that comment, there remains a relative scarcity of research on the topic of international students and their families.

While, overall, there is little published research on the families of international students, we believe (based on our expertise in teaching cross-cultural diversity issues, our professional interactions with the families of international students, and our own experiences as international students with families) that the following frameworks and multicultural literature on the experiences of immigrant groups in the United States may be relevant and helpful in conceptualizing and understanding the factors that mediate, both individually and interactively, the process of adjustment for the families of international students. Perhaps the most salient of these factors include those related to membership in individualistic versus collectivistic cultures, acculturation to the United States, and the family life cycle with its associated developmental tasks. We discuss each of these factors in the following sections.

Individualistic Versus Collectivistic Cultures

A significant factor that influences family adjustment to life in the United States has to do with family membership in either individualistic or collectivistic cultures (Helms & Cook, 1999; Hui & Triandis, 1986). Simply defined, *individualistic* cultures, such as those found in the United States and other Western societies, tend to emphasize qualities such as independence, self-reliance, and satisfaction of personal needs and goals, whereas *collectivistic* cultures, such as those found in Asia and Latin America, tend to emphasize the interdependent self and are other-focused, group-oriented, and emphasize group rather than individual needs (Hui & Triandis, 1986). More than 80% of international students in the United States are from Asia (58%), Latin America (12%), Africa (6.4%), and the Middle East (5.5%), regions that have a predominantly collectivistic orientation (Institute of International Education, 2005). These students and their families are confronted with the challenges of functioning in an academic and cultural environment that espouses individualistic values and, hence, may have a more difficult time adjusting to life in the United States than families from countries that are more culturally similar (Heggins & Jackson, 2003).

The clash between individualistic and collectivistic values is a thread that weaves through and permeates every aspect of the adjustment of international families, both in terms of their interactions with the larger host culture and in terms of its impact on family dynamics. For example, within families with adolescents, in particular, difficulty arises when parents are raised with a collectivistic outlook on life with its emphasis on obedience and conformity to parental expectations and group norms while their adolescent children are exposed daily through the school environment to a host culture that promotes individualistic values such as autonomy, freedom of choice, and independence of thought (Sankar-Gomes, 2005).

Acculturation to the United States

Acculturation is defined as the process of psychological and behavioral change, undergone willingly or unwillingly by individuals who come into contact with a new culture (Marin, 1992, as cited in Ponterotto, Casas, Suzuki, & Alexander, 2000). These changes include (a) external observable behavioral signs of accommodating to the new culture such as language use, dress, food preferences, and participation in ethnic activities, and (b) internal aspects such as shifts in cognitive beliefs, values, attitudes that are more in tune with those of the host culture, and changes in the degree of affiliation, preference, and feelings toward the host culture compared with their own (Padilla, 1980; Sodowsky, Kwan, & Pannu, 1995; Ward, 1996). Research suggests that individuals who relocate to a new cultural environment adapt more quickly in peripheral, visible, or behavioral elements such as food, language usage, and clothes and resist changes in core or invisible elements of ethnic loyalty and cultural values, which are likely to remain stable (Ward, 1996). Such a pattern is also likely to hold true for international students and their families who are sojourners in the United States.

Several factors moderate the degree of acculturative stress, in particular, the cultural distance between the host culture and the home culture of international student families in terms of cultural practices, language fluency and educational experiences, geographical distance and dissimilarity between the two cultures (Zhang & Rentz, 1996), and physical differences related to skin color and other facial features (Berry, 1997; Poyrazli et al., 2001; Wan, 2001; Ward, 1996). For instance, European students and their families may adjust more easily to the United States because of their Caucasian features and color of their skin, whereas families from Africa, South America, and Asia are distinguishable by their physical features and skin color, and thus may experience subtle discrimination and prejudice that may not facilitate easy adjustment (Berry, 1997; Segal, 1998). Nonacceptance by the dominant culture and the complexity of living in two cultures may lead these students and their family members to feel marginalized and alienated and to experience a sense of identity confusion and intrapsychological conflict.

International students and their family members may adopt different acculturation strategies when confronted with the issue of adaptation to a new country (McCarthy, 2005; Moore & Constantine, 2005). Berry (1997) described four possible acculturation outcomes for immigrants that may have useful implications for the adjustment of international student families: separation, assimilation, biculturalism, and marginalization. Some family members may have minimal contact with the host culture outside of the academic setting, either because of a lack of opportunity or because of an inability or unwillingness to step out of their comfort zone, especially if lack of fluency in the English language is an issue. Families from more traditional, collectivistic societies may, for example, pursue a *separation* or isolationist strategy in the face of a clash between their own cultural values and those of the United States. They may socialize only within their own ethnic communities and limit their social interactions with the host culture to ensure that their families maintain their cultural heritage. On the other hand, their children and adolescents are exposed to a larger degree to the host culture through their network of peer relationships in school. They become relatively adept consumers of U.S. culture and are more likely to desire and pursue *assimilation* to the host culture (Bemak & Chung, 2003). These differences in acculturation and exposure to the host culture among family members may exacerbate normal sources of family conflict (Larson & Ovando, 2001). One must also bear in mind that acculturation efforts of international students and their families who plan to be in the United States only during the period of their studies and return to their home country (sojourners) are likely to be different from those who plan to settle in the United States after graduation (Yoon & Portman, 2004).

In the past, acculturation was viewed as a unidimensional, linear process in which individuals became assimilated to the host culture only through the gradual process of giving up their own ethnic identity. However, more recent conceptualizations such as Berry's (1997) model suggest that it is possible for individuals to retain their ethnic identity and behaviors while acquiring competence in the host culture. Hence, individuals could pursue a *bicultural* strategy, in which they can function effectively in both the host culture and their ethnic culture, have a strong sense of belonging or affiliation with both, and be able to alternate or switch behavior according to the demands of the cultural contexts (LaFromboise, Coleman, & Gerton, 1993; Rotheram-Borus, 1993). Research with various immigrant groups has generally suggested that a tendency to isolate oneself from the host culture is associated with greater stress, and that an integrationist or bicultural approach is usually the most adaptive strategy, while total assimilation into the dominant culture is more likely to be related to psychological maladjustment and psychosomatic problems (see Berry, 1997; Coll & Magnuson, 1997; Rotheram-Borus, 1993; Ward, 1996).

Findings generated in the literature on immigrant cultures have significant relevance for the psychological adjustment of the families of international students. Counselors need to be aware of the differences in acculturation strategies that international student families adopt in negotiating the dual-culture context they are confronted with on a daily basis. Differences in these strategies (whether they are bicultural, assimilation, or separation strategies) greatly shape and affect the well-being of these families.

The Family Life Cycle and Developmental Tasks

A third factor that impinges on the adjustment of international student families has to do with the family life cycle, as well as the specific developmental tasks and challenges associated with each stage of the life cycle. According to Carter and McGoldrick (1999) and Lambie (2000), the family life cycle includes predictable events and stages that occur in the development of all families. The family life cycle approach is based on the assumption that no individual's behavior can be understood without first understanding his or her role in the family as well as the current stage of the life cycle of the family. Life cycles are marked by nodal events that usher in the beginning of a new stage and bring with them the normal ups-and-downs that have an impact on how all families generally, and international student families specifically, navigate various environmental demands.

A comprehensive review of the literature revealed no studies on the family life cycle as it relates to international students and their families. Although the family life cycle model was developed in a Western, individualistic context, it is our belief that it can provide a valuable framework for understanding the adjustment of families of international students.

Each international student family is faced with transitional periods (interspersed with plateau periods of relative stability and predictability), when the occurrence of a life event demands changes in the structure and function of the family. Such transitional periods may result in a successful adjustment or, conversely, may bring with them anxiety, uncertainty, a sense of loss, and other dysfunctional outcomes. Transition periods may be triggered by either nonnormative, unexpected events (such as relocation or loss of income and status) or normative, expected events (such as the birth of a child or a child entering adolescence). For families of international students, we believe that relocation to a new country could be conceptualized as a nonnormative life event that may exacerbate the stresses associated with normal transitions in the family life cycle and place inordinate demands on the structure and function of the family.

In applying the family life cycle framework to the experiences of the families of international students, it is clear that passage through the various stages of the family life cycle will exert varying demands that will most likely compound the stresses of adjustment to the host country. Related to the family life cycle, and interacting with it, are also various age-related developmental tasks (Broderick & Blewitt, 2003) faced by one or more family members during any given phase of their lives that must be successfully navigated for individuals to move to the next developmental phase. In addition, international student families have to manage not only developmentally appropriate tasks but also changing gender roles for a successful adjustment process.

For example, in *Stage 1, The Newly Married Couple*, individuals must deal with issues of attachment, realignment of relationships with family and friends to include the spouse, and the development of common goals. In the case of international students, newly married couples who are negotiating marital adjustment issues have the added acculturative stress of adjusting to a new environment.

For spouses, especially those from collectivistic cultures, who have left a strong extended family network and social support in their home country, there may be an even greater sense of isolation and grief over loss of emotional ties with the home culture, especially if their marital partner becomes immersed in the academic environment. Spouses who have given up their own professional career to accompany their partner may also experience a loss of social status, productivity, and professional self-esteem (Juntunen et al., 2003). The issue is complicated if it is the female who is the international student and the male who is dependent on her, particularly if they belong to a hierarchical culture in which traditional gender roles are strictly observed.

In *Stage 2, Families With Young Children Ages 0-5*, developmental tasks include adjusting the marital system to make space for children, sharing of responsibilities for child rearing, managing financial and household tasks, and realigning relationships with friends and family to include parenting and grandparenting roles (Carter & McGoldrick, 1999). International students and their partners have to learn how to love and nurture their children within the limited resources and time constraints of international student life. International students also have to cope with the added stress of parenting in an unfamiliar cultural environment as they negotiate the stresses of their own academic and social adjustment. For those from collectivistic cultures in which there is much support for child care from the larger extended family in their home country, parenting can be an especially isolating process, especially for the spouse, who may not have connections with the larger academic community that the international student may enjoy. As Mori (2000) stated, spouses of international students, who come

to the U.S. specifically to support their husbands or wives in actualizing their academic and career dreams, and thus (do not belong) directly to the school environment (especially if they are the mothers of small children) are even more socially isolated than the international students. (p. 143)

Schools may serve as the entry point into life in the United States for international student families with school-age children. Willingly or not, these children are thrust into the daily life of schools, school-age peers, and teachers and are required to make adjustments to a new way of functioning. In *Stage 3, Families With Elementary-Age Children 6-12,* and *Stage 4, Families With Adolescents Ages 13-19,* international students, while having to negotiate their own academic adjustments to U.S. higher educational institutions, are also, along with their spouses and school-age children, confronted by the daunting task of managing differences in classroom procedures, teacher–student interactions, and pedagogy in U.S. schools (Lin & Yi, 1997). Besides the normal stresses of learning the ropes to survive the school day, including expectations related to time, getting excuse notes, using school lockers, and moving from class to class (Bemak & Chung, 2003; Juntunen et al., 2003), children of international students may experience more fundamental cultural barriers that may be just as challenging. For example, these children may struggle with an education system in the United States that values and rewards behaviors such as assertiveness, verbal fluency, and individual competitiveness (Gollnick & Chinn, 2006). These behaviors and attitudes may conflict sharply with values such as obedience, conformity, harmony, cooperation, and working for group rather than individual priorities (Banks & Banks, 2003) that have been instilled in them in their home culture. Children from cultures in which the teacher–student relationship is more authoritarian than democratic and communication more linear than egalitarian may not understand or feel comfortable with teacher expectations of verbal participation in class discussions or classroom interactions that may be perceived as disrespectful or challenging of authorities (Gibbs & Huang, 1998; Sue & Sue, 2003). Some studies have suggested that older children and children with extensive schooling in their home countries tend to do better academically than children who are younger and have had limited school experience; indeed, among older students, there is a strong positive correlation between academic success and literacy skills acquired in the primary language (Ovando & Collier, 1998; Ovando & McLaren, 2000). Such findings have clear implications for school personnel who work with these children.

For international students and their spouses, a variety of factors may influence their interaction with their children's schools, including their motives for moving to the United States (brief sojourn vs. eventual permanent residency), their perceptions of U.S. schools, their understanding of the nature of parent–teacher interactions, their views on parental versus school responsibility for children's learning, and their knowledge of school procedures, all of which in turn will affect their children's school adjustment (Juntunen et al., 2003). International students who come from countries where home–school collaboration is not customary may have different cultural expectations of the type and degree of involvement in their children's progress; however, these might be misinterpreted by the schools as a lack of care or concern (Juntunen et al., 2003).

Although international families with school-age children face significant challenges, the families in Stage 4, with adolescents ages 13–19, face far greater developmental and psychological challenges. The normal developmental tasks of adolescence may be exacerbated when students enter the United States during the middle and high school years, particularly when the decision to leave the home country may not have involved them (Larson & Ovando, 2001). In addition, the adolescent, for whom peer relationships are critical, may fiercely resent the parent who is seen to be severing established relationships in the home country while not contributing to and, in some cases, severely limiting the forging of new bonds in the host country.

Issues of identity development that become salient at this stage (Erikson, 1968) may be especially challenging for the adolescent children of international students who come from collectivistic societies. Unlike their parents who have established and usually retain their core identity and ethnic values, children of international students, like children of U.S. immigrants, are faced with the complex and confusing developmental tasks of establishing an identity in two different worlds with often conflicting values systems—a home culture that stresses

121

individual sacrifice for group priorities, harmony, and conformity to parental expectations, and the host culture of the schools that promotes individual autonomy, assertiveness, and personal choice. A review of the literature on the experiences of immigrant children suggests that living in a dual-cultural context may make the process of integration of a clear ego identity rather challenging and that some children may struggle with a sense of marginality, confusion, and ambivalence as they attempt to forge their identity and to bridge and reconcile two disparate sets of values and practices (Bernal & Knight, 1993; Coll & Magnuson, 1997; Sankar-Gomes, 2005; Segal, 1998). However, the degree to which this may be applicable for international student families may depend on factors such as adolescents' age of entry into the United States, length of stay and hence exposure to the host culture, and the degree to which they are grounded in their own cultural community.

International students and their partners may find the stresses of parenting children in an unfamiliar culture challenging, given that they are undergoing their own developmental crises. They have to learn to manage their children's increasing independence and deal with increasing cultural conflicts as their children are increasingly exposed to the host culture. Teenagers, who are experiencing the pressure of peer influence, may respond very differently from younger children who view their parents as being the source of authority over their lives. The generation gap widens when parents have limited socialization opportunities with the host culture (other than through academic interactions) and when their children establish a stronger network of peer relationships through school and become more adept consumers of U.S. culture (Bemak & Chung, 2003; Coll & Magnuson, 1997).

Intergenerational conflict between parents and adolescents may also arise over involvement in school activities. There may be a cultural difference in the valuing of extracurricular activities such as music or sports, which some international families may perceive as a distraction from academic work. Many international students feel intense pressure to do well, to serve as role models, and to live up to the expectations of their families in their home country; unfortunately, these pressures to perform well academically may be passed on to their children. In addition, parents from more traditional cultures with strict rules about gender interactions may have concerns about the negative influence of Western values on their adolescent children and thus may curtail their peer interactions and involvement in extracurricular and, in particular, coeducational, activities. Some international students, such as those from Asian cultures, may frown on American values and perceive them as "corrupting" their children, as promoting freedom to experiment with different lifestyles and sexual activity, and as encouraging disrespect for elders, traditions, and customs. Thus, parents from collectivistic cultures may adopt a defensive and conservative stance in their parenting. They believe increasing control and hypervigilance are necessary to limit their children's exposure to the process of Americanization, whereas their children react with a corresponding defiance of such strictures. While literature in this area has focused on immigrant populations (e.g., Almeida, 1996; Coll &

Magnuson, 1997; Hines, Garcia-Preto, McGoldrick, Almeida, & Weltman, 1992; Segal, 1998), it is logical to assume that international students, whose status in the United States is temporary, may be even more likely to curtail their children's attempts at independence or other behaviors that they see as unhealthy or culturally inappropriate. Often these may lead to intense intergenerational conflict within these families and extreme confusion in the adolescent who is straddling two different worlds.

While most international students and their families are best described in these first four stages of the family life cycle, they may also find themselves in *Stage 5, Families Launching Children (20 and Over)*, when they have to renegotiate their roles with adult children or adjust to being away from their adult children who may have remained behind in their native country. During *Stage 6, Families in Later Life*, international student families may have to deal with the complications of homesickness for their extended families (Poyrazli et al., 2001), caring for aging parents who may have remained in their home countries, and contending with the impact of sickness and death in their family and friends far away. This is a particularly acute source of guilt and anxiety for many international students from collectivistic cultures, especially oldest sons, who are duty-bound to care, both physically and financially, for their parents despite their own severely limited resources as international students.

There are, of course, limitations to the family life cycle approach with its strict focus on stages and a somewhat limited emphasis on interindividual variation. Nevertheless, it is a useful model to help counselors understand how life changes can affect the families of international students.

Intervention With Families of International Students: General Considerations

The complex needs of the families of international students demand a multidimensional, collaborative, and proactive response from school counselors, counselors, psychologists, and other helping professionals (Sandhu, 1994). Cultural competence on the part of counselors is critical when dealing with international students and their families and must underlie everything they do with their clients (Pederson, 2004; Sue & Sue, 2003). Most writers in the area of multicultural counseling have delineated specific areas of cultural competencies, which we believe have much to offer in working with international students and their families: (a) awareness of one's own assumptions, values, and biases; (b) knowledge and understanding of human differences in race, culture, religion, gender, and sexual orientation; and (c) development of culturally sensitive intervention and therapeutic skills (Arrendondo et al., 1996; Constantine & Ladany, 2001; Ponterotto, Alexander, & Grieger, 1995; Sue & Sue, 2003).

Counselors' awareness of their own prejudices, biases, and evaluations of appropriate or healthy behaviors, attitudes, and values is the key first step in providing a culturally sensitive environment in which the international student can feel comfortable and unconditionally accepted. Smith, Richards, Mac Granley, and Obiakor (2004) stated that at the simplest level, practicing multiculturalism involves (a) challenging one's own assumptions of reality, (b) valuing others so as to not impose one's notions of what are appropriate and healthy values/behaviors on others, and (c) being genuine and open and minimizing defensiveness in all interactions. Smith and Draper (2004) described a contextual approach to counseling culturally diverse clients that can be used effectively with international students and their families. Extrapolating from a relational perspective, Smith and Draper suggested that counselors view their clients not as individuals but as "interactive agents in the contexts of multiple relationships, past, present and potential" (p. 316). By adopting a relational perspective or an "other-focus," counselors will begin to realize how their own preconceived ideas and negative judgments of their international clients' worldviews may be barriers to effective interactions with them. As a result, they may become more open to being taught by their clients, become less defensive, view the counseling session as a mutually enriching experience, and appreciate the rich histories and unique behaviors of international students and their families.

Counselors should be willing to be challenged to examine their own cultural assumptions and expectations about the counseling process, which may clash with deeply ingrained values of international families from collectivistic cultures such as those in Asia. For instance, in collectivistic cultures, seeing a counselor may be viewed as a stigma, and self-disclosure about family problems may be a cultural taboo (Leong & Chou, 1996; Lin & Yi, 1997; Paniagua, 1998); such actions may evoke considerable anxiety in clients. Several authors have addressed the tendency for international students to present with somatic complaints such as headaches, loss of appetite, and sleeplessness (Mori, 2000; Zhang & Dixon, 2003). Concerns about treatment of these complaints as well as a lack of perceived access to free and comprehensive health care (Harju, Long, & Allred, 1998) may exacerbate these complaints and delay treatment. Although some have cautioned against an overemphasis on somatization of psychological problems (Yoon & Portman, 2004), counselors must be sensitive to these issues and work at the pace of clients, by building trust and rapport, respecting their privacy, reassuring them of confidentiality, and not pushing for quick self-disclosure or addressing personal and emotional issues too soon.

Clients' perceptions and expectations of the counselor's role may also have to be explored and understood. International students and their families may come from cultures in which the counselor may be viewed as the expert or authority figure; as such, they may expect specific directives and may struggle with the ambiguity of counseling sessions. In such situations, therefore, it has often been recommended that counselors adopt a more structured, problem-solving, solution-focused approach, with an emphasis on concrete strategies (e.g., study skills and homework supervision; see Paniagua, 1998; Thomas & Althen, 1989; Yuen & Tinsley, 1981), although Yau (2004) cautioned against overgeneralizing this approach to all international students.

Finally, there is potential for misunderstanding based on cultural differences in communication styles between counselors and their clients. Multicultural counseling experts (e.g., Paniagua, 1998; Sue & Sue, 2003) have suggested that in some cultures, a lack of eye contact may not be rude but a sign of respect, a lack of emotional expression may not signal inhibition but may be an indicator of maturity, and a tendency toward conformity should not necessarily be considered a sign of passivity. Counselors would also be wise to refrain from making judgments about parenting styles that differ from the dominant culture. For example, some international students and their spouses may use shame, guilt, or harsh methods of discipline (e.g., corporal punishment) that may be culturally appropriate in their home country but may be seen as ineffective or inappropriate by a Western counselor (Gibbs & Huang, 1998). Again, counselors should be careful to remember that international students are not monolithic groups and, therefore, to avoid making broad, and possibly untrue, assumptions and overgeneralizations about international students and their families (Yoon & Portman, 2004).

Interventions for Families of International Students: Specific Strategies for School Personnel

Given that families of international students are most likely to have school-age children in K-12 schools, we now present several effective strategies for school personnel, including counselors, psychologists, social workers, and others who are in a helping relationship with these children. Strategies may be conceptualized along two dimensions: (a) academic and school culture issues and (b) family and parenting issues.

Academic and School Culture Issues

For newly arrived international families, counselors could develop a systematic transition plan to help ease their academic transition into an unfamiliar setting (Baird, 1997), monitor their progress on a regular basis, teach students basic survival skills, and help demystify school processes by alerting them to school rules and procedures. They can also educate parents about the nature and purpose of teacher conferences and ways in which they can get involved in their children's education. Counselors could help explain expectations for classroom behavior and verbal participation in discussion, especially if the student comes from a culture in which the teacher–student relationship varies from that of the host culture. Generally, it is best to adopt a proactive stance with regard to parents and families so that home–school interactions are not fueled by urgency and crisis (Sandhu, 1994). One way this might be done is to hold parent training workshops, language lessons, training in daily skills (e.g., car care), and field trips that include all family members (Gollnick & Chinn, 2006; Wilen & Diaz, 1998).

Generally, counselors should model an attitude of respect for diversity and act as "cultural brokers" in translating school culture to international families and educating school personnel about the cultural norms and practices of international students in their setting. Counselors should also be advocates for international students and their families by promoting an understanding among school personnel of the factors that affect acculturative stress in international students, including loss of social support, culture shock and culture conflicts, language barriers, and psychological damage arising from encounters with racial discrimination within schools in the form of racial slurs and ethnic group segregation (Juntunen et al., 2003).

Counselors should act as proactive change agents and focus on creating a school climate that values and celebrates diversity. Research has shown that a bicultural strategy predicts emotional well-being and positive outcomes better than complete assimilation, and that retaining one's cultural roots is a key ingredient for both personal and academic success (LaFromboise et al., 1993). Counselors can help the children of international students by finding ways in which they can remain grounded within their own ethnic identity and see it affirmed within an inclusive school climate. Counselors can promote a school culture that values and celebrates diversity through consultation with teachers about classroom activities and coordinating Diversity Appreciation Days that pay tribute to cultural traditions and practices. There has been much criticism about the tendency in the counseling field to identify adjustment issues and overemphasize pathology rather than perceive international students and their families as having unique strengths, such as being bilingual, bringing rich and diverse perspectives to U.S schools, and being an important resource for other students and adults (Leong & Chou, 1996; Pedersen, 1991; Sandhu, 1994). School personnel can create opportunities for students and their families to be cultural informants about traditions, food, clothing, and holiday practices.

Teachers can develop lesson and unit plans that incorporate information and experiences from their international families' home life and country to help instill a sense of belonging rather than a heightened sense of difference and alienation (Bemak & Chung, 2003). In addition, they can also be encouraged to include multicultural perspectives in the classroom through adopting teaching methods that are culturally sensitive, for example, storytelling, use of colorful decorations, words in students' native language, and instructional materials that reflect the culture of students (Banks & Banks, 2003; Gollnick & Chinn, 2006; Tiedt & Tiedt, 1999). Simple ways of showing respect for others' cultures include pronouncing names correctly and not using English nicknames instead of native names unless specifically asked to do so, asking students about their countries, learning key phrases in their native language, and being sensitive to culturally unique forms of clothing, such as the *hijab* (head coverings for religious reasons). Teachers can use cooperative learning strategies that will encourage peer interaction and opportunities for socialization with U.S. peers and that are based on interpersonal relations rather than competition (Banks & Banks, 2003; Bemak & Chung, 2003; Gollnick & Chinn, 2006).

With regard to language use, it is important to build on students' strengths rather than to focus on language deficiency and to understand that deficits in language do not necessarily reflect limited intellectual potential (Gollnick & Chinn, 2006; Wilen, 1998). Instead, school personnel should be sensitive to and acknowledge the unique challenges that children of international students face in moving to a new country, not being fluent in the host country language, and then receiving formal education in that language (Roysircar, 2004). Fears about speaking in class may be rooted in a cultural upbringing that stresses listening and quiet absorption from an authoritative figure rather than critical questioning and self-discovery methods. In addition, children may have fears about their accent being ridiculed and of being perceived as less eloquent than their peers; they may, therefore, hold back from asking questions or making comments, which further reinforces their sense of being isolated and disconnected from their setting (Roysircar, 2004). Children of international students who are learning the language may understand much more than may be apparent; indeed, their nonverbal language can help them communicate with peers and adults in a way that may not be possible with oral language alone. It is especially important for counselors and teachers to refrain from overtly rejecting students' native language by insisting that they use English in the school setting and that they gently model appropriate usage instead of sharply correcting errors (Banks & Banks, 2003; Wilen & Diaz, 1998). Classroom teachers and speech pathologists can also help the families of international students by providing English language classes free of charge and setting up social events in which they are given the opportunity to interact with U.S. students and their families (Pilon, 1998; Wan, 2001). When counselors support and advocate for the right of children to use their native tongue freely, they will help create a more inclusive school climate that respects diversity and supports their students' cultural identity (Bemak & Chung, 2003).

Family and Parenting Issues

It is important that international students and their families work toward gaining mastery of the skills and competencies needed to function in, and adapt to, a new culture; however, counselors and other helping professionals must communicate this to families without diminishing their culture in any way or at the expense of their own cultural skills, knowledge, and identity (Bemak & Chung, 2003). It is also important that counselors refrain from indiscriminately promoting Western ideals such as adolescent autonomy and individuation, as this may run counter to cultural norms that promote family interdependence and harmony (Sankar-Gomes, 2005). School professionals must be culturally sensitive to traditional hierarchical family structures in helping international families negotiate changes in family dynamics as a result of varying acculturation rates of parents and children. For example, for families from patriarchal societies, the father is recognized as the head of the family and should be approached and consulted rather than the mother (Sue & Sue, 2003). Counselors and other school personnel should also be vigilant against creating situations in which children (who may be more proficient in the norms and values of the dominant culture) are asked to be cultural brokers or translators for parents who do not speak English. Such practices as asking children to complete school forms and translate documents may lead to undermining of parental authority and may reinforce intergenerational conflicts over issues such as gender roles, religious practices, discipline and punishment, school parties, and sleepovers, and, hence, leave parents feeling frustrated and powerless (Bemak & Chung, 2003). This can be especially problematic if the parents are conservative and are concerned about protecting their children from what they see as the corrupting influences of Western culture.

Counselors must also guard against doing anything that circumvents or undercuts the parenting provided by international students and their spouses. Parenting practices that may seem unusual to an untrained eye may be perfectly appropriate in other cultural settings, for example, parental insistence on hours of homework, requiring children to study their textbooks (even when there is no test to study for), and expecting them to take on household chores or child-care responsibilities. Counselors can, of course, intervene to help children balance work and home responsibilities and can work with parents to develop compromises so that students are not overwhelmed with multiple demands on their time and energy (Bemak & Chung, 2003). Parents may be encouraged to participate in their children's lives by using them as cultural resources to train school staff or by asking for their involvement in cultural activities. Seeing their parents participating in school in this way might help children value them more, help them offset feelings of embarrassment about having parents who are "different" (because they still wear traditional clothing or speak accented English, for example), and rekindle their sense of ethnic and national pride (Gollnick & Chinn, 2006).

Again, a proactive approach to mental health is ideal, with workshops and training sessions being held periodically, to ensure that international students and their families develop the skills to help themselves without having to resort to external resources (Gollnick & Chinn, 2006). Feelings of isolation may be addressed by encouraging family involvement in home and community activities, reaching out to international students and their families, encouraging them to maintain contacts with others from their home country (Tseng & Newton, 2002), and arranging home visits to local American families, particularly around holidays such as Thanksgiving (Bemak & Chung, 2003). Counselors and other school professionals must remain alert to signs of unhappiness or depression, such as changes in appearance, behavior, and school performance, all of which may signal a need for intervention. For example, some cultural groups (e.g., Asians) are more susceptible to internalizing problems, for which they seek the support of their immediate social networks instead of relying on outsiders and other professionals (Heggins & Jackson, 2003). Many of the strategies discussed in the preceding sections can also be used to help promote a sense of self-worth, pride, and confidence and to address intrapersonal issues among families of international students. As the families become more comfortable in the host culture, counselors can reinforce this by continuing to provide basic information about school activities and by stressing the potential for taking on leadership and mentoring roles for other new international families.

Case Scenario: Practical Applications

The following case scenario, along with a sample plan for working with the client and her family, is presented to illustrate some of the issues that have been discussed in this chapter. Although we offer a potential course of action, readers are encouraged to look for alternative solutions to the problem. It might also be helpful for readers to engage in small-group discussions about possible responses to the case scenario and to generate, collaboratively, additional cases that might be used for class discussion.

Tanya Lee, age 14, is an Asian student in the eighth grade. Her parents have moved to the United States so that her father can complete a doctorate in chemistry at the local university. His written English is adequate, but he speaks heavily accented English; his wife speaks no English at all. Tanya has studied English in Taiwan but is not fluent in the language. After spending 3 weeks with Mr. Lee's brother in New York, the Lees have just arrived at a new school district in Anytown, USA, and are eager to get Tanya settled in school.

Within 3 weeks of beginning school, Tanya's teacher refers her for a comprehensive evaluation, saying that she is not achieving in the regular classroom, that she is overly sensitive, and that she has "significant social–behavioral deficits." The teacher narrative indicated that on two occasions, Tanya burst out crying uncontrollably after her classmates called her "Ching Ching Chong" and "stretched their eyes to look Oriental." After delays of several months, during which Tanya's performance in the classroom becomes increasingly worse, she is finally tested. Results of tests of intelligence and academic achievement given to Tanya indicate that she has an IQ of 48 and that her reading achievement is also significantly low. However, her achievement in math is high average, as is her ability to adapt to environmental demands (e.g., dressing appropriately for the weather, handling money). The assessment team decides that regular education does not provide what Tanya needs and makes the determination that she needs to have special education help. The team schedules a placement meeting, and the chairperson sends home a letter of permission for the parents to sign. Neither parent is able to attend the meeting because of other conflicts; Mr. Lee leaves several messages for the school but does not have his calls returned. One teacher in the staff lounge is heard saying, "Not like they'd be able to communicate or anything, anyway . . . what's the point of wasting everyone's time?"

Tanya is placed in the only classroom where there is "a vacancy." This is a self-contained classroom with three children with severe mental retardation, one child with multiple disabilities and two with autism. Tanya comes home miserable each day from school, crying and saying that she hates being around "those children." She does not sleep well and has begun to lose weight. She is given worksheets to do everyday while the teacher and her assistant work on self-help skills with the other students. Her parents finally summon the courage to speak to the principal and arrive at his office at the end of the school day. He says there are 148 children waiting in line to be tested for placement and adds, "You know, we have to take care of our own first." When questioned, he pats Mr. Lee on the shoulder and says, "You Orientals are pretty smart . . . good at math and computers . . . I really think she'll be okay." He says, "Anyway, a little longer in that classroom is not going to hurt and Tanya's IQ scores are very similar to those of her classmates." Mr. and Mrs. Lee leave the principal's office feeling confused and helpless. The principal is heard talking to the counselor, saying, "Oh you know, those folks aren't going to complain. When have you heard a Chinese parent complain? Just back me on this, okay?"

Potential Responses to the Case of Tanya

The following responses to Tanya's concerns and those of her family are suggested by the particulars of her case as well as broader factors that are likely to inform problem solution. Although counselors and other helping professionals should, ideally, function in a proactive, preventative role, it is clear that in this situation, their immediate efforts should focus on issues of racial discrimination, intolerance for diversity, and the lack of cultural awareness that appear to be rampant in this school. The principal not only lacks sensitivity to Tanya's needs but is clearly engaging in extreme acts of discrimination against her and her family. As the academic leader of the school, the principal's values and attitudes may be conveyed to other school personnel, and efforts should be made to guard against this happening. The school psychologist, who is relatively inexperienced, could work with the counselor and other teachers to address Tanya's most immediate needs. First, it is important that Tanya have a complete physical to rule out physical causes for her sleeplessness and weight loss. Next, her feelings of isolation and the acculturative stress that she is clearly experiencing are obviously compounded by the fact that she is an adolescent; as such, these must be placed at the forefront of the counselor's efforts. The counselor could serve as an advocate for Tanya and her family and help protect her against further attacks from the adults and children around her. The counselor and the school psychologist could hold diversity awareness sessions and sensitivity training in all of the classrooms, conduct staff development programs about cultural diversity for the adults, and generally do everything they can to promote a school climate that is characterized by respect for, and appreciation of, diversity in all its forms.

Tanya could be scheduled for counseling sessions with the school counselor, twice a week to begin with, and then tapering off, depending on her progress. The counselor could begin by taking a detailed cultural history and by meeting with her parents and other school professionals as well. The counselor could focus, first, on building trust and rapport with Tanya, and then on working with Tanya to build back her self-confidence. It is also important to help Tanya find ways in which she can achieve success (academic or otherwise), give her some strategies that she can use to handle negative comments from her peers, and in general, help her develop coping skills to address her situation. Finally, Tanya's mother, and father (if necessary), could be enrolled in English language classes, free of charge, that are often held at the local public library or at local community agencies.

Tanya needs to be retested using appropriate, culturally sensitive measures, in this case, measures that do not rely on the English language or that use non-verbal or language-free approaches to assessment. An interpreter and translator could be used during the testing so that Tanya and the examiner are able to communicate with each other. Once the assessment team has made its determination of eligibility for special services or accommodations, they need to work with Tanya's parents (using an interpreter and translator, if necessary) to determine the best educational and related options for her. Tanya might benefit most from placement in a regular education class with several hours a week in the ESL classroom, using strategies that have been found to work best for children who are learning a second language. As with other children in Tanya's situation, an older college student, perhaps one who is Asian American, could be assigned to function in the role of Big Sister and to provide her with the moral support that she desperately needs.

Tanya's new teachers could be encouraged to work on including her with her American peers as much as possible, to incorporate material from her home culture on their daily and weekly lesson plans (e.g., they could include a unit on Taiwan), and might consider inviting Tanya's family to come to the school to share items, books, and food from their culture. All teachers who interact with Tanya should be encouraged to follow similar strategies in working with her.

Summary

As the international student population in the United States continues to increase, so too does the number of students who bring their families, including their spouses and children, with them. The families of international students are an important population with multidimensional needs. Counselors, psychologists, and other helping professionals are in a unique position to collaborate with each other in the provision of services to these individuals, and by so doing, to help facilitate an effective transition to a new way of life. However, despite the attention that has been paid to addressing the needs of international students themselves, their families have remained largely ignored (National Center for Education Statistics, 2002). There have been some isolated, and often incidental, attempts at addressing their needs but few systematic attempts at theory building (Pederson, 1991), and minimal efforts to train counselors and other helping professionals to work with this population. There is much that remains to be done, in both research and practical arenas.

This chapter provided an overview of the adjustment process faced by the families of international students, offered some ways to conceptualize salient issues, described interventions that may be successful with both spouses and children of international students, and used a case scenario to illustrate practical applications of relevant concepts. It is hoped that counselors and other helping professionals will seriously consider the challenges faced by the families of international students, develop research studies to further examine their adjustment to life in the United States, generate findings that will inform both their actions as well as those of their colleagues, and in so doing, benefit this vulnerable but important population.

References

Almeida, R. (1996). Hindu, Christian, and Muslim families. In M. McGoldrick, J. Giordano, & J. K. Pearce (Eds.), *Ethnicity and family therapy* (2nd ed., pp. 395-426). New York: Guilford Press.

Andrade, M. S. (2006). International students in English-speaking universities: Adjustment factors. *Journal of Research in International Education, 5,* 131-154.

Arrendondo, P., Topirek, R., Brown, S. P., Jones, J., Locke, D. C., Sanchez, J., & Stadler, H. (1996). Operationalization of the multicultural counseling competencies. *Journal of Multicultural Counseling and Development, 24,* 42-78.

Baird, C. T. (1997). A systematic transition plan for new students. *Professional School Counseling, 1,* 69-70.

Banks, J. A., & Banks, C. A. M. (2003). *Multicultural education: Issues and perspectives* (5th ed.). Hoboken, NJ: Wiley.

Bemak, F., & Chung, R.C. (2003). Multicultural counseling with immigrant students in schools. In P. B. Pederson & J. C. Carey (Eds.), *Multicultural counseling in schools* (pp. 84-104). Boston: Allyn & Bacon.

Bernal, M. E., & Knight, G. P. (Eds.). (1993). *Ethnic identity: Formation and transformation among Hispanics and other minorities* (SUNY Series, United States Hispanic Studies). Albany, NY: SUNY Press.

Berry, J. W. (1997). Immigration, acculturation, and adaptation. *Applied Psychology: An International Review, 46,* 5-68.

Broderick, P. C., & Blewitt, P. (2003). *The life span: Human development for helping professionals.* Upper Saddle River, NJ; Merrill Prentice Hall.

Carter, B., & McGoldrick, M. (Eds.). (1999). *The expanded family life cycle: Individual, family, and social perspectives* (3rd ed.). Boston: Allyn & Bacon.

Chittooran, M. M. (2006). *Cross-cultural adjustments for families of international students.* Unpublished manuscript, Department of Educational Studies, Saint Louis University.

Chittooran, M. M., & Singaravelu, H. (2004). Children of international students: Guidelines for school professionals. In A. S. Canter, L. Z. Paige, M. D. Roth, I. Romero, & S. A. Carroll (Eds.), *Helping children at home and at school: II. Handouts from your school psychologist* (pp. 39-42). Bethesda, MD: National Association of School Psychologists.

Coll, C. G., & Magnuson, K. (1997). The psychological experience of immigration: A developmental perspective. In A. Booth, A. Crouter, & N. S. Landale (Eds.), Immigration and the family: Research and policy on U.S. immigrants (pp. 91-131). Hillsdale, NJ: Erlbaum.

Constantine, M. G., & Ladany, N. (2001). New visions for defining and assessing multicultural counseling competence. In J. G. Poterotto, J. M. Casas, L. A. Suzuki, & C. M. Alexander (Eds.), *Handbook of multicultural counseling* (2nd ed., pp. 482-498). Thousand Oaks, CA: Sage.

Crano, S. L., & Crano, W. D. (1993). A measure of adjustment strain in international students. *Journal of Cross-Cultural Psychology, 24,* 267-283.

Erikson, E. H. (1968). *Identity, youth, and crisis.* New York: Norton.

Gibbs, J. T., & Huang, L. N. (1998). *Children of color: Psychological interventions with culturally diverse youth* (2nd ed.). San Francisco: Jossey-Bass.

Gollnick, D. M., & Chinn, P. C. (2006). *Multicultural education in a pluralistic society* (7th ed.). Upper Saddle River, NJ: Pearson Education.

Harju, B. L., Long, T. E., & Allred, L. J. (1998). Cross cultural reactions of international students to US health care. *College Student Journal, 32,* 112-120.

Hechanova-Alampay, R., Beehr, T. A., Christiansen, M. D., & Van Horn, R. K. (2002). Adjustment and strain among domestic and international student sojourners. *School Psychology International, 23,* 458-474.

Heggins, W. J., III, & Jackson. J. F. L. (2003). Understanding the collegiate experience for Asian international students at a midwestern research university. *College Student Journal, 37,* 379-391.

Helms, J. E., & Cook, D. A. (1999). *Using race and culture in counseling and psychotherapy: Theory and process.* Needham Heights, MA: Allyn & Bacon.

Hines, P. M., Garcia-Preto, N., McGoldrick, M., Almeida, R., & Weltman, S. (1992). Intergenerational relationships across cultures. *Families in Society: The Journal of Contemporary Human Services, 73,* 323-338.

Hui, C. H., & Triandis, H. C. (1986). Individualism–collectivism: A study of cross-cultural researchers. *Journal of Cross-Cultural Psychology, 17,* 131-152.

Institute of International Education. (2005). *Open Doors annual report, 2005.* Retrieved August 25, 2006, from http://opendoors.iienetwork.org

Juntunen, C. L., Atkinson, D. R., & Tierney, G. T. (2003). School counselors and school psychologists as school–home–community liaisons in ethnically diverse schools. In P. B. Pederson & J. C. Carey (Eds.), *Multicultural counseling in schools* (pp. 84-104). Boston: Allyn & Bacon.

Klomegah, R. Y. (2006). Social factors relating to alienation experienced by international students in the United States. *College Student Journal, 40,* 303-316.

LaFromboise, T., Coleman, H. L. K., & Gerton, J. (1993). Psychological impact of biculturalism: Evidence and theory. *Psychological Bulletin, 114,* 395-412.

Lambie, R. (2000). *Family systems within educational contexts: Understanding at-risk and special-needs students* (2nd ed.). Denver, CO: Love Publishing.

Larson, C. L., & Ovando, C. J. (2001). *The color of bureaucracy: The politics of equity in multicultural school communities.* Belmont, CA: Wadsworth/Thomson Learning.

Leong, F. T. L., & Chou, E. L. (1996). Counseling international students. In P. B. Pedersen, J. G. Draguns, W. J. Lonner, & J. E. Trimble (Eds.), *Counseling across cultures* (4th ed., pp. 210-242). Thousand Oaks, CA: Sage.

Lin, G. J., & Yi, J. K. (1997). Asian international students' adjustment: Issues and program suggestions. *College Student Journal, 31,* 52-63.

McCarthy, J. (2005). Individualism and collectivism: What do they have to do with counseling? *Journal of Multicultural Counseling and Development, 33,* 108-117.

Moore, J. L., & Constantine, M. G. (2005). Development and initial validation of the collectivistic coping styles measure with African, Asian, and Latin American international students. *Journal of Mental Health Counseling, 27,* 329-347.

Mori, S. (2000). Addressing the mental health concerns of international students. *Journal of Counseling & Development, 78,* 137–144.

National Center for Education Statistics. (2002). *Digest of educational statistics, 2002.* Retrieved August 25, 2006, from http://nces.ed/gov/edstats/

Ovando, C. J., & Collier, V. P. (1998). *Bilingual and ESL classrooms: Teaching in multicultural contexts* (2nd ed.). Boston: McGraw-Hill.

Ovando, C. J., & McLaren, P. (Eds.). (2000). *The politics of multiculturalism in bilingual education: Students and teachers caught in the cross fire.* Boston: McGraw Hill.

Padilla, A. M. (1980). *Acculturation: Theory, models and some new findings* (3rd ed.). Boulder, CO: Westview Press.

Paniagua, F. A. (1998). *Assessing and treating culturally diverse clients* (2nd ed.). Thousand Oaks, CA: Sage.

Pedersen, P. B. (1991). Counseling international students. *The Counseling Psychologist, 19,* 10–58.

Pederson, P. B. (2004). The multicultural context of mental health. In T. B. Smith (Ed.), *Practicing multiculturalism: Affirming diversity in counseling and psychology* (pp. 17–32). Boston: Pearson.

Pilon, B. (1998). Immigrant teenagers: Helping them adjust to their first year—recommendations for parents. In *Helping children at home and school: Handouts from your school psychologist* (pp. 489–492). Bethesda, MD: National Association of School Psychologists.

Ponterotto, J. G., Alexander, C. M., & Grieger, I. (1995). A multicultural competency checklist for counseling training programs. *Journal of Multicultural Counseling and Development, 23,* 11–20.

Ponterotto, J. G., Casas, J. M. Suzuki, L. A., & Alexander, C. M. (Eds.). (2000). *Handbook of multicultural counseling* (2nd ed.) Thousand Oaks, CA: Sage.

Poyrazli, S., Arbona, C., Bullington, R., & Pisecco, S. (2001). Adjustment issues of Turkish college students studying in the United States. *College Student Journal, 35,* 52–63.

Rotheram-Borus, M. J. (1993). Biculturalism among adolescents. In M. E. Bernal & G. P. Knights (Eds.), *Ethnic identity: Formation and transformation among Hispanics and other minorities* (SUNY Series, United States Hispanic Studies, pp. 81–102). Albany, NY: SUNY Press.

Roysircar, G. (2004). Counseling and psychotherapy for acculturation and ethnic identity concerns with immigrant and international student clients. In T. B. Smith (Ed.), *Practicing multiculturalism: Affirming diversity in counseling and psychology* (pp. 255–275). Boston: Pearson.

Sam, D. L. (2001). Satisfaction with life among international students: An exploratory study. *Social Indicators Research, 53,* 315–337.

Sandhu, D. S. (1994). An examination of the psychological needs of the international students: Implications for counseling and psychotherapy. *International Journal for the Advancement of Counseling, 17,* 229–239.

Sankar-Gomes, A. (2005). *A comparative study of the relationship between dimensions of separation-individuation adjustment and White and Asian Indian college undergraduates.* Unpublished doctoral dissertation, University of Iowa.

Segal, U. (1998). The Asian Indian-American family. In C. H. Mindel, R. W. Habestein, & R. W. Wright Jr. (Eds.), *Ethnic families in America: patterns and variations* (4th ed., pp. 331-360). Upper Saddle River, N.J: Prentice Hall.

Smith, T. B., & Draper, M. (2004). Understanding individuals in their context: A relational perspective of multicultural counseling. In T. B. Smith (Ed.), *Practicing multiculturalism: Affirming diversity in counseling and psychology* (pp. 311-324). Boston: Pearson.

Smith, T. B., Richards, P. S., Mac Granley, H., & Obiakor, F. (2004). Practicing multiculturalism: An introduction. In T. B. Smith (Ed.), *Practicing multiculturalism: Affirming diversity in counseling and psychology* (pp. 3-16). Boston: Pearson.

Sodowsky, G. R., Kwan, K. K., & Pannu, R. (1995). Ethnic identity of Asians in the United States. In J. G. Ponterotto, J. M. Casas, L. A. Suzuki, & C. M. Alexander (Eds.), *Handbook of multicultural counseling* (pp. 123-154). Thousand Oaks, CA: Sage.

Sue, D. W., & Sue, D. (2003). *Counseling the culturally diverse: Theory and practice* (4th ed.). New York: Wiley.

Thomas, K., & Althen, G. (1989). Counseling foreign students. In P. B. Pedersen, J. G. Draguns, W. J. Lonner, & J. E. Trimble (Eds.), *Counseling across cultures* (3rd ed., pp. 205-241). Thousand Oaks, CA: Sage.

Tiedt, P. L., & Tiedt, T. M. (1999). *Multicultural teaching: A handbook of activities, information, and resources* (5th ed.). Boston: Allyn & Bacon.

Tseng, W., & Newton, F. B. (2002). International students' strategies for well-being. *College Student Journal, 36,* 591-598.

Wan, G. (2001). The learning experience of Chinese students in American universities: A cross-cultural perspective. *College Student Journal, 35,* 28-44.

Ward, C. (1996). Acculturation. In D. Landis & R. S. Bhagat (Eds.), *Handbook of intercultural training* (2nd ed., pp. 124-147). Thousand Oaks, CA: Sage.

Wilen, D. K. (1998). Limited English proficiency: A handout for teachers. In *Helping children at home and school: Handouts from your school psychologist* (pp. 481-483). Bethesda, MD: National Association of School Psychologists.

Wilen, D. K., & Diaz, B. (1998). Second language acquisition: A handout for educators. In *Helping children at home and school: Handouts from your school psychologist* (pp. 489-492). Bethesda, MD: National Association of School Psychologists.

Wilton, L., & Constantine, M. (2003). Length of residence, cultural adjustment difficulties, and psychological distress symptoms in Asian and Latin America international college students. *Journal of College Counseling, 6,* 177-187.

Yau, T. Y. (2004). Guidelines for facilitating groups with international college students. In J. L. DeLucia-Waack, D. A. Gerrity, C. R. Kalodner, & M. T. Riva (Eds.), *Handbook of group counseling and psychotherapy* (pp. 253-264). Thousand Oaks, CA: Sage.

Ying, Y. (2003). Academic achievement and quality of overseas study among Taiwanese students in the United States. *College Student Journal, 37,* 470-481.

Yoon, E., & Portman, T. A. (2004). Critical issues and literature on counseling international students. *Journal of Multicultural Counseling and Development 32,* 33-34.

Yuen, R. K., & Tinsley, H. (1981). International and American students' expectancies about counseling. *Journal of Counseling Psychology, 28,* 66-69.

Zhang, N., & Dixon, D. N. (2003). Acculturation and attitudes of Asian international students toward seeking psychological help. *Journal of Multicultural Counseling and Development, 31,* 205-222.

Zhang, N., & Rentz, A. L. (1996). Intercultural adaptation among graduate students from the People's Republic of China. *College Student Journal, 30,* 321-328.

Chapter 7

Returning Home and Issues Related to Reverse Culture Shock

S. Alvin Leung

Each year, thousands of students leave their home countries to study overseas. Some of these students are involved in short-term academic exchanges, and others stay in a host country for a longer period of time to pursue undergraduate or postgraduate training. Upon graduation, some students continue to seek advanced academic training, internship experience, or even career opportunities in their host countries. Eventually, some international students choose to stay in their host country and make it their adopted home, but many would return to their original home country to start a "new life" after being away for a significant period of time.

"Returning home" seems to be a natural turning point to the lives of international students. Whereas going abroad to study involves many social, psychological, and cultural adaptations (Dion & Dion, 1996), returning to a once familiar place is expected to be less of a challenge. Indeed, to many international students, returning home is the beginning of an exciting new phase of their life development. They are to be reunited with family members and their home community. This is also a turning point at which many international students have to make a transition into a career, to apply what they have learned overseas to a work position at home (e.g., Pedersen & Lee, 2000).

However, many international students experience a lengthy period of adjustment as they reintegrate into their home community. The psychological stress involved in reentering one's home country after living abroad is called *reentry shock* or *reverse culture shock* (N. J. Adler, 1981). Reverse culture shock is defined by Gaw (2000) as "the process of readjustment, reacculturation, and reassimilating into one's own home culture after living in a different culture for a significant period of time" (p. 84). Reverse culture shock could trigger a range of unpleasant feelings, including confusion, loneliness, depression, anger, and despair. For example, in a study by Gaw (2000) on the reentry experience of U.S. college students who had studied abroad, it was found that the most often reported problems were loneliness, college adjustment, career choice, alienation, depression, and difficulty studying. This suggests that if a former international

137

student is unable to cope with the psychological impact of reverse culture shock, it could result in deteriorating work performance and interpersonal relationships, as well as other psychological distress that might inhibit individual functioning. Many authors (e.g., Martin, 1984; Wang, 1997; Ward, Bochner, & Furnham, 2001) believe that the stress involved in moving back home is stronger than the stress involved in entering a new culture, partly because reverse culture shock is often unexpected and contrary to our belief that home is familiar.

Comprehensive counseling service should seek to strengthen the resilience of international students to deal with the impact of reverse culture shock as they return home (Arthur, 2004). The purposes of this chapter are to help counseling and educational professionals understand the psychological process of reverse culture shock and its impact on international students and to examine counseling strategies that could help international students make a smooth transition as they reenter their home community. Accordingly, this chapter is divided into two sections. In the first section, relevant conceptual and empirical literature related to reverse culture shock is reviewed and examined. In the second section, counseling interventions to help international students cope with reverse culture shock are discussed.

Perspectives on Culture Shock and Adaptation

Conceptually, reverse culture shock is viewed as a special case of culture shock (e.g., Gullahorn & Gullahorn, 1963). Culture shock has been an important area of inquiry in the cross-cultural literature, and a number of conceptual models have been offered to explain its impact on individuals who travel across cultures. Partly based on Pedersen's (1995) classification of models of culture shock, I review three major perspectives of culture shock: conflict perspective, stage perspective, and acculturation perspective. Each of these perspectives focuses on different facets of the culture shock experience, and in unity they help us to understand the joy and struggle of sojourners reentering their home cultures.

Conflict Perspective

The first conceptual model on culture shock can best be described as a conflict perspective. According to this perspective, changes in cultural context often trigger a range of negative reactions such as anxiety, fear, insecurity, and sense of loss. Culture shock or reverse culture shock is understood in terms of internal psychological conflicts, misperceptions, miscommunication, one's inability to pick up culturally different behavioral cues, and/or behavioral deficits (e.g., Stephan & Stephan, 1992). Conflict perspective focuses on the negative impact of culture shock, and sojourners are viewed as vulnerable to the stress involved.

The account by Wang (1997) on reverse culture shock is an example of a conflict perspective. Wang suggested that reentering one's own culture often involves conflicts between past and present. There is conflict between a self-concept and identity that are parts of one's past and the present self-concept and identity that are shaped by the cross-culture life experience. When international students travel abroad to study, they encounter many social and interpersonal experiences that are challenging to them initially. In the process of adaptation, many students are able to manage the new cultural environment through developing a new set of values, attitudes, and beliefs, as well as a different way of responding and behaving. Over time, the experience is integrated into a new system of self-concept and identity. In many ways, the returnee is no longer the person who left home a few years ago; however, whether "home" approves of the new identity is questionable. As international students reenter their home culture, they are confronted with an existential question of who they are. To individuals who were once familiar with the returnee, they might experience dissonance as they find the returnee thinking and behaving more like a foreigner than a local person. Mediating between using a "new self" or "old self" in interacting with the home cultural environment is a challenge to many returning international students.

Another source of conflict is between the returnee's perceptions of the past and present home environment. Wang (1997) speculated that "disconfirmed" expectation is often involved in reentering. There is a tendency for returnees to idealize the home environment, especially among students who have long anticipated this return trip. However, what they find and experience may be quite different from their idealized image. They may find relationships, values, and attitudes to be different from what they used to be and the social and cultural scenes to be alien and unfamiliar. The returnee may find out that in the passage of time, their home culture has naturally evolved to become different from when they left home. This is a frustrating experience to many returnees, as they have to adjust and modify their expectation and to adapt to the realities of the home culture.

Wang (1997) suggested that a sense of loss is a major theme in reverse culture shock. Reverse culture shock is a process of coping with grief over losing one's ideal home culture that is buried in the past, and in losing the familiar host culture that the student has abandoned in choosing to return home.

The concept of conflict perspective is limited because it puts too much weight on negative reactions and consequences. It fails to take into account that culture shock may be a temporary or transitional reaction, and many individuals are able to effectively turn that into a positive, growth-inducing life event (Pedersen, 1995). Many individuals are able to adapt quickly without experiencing the expected turmoil of culture shock or reverse culture shock.

Stage Perspective

The second perspective on culture shock is the stage perspective (e.g., P. S. Adler, 1975; Gullahorn & Gullahorn, 1963; Lysgaard, 1955). According to stage models, sojourners have to progress through a series of stages in their adaptation to a new culture. The number of stages proposed varies across different theories, but the general assumption is that there is a decline in personal functioning before the sojourner bounces back (e.g., Ying, 2005). Most stage theories assume that there is an initial *excitement* stage in which the individual is consumed by the excitement of entering a new culture, and very little dissonance is experienced. The process of psychological adaptation moves on to a middle or *confusion* stage as the individual continues to immerse in the new cultural environment. Feelings of excitement are replaced by feelings of frustration when the person finds that his or her familiar ways of coping and relating are no longer effective. The perception that one is not functioning effectively in the new cultural environment may lead to self-double and in some cases an identity crisis (Wang, 1997). The third is a *reintegration* stage in which the person reestablishes his or her psychological equilibrium by assimilating into oneself a new set of values and behavior instrumental to functioning in the host cultural setting. Some scholars characterize the progression through stages of cultural adaptation as a U-curve adjustment process. According to the U-curve hypothesis, a person will experience reduced functioning and psychological discomfort in progressing from the initial phase to the confusion phase, and functioning will gradually be restored through effective coping and psychological adaptation as the person moves toward the reintegration phase of adaptation.

According to a stage perspective of culture shock, reverse culture shock is an expansion of the U-curve process in that a person experiences further symptoms of culture shock in returning to the home culture. The person passes through the stages of culture shock (e.g., Storti, 2001), which if viewed using the three-stage model as mentioned above, are the initial excitement stage, confusion stage, and reintegration stage. Similar to the process of entering a new cultural environment, at the initial stage, the returnee is filled with excitement and anticipation and is eager to meet and interact with the home culture. However, as reality sets in, the returnee soon finds the home culture to be different from what it is used to be, and his or her repertoire of behavior is suddenly insufficient for dealing with the new environment. This is a period of questioning and reexamination in which a range of emotions including frustration, anger, alienation, disappointment, and a sense of being inadequate might surface. These emotions can become quite overwhelming to returnees. Whereas many returnees hope that the confusion stage will pass quickly, Wang (1997) pointed out that many returnees have little idea that reverse culture shock "is measured in years, not days" (p. 119).

Returnees enter a reintegration stage when they are able to integrate the elements of the present home culture with those of the host culture. Reintegration is a stage in which returnees see the bad and good elements of both cultures, and in the process they discover that they have the autonomy in using a range of behavior to deal with diverse social situations (Pedersen, 1995). The increase in cognitive complexity, along with the increase in behavioral autonomy, could lead to more effective functioning, both interpersonally and psychologically.

Viewing the entire experience as a whole, some scholars have used the W-curve hypothesis to describe the process of entering a new culture as well as returning to one's home culture. The U-curve and W-curve hypotheses have received mixed support in the empirical literature (e.g., Church, 1982; Coschignano, 2002; Pedersen, 1995). Overall, stage perspective suffers from at least two limitations (Ward et al., 2001). First, in reality, the cultural adaptation process is seldom a smooth, simplistic linear process characterized by sequential stages. The process of adaptation could be a transformation process with many ups and downs. Second, the U-curve and W-curve perspectives do not take into consideration that upon reentering a home culture, a range of psychological dimensions (e.g., personality, expectation) is involved. Within the same person, the status of different psychological dimensions and their interactions with the overall adjustment process affects the outcome of adaptation. Third, a stage model does not take into consideration characteristics of the unique cultural context to which one is returning. For example, a supportive family environment and the existence of good career opportunities for the returnee would greatly facilitate the transition process. Consequently, a U- or W-curve might be an overly simplistic way of looking at the process of culture shock.

Acculturation Perspective

Acculturation has been widely used in the literature as an encompassing variable to account for the cultural adaptation process. Acculturation is a process in which individuals adopt attitudes, values, and behavior of a host culture to effectively cope with the demands involved in living in the new environment (Berry, Trimble, & Olmedo, 1986). According to Berry (1980), the most central aspect of acculturation involves a sojourner's cultural identity. Intercultural contacts are likely to create changes in one's cultural identity, the status of which could be assessed through asking two key questions. The first question is whether a person considers it important to maintain the values, practices, and tradition of his or her own culture. The second question is whether a person considers it important to take on the values, practices, and behaviors of the host culture. The answers to these two questions would result in four different scenarios that Berry (1980) called positions or styles of acculturation. The first position is that of an *integrationist* who maintains his or her own cultural values and identity, yet at the same time is willing to accept the values and practices of the host culture. The second position is that of the *assimilationist* who abandons his or her own cultural values and practices and takes on those of the host culture, in the process, reanchoring his or her identity in the host culture. The third position is that of a *separationist* who strongly maintains the values and practices of his or her own culture and rejects the values and practices of the host culture. The fourth position is that of the *marginalist* who chooses not to affiliate with values and practices of their own culture as well as those of the host culture.

The four positions of acculturation are used to understand the experiences of international students reentering their own cultures (e.g., Pedersen, 1995). Leong and Leung (2004) used Berry's (1980) model to analyze the experience of Asian academics who returned from studying in the United States to teach in their own culture. They suggested that among the four positions, the assimilationists have the most difficult time adjusting to lives in their home culture because in many ways they have rejected values and traditions at home and have adopted Western-oriented values and practices. Consequently, they are most likely to experience a large dose of reverse culture shock. On the other hand, international students who are traditionalists have to make the least adjustment in returning home because they have engaged in the least amount of change in their cultural identity. The integrationists who combine values and practices of both the home and host culture would also experience some degree of acculturation stress, as they might not be able to find avenues where their multicultural identities are recognized and appreciated. Lastly, moving back home might not create a significant dose of reverse culture shock for international students who are marginalists because they do not affiliate with either set of values from home or host culture.

Berry's (1980) classification provides a useful framework for understanding the cultural conflicts that international students experience. Many cross-cultural scholars (e.g., Dion & Dion, 1996; Leung & Chen, 2004; Yang, 2003) have observed that possessing a multicultural identity and orientation is a key characteristic of individuals who are exposed to traditional and Western cultures. It is not suggested that all international students are integrationists, but it seems likely that many students have integrated some of the values and practices of the host culture into their self-identity. The coexistence of traditional and modern values in the cultural identity of international students is both a blessing and a challenge. The multicultural exposure of international students, along with their ability to understand diverse cultural perspectives, has enabled many returning international students to make positive contributions to their home communities. However, the coexistence of modernity and traditionality in one's identity is likely to create a certain degree of conflict and dissonance at different stages of the reentry process (e.g., Yang, 2003). The resolution of such conflict is a task that many former international students have to confront in their developmental journeys.

The positions of acculturation by Berry (1980) could also be used as a convenient framework in reentry training to help international students understand changes and transformation in their own cultural identity during their journeys abroad. Furthermore, this concept may help students actively look for ways that their multicultural identities could be expressed and appreciated at home in their future developmental paths.

Summary

Reverse culture shock is an experience that many international students undergo in reentering their home culture. The conflict perspective allows one to see the unpleasant psychological struggles involved in the reentry process. The stage perspective maintains that reverse culture shock is often a long process that may be viewed as sequential stages and that many international students do get better after they hit a low point. The acculturation perspective sees reverse culture shock as a function of one's position on acculturation and accounts for individual differences in the experience of reverse culture shock. Overall, reverse culture shock is not necessarily a negative experience, even though negative emotions are often involved. Through their resiliency, perhaps with the help of a counselor and supportive friends, many international students are able to consolidate their multicultural identity and move positively into the future.

Counseling Interventions

In this section, I highlight two types of counseling interventions to assist international students in their reentry process. The first is a prevention intervention that is often called *reentry training* (e.g., Wang, 1997). Reentry training should target all international students who aspire to return home upon completing their academic study. Second, for international students who need additional help in resolving issues surrounding their reentry, *personal counseling* may be necessary. A case scenario is used to illustrate counseling strategies to work with international students struggling with issues related to reentry.

Reentry Training

The literature suggests that psychological preparation is instrumental to making a smooth reentry transition (Arthur, 2004; Pedersen, 1995; Wang, 1997; Ward et al., 2001). Psychological preparation could best be done through reentry training while international students are still contemplating their move back to their home country. Wang (1997) suggested that reentry training should be a part of an overall intervention helping sojourners to process their cross-cultural experience at different stages of their journey abroad and back home. According to Wang, reentry training should be structured to achieve the following goals: (a) to convince international students that reverse culture shock is real and that it affects all international students returning home permanently to varying degrees; (b) to encourage international students to identify and evaluate all the internal and external changes that have taken place while they study abroad and how those changes might affect their reentry experience; (c) to encourage international students to start "worrying" about their return; and (d) to convince international students that they could take steps to turn the pains of reentry into positive growth and development.

Reentry training should be conducted using a group format. The leader of the reentry group should be someone who is familiar with the international student population and has experience in working with them. The leader should also be someone who has received training in counseling. The reentry process involves many personal and growth-related issues, so group leaders must possess counseling skills to help members to cope with these issues constructively.

Reentry training should be conducted using a semistructured format with a balanced distribution of time between presentation of ideas and information and personal experience processing. On the basis of the goals of reentry training suggested by Wang (1997), I offer several strategies.

First, reentry training should provide international students with relevant facts about reentering one's home culture. It involves gathering more information about what is happening at home, such as news, weather, politics, and cultural and social events. More important, international students should be informed of the psychological impact of reentering and the diverse emotions that might emerge in the process. International students could be encouraged to read articles, books, and Web resources related to cultural adjustment and reverse culture shock (e.g., Storti, 2001) to prepare for their future reentry experience.

Second, experts should be invited to share their personal experience of reentry. Wang (1997) observed that many sojourners do not believe that reverse culture shock can happen to them, and so individuals who have had the experience are instrumental in "waking up" participants to the realities. International students possessing the experience of reentering their home culture and have returned to the campus are ideal candidates to share their joys and pains of reentering.

Third, culture assimilator or critical incidents (e.g., Cushner & Brislin, 1996; Pedersen, 1995) may be used in reentry training to facilitate discussion and exploration. Critical incidents are designed to sensitize individuals to diverse cultural values and practices and to prepare individuals moving to a different culture. Critical incidents are short stories or vignettes portraying cross-cultural interactions or experiences in which cultural clashes, misunderstandings, and mistaken perceptions or attributions are involved. After reading a critical incident, a person is asked to provide an alternative interpretation or response to the situation. Pedersen (1995) identified several multicultural competencies that can be developed in using critical incidents in cross-cultural training, including the ability to use multiple information sources in a cultural environment, cultural awareness and understanding, effective interpersonal communication, and effective problem solving in multicultural interactions. Critical incidents can be used as strategies in reentry training to sensitize international students to issues that they may encounter in their journey back home. Group leaders can use critical incidents as stimuli to elicit group discussion and sharing, to encourage cognitive and affective exploration, and to foster interpersonal learning in a group context. In addition to using critical incidents developed by Pedersen (1995), counseling practitioners could also consult Cushner and Brislin (1996) and Wang (1997) for additional examples of critical incidents to be used in working with sojourners returning home.

Fourth, reentry training can be used to expand the interpersonal network of international students returning home. When international students return home, they have to abandon their existing network of support and become reacquainted with relatives and friends they have at home. Many international students feel alienated after they return home because there are very few who understand their experience. Reentry training should help international students identify individuals at home who might become a part of their future personal and professional support network. These individuals could help the returnees anticipate difficulties they might encounter during reentry, as well as to serve as advisors should these difficulties emerge. Reentry training leaders could identify former graduates who have returned to the same region that students could count on as resource persons. Members of the reentry training group could also serve as support to each other, especially if they are returning to the same region.

Fifth, training should help and encourage reentering international students to engage in practical actions. Preparation could be in the form of taking tangible actions, such as deciding on a place to stay at home, making address changes, packing, and making travel arrangements. Of equal importance is taking steps to say goodbye to a campus and to friends and teachers who have important developmental meanings for the students. Saying goodbye is always a difficult process that cannot be accomplished in a short time. Reentry training should help students understand what it takes to say goodbye, to inform friends on campus and at home of their pending departure, to visit places and friends, and to communicate in ways they feel appropriate and desirable.

Sixth, reentry training should also help students to look into the future and to engage in steps toward planning their careers. When international students return home, many are also changing their status from being a student to a career person. Being away from home, many students might not have a job waiting for them upon their return, and some might be struggling with concerns related to career choice and how to translate their academic experience into a meaningful career. Indeed, one of the most important tasks in returning home is to identify future goals and a life mission. Career planning issues of international students are complicated by parental expectations, as parents often have high expectations of their children who have studied abroad, expecting them to move rapidly to a "good" career after graduation. Consequently, career and life planning issues should be a core component of reentry training. If needed, counselors can refer students to career counselors on campus to work on more specific career-related needs and concerns (Leong & Brown, 1995).

Ward et al. (2001) and Westwood, Lawrence, and Paul (1986) have suggested that there is a responsibility for host educational institutions to offer reentry preparation programs to international students. Reentry training should be a regular service offered to international students. International student advisors and counselors could offer workshops and seminars on reentry to international students planning to return home. Follow-up interventions should also be organized by using the international student networks that exist in different regions that students are returning.

Individual Counseling With Clients Experiencing Reverse Culture Shock

In this section, a counseling case is described. The purpose of this case analysis is to discuss treatment processes and strategies in counseling international students who are experiencing a special case of reverse culture shock. In addition to using theories and concepts related to reentry, an existential–humanistic counseling approach is used as an adjunct theoretical lens (e.g., Ivey, D'Andrea,

145

Ivey, & Simek-Morgan, 2002), focusing on the understanding of individual-phenomenological experience, identification of personal and cultural meanings, and facilitation of personal growth in the context of one's cultural environment.

Nancy is a 26-year-old Chinese female now living in Hong Kong. After she graduated from high school, Nancy traveled to the United States and studied at a major university in the Midwest. She received an undergraduate degree in economics and then continued in a Master's of Business Administration (MBA) program at the same university. About a year ago, upon receiving her MBA degree, she returned to Hong Kong and worked in her father's company as an assistant manager. Nancy's father was the owner of a manufacturing company with factories in the Chinese mainland but maintained its business office in Hong Kong.

Nancy was referred by a family physician to consult a counselor in private practice. The physician found Nancy to be suffering from mild depression and suggested that Nancy seek help from a counselor. Nancy had never seen a counselor before, but she felt that there were things that she had to sort out so she followed up on the suggestion.

Nancy was quiet at the beginning of therapy, and the counselor had to work hard to encourage her to talk. However, after trust developed, Nancy was quite willing to share her experience and concerns. Nancy reported that she had been quite unhappy since her move back home. Nancy perceived her upbringing to be typical of most middle-class children in Hong Kong. She did well in school and was obedient to her parents, who sent her oversea to study even though she had a good chance of entering one of the local universities.

Nancy's life changed quite drastically after she went to the United States. She met many new friends, and she enjoyed her independence without being "bothered" by her parents, who tended to be overprotective. Nancy felt that the experience as an international student away from home was instrumental in building her self-esteem and confidence. Interpersonally, Nancy felt that she was able to mingle well with Chinese students on campus, but unlike some of her fellow international students whose social lives were confined to a circle of friends from their own cultures, Nancy made many friends from different places, including friends from the United States. She liked the U.S. culture and had often thought about getting a job there after receiving her MBA.

Nancy's memories of her time as an international student were mostly positive. One of her regrets was a relationship that did not work out. She had steadily dated a boyfriend who was also Chinese and from Hong Kong. However, when her boyfriend moved to another university for graduate study, the relationship started to deteriorate and they eventually broke up. Nancy felt that she had already overcome the pains involved in this relationship when she returned to Hong Kong.

For Nancy, moving back to Hong Kong was very hard; she returned at the urging of her parents, who wanted her to come home to help with the family business. Nancy cared about her parents but had always felt that they wanted to control too much of her life. Her parents often had strong opinions, and it was hard for Nancy to talk to them. She had told them about her desire to stay in the United

States and to get some work experience there. However, she was not able to locate a job at the time of graduation, so she reluctantly returned to Hong Kong.

When Nancy talked about her move back to Hong Kong, there were tears and grief in her eyes. She felt that being an international student was the best time of her life, and now it had become a memory. Nancy felt trapped, especially now that she had to stay with her parents. Nancy did not participate in any reentry training program before she returned to Hong Kong because she was too overwhelmed with the task of moving after a decision was made to return home.

Nancy was not thrilled about her job and the arrangement to work for her father. In contrast to her extroverted interpersonal style while she was in international student, she was quite withdrawn socially and felt alienated. She had occasional contacts with a few friends, most of them former international students who had returned to Hong Kong from the same university. Nancy felt that having the same experience helped them bond together. Nancy became a Protestant Christian when she was an international student, but now she was unable to find a church in which she felt comfortable so she had not gone to church for a long time.

Nancy was unhappy and sad. She had lost weight, and her appetite was low. She found herself crying sometimes at night. She was unwilling to tell her parents about her feelings because she was afraid that they would become worried and overreact. She was unsure if her depressed feelings were connected to her move back to Hong Kong. She felt that she had already managed the transitions and that the move was all behind her.

The counselor worked with Nancy collaboratively to decide on the general direction of counseling. They decided that the most immediate goal was to help Nancy cope with her depressed feelings and to find out what was bothering her. The long-term goal was to help Nancy develop a more positive lifestyle in Hong Kong and to explore and make decisions on her future life direction.

The counselor felt that much of Nancy's emotional toil was related to the process of reentering a home culture after studying abroad. To some extent, Nancy was still experiencing a significant amount of grief over departing from a campus and a university experience that had allowed her to grow and mature. Through her years as an international student, she had adopted many Western-oriented values and was not able to fit in upon returning to a Chinese society. Her relationship with her parents was a major source of stress. Nancy resented her parents, who were traditional in their values and parental style, but she was not able to communicate and negotiate with them to get what she wanted. She had experienced the freedom to be herself when she lived away from home. Now, she had to struggle between being an obedient daughter who put her needs behind family expectations and being a "modern" person who put individuality and self-development ahead of collective needs.

The counselor used the following six general strategies in working with Nancy:

1. The counselor recognized the importance of a therapeutic alliance and the need to be empathic, accepting, and genuine (Ivey et al., 2002;

Sandhu, Leung, & Tang, 2003). The counselor used a range of listening and microcounseling skills, trying to understand Nancy's subjective experience and responding in ways to communicate empathic understanding (Egan, 2002; Ivey et al., 2002). Through this process, Nancy was able to narrate her life story with the encouragement of the counselor. Perhaps because of her exposure to Western-oriented values and practices, self-disclosure in a therapeutic encounter was not difficult for Nancy once trust was established. The counselor encouraged Nancy to allow her emotions to come out during the therapy process. Slowly Nancy learned to use therapy time to express, understand, and work through her emotions.

2. The counselor assured Nancy that many individuals experienced negative affect upon returning home from a host culture (e.g., Wang, 1997). Nancy was unsure of how her depression was related to coming home. In the process of exploration, Nancy recognized the connection and began to see her emotional reactions as a part of a "reentry shock" that could become overwhelming to many individuals.

3. The counselor encouraged Nancy to talk about the different aspects of her experience as an international student, including her romantic relationship that did not work out and the struggles she went through in deciding to come home. The counselor told Nancy that although talking about the past would not change things, it might change how she viewed these experiences. Through this process, Nancy became more aware of her thoughts and feelings toward events in the past. Recognizing her sense of loss (Wang, 1997) in moving away from a place that had so much meaning to her, Nancy was able to appreciate her cross-cultural experience and to realize that it had made her a stronger person.

4. The counselor encouraged Nancy to become more active socially. First, Nancy was able to find an English-speaking church in which many members had similar experiences and life orientations as Nancy's. She was able to establish herself in a supportive community in which her multicultural identity was accepted. Second, she formed a support group with several friends who were peers from the same university. They shared similar experiences in returning home and were able to provide support to each other.

5. The counselor challenged Nancy to expand and make use of her communication channels with her parents, to share with them her thoughts and beliefs. The counselor also encouraged Nancy to separate "being disobedient" from "not having the same view." Through the process, Nancy identified guilt as well as love toward her parents (Ho, 1996). The counselor also used a range of dialogue and role-play techniques that are often used in humanistic–existential approaches (Ivey et al., 2002), helping Nancy to explore the conflicting parts of herself, as well her perceptions of her parents' expectations and intentions. This

process helped Nancy to integrate the different aspects of self, and as she became more aware of her needs and her parents' perspectives, Nancy was able to communicate effectively with her parents.

6. The counselor engaged Nancy in a process of examining her needs, her desires, and her dreams. It seemed that Nancy had not been forthcoming about telling her parents what her needs were because she felt that she had to follow their expectations. The counselor suggested to Nancy that it was important for her to make a conscious choice between following her own path and the path expected of her, between putting a priority in self-development and in fulfilling parental wishes (Kwan, 2000; Sandhu et al., 2003). Through the process, Nancy decided that she would seek a job away from her father's company but would continue to stay with her parents for the time being because it was important for her to be close to them. Nancy's parents eventually agreed to this arrangement. Recognizing that it would always be a balancing act to negotiate between her needs and wishes and her parents' expectations (especially when she decided to stay with her parents), Nancy hoped that the personal growth and awareness she gained in the process of counseling, and the interpersonal skills and strengths she acquired (e.g., through the use of dialogues techniques and exercises), would enable her to communicate with her parents and to resolve future differences and conflict.

Summary

In this chapter, reverse culture shock was examined from a personal growth orientation based on three core beliefs. First, reverse culture shock is not treated as merely a deficit or psychological problem; rather, it is viewed as part of a developmental transition that a person experiences in moving back to one's culture of origin. Second, the immediate experience of a person is understood in terms of the overall cultural experience, and individuals reentering a culture are encouraged to find ways in which their multicultural identities can be expressed and appreciated. Third, individuals reentering their home cultures are invited to adapt, adjust, compromise, and make life decisions with full understanding of the conflicts embedded in their unique cultural context. Overall, I want to make the point that traveling across cultures is a process involving joy and pain. Reverse culture shock is a challenge that can be overcome, and in walking this path, one can experience personal growth and development.

References

Adler, N. J. (1981). Re-entry: Managing cross-cultural transitions. *Group and Organizational Studies, 6,* 341-356.

Adler, P. S. (1975). The transitonal experience: An alternative view of culture shock. *Journal of Humanistic Psychology, 15,* 13-23.

Arthur, N. (2004). *Counseling international students: Clients from around the world*. New York: Kluwer Academic/Plenum.

Berry, J. W. (1980). Acculturation as varieties of adaptation. In A. M. Padilla (Ed.), *Acculturation: Theory, models, and some new findings* (pp. 9-25). Boulder, CO: Westview Press.

Berry, J. W., Trimble, J. E., & Olmedo, E. L. (1986). Assessment of acculturation. In W. J. Lonner & J. W. Berry (Eds.), *Field method in cross-cultural research* (pp. 291-324). Thousand Oaks, CA: Sage.

Church, A. T. (1982). Sojourner adjustment. *Psychological Bulletin, 91*, 540-572.

Coschignano, D. M. (2002). Crossing borders: A descriptive analysis of the re-entry experiences of twenty adult United States citizens from Hawaii, Colorada, and California. *Dissertation Abstracts International, 62*, 5428.

Cushner, K., & Brislin, R. W. (1996). *Intercultural interactions: A practical guide* (2nd ed.). Thousand Oaks, CA: Sage.

Dion, K. L., & Dion, K. K. (1996). Chinese adaptation to foreign culture. In M. H. Bond (Ed.), *The handbook of Chinese psychology* (pp. 457-478). Hong Kong: Oxford University Press.

Egan, G. (2002). *The skilled helper: A problem-management and opportunity-development approach to helping* (7th ed.). Pacific Grove, CA: Brooks/Cole.

Gaw, K. F. (2000). Reverse culture shock in students returning from overseas. *International Journal of Intercultural Relations, 24*, 83-104.

Gullahorn, J. T., & Gullahorn, J. E. (1963). An extension of the U-curve hypothesis. *Journal of Social Issues, 19*, 33-47.

Ho, D. Y. F. (1996). Filial piety and its psychological consequences. In M. H. Bond (Ed.), *The handbook of Chinese psychology* (pp. 155-165). Hong Kong: Oxford University Press.

Ivey, A. E., D'Andrea, M., Ivey, M. B., & Simek-Morgan, L. (2002). *Theories of counseling and psychotherapy: A multicultural perspective* (5th ed.). Boston: Allyn & Bacon.

Kwan, K. K. (2000). Counseling Chinese people: Perspectives of filial piety. *Asian Journal of Counselling, 7*, 23-41.

Leong, F. T. L., & Brown, M. T. (1995). Theoretical issues in cross-cultural career development: Cultural validity and cultural specificity. In W. B. Walsh & S. H. Osipow (Eds.), *Handbook of vocational psychology* (2nd ed., pp. 143-180). Mahwah, NJ: Erlbaum.

Leong, F. T. L., & Leung, K. (2004). Academic careers in Asia: A cross-cultural analysis. *Journal of Vocational Behavior, 64*, 346-357.

Leung, S. A., & Chen, P. H. (2004, July). *Challenges in teaching multicultural counseling in Chinese communities*. Paper presented at the Annual Convention of the American Psychological Association, Honolulu, HI.

Lysgaard, S. (1955). Adjustment in a foreign society: Norwegian Fulbright grantees visiting the United States. *International Social Science Bulletin, 7*, 45-51.

Martin, J. N. (1984). The intercultural re-entry: Conceptualization and directions for future research. *International Journal of Intercultural Relations, 8*, 115-134.

Pedersen, P. (1995). *The five stages of culture shock: Critical incidents around the world*. Westport, CT: Greenwood Press.

Pedersen, P., & Lee, K. S. (2000). "Happy hell or lonely heaven": Quality-of-life factors in the reentry of Taiwan graduates after study abroad. *Asian Journal of Counselling, 7*, 67-84.

Sandhu, D. S., Leung, S. A., & Tang, M. (2003). Counseling approaches with Asian Americans and Pacific Islander Americans. In F. D. Harper & J. McFadden (Eds.), *Culture and counseling: New approaches* (pp. 99-114). Boston: Allyn & Bacon/Longman.

Stephan, C. W., & Stephan, W. G. (1992). Reducing intercultural anxiety through intercultural contact. *International Journal of Intercultural Relations, 16*, 89-106.

Storti, C. (2001). *The art of coming home*. Yarmouth, ME: Intercultural Press.

Wang, M. M. (1997). Re-entry and reverse culture shock. In K. C. Cushner & R. W. Brislin (Eds.), *Improving intercultural interactions: Modules for cross-cultural training programs* (Vol. 2, pp. 109-128). Thousand Oaks, CA: Sage.

Ward, C., Bochner, S., & Furnham, A. (2001). *The psychology of culture shock*. Philadelphia: Taylor & Francis.

Westwood, M. J., Lawrence, W. S., & Paul, D. (1986). Preparing for re-entry: A program for the sojourning student. *International Journal for the Advancement of Counselling, 9*, 221-230.

Yang, K. -S. (2003). Methodological and theoretical issues on psychological traditionality and modernity research in an Asian society: In response to Kwang-Kuo Hwang and beyond. *Asian Journal of Social Psychology, 6*, 263-285.

Ying, Y. W. (2005). Variation in acculturation stressors over time: A study of Taiwanese students in the United States. *International Journal of Intercultural Relations, 29*, 59-71.

Part II

Characteristics of International Students From Around the World

Chapter 8

Counseling International Students From Latin America and the Caribbean

Edward A. Delgado-Romero and Samuel Sanabria

Although definitions range on which countries comprise Latin America, it is generally understood that Latin America includes Mexico, Central America, South America, and the Caribbean. According to the Institute of International Education (2003), the College Board Annual Survey of Colleges for 2002/2003 for the fall 2001 enrollment listed a record total of 582,996 international students attending colleges and universities in the United States; of these, 68,358 (12% of the total) were from 45 countries in Latin America.[1] Of the top 15 countries of origin, Mexican students (7th at 12,518 students), Brazilian students (12th at 8,972 students), and Colombian students (15th at 8,068 students) represent the majority of international students from Latin America. Other Latin American countries with over 1,000 students in the United States include (in order from most to least number of students) Venezuela, Jamaica, Argentina, Peru, Trinidad and Tobago, Ecuador, Bahamas, Chile, Panama, Haiti, Guatemala, and Honduras.

Although the popular misconception is that Latin America is composed of only Spanish-speaking Latino/a people, the reality is that people from Latin America represent indigenous, African, European, and Asian heritage and speak an array of languages. For example, in general, Brazilians speak Portuguese, Venezuelans speak Spanish, Haitians speak Haitian Creole, and 40% of Guatemalans speak one of the 23 Amerindian languages such as Quiche or Kekchi. Each one of the 45 different countries reflects a unique political, economic, social, religious, and cultural constellation, and there is rich within-group diversity. In addition, each country has a unique history relative to the United States; for example, Cuba, which the United States has boycotted since the 1950s, versus Mexico, which has free trade agreements and shares a common border with the United States. Therefore, Latin American international students represent a highly diverse group with respect to culture, history, and experiences with the United States.

---

[1]It should be noted that the term *Latin America* refers to a common history of conquest and colonialism, first by the Roman empire (i.e., Latin) and then by Spain, Portugal, and France, among other European countries. Latin America also refers to countries where romance languages (those derived from Latin) are spoken.

Latin American international students may share some common experiences in U.S. institutions of higher education even though they originate from diverse cultural, social, religious, and political backgrounds (Thomas & Althens, 1989). Garcia-Preto (1996) offered a framework of similarities of those who have origins in Latin American countries that include the following:

- A history of conquest and oppression
- Struggle for liberation
- Domination by White European immigrants
- Destruction of indigenous cultures, religions, and people
- The impact of slavery and racial mixing that resulted in *mestizo* (racially mixed) people
- A struggle for social justice

Delgado-Romero and Rojas (2004) added that Latin Americans might share:

- The influence of European languages (Spanish, Portuguese, French, English, Dutch, German)
- An often ambivalent relationship with U.S. foreign policies and political intervention in the history of Caribbean and Central and South American countries[2]
- A history of Roman Catholicism religious dominance
- An emphasis on family unity, welfare, and honor (*familismo*); a preference for close personal relationships (*personalismo*); and respect (*respeto*) for elders and authority figures

There has been recent attention given to the internationalization (Leong & Ponterroto, 2003) and globalization (Leong & Blustein, 2000) of counseling as well as to the issues facing international students as they adjust to institutes of higher education in the United States (e.g., Komiya & Eells, 2001; Mori, 2000; Tatar & Horenczyk, 2000). However, this attention has often been given to international students in general and can obscure important differences for specific national groups (e.g., Byon, Chan, & Thomas, 1999; Swagler & Ellis, 2003) or between international student populations (e.g., Wilton & Constantine, 2003). Consequently, what is written about international students may be of limited practical use for counselors working with specific populations such as Latin American international students. Similarly, Delgado-Romero, Galván, Maschino, and Rowland (2005) found over a 10-year period (1990–1999) that international populations composed only 4% of the population in counseling research. This lack of inclusion is problematic because it reflects a lack of focus on international clients. Additionally, Delgado-Romero and colleagues stated that this finding potentially represents a confound

---

[2]For example, as we prepare this chapter there are riots in Argentina protesting a visit by the U.S. president.

in research whereby international research participants might be "forced" into U.S. racial and ethnic categories rather than treated as a separate population. Given that Latino/a Americans are the largest minority population in the United States, the unique issues of international students from Latin America may be lost if subsumed in this growing population. Historically, counselors have not been adequately prepared to work with international students in general (Fouad, 1991) and specifically with Latin American international students. Therefore, we focus specifically on Latin American international students in this chapter by exploring some of the barriers experienced by this population, including language and relationship barriers as well as family expectations. We introduce three case scenarios to illustrate the struggles some Latin American international students encounter in the college setting. We conclude with recommendations for counselors.

Latin American International Students and Higher Education in the United States

International students from Latin America potentially face many challenges on campuses of higher education in the United States. In addition to the challenges of adjusting to college life, which includes living away from home, making new friends, and becoming accustomed to new rituals, international students face the pressures of living in a country whose customs are different from those with which they are familiar (Boyer & Sedlacek, 1989). A part of being in an unfamiliar culture is learning new roles, and for Latin American international students who are in the United States for a specific time period, that means having to learn these new roles quickly, both inside and outside of the classroom. Thus, many Latin American international students might experience cultural shock, even those who are from countries that are U.S. territories or where English is spoken (Soto-Carlo, Delgado-Romero, & Galván, 2005). Factors that might affect acculturation or adaptation to U.S. culture include previous experience with U.S. culture; English fluency; the presence (or lack of) family, friends, and other international students; faculty attitudes and the degree of faculty sensitivity to international student issues; and campus and community support and resources.

Language Proficiency

Like other international students, many Latin American students face linguistic, academic, interpersonal, financial, and intrapersonal problems (Mori, 2000). They may also feel homesick and be concerned or distracted when crises happen at home (e.g., political and economic destabilization in Venezuela, the ongoing civil war in Colombia, or hurricanes in Puerto Rico) that may be virtually ignored by the U.S. media. At the same time, many Latin American international students may view a return to their home countries without their college degree as a sign of failure and feel immense pressure to achieve at a high level on a compressed timeline. Some of the most serious problems can be language issues, experiences with race and racism, relationship issues, and acculturative stress.

Language difference is probably the most significant barrier for international students (Mori, 2000). Given that many Latin American international students do not have English as a first language (see Table 8.1), language difficulties may prohibit these students from adequately performing in their classes or developing a social support system. Latin American students who have English as a second language (ESL) may encounter a variety of academic problems. For example, ESL students may have difficulties understanding lectures, reading textbooks, taking notes, completing exams, and speaking in class. Fluency in the English language may also have a direct effect on the adjustment process of international students (Kagan & Cohen, 1990). An exclusive focus on English fluency may contribute to feelings of dehumanization and alienation, especially in the therapy process (e.g., Thompson et al., 2003). Furthermore, even for students from countries that have English as an official language (e.g., Belize, Trinidad) or are officially bilingual (e.g., Puerto Rico), the transition to formal academic English may be difficult (see Soto-Carlo et al., 2005).

According to Yeh and Inose (2003), English language proficiency is related to the level of stress for international students. In particular, those students who have strong language proficiency in the English language reported less stress in adjusting to the new culture. A higher level of language proficiency, that is, frequency of use, fluency, and degree of comfort using the language, may reduce the stress some international students have when engaging in conversations with U.S. students. Barratt and Huba (1994) claimed that international students who have a high level of English proficiency experience less embarrassment and are less self-conscious about their accent or ethnic background. They also asserted that higher levels of English proficiency help international students in the academic setting because they are more likely to speak in class and participate in discussions. Because Latin American international students represent a variety of cultures and speak an array of non-English languages, adjusting to the U.S. culture may further be complicated if level of English proficiency is low. In addition, the issues of accents may be very salient for Latin American international students given the potential stereotypical associations of a Spanish accent with negative characteristics (e.g., lack of intelligence, illegal status, a tendency toward emotional outbursts) in the U.S. media.

Identity Issues

Latin American international students also need to understand the slang and idioms that are used in the United States. For example, phrases like "get out of here" or "that's bad" may be perceived literally as negative comments. Counselors should help Latin American international students learn more about American or regional idioms and college slang (Lacinda, 2002). Latin American international students can increase their understanding of American idioms by asking native speakers the meaning of the phrases they use, or they may find that a less embarrassing way is to visit Web sites such as www.eslcafe.com, which is designed to introduce American slang to international students (Sperling, 2005). Counselors

Table 8.1

Languages Spoken in Latin American Countries

General Area	Country	Language Spoken
Caribbean	Antigua & Barbuda	English (official), local dialects
	Aruba	Dutch (official), Papiamento, English, Spanish
	Bahamas	English, Creole
	Barbados	English
	Cayman Islands	English
	Cuba	Spanish
	Dominica	English (official), French patois
	Dominican Republic	Spanish
	Grenada	English (official), French patois
	Guadeloupe	French (official), Creole patois
	Haiti	French (official), Creole (official)
	Jamaica	English, patois English
	Martinique	French, Creole patois
	Puerto Rico	Spanish, English
	St. Kitts and Nevis	English
	St. Lucia	English (official), French patois
	St. Vincent and the Grenadines	English, French patois
	Trinidad & Tobago	English (official), Hindi, French, Spanish, Chinese
	Virgin Islands	English (official), Spanish, Creole
Central America	Belize	English (official), Spanish, Mayan, Garifuna, Creole
	Costa Rica	Spanish (official), English
	El Salvador	Spanish, Nahua
	Guatemala	Spanish 60%, Amerindian languages 40% (23 officially recognized Amerindian languages, including Quiche, Cakchiquel, Kekchi, Mam, Garifuna, and Xinca)
	Honduras	Spanish, Amerindian dialects
	Nicaragua	Spanish (official), English, indigenous languages
	Panama	Spanish, English
North America	Mexico	Spanish, various Mayan, Nahuatl, and other regional indigenous languages
South America	Argentina	Spanish (official), English, Italian, German, French
	Bolivia	Spanish (official), Quecha (official), Aymara (official)
	Brazil	Portuguese (official), Spanish, English, French
	Chile	Spanish
	Colombia	Spanish
	Ecuador	Spanish (official), Amerindian languages (especially Quechua)
	French Guiana	French
	Guyana	English, Amerindian dialects, Creole, Hindi, Urdu
	Paraguay	Spanish (official), Guarani (official)
	Peru	Spanish (official), Quechua (official), Aymara
	Suriname	Dutch (official), English, Sranang Tongo, Taki-Taki, Hindustani, Javanese
	Uruguay	Spanish, Portunol, or Brazilero
	Venezuela	Spanish (official), various indigenous dialects

Note. From Office of the Director of Central Intelligence (n.d.). Retrieved December 7, 2006, from https://www.cia.gov/cia/publications/factbook/fields/2098.html

may also help by normalizing the ever-changing nature of English slang and regional variations.

In addition to language, international students are also faced with identity issues. For example, upon entry into the United States, Latin American students are often confronted with new notions of race (e.g., a focus on Black and White; see Perea, 2000) and a new ethnic conceptualization of being "Hispanic" or "international" rather than being identified nationally. This potential loss of identity and the imposition of a new identity can be stressful, especially if Latin Americans are lumped together with people from countries that they have traditionally had conflict with or feel animosity toward (Shorris, 1992) or if Latin Americans have internalized prejudices against U.S. Hispanics/Latinos or African Americans. Because international students may experience initial difficulties adapting to the host social culture, there may be a tendency to stay within their own nationality and language groups as a response to a hostile environment. Unfortunately, some U.S. citizens may see this behavior as international students isolating themselves rather than a normal and expected reaction to unfamiliar surroundings. Optimally, the focus should be on improving the environment for international students rather than blaming the victim (Yoon & Portman, 2004).

Relationship and Reentry Concerns

For a member of a collectivist culture, identity issues are grounded in familial relationships. Latin American international students have left their home country to study in the United States, leaving behind significant people including family, relatives, and friends who have been a large influence on their sense of identity (Yeh & Inose, 2003). This newly adopted transitional experience of being away from loved ones is likely to alter their sense of self and, therefore, exacerbate their level of stress. As a result of their transitory state, Latin American international students are forced to create their own social networks to satisfy their need for validation (Lacinda, 2002). Forming social groups may play an important part in satisfying a need for interdependence, which is part of many Latin American cultures. Belonging to a group may help these students adjust to a new culture, develop close relations, and establish social networks. Ultimately, group membership may help students work through stressful experiences and mental health issues. Counselors may consider forming formal groups or facilitating informal groups to assist this process.

For many Latin Americans, family is a significant part of life and a necessity for love, happiness, and fulfillment. Latin American families typically not only include blood relatives but also are often extended to include friends, neighbors, and coworkers (Sue & Sue, 2003). Latin American international students, having a deep respect and appreciation for family and friends, may struggle with the individualistic orientation, nonpermanence of friendships, and differing values placed on relationships in the United States (Aubrey, 1991). For example, some Latin American students may confuse the amicable and sociable nature of their fellow U.S. students as invitations to serious or romantic relationships (Mori, 2000). U.S. students may view phrases such as "come over some time," "let's get together soon," or "how are you?" as social politeness, whereas Latin American students, hearing these phrases as genuine requests for friendship, may be offended when U.S. students do not wait for a response (Lacinda, 2002). These communication differences can introduce confusion into the already difficult process of establishing and developing social networks, and the greater the cultural difference between students, the greater difficulties the student will have in learning the customs of the host country. In addition to different ideas in friendships, Latin American international students may experience ethnic or racial discrimination that may leave them disillusioned in developing relationships.

Adjusting to the dominant U.S. culture usually consists of relinquishing characteristics of cultural origins and associating with the host culture, which can be a stressful process. This acculturative stress (Boyer & Sedlacek, 1989) can be a lonely experience that other students, even U.S. racial and ethnic minorities, do not experience. Complicating acculturative stress is the issue of the future and what will happen after graduation. For example, some Latin American international students intend to return to their home countries after graduation (sometimes referred to as *sojourners* in the literature), whereas other students plan to stay in the United States (immigrants), and others are undecided and exploring options. Thus plans for the future may also affect the willingness of an individual to either accept or reject cultural values, beliefs, traditions, customs, and mental health practices (such as counseling) found in the United States that are different from those found in Latin American countries. The decision whether to stay in the host country or return home is often difficult. Students have to consider future career plans while recognizing the changes to their identity. Exposure and assimilation to a different culture may alter values, beliefs, traditions, and customs, which can make the decision to return home challenging (Mori, 2000; see also chapter 7). Fortunately, this topic, with all of its life-changing implications, seems perfectly suited for counseling.

Latin American Students and Counseling

Despite the fact that Latin American international students experience more adjustment problems than domestic students, they are less likely in general to seek counseling services (Mori, 2000). This can be the result of Latin American international students' perceptions of counseling, as well as the lack of availability of culturally competent counselors. Cultural influences often prevent Latin American international students from considering counseling. For example, working through personal problems or issues is usually reserved for extended family or friends because there is a strong cultural value placed on not discussing personal problems with strangers (Sue & Sue, 2003). Also, many Latin American cultures place a value on "saving face" (known in Spanish as ¿que diran?—literally "what will others say?") and maintaining prestige and dignity. By discussing personal problems with nonfamily members, Latin American international students may feel that they will be judged or looked down on. In addition, many Latin American international students may be familiar with psychology and therapy as the treatment and remediation of psychopathology and therefore may not be aware of the normal developmental focus of counseling. They may believe that counseling is for the mentally ill or "crazy" people and attach a strong negative stigma to therapy. Consequently, the Latin American student may turn to campus personnel with whom they have close contact (e.g., housing, financial aid, international services staff). Therefore, it is important for counselors to reach out and consult with other student services personnel to help them understand why and how to refer Latin American international students for counseling if appropriate.

It is important to keep in mind that not all Latin American international students experience the same barriers to developing relationships and social networks. Addressing these difficulties is an important step in assisting Latin American international students to construct relationships and develop social networks (Hayes & Lin, 1994). We note that it cannot fairly be said that Latin American international students are averse to therapy in general when many lack access to bilingual and bicultural counselors with an international perspective who are competent to understand and work with the issues presented by these students.

There is very little written about counseling Latin American international students in the counseling literature and even less research. We highlight two counseling research studies involving Latin American international students. First, Wilton and Constantine (2003) found that Latin American international students reported higher levels of psychological distress than did their Asian peers. Length of residence was negatively associated with psychological distress symptoms, and acculturative distress and intercultural competence concerns were positively related to psychological distress in both Latin American and Asian international students. Wilton and Constantine administered a cultural adjustment difficulties checklist and a general psychological distress checklist to a group of 65 Cuban, Mexican, Peruvian, and Dominican students (as well as to 125 Asian international students). The researchers felt the results of the study indicated that risk factors (lower enrollment, higher attrition, lack of social support) should be investigated for Latin American international students.

Soto-Carlo et al. (2005) undertook a qualitative study with Puerto Rican Islanders[3] who came to the United States for graduate study. They found six major themes: (a) Islanders came to the United States because their graduate programs were not available in Puerto Rico, not because they felt Puerto Rican education was inferior; (b) although Puerto Rico is officially bilingual, Islanders struggled with English (especially academic English reading and writing); (c) cold weather was a challenge, both because it was unfamiliar and because the cold weather reminded Islanders they were not at home; (d) the lack of traditional food, music, and cultural events as well as physical separation from family also

---

[3]Puerto Ricans are U.S. citizens given that Puerto Rico is a U.S. territory. However, this research found that because of strong identification of Puerto Rican nationalism, Islanders (as opposed to Puerto Ricans who live in the United States) often identify as international students. We believe their experiences are instructive given the expected familiarity and experienced difficulties with U.S. mainland culture.

led to isolation; (e) Islanders encountered ignorance of Puerto Rican heritage (e.g., one graduate student was asked, "Do they even have universities in Puerto Rico?"; Soto-Carlo et al., 2005, p. 292) and discriminatory attitudes; and (f) Islanders felt a strong sense of nationalism and often identified more closely with international students than they did with U.S. Latinos.

In the next section we turn our attention to what a counselor should do who desires to be multiculturally competent when working with Latin American international clients. We start by providing some brief counseling scenarios.

Case Scenario 1

Juliana is a Colombian student from the coastal city of Cartagena, Colombia. Her skin is very dark, and even though her family calls her *"la negrita,"* she has never thought of herself as racially different from other Cartageneras or Colombianas. Juliana says that the African American students in the college she attends in the eastern United States become angry with her when they approach her and she immediately denies she is Black. The Latino students at the university are mostly second-generation Mexican American students who speak little or no Spanish and have different customs, food, music, and dance than those with which Juliana is familiar. Juliana also finds that she is not making any White friends either, and her attempts to join study groups are constantly rejected. Consequently, Juliana feels confused, isolated, and angry. In addition, as the weather begins to change, Juliana finds herself increasingly unable to concentrate on her classes, has frequent headaches, and often wants nothing more than to return home to Cartagena. However, she knows her parents expect her to get her degree in the United States. A concerned resident assistant in international housing referred her to counseling because of her frequent absence in class caused by headaches.

Juliana's story highlights several aspects of adjustment for Latin American international students. First, it highlights the sudden and confusing change in racial and ethnic perception that some Latin Americans undergo upon entry to the United States. Juliana finds that people identify her mainly by the color of her skin rather than by her country and hometown. If anyone identifies her ethnically, she is classified as "Hispanic," a term that has no meaning for her. Second, the story also highlights that Latin Americans must navigate relationships with several groups—Whites, African Americans, Hispanic Americans, and other minority groups—and that rejection from all groups is possible. Juliana's counselor might consider exploring the meaning of race and ethnicity in the United States along with possible sources of social support and perhaps even help Juliana think about transferring to a university where there is a stronger Colombian or South American presence. Finally, it should be noted that for someone from a tropical country, even the mildest winter in the eastern United States might be a shock; counselors should check in to make sure their clients are prepared to deal with winters both physically (e.g., warm clothing) and psychologically (e.g., alert for signs of depression). It should be noted that Juliana never used the word *depression* and may describe her increasing symptoms of depression somatically or pass them off as being homesick. Juliana may describe her feelings in Spanish as *"Me siento ída, distraída, agotada, triste, sin ganas de nada, sentimental* or *me enojo por nada.*"[4] According to the American Counseling Association's multicultural counseling competencies (e.g., Arredondo et al., 1996), Juliana's case can be conceptualized by focusing on the relevant awareness, knowledge, and skills needed. For all the case scenarios, we discuss each of these in turn.

Awareness: The counselor should be aware of the intersection of race, ethnicity, gender, nationality, and identity; their own attitudes toward race and acculturation; and the unique experiences of Colombian international students when compared with U.S. Latinos or U.S. racial or ethnic minorities.

Knowledge: The counselor should understand how identity may be transformed upon entry into the United States, the unique history and traditions of Colombians, the history of discrimination in the United States based on skin color, and culturally sensitive approaches to depression.

Skills: The counselor should have skills that permit a systemic and environmental (vs. individualistic) conceptualization of the client issues (see Yoon & Portman, 2004), facility and comfort in exploring oppression and discrimination, culturally sensitive diagnostic skills, and working knowledge and connections to possible resources in the community.

Case Scenario 2

Amado is a 35-year-old graduate student from the city of Tepic in the state of Nayarit, Mexico. He had a previously successful career as an accountant and decided to get his PhD in business in the United States. Amado is also a gay man who led a very closeted life while in Mexico. At his university in the United States, Amado has found a sexual openness and liberal attitude that he views as refreshing, and he and his partner are active members of the campus LGBT (lesbian, gay, bisexual, and transgender) group. Amado has a very strong accent and finds that people often do not understand what he says, and the students he teaches in his courses are often critical and aggressive about his English. In addition, Amado is facing pressure from his family to return home to care for his elderly parents. His siblings are married with children, so the responsibility for the parents falls on him. Amado was referred to counseling through a university nurse when he came to the health center for a chronically upset stomach.

Amado comes to counseling, like Juliana in the previous scenario, because of physical symptoms. Latin American clients may not understand what counseling is and see counseling as something that only "crazy people" do. Thus, the only legitimate way to obtain support may be through a physical problem. Counselors should be sensitive to this dynamic while explaining the purpose and goals of counseling. It should be noted that some Latin American students may be familiar with therapy and be comfortable seeking out help.

---

[4]We thank Nallely Galván from the University of Illinois (personal communication, October 24, 2005) for providing these typical Spanish expressions from her practice with Latin American international clients, which roughly translated means "I feel gone (or not there), distracted, drained, sad, do not want to do anything, sentimental (nostalgic), and I get mad or annoyed about everything."

Amado has found a very liberal atmosphere at his university and is able to express his sexual orientation openly for the first time in his life, which he finds liberating. At the same time, his parents and siblings are encouraging a traditional role of caretaker on him because he is not married and does not have children. This situation results in a great deal of stress and anxiety for Amado that is exacerbated by aggressive and hostile reactions to his strong Spanish accent (e.g., Lacinda, 2002). Counselors should help Amado explore this difficult situation with sensitivity to Amado's need for a continued relationship with his family, regardless of their homophobic views. For example, counselor questions like "What is best for *you*?" emphasize an individualistic orientation over a collectivistic one. Because his family may have accused Amado of being selfish, counselors may unwittingly contribute to this dynamic by emphasizing the self. At the same time, counselors must realize that Amado is being pressured to be selfless or self-sacrificing, and this dichotomous thinking (selfish vs. selfless) might guarantee a negative outcome for Amado.

Awareness: The counselor should be aware of the intersection of gender, ethnicity, sexual orientation, nationality, and identity; her or his own attitudes toward race and acculturation; their own attitudes toward gay men; and the unique experiences of Mexican international students when compared with U.S. Mexicans or Hispanics.

Knowledge: The counselor should understand traditional Mexican familial structure and the role of interdependence (vs. individuation), traditional and contemporary roles regarding gay men, the unique history and traditions of Mexicans (perhaps even considering indigenous traditions), the history of discrimination in the United States based on sexual orientation, and culturally sensitive approaches to depression.

Skills: The counselor should have skills that permit a systemic (vs. individualistic) conceptualization of the client issues, focusing on family relationships and expectations, means to communicate a gay-affirming stance, an openness to discussing issues pertaining to sexual orientation, facility and comfort in exploring oppression and discrimination, culturally sensitive diagnostic skills, and working knowledge and connections to possible resources in the community.

Case Scenario 3

Khym, a graduate student in student affairs at a U.S. southeastern university, is from the Caribbean Island of St. Kitts in the West Indies. She came to counseling because she stated, "I don't understand Americans," and she was seeking someone to explain some confusing behavior. Khym has left behind a fiancé in St. Kitts and is worried about the long-term prospects of the relationship. During the record-setting hurricane season, she is constantly concerned about her family and friends in St. Kitts, but she finds that her faculty and fellow students are oblivious to the danger to her country and only seem concerned about hurricanes that threaten the United States. Her academic program is predominantly White, and she tends to study with and socialize with people in the program. At a club, she was shocked when an African American male mocked her Island accent and accused her of not really being Black. In addition, in her program, classes are primarily focused on discussion and writing papers, unlike the more formal education (in which faculty lecture and give tests) that she was used to in St. Kitts. To top it off, her faculty advisor insists that Khym call her by her first name, and this feels completely uncomfortable to her. As a student affairs student, Khym knew about counseling from an outreach she attended, and she decided to see if a counselor could help her understand Americans.

Although she comes from an English-speaking country, Khym is experiencing culture shock on several levels. First, she is struck by the provincial worldview of American media and the limited interest and information that many faculty and students have about other countries. Consequently, this leaves Khym feeling alone with her concerns for the safety of her family. Second, she has left a significant relationship and put it on hold for several years (which may seem like an eternity). Third, despite the fact that St. Kitts also has a history that includes colonization and slavery, both African Americans and Whites may assume that she has some privilege by virtue of her accent and her international student status. Khym may have also internalized stereotypes about African Americans and may have unexamined prejudicial views against African Americans. Finally, the U.S. educational system may be a challenge for an international student to navigate (and often is a challenge for even U.S. citizens to navigate), especially doctoral programs that focus on independence while emphasizing writing and discussion and deemphasizing test taking and lecturing. It cannot be assumed that international students are familiar with the teaching styles of U.S. faculty and academic training programs.

Khym presented to counseling as searching for a guide to understand her experience in the United States. It is important that the counselor has examined his or her own attitudes about the United States so that the counselor can facilitate a critical discussion about life in the United States for an international student rather than feeling a need to defend it. Once a strong alliance is formed, the counselor may be able to help Khym delve deeper into her concerns about her relationships and the meaning of racially charged interactions in the United States. It is also important that the counselor not be distracted by the relatively detached presentation of the client (e.g., needing to understand Americans) and to realize that addressing this externalized concern may represent an opportunity for the client and counselor to explore personal identity and other issues.

Awareness: The counselor should be aware of his or her own attitudes about the United States (e.g., beliefs about the superiority of U.S. education), marginalization of international perspectives by many Americans and American institutions (e.g., media), potential tension between international African-descended people and African Americans, and the unique experiences of Caribbean Islander international students when compared with African Americans or African international students.

Knowledge: The counselor should understand English and French colonial educational systems, the history of Caribbean Islands such as St. Kitts (with an understanding of the effects of slavery), potential resources in the university (e.g., international programs) and the community, and racial identity development in an international and U.S. context.

Skills: The counselor should have skills that permit an honest and critical examination of life in the United States, openness and facility in discussing racial incidents, ability to take a systemic perspective, and ability to balance and transition from a role as a "guide" to the role of a therapist.

In interactions with any client, counselors should have first explored their own cultural heritage and examined their values so that they do not impose their values on a client. It should be noted that the Latin American international student is not the only person bringing culture into the counseling session, the counselors also bring their own culture with them.

Recommendations

This chapter highlights the significance of providing appropriate counseling services to Latin American international students. However, one of the greatest challenges in providing these services stems from the lack of research and resources available to counselors. Much of the research that is available focuses on the general Latin American population or on the broad spectrum of immigrants in the United States. It is difficult to draw any conclusions on how to work with Latin American international students based on the generalized information. It is our hope that this chapter will shed light onto some of the potential issues faced by Latin American international students. The following sections offer suggestions on how to provide appropriate counseling services to Latin American international students.

Social Networks

In working with Latin American international students in an individual counseling setting, it is important to consider the importance of social connectedness. Because many Latin American international students may be experiencing feelings of loneliness, isolation, and stress, counselors should work toward promoting integration and a sense of community around campus. This can be accomplished by providing information about various on- and off-campus organizations that include other Latin American or international students. Counselors should also be prepared to discuss the struggles the international student faces trying to fit in, in addition to discussing how the student may develop fulfilling interpersonal relationships.

Peer Programs

Utilizing peers to aid international students can circumvent the stigma associated with getting help. Counselors may encourage Latin American international students to consider joining a peer program that would match them with a U.S. student to help acclimate them to the university and the community. By joining a peer program, international students from Latin America may be introduced to other students from the United States, which can help alleviate the stress of trying to develop a social network in a different environment. University counseling centers can work with various campus departments, including the department of international student affairs, to help develop peer programs for international students if one is not available (Yeh & Inose, 2003). Likewise, Jacob and Greggo (2001) recommended that counseling centers consider developing alternative counseling programs, similar to peer programs, that would have graduate-level counselors work with Latin American international students in "noncounseling" environments. A less formal style of counseling may help the Latin American student feel comfortable while helping graduate-level counseling students develop a higher level of cultural awareness.

Smith, Chin, Inman, and Findling (1999) advocated for the use of international student outreach and support groups on campus. They believe that support groups can provide international students with opportunities to meet with other students who are experiencing the same difficulties adjusting to a new environment while minimizing the stigma of receiving counseling. This may be particularly helpful for Latin American international students interested in talking to others about their feelings yet worried about violating cultural values by expressing personal issues that are usually reserved for the family circle or the church. Latin American international students may initially participate in these groups and gain comfort in hearing others share their experiences. Support groups can also be conducted bilingually, giving Spanish-speaking students an opportunity to speak comfortably in their native language while at the same time providing an environment in which they can practice English. This would have to be monitored closely and modified as needed because not all Latin American students speak Spanish.

Counselors should constantly monitor their own views and expectations about living in the United States. Because of unconscious or unexamined beliefs about the superiority or importance of the United States, counselors may expect or reinforce acculturation as a desirable outcome. These attitudes may not meet the needs of all clients, especially those who feel ambivalent about U.S. society or those who primarily wish to return home with an education. Similarly, counselors should seek to find cultural strengths rather than focus exclusively on challenges. Doing so may entail becoming knowledgeable about local Latin American communities or festivals. For example, the first author (Delgado-Romero) affiliated with a Colombian social group in a nearby urban area; this group has served as a lifeline for many international students.

University Resources

In addition to helping the international student develop social networks in the community, counselors should inform the student about existing associates. Counselors may want to work with sources (individuals or groups) that can assist the student either directly or indirectly with the adjustment process. These sources may include various student organizations, clubs, offices of international affairs, ESL instructors, peer programs, and other available networks (Yeh & Inose, 2003). For the counselor, working with these groups may be an excellent opportunity to better understand the resources available but not currently used by the client. For instance, a university's department of international affairs may have information on various workshops on campus that are geared toward help-ing international students better adjust to American culture. Because language flu-ency is a significant predictor of stress with many international students and contributes to comfort level in interacting with the majority culture, it may be a good idea to encourage Latin American international students to participate in pro-grams of this nature. Unless the client is directly notified of these workshops, the workshops may be unattended.

In addition to these workshops, entities working with international students from Latin America may offer insight into some of the personal struggles faced by this population. By meeting with faculty advisors, sponsors, the office of interna-tional affairs, and others working closely with the student, counselors can get a bet-ter understanding of the client's needs and personal background. It is important to secure the client's informed consent before soliciting help from these entities.

College counselors may also want to encourage various departments on cam-pus that have interactions with international students to educate these students on counseling services that are available to them. For example, student orientation that includes information on counseling services on campus may help international students make the decision to seek services sooner (Hayes & Lin, 1994) and gives them an opportunity to ask questions about the different types of services available, which may help reduce the stigmatization associated with counseling.

International Student Centers

Counselors can also become involved in international students centers on cam-pus to obtain a better understanding of the resources available to Latin American international students on campus. Many of these centers offer a variety of activ-ities that help international students adjust to their new environments and de-velop social networks on campus. Activities such as socials, learning institutes, and volunteer services are great ways to bring the Latin American international student populations together with U.S. students and other international students. By associating with the international student center on campus, counselors can learn about the challenges and strengths of international students.

Sociocultural and Family Expectations

Before working with Latin American international students, counselors should have a thorough understanding of their cultural heritage as well as their familial expectations. Many international students who attend U.S. universities do so with the understanding that they will go back to their home country and work. Some international students, who may have acculturated to the dominant culture, struggle with wanting to stay in their host country. Whether for political, social, or economic reasons, the decision of whether to go back to their country can be a difficult one, especially when family expectations play an important role in the decision-making process. It is important that counselors discuss the various options available to the client, keeping in mind any and all social and political consequences. For example, the decision to stay in the host country may have significant effects on the international student's relationship with his or her family. As a result, it is likely that the student will experience personal distress and develop feelings of isolation. Given that personal identity is largely associated with the relationship developed with significant others, the client may also experience difficulty with sense of self. The counselor may want to assess the following questions with the client: How will staying in the host country affect the client's relationship with his or her family? Will his or her family suffer financial hardship? Will the client be able to continue to live within the dominant culture and not lose his or her cultural identity? Is the client receiving governmental support for attending an American university? If so, how will the decision affect the client's financial security or relationship with his or her home country? Will the client experience shame or guilt by deciding to stay in the host country? What part of the host country's values is most attractive to the client? Do these values complement the client's own cultural values? These are just a few questions that counselors should explore to help the client better understand the consequences of his or her decision.

Summary

As previously mentioned, there are insufficient resources available for counselors interested in working with Latin American international students. This poses a problem not only for counselors but also for those Latin American international students who are in need of appropriate and effective services. Given that many of these students are less likely to seek counseling services and more likely to forgo opportunities for self-assessment, it is important that we develop an appropriate theoretical and practice foundation to reach out to this population and to better understand their emotional, psychological, and social needs. Although there are studies on international students, as a whole, they are not enough to meet the psychological and social needs of this specialized group. Even the category of Latin American is an overly broad generalization that may provide limited information for an individual client. For example, consider our case scenarios. Suppose Juliana, Amado, and Khym were seen on intake. Is the general category of Latin American helpful? We think not. It is our hope that the information provided in this chapter will be used as a catalyst for further investigation into the needs, challenges, and strengths of international students from Latin America.

References

Arredondo, P., Toporek, R., Brown, S., Jones, J., Locke, D., Sánchez, J., et al. (1996). Operationalization of multicultural counseling competencies. *Journal of Multicultural Counseling and Development, 24,* 42–78.

Aubrey, R. (1991). International students on campus: A challenge for counselors, medical providers, and clinicians. *Smith College Studies in Social Work, 62,* 20-33.

Barratt, M. F., & Huba, M. E. (1994). Factors related to international undergraduate student adjustment in an American community. *College Students Journal, 28,* 422-436.

Boyer, S. P., & Sedlacek, W. E. (1989). Noncognitive predictors of counseling center use by international students. *Journal of Counseling & Development, 67,* 404-407.

Byon, K. H., Chan, F., & Thomas, K. R. (1999). Korean international students' expectations about counseling. *Journal of College Counseling, 2,* 99-110.

Delgado-Romero, E. A., Galván, N., Maschino, P., & Rowland, M. (2005). Race and ethnicity: Ten years of counseling research. *The Counseling Psychologist, 33,* 419-448.

Delgado-Romero, E. A., & Rojas, A. (2004). Other Latinos: Counseling Cuban, Central and South American clients. In C. Negy (Ed.), *Cross cultural psychotherapy: Toward a critical understanding of diverse client populations* (pp. 139-162). Reno, NV: Bent Tree Press.

Fouad, N. A. (1991). Training counselors to counseling international students: Are we ready? *The Counseling Psychologist, 19,* 66-71.

Garcia-Preto, N. (1996). Latino families: An overview. In M. McGoldrick, J. Giordano, & J. K. Pearce (Eds.), *Ethnicity and family therapy* (2nd ed., pp. 141-154). New York: Guilford Press.

Hayes, R. L., & Lin, H. -R. (1994). Coming to America: Developing social support systems for international students. *Journal of Multicultural Counseling and Development, 22,* 7-16.

Institute of International Education. (2003). *Open Doors 2002 report.* Retrieved August 20, 2003, from http://opendoors.iienetwork.org/?p=25182

Jacob, E. J., & Greggo, J. W. (2001). Using counselor training and collaborative programming strategies in working with international students. *Journal of Multicultural Counseling and Development, 29,* 73-88.

Kagan, H., & Cohen, J. (1990). Cultural adjustment of international students. *Psychological Science, 1,* 133-137.

Komiya, N., & Eells, G. T. (2001). Predictors of attitudes toward seeking counseling among international students. *Journal of College Counseling, 4,* 153-160.

Lacinda, J. G. (2002). Preparing international students for a successful social experience in higher education. *New Directions for Higher Education, 117,* 21-27.

Leong, F. T. L., & Blustein, D. L. (2000). Towards a global vision of counseling psychology. *The Counseling Psychologist, 28,* 5-9.

Leong, F. T. L., & Ponterotto, J. G. (2003). A proposal for internationalizing counseling psychology in the United States. *The Counseling Psychologist, 31,* 381-395.

Mori, S. C. (2000). Addressing the mental health concerns of international students. *Journal of Counseling & Development, 78,* 137-144.

Perea, J. F. (2000). The Black/White binary paradigm of race. In R. Delgado & J. Stefanic (Eds.), *Critical race theory: The cutting edge* (2nd ed., pp. 344–353). Philadelphia: Temple University Press.

Shorris, E. (1992). *Latinos: A biography of the people.* New York: Norton.

Smith, T. B., Chin, L. C., Inman, A. G., & Findling, J. (1999). An outreach support group for international students. *Journal of College Counseling, 2,* 188–190.

Soto-Carlo, A., Delgado-Romero, E. A., & Galván, N. (2005). Challenges of Puerto Rican Islander students in the US. *Latino Studies Journal, 3,* 288–294.

Sperling, D. (2005). *Dave's ESL café.* Retrieved October 16, 2005, from http://www.eslcafe.com

Sue, D. W., & Sue, D. (2003). *Counseling the culturally diverse: Theory and practice* (4th ed.) New York: Wiley.

Swagler, M. A., & Ellis, M. V. (2003). Crossing the distance: Adjustment of Taiwanese graduate students in the United States. *Journal of Counseling Psychology, 50,* 420–437.

Tatar, M., & Horenczyk, G. (2000). Counseling students on the move: The effects of culture of origin and permanence of relocation among international college students. *Journal of College Counseling, 3,* 49–62.

Thomas, K., & Althens, G. (1989). Counseling foreign students. In P. B. Pedersen, J. G. Draguns, W. J. Lonner, & J. E. Trimble (Eds.), *Counseling across cultures* (3rd ed., pp. 205–241). Honolulu: University of Hawaii Press.

Thompson, C., Issac, K., Delgado-Romero, E. A., Korth, B., Hwang, B. & Vandiver, B. (2003, August). *Psychotherapy research using critical methodology: A focus on racism.* Paper presented at the Annual Convention of the American Psychological Association, Toronto, Ontario, Canada.

Wilton, L., & Constantine, M. G. (2003). Length of residence, cultural adjustment difficulties, and psychological distress symptoms in Asian and Latin American international college students. *Journal of College Counseling, 6,* 177–186.

Yeh, C. J., & Inose, M. (2003). International students' reported English fluency, social support satisfaction, and social connectedness as predictors of acculturative stress. *Counseling Psychology Quarterly, 16,* 15–28.

Yoon, E., & Portman, T. A. A. (2004). Critical issues of literature on counseling international students. *Journal of Multicultural Counseling and Development, 32,* 33–44.

Chapter 9

Counseling International Students From East Asia

Hung-Bin Sheu and Mary A. Fukuyama

his chapter provides an overview of how to counsel East Asian international students at universities and colleges in the United States. Following
a brief summary of the demographics of this population, we discuss core
Asian cultural values in relation to assessment and counseling and present a literature review of counseling issues for this group. Acculturation, adjustment,
and help-seeking attitudes/behaviors are explored in conjunction with implications for counseling. Case studies are introduced to illustrate the major themes
in working with East Asian international students. The chapter concludes with recommendations for clinical practice with international students from East Asia.

Overview

The number of international students in American colleges and universities has
grown steadily since the end of World War II, and students from Asia constitute
a significant proportion of this population. According to the National Center for
Education Statistics (2001), from the year 1980 to 2000, the number of international students from Asia increased from 94,640 to 280,146, or about 54.4% of the
entire international student population studying in the United States in 2000.
Among these Asian students, 64.3% came from East Asia (China, Japan, South
Korea, and Taiwan). The same survey also revealed that three of the leading countries were China (63,211), South Korea (49,046), and Japan (46,810). In 2003 another survey showed the same trend, that four of the top five countries sending
students to the United States were, again, China, South Korea, Japan, and Taiwan
(Jacobson, 2003). These statistics suggest that a significant proportion of international students may have East Asian cultural backgrounds.

It is important to note the "diversity within diversity" when approaching East
Asians. Each country of origin has its unique culture, history, language, customs,

We are grateful for input and suggestions from the University of Florida Counseling Center Staff and
from Sang Min Lee and William E. Sedlacek.

and subsequently, differing worldviews. Additionally, these countries have centuries of history in relating to each other, and not all of it is pleasant. It is a history that includes military occupation during wartime (e.g., the Japanese invasion of China and Korea in the early 20th century, British occupation of Hong Kong for almost a century) and political divisions and tensions (e.g., North vs. South Korea, mainland China vs. Taiwan). Some of these political and military conflicts still remain and sometimes escalate. Recent events that have affected the stability of East Asia include China's test-firing missiles before the Taiwan presidential elections in 1996, Britain's handover of Hong Kong to China in 1997, military exercises conducted by China and Taiwan in the Taiwan Straits, development and test-firing of the North Korean ballistic missile program and nuclear weapon program, and the economic development in China (e.g., Bullard, 2000; Niksch, 2005). These factors as well as political, economic, and military issues have certainly influenced some East Asians' decisions to migrate to other countries and to study abroad, which at times can make the adjustment of East Asian international students more complicated and difficult. Knowledge of the history of East Asia can add to understanding international students from these countries.

Over the past few decades, counseling practitioners and researchers have documented difficulties that international students must overcome to succeed in cross-cultural adaptation and adjustment. These challenges include fitting into new cultural and social norms, developing a new identity, dealing with language barriers, coping with financial concerns, and encountering classroom communication difficulties (e.g., Arthur, 1997; Brinson & Kottler, 1995; Collins, Simons, Bamford, & Blazes, 1994; Lewthwaite, 1996). Despite these adjustment barriers and stressors, few empirical studies have been conducted with this population. The incredible diversity within this group has posed challenges for researchers and has slowed down the accumulation of knowledge of these international students' psychological needs. The scarcity of empirical research is especially true when we focus on international students who have East Asian cultural backgrounds. As a result, we draw on both conceptual and empirical work for our review on counseling East Asian international students. Also, it is rare that empirical research emphasizes only international students from these regions. Thus, we cite literature on mental health issues of Asian Americans when relevant and appropriate. Because a separate chapter is devoted to South Asians (see chapter 10), this chapter focuses primarily on East Asian international students from China, Korea, Japan, and Taiwan. We do not intend to slight other East Asian countries that also are represented among Asian international students, such as Singapore, Indonesia, Thailand, Malaysia, and the Philippines, but because of space limitations, we focus on the four countries noted above.

East Asian Cultural Values

I just cannot understand why putting the family's interest before one's own is not correct or normal in the dominant American culture. . . . When you are young, you depend on your parents; when you are an adult, your parents may need to depend on you. What is wrong with this interdependence? . . . In my country that kind of assertiveness [teaching clients to be assertive to their parents] is considered aggressive and immoral. . . . It is all right for everyone to stand up for one's own rights, but one is required to do it in an indirect, subtle way, lest it causes others to 'lose face,' especially when one is dealing with one's elders. (Zhang, 1994, p. 80)

The above quote was written by an international student from East Asia who was enrolled in a counseling graduate program of a U.S. university. It vividly describes the culture shock that an international student with East Asian cultural background may experience. It also shows some of the differences between East Asian and U.S. American culture and how an East Asian international student may think differently from his or her U.S. peers. In the helping professions, culturally diverse clients inevitably come to counseling with their cultural and ethnic heritages that guide their responses, thinking, and emotions and partially influence their help-seeking behaviors. It is difficult, if not impossible, for a counselor to build a therapeutic alliance with international student clients and have successful outcomes without considering the students' cultural heritages. To work effectively with East Asian international students on their problems, a counselor first needs to understand and respect the students' cultural values so that he or she can modify clinical approaches or develop new treatment models to help those with this particular cultural background (Cadieux & Wehrly, 1986; Dillard & Chisolm, 1983).

Although international students from East Asia are composed of many different subgroups, they share some cultural patterns and a sense of commonality (Chung, 1992; D. W. Sue & Sue, 2003). Most East Asian countries are influenced by Buddhism, Confucianism, and Taoism that emphasize such traits as silence, non-confrontation, moderation in behavior, self-control, patience, humility, and simplicity (Sodowsky, Kwan, & Pannu, 1995; Uba, 1994). These philosophies also value filial piety, restraint in emotional expression, respect for authority and elders, well-defined social roles and expectations, fatalism, inconspicuousness, conformity to norms, and the centrality of family relationships and responsibilities (Chung, 1992; B. S. K. Kim, Atkinson, & Yang, 1999). The core cultural values of East Asians are summarized and contrasted with those of U.S. Americans in Table 9.1.

Comparison of Individualist and Collectivist Cultures

Major cultural differences between U.S. and East Asian cultures can be found in the contrast between individualism and collectivism, and many social adjustment issues are related to understanding these anthropological concepts (U. Kim, Triandis, Kâğitçibaşi, Choi, & Yoon, 1994). Although cultures may vary in terms of emphasis, in general, Northern European and English-speaking societies are individualistic, whereas Asian, Latin American, and Islamic societies are collectivistic. This social construction influences social relationships, and interpersonal communication patterns widely (Chen, Brockner, & Chen, 2002). In child-rearing practices, for example, individualists emphasize mastery training and social

Table 9.1

Contrasting Values Between East Asian Culture and U.S. Culture

East Asian Culture	*U.S. Culture*
• High-context culture—situation	• Medium low-context culture—individual
• Environment-centered—the greatness of nature	• Individual-centered—the greatness of humanity
• Family and group focus, interdependence	• Individual focus, independence
• Hierarchical relationships	• Equality of relationships
• Restraint of emotions = maturity	• Emotional expression = healthy
• Counselors should provide solutions	• Clients develop solutions through introspection
• Mental illness is shameful and represents family failure	• Mental illness is the same as any other problem

Note. Adapted from Chung (1992), Sodowsky et al. (1995), and D. W. Sue and Sue (2003).

competency, whereas collectivists promote dependency. Peer influence is stronger among individualists, whereas parental influence is stronger among collectivists. Individualist societies are egalitarian, are democratic, and value human rights, whereas collectivist societies are hierarchical, are authoritarian, and emphasize harmony and security. Individualists use guilt, whereas collectivists use shame as a method of social control; hence East Asians tend to be concerned with "saving face." Individualists value honesty and genuineness, whereas collectivists may feel compelled to hide the truth or lie to save face for the family or group.

Collectivists are more likely to differentiate between the in-group and out-group. An *in-group* is a set of people with whom one belongs, identifies, or feels a shared fate of some kind. The in-group includes one's primary group, such as relatives, friends, and close associates and sometimes extends to one's career group or even national identity. The *out-group* effectively names "the other" as all people not belonging to the in-group (Myers, 1996).

Collectivists make a distinction between the way they treat members of the in-group versus out-group, including friendliness and politeness reserved for in-group members, hoarding information for in-group use, and using exclusive in-group language. There is a sense of long-term obligation, commitment, and reciprocity to the in-group that is absent in the relationships of many individualists. Individualists, in comparison with collectivists, treat in-group and out-group members fairly similarly. This is seen in information sharing, language use, and dealing with conflict. Generally speaking, individualism is more egalitarian.

Collectivist relationships are characterized by loyalty and obligation. Friendships are kept within the in-group, and relationships are an end in themselves. Individualists tend to see relationships opportunistically, and friendships are by personal choice and unconstrained by in-group ties. One of the implications of this distinction is that East Asian international students may misunderstand initial friendliness from their U.S. counterparts. They may feel that they are being included as an in-group member with long-term benefits when, in fact, they are being treated in a friendly but casual manner with no long-term obligations. East

Asian students then complain that their "friends are not really friends and they disappear after a few months." In-group norms may also influence marital selection by applying intense pressure to choose a husband or wife within the group.

The U.S. educational system encourages and rewards individualism and initiative. East Asian international students who have participated in educational systems that are hierarchical and collectivistic may be at a loss initially when enrolling in U.S. higher education. They may expect more direction from their faculty and may not understand the interactive and competitive nature of the U.S. classroom. They may also find American informality in the classroom to be disturbing in comparison with more formal relations between instructors and students in their countries of origin. Students may be waiting for their instructors to give them direction, while their professors may be waiting for them to take individual initiative. Some of these cultural differences are discussed in case examples later in the chapter.

Collectivist families are by nature "enmeshed" but not necessarily harmonious. The sense of family loyalty and obligation often transcends the actual feelings members have for each other, and disharmonies could develop because of the lack of emotional expression or communication. Many Asian families show a high degree of involvement in each other's activities but not necessarily in friendship or cordial social relationships. Sex role differentiation is also greater in collectivistic than in individualistic societies in terms of family roles and work. Family life is discussed further in the next section.

Hierarchical Structure and Family

East Asian international students come from a hierarchical social structure in which authority, leadership, and responsibility are at the top. These students tend to behave passively toward their superiors and their elders, as well as await instructions. Obedience and compliance are often treated as virtues. For international students who come from East Asian countries influenced by Confucianism, five major prototypes of interpersonal relationships underlie their society: superior–subordinate, parent–child, husband–wife, siblings, and friends (Chung, 1992). These relationships are organized in a vertical order and status so that the structure of society is hierarchical, a sharp contrast to the egalitarian and horizontal social structure of U.S. culture. Every individual in this hierarchical structure has distinct obligations to the other in a particular relationship. For example, the ruler or superior takes care of the needs of subordinates, whereas subordinates are required to present their loyalty to the ruler. Some relationships require love and caring, whereas others require protection, provision, loyalty, and filial piety.

Three of the five basic relationships lie in the family, which shapes the self-identity of East Asian international students. Family kinship is the paramount relationship and primary socializing agent. The American notion of individualism is often not rewarded. Family identity is achieved by the interdependence of family members, by individuals' seeking the "honor" and "good name" of family, and by reciprocal duties and obligations that surpass individual desires (Sodowsky et al., 1995). Just like the aforementioned quote from an East Asian student, these duties include obligations of parents to children and adult children to elderly parents. East Asian international students regard the family as the basic social unit, and family relationships are the prototypes for all relationships, such as those between teacher and student, employer and employee, and host and guest. Because family is so highly valued and the authority of parents respected, if East Asian international students are somehow failing to meet family expectations, they may hide this information from their parents.

Well-Defined Social Roles

The role of each member in the East Asian family network and hierarchical social structure tends to be clear and apparent and can rarely be changed (Paniagua, 1994). Each individual has distinct obligations to the other in a particular relationship. For example, the father functions as the dominant person taking care of the economic and physical needs of the family, and his authority is supreme and preeminent. On the other hand, women and children are expected to respect the authority of men and parents. Among traditional East Asian societies, the duty of children is to be good and to respect their parents. Their desires are decided by their parents, and any attempt to resist parents' expectations or decisions is regarded as a threat to the parents' authority and will be punished. Social control is achieved through family demands for fulfillment of obligation and compliance, and these social roles are determined by the established family network. If these expected behaviors determined by roles are not observed, the major means of punishment are to arouse moral guilt and to make the person feel ashamed. Because of these clear definitions of behavioral patterns and obligations, the self-identity of East Asian international students tends to be defined by their social role and relationships with others (Hwang, 1987, 1997), which is drastically opposed to the independent self of White Americans.

Public Repression of Problems

In general, East Asian international students tend to restrict discussion of personal problems, including physical and mental illnesses. Members of the family are not encouraged to express their problems to people outside the group, especially to strangers. One way to fulfill one's family obligation is not to create problems (Chung, 1992). Violation of this duty may cause a loss of support from the family and may lead to a sense of shame and guilt. These mechanisms play an important role in prohibiting East Asian international students from expressing and admitting their problems in settings outside their family, such as in counseling. Seeing a counselor or other mental health professional may be frightening for an East Asian international student because of the stigma attached to mental illness. To alleviate client worries and anxiety, a counselor can show his or her understanding of the clients' concerns, explain confidentiality, normalize problems (i.e., the client is not crazy), and clarify the role of counselor.

Value of Harmony

Harmony plays a vital role in affecting East Asian international students' behaviors in various social interactions (Chung, 1992). It is highly valued at different levels, such as in the universe, nature, society, family, or individual. All the philosophies of Confucianism, Taoism, and Buddhism provide ideas and evidence for supporting the practice of forbearance (Hwang, 1997), which functions to achieve the status of interpersonal harmony. Forbearance means not only to control and suppress one's desires, emotions, and psychological impulses but also to give up one's personal goals for maintaining a harmonious relationship. Restraint of feelings and emotions, self-control, and cooperation with others are all associated with this value.

Indirect Forms of Communication

Communication problems are one of the barriers to a constructive therapeutic relationship, especially in a cross-cultural context. When engaged in verbal communication, East Asian international students usually are less assertive, appear reserved, and avoid offending others. Silence and lack of eye contact often occur when East Asian international students listen or speak to people of authority, such as parents, instructors, elders, and supervisors (Chung, 1992; D. W. Sue & Sue, 2003). One-way communication from an authority figure to people in a group is also more the norm in Asian society. These indirect forms of communication, regarded as a sign of respect in Asian society, could be easily misunderstood by non-Asian counselors as passive or lacking self-confidence.

Loss of Face

Loss of face has been identified as a key component in moderating the social behaviors and relationships among East Asian international students (S. Sue, 1996). According to Hwang (1997), face is defined as "an individual's awareness about a public image formed in others' minds" (p. 22). In the context of East Asian culture, face means more than reputation and renown, and loss of face means that people feel ashamed by perceiving the inadequacy of their behaviors according to their relative role positions. Shaming an individual will make that person feel he or she is "losing face," so it is important to help East Asian clients protect their dignity and self-esteem in counseling through saving face. Furthermore, a family member's mental illness represents family failure and makes the entire family lose face. This cultural factor may be related to how individuals with an East Asian cultural background cope with difficulties, because denial of a problem could serve as a way to save face. This hypothesis was partially supported by a study (Sheu & Sedlacek, 2004) that found evidence for the tendency of Asian Americans to use avoidant coping strategies. Therefore, East Asian international students may experience difficulties expressing their psychological or academic problems in a more public venue.

The presenting problems of clients need to be understood, diagnosed, and treated with knowledge of the specific cultural context of the person asking for help (Root, 1985). Thus, becoming familiar with these cultural values will help to decrease the premature termination rate and produce positive counseling outcomes when working with clients who have East Asian cultural backgrounds. A case example that demonstrates the clash between East Asian cultural values and U.S. cultural values is presented below.

Case Scenario

Ms. Kim, an international student from South Korea, was referred to counseling by her instructor after she failed her classes and showed signs of depression. She has not told her parents that she is having difficulties with school and is quite afraid of having to return home without her degree. After spending a few years in the United States, Ms. Kim has learned to enjoy the freedom and individualism that is encouraged in U.S. culture. However, she is worried that her lifestyle might not be acceptable to or approved by her parents. Moreover, her mother has been pressuring her to return home and get married, when in reality, she is quite happy living independently. Ms. Kim wonders how much she has to sacrifice to maintain her family ties.

First, the counselor needs to get a good sense of what is causing Ms. Kim's academic difficulties and personal problems. It is also important that the counselor gains knowledge about the cultural value of independence versus interdependence and try to understand where Ms. Kim stands on this continuum. The counselor may want to help the client explore her acculturation experiences and articulate what independence and interdependence mean to her at this point. It will be helpful that the counselor shows empathy to Ms. Kim's fear of academic failure, explore with her what is underneath the fear, and process related emotions (e.g., shame, guilt) in a culturally sensitive way. In addition to engaging Ms. Kim in self-exploration activities and conveying empathy, the counselor can also provide Ms. Kim with communication skills training. The counselor can role-play with Ms. Kim on how she could talk to her parents about her desires and academic issues and how to deal with tensions between her and her parents. Moreover, stress management skills and social support groups are helpful as the client can learn how to soothe herself and seek help as the need arises. Finally, the counselor may want to work with other professionals (e.g., academic advisor, staff at the international center) to develop strategies for improving Ms. Kim's adjustment and academic performance.

Acculturation, Adaptation, and Help-Seeking

The difficulties that international students face in adapting to U.S. higher education are well documented (Hayes & Lin, 1994; Kaczmarek, Matlock, Merta, Ames, & Ross, 1994; Sandhu, 1997; Yeh & Inose, 2002). In addition to the typical developmental concerns that every student may share, international students encounter additional stressors because of the demands of cultural adjustments (Mori, 2000). Those difficulties include language, academic, interpersonal/intrapersonal, and financial problems, all of which constitute unique sources of stress and apply to East Asian international students. For example, it is not uncommon to hear East Asian international students report that they only understand a small portion of classroom lectures and discussions and, because of that, leave school everyday frustrated and exhausted. The language barriers have a significant impact on East Asian international students' adjustment as effective communication is required in almost every aspect of their new experiences in the United States. These barriers can also present a special challenge to practitioners who work with students and clients from this population.

Research has indicated that international students from non-Western countries experience significantly more adaptation difficulties than those from Western countries (Surdam & Collins, 1984). For example, Yeh and Inose (2003) studied a group of international students from Asia and found that Asian international students, compared with their counterparts from Europe, Central/Latin America, and Africa, seemed to experience higher acculturative stress. This study also found that English fluency, social connectedness (i.e., level of interpersonal closeness and difficulty in maintaining this sense of closeness), and satisfaction with social support were predictive of lower acculturative stress experienced by international students. In another study (Yeh & Inose, 2002), a sample of 274 Chinese, Japanese, and Korean immigrant junior high and high school students reported that communication difficulties were the most common problem, and the use of social support networks was the most frequently reported coping strategy.

Given the increasing diversification of the U.S. society, East Asian international students might find it difficult to deal with diversity issues (e.g., race/ethnicity, sexual orientation) as they strive to fit in the academic environment, in particular, and the mainstream society in general. A study by Sheu and Sedlacek (2005) showed that attitudes toward diversity might have a negative effect on general life satisfaction for Asian American college students, whereas this effect was not present for their White American and African American counterparts. While more research is needed to shed light on these racial differences, the negative effect of diversity on life satisfaction for Asian Americans may be due to Asian cultural values, such as harmony and well-defined social roles, which place conformity to group norms over individual differences. In other words, East Asian international students with these cultural values may find it difficult to deal with diversity issues that require tolerance of uncertainties and ambiguities.

The acculturation level of East Asian international students is associated with how they manifest their adjustment stress and their attitudes toward seeking psychological help. According to Mori (2000), some of the symptoms that international students may experience in coping with adjustment stress include physiological responses (e.g., physical tension, blushing, an increase in blood pressure and heart rates), cognitive fatigue, and psychological symptoms. For those East Asian international students who are less acculturated, the culture-bound syndromes identified by the *Diagnostic and Statistical Manual of Mental Disorders* (4th ed., *DSM-IV;*

American Psychiatric Association, 1994) may be particularly relevant to practitioners because such individuals are more likely to experience psychological distress in ways that are linked to their cultures. Research showed that most counseling graduate students felt less confident in dealing with the culture-bound syndromes, probably because of the lack of training in this area (Sheu & Lent, in press).

Empirical research has supported the hypothesis that more acculturated Asian American college students perceived counseling professionals more favorably as sources of help for personal/emotional issues compared with their less acculturated counterparts (Atkinson & Gim, 1989; Tracey, Leong, & Glidden, 1986). Zhang and Dixon's (2003) study with 170 Asian international undergraduate and graduate students (the majority of them were from China, South Korea, and Japan) also supported this hypothesis. These authors found a positive relationship between acculturation level and help-seeking attitudes. Specifically, the more acculturated Asian students were, the less stigma they had toward seeking psychological help and the more confidence they had in mental health practitioners. These findings suggest that acculturation levels of East Asian international students may be related to their adjustment, coping strategies, and willingness to seek help.

Finding social support is a key issue for many students. Some international students will naturally gravitate to "home culture" support systems, such as the Chinese club or Korean church. Although these groups are often a good source of support, they may also be a source of stress, especially when the students are experiencing personal problems that they do not want to reveal to their own cultural group. Finally, matching counselor and client on such demographics as gender or race/ethnicity could be helpful. If clients express preferences that can be met, doing so may increase the chances of forming a successful counseling relationship and obtaining favorable outcomes.

In addition to acculturation, several issues are also related to East Asian international students' adjustment. Most international students come to the United States with specific career plans. They may be supported by their governments or companies to achieve specific career goals. Not making progress in their academic programs can lead to a crisis, and it is not unusual for international students to be referred to counseling by concerned faculty. Counselors may need to intervene as advocates on behalf of their clients in terms of dealing with institutional barriers to success. Because of greater academic stress, international graduate students can benefit from coaching on how to work with their faculty advisors, establish support system, and reduce and manage stress. In situations in which East Asian international students cannot continue in their course of study, counselors need to help them find acceptable alternatives (e.g., transferring to another university, returning to home country). Because these issues are quite common among international graduate students, a case study is presented to illustrate.

Case Scenario

Mr. Chen, a 30-year-old man from Taiwan, has studied engineering for 4 years with his advisor and comes to counseling feeling frustrated with his lack of progress on his doctoral dissertation. He complains that his advisor only wants him to work on faculty projects funded by his grant. Mr. Chen does not feel that it is appropriate to confront his advisor out of respect for authority. Yet he is discouraged and wonders when he will be able to complete his degree. At some level, he is beginning to feel exploited.

The counselor may want to assess initially what has worked and not worked well for Mr. Chen in his graduate studies. What are his strengths and weaknesses? Second, what is the milieu in which he is working; how do his peers deal with this particular faculty member? Finding out the group norms for relating to professors helps clarify expectations. Third, a two-chair technique that role-plays communicating with his advisor could clarify the client's expectations as well as develop empathy for his advisor's position. This exercise also allows Mr. Chen to deepen his understanding of himself. Additionally, the counselor may engage in helping Mr. Chen understand the concept of assertiveness and work with him to develop confidence in speaking with his advisor. Exploring his fears of consequences may also aid in developing effective strategies. As another resort, Mr. Chen may need to consider changing advisors if the working relationship with the current advisor is not salvageable. Doing so may be extremely difficult for someone from a collectivist culture who values harmony and loyalty; therefore, it is important that the counselor be sensitive to and respects Mr. Chen's cultural values throughout the process. The counselor may need to educate Mr. Chen about the norms in U.S. higher education that allows for change in academic committees, depending on specific department's standards, of course. Finally, some institutions provide ombudsman services to help mediate student–faculty complaints.

Implications for Assessment

Because of within-group differences in histories, languages, and acculturation levels for East Asian international students, proper assessments are crucial before counselors can develop treatment plans with clients from this population. Several factors involved in effective assessment are discussed in this section.

What Should Be Assessed?

Atkinson and Gim (1989) pointed out that the help-seeking behavior of many Asian American groups depends on both their acculturation level and cultural values. Most models about acculturation level and racial identity are progressive and sequential. It is suggested that counselors be familiar with the general model of racial/cultural identity development (e.g., D. W. Sue & Sue, 2003) and a model of Asian American identity development (e.g., J. Kim, 1981). These models will increase counselors' knowledge of psychological distress, mechanisms, environmental factors, and personal coping methods involved in the acculturation process of East Asian international students.

Understanding the concept of worldview, in addition to specific cultural values and acculturation level, is another important aspect of assessment (Sodowsky,

Maguire, Johnson, Ngumba, & Kohles, 1994; D. W. Sue & Sue, 2003). Worldview helps counselors understand the way the clients perceive their problems and will enable counselors to find appropriate solutions within a specific cultural context. The information derived from evaluating acculturation level and world-views of East Asian clients in the first few sessions should be used to guide subsequent treatment plans.

Moreover, Pedersen (1991) pointed out the importance of reliably and properly assessing international student adjustment. Unfortunately, few instruments have been developed for this purpose. One of the examples is the Student Adaptation to College Questionnaire (Kaczmarek et al., 1994); however, its psychometric properties for a particular group of international students, such as East Asians, warrant more empirical scrutiny. Another useful tool is the noncognitive assessment model (Sedlacek, 2004). The eight noncognitive variables include positive self-concept, realistic self-appraisal, successfully handing the system (racism), preference for long-term goals, availability of strong support person, leadership experience, community involvement, and knowledge acquired in a field. Although this model was originally developed to more properly assess potentials of minorities (e.g., students of color, women, people with disabilities, athletes), it has implications for international students as well because positive attributes on these eight factors can significantly add to the cross-cultural adjustment.

While assessment tools are often used to identify clients' difficulties or presenting issues, let us not forget it is equally important to assess clients' strengths and assets. Recent development in positive psychology encourages practitioners to move toward a complementary focus on human weaknesses and strengths (Lopez, Snyder, & Rasmussen, 2003). This may prove to be especially relevant when working with East Asian international students as the non-Asian counselor may not immediately recognize their clients' unique strengths that stem from their cultural experiences. Identifying the existence of strengths and weaknesses will enable counselors to develop working hypotheses and design appropriate treatment plans. Therefore, it is vital that the counselor conducts a thorough assessment on both resources that clients can draw on and symptoms from which clients suffer.

Language and Cross-Cultural Communication

English fluency is a main concern in assessment because it is often identified as one of the predictors of adjustment satisfaction (Surdam & Collins, 1984; Yeh & Inose, 2002, 2003). Because most East Asian international students' use of English may be not adequate on arrival in the United States, they are particularly at risk and may benefit from receiving mental health services in their own Asian language. It would be most helpful if counseling professionals speak their East Asian clients' language; however, this is often not the case. In situations in which enlisting the service of interpreters is necessary, properly trained interpreters must work closely with the counselor as a team to avoid miscommunication and loss of clinical data (Hong & Ham, 2001).

At times, East Asian clients may give affirmative answers just to be polite when they cannot understand the counselor's questions, especially in situations in which the counselor is seen as an authority figure (Diller, 1999; D. W. Sue & Sue, 2003). Response set is another confounding variable. In East Asian cultures, people are encouraged to regard moderation in behavior as a virtue (Chung, 1992; Sodowsky et al., 1995). Therefore, East Asian clients may be inclined to use the middle position when responding to an inventory with Likert scales.

Because of the cultural values of self-control, suppression of emotions, and not losing face, it may be unrealistic for counselors to expect East Asian international students to express their concerns without hesitation in the first session (Paniagua, 1994). In fact, focusing on intense feelings may increase a client's anxiety. East Asian clients, especially women, may appear less assertive and autonomous, as well as more conforming, inhibited, dependent, and submissive. These characteristics and the lack of eye contact could be misunderstood as indication of dishonesty, low confidence, or attention problems. Also, because of the differences of communication styles, non-Asian counselors need to pay attention to the end of the conversation, because East Asian clients may have the tendency to bring up important issues at the end rather than place main points at the beginning of a session.

To make an assessment more complete, counselors are encouraged to consider contextual factors (e.g., role status, gender) in the counseling setting because East Asian clients' verbal and nonverbal responses are more implicit and depend more on situations and relationships in which the interactions take place.

Expressing Psychological Problems in Somatic/ Physiological Terms

To avoid feelings of shame, humiliation, and guilt, East Asian clients tend to express mental illness in somatic terms, such as headaches, chest pains, fatigue, and loss of appetite. Thus, these clients may first seek help from medical professionals rather than mental health professionals (Root, 1985). This special form of reporting emotional/psychological problems as physical complaints could be deemed as a defense mechanism because it is safer and more acceptable by East Asian cultural norms. For East Asians, mind and body are not split off as in Western medicine, and emotional, physical, and mental concerns are seen as intimately linked. It will be helpful to offer East Asian international students opportunities to talk about physical symptoms, acknowledge them, and inform them that medical consultation can be arranged if they need it (Paniagua, 1994; D. W. Sue & Sue, 2003). Moreover, it is important that counselors familiarize themselves with those culture-bound syndromes associated with East Asian cultures and seek out consultations when they are unable to make proper assessment. Some of the syndromes consist of *shen-k'uei* (i.e., severe anxiety associated with the discharge of semen, whitish discoloration of the urine, and feelings of weakness and exhaustion); *hwa-byung* (i.e., a Korean folk syndrome caused by the suppression of anger, with symptoms including fatigue, panic, fear of impending death, dyspnea, and generalized aches and pains); and *taijin kyofusho* (i.e., a culturally distinctive phobia in Japan refer-ring to an individual's intense fear that his or her body, its parts, or its functions displease, embarrass, or are offensive to other people in appearance, odor, facial expressions, or movement). (These syndromes are discussed in more detail in the *DSM-IV*; see American Psychiatric Association, 1994, pp. 844-849.)

Implications for Counseling

With the knowledge of East Asian cultural values and worldviews, as well as proper assessment of the acculturation levels and adjustment difficulties of East Asian international students, the next step is to incorporate these factors into treat-ment plans to make the counseling process more relevant to this population.

Therapeutic Structuring in the First Session

For East Asian international students, counseling could be a foreign and unfamil-iar experience. Most East Asian clients have little or no understanding about terms such as *counseling, therapy, psychodynamic therapy, cognitive-behavior therapy,* and so forth. Before providing subsequent professional services, it may be a good idea for counselors to give a brief introduction about counseling and encourage the client to ask questions. In other words, less acculturated East Asian clients could benefit from some education on the significance, practices, and procedures of counseling (Paniagua, 1994; Sandhu, 1997). Moreover, similar to medical service professionals, the counselor could be seen by East Asian clients as an expert or authority who tells them what is wrong and provides solutions. To increase the possibility that East Asian clients will return for the following sessions, it may help for the counselor to exhibit his or her expertise through men-tioning prior successful experiences with similar clients and problems, display-ing diplomas, licenses, or books, and using a professional title (e.g., "I'm Doctor..."). Because East Asian international students may lack knowledge about mental health services, counselors should also actively inform these clients about their rights and obligations in the counseling process, such as costs involved in counseling and assessment, the length of counseling, the nature and purpose of confidentiality, and benefits and risks of treatment (Corey, Corey, & Callanan, 1997). These prologues help the clients reduce their anxiety about counseling, prepare them for what is about to happen in counseling, recognize the coun-selor's expertise, and build a trusting relationship.

In multicultural counseling, it is recommended that in the first session the counselor demonstrate his or her credibility to solve problems and be perceived as giving something directly beneficial to the client (Lefley, 1989; S. Sue & Zane, 1987). It is important to give East Asian clients the impression that a tentative so-lution to the problem is possible and instill the sense of hope (Paniagua, 1994). Therefore, it is a good strategy that counselors focus on increasing the clients' "self-efficacy or agency thinking," which are thoughts clients have about their ability to pursue desired goals (Snyder, Michael, & Cheavens, 1999). For example, this could be accomplished by saying that "coming to therapy represents your desire for recovery, and by working together, your problems could be solved in the near future." An assurance at the first session will meet the needs of East Asian clients for protection and provision from an authority figure. In addition, it will increase the probability that the clients will continue to show up. Of course, the counselor needs to do so in a genuine way and provide services within the boundaries of his or her competence.

Therapeutic Relationship

For East Asians, the interaction distance (proxemics) depends on the nature of the relationship. In the therapeutic relationship, it is suggested that the counselor sits first and allows the East Asian client to set the interaction distance (assuming that the chairs are movable; Chung, 1992). It may take East Asian clients more time to build a trusting relationship because most of their social relationships are developed slowly, and the counselor is an outsider at the beginning. It could be helpful for the counselor to first establish a therapeutic relationship and then develop a mutually acceptable plan for change if the counselor and client can make their implicit value differences explicit (Sodowsky et al., 1994). In other words, openly discussing the cultural differences between the counselor and the client could play an important role in building the therapeutic relationship.

One way to explore the saliency of culture is to ask East Asian clients how they might solve this particular problem if it were occurring in their home country. The counselor may play a role of cultural broker or bridge in explaining cultural differences in some circumstances, for example, discussing the differences in friendship patterns between Americans and Taiwanese. In other cases, the counselor may be a coach who encourages East Asian clients "to make mistakes" in speaking English to improve their language proficiency. In addition, most East Asians are accustomed to relationships that are clearly defined (Hwang, 1997). Thus, the formal relationship and therapeutic framework (e.g., regulation and consistency of meeting) established at the first session is expected to continue throughout the therapy process.

Treatment Models

Because of cultural expectations and the lack of experiences with mental health service, East Asian international students could expect counselors to take an active and directive role and offer clear and concrete advice. Therefore, solution-focused, cognitive, and behavioral approaches are generally recommended because these approaches are more tangible, concrete, short term, and future oriented and do not emphasize the deep exploration of internal conflicts, which could arouse feelings of shame and guilt in this population (Paniagua, 1994; D. W. Sue & Sue, 2003).

However, these directive approaches and related techniques must be offered with caution. Sometimes advice given by counselors could imply that clients cannot solve the problems by themselves and are not responsible for the solutions. If counselors, instead of clients, do most of the work in counseling, these solutions from counselors could decrease clients' sense of competency. Thus, except for specific behavior disorders, counselors working with East Asian clients may need to consider a shift from a medical or enlightenment model at the beginning to a compensatory or moral model in the later sessions (Brickman et al., 1982). The former models imply that clients are not responsible for solving their problems, and the latter models suggest that clients are their own agents of change. This shift of treatment models may help to achieve the two goals of ensuring clients' presence in counseling and increasing their sense of competency and hope simultaneously.

Finally, harmony plays a vital role in influencing East Asians' behaviors (Sodowsky et. al., 1994). Self-control, cooperation with others, shame, and obedience serve as means of maintaining this value. "Confrontation" means the vertical relationship (e.g., between East Asians international students and their elders or between these students and counselors) has been changed into a horizontal one, which is often not valued in the East Asian society. Therefore, conflict or confrontation techniques, rather than helping East Asian clients, may violate their cultural values and should be used only after a solid counseling relationship has been established (Ho, 1976).

Recommendations for Working With East Asian International Students

Recommendations for Counselors

To bring about positive outcomes, counselors need to familiarize themselves with those factors that contribute to a productive therapeutic relationship and East Asian clients' involvement in counseling. It is also important that counselors be able to translate their knowledge and awareness into behaviors in sessions. According to a model of multicultural counseling competencies (Roysircar, Arredondo, Fuertes, Ponterotto, & Toporek, 2003), we recommend the following:

Awareness

- Be aware of the counselor's own cultural values and how they are different from the East Asian client's cultural values.
- Recognize the importance of taking cultural factors (e.g., acculturation level, ethnic identity, worldviews) into account in case conceptualization.
- Be aware of how East Asian international students may respond to counseling techniques differently because of their cultural backgrounds.

Knowledge

- Become knowledgeable about histories and cultures of East Asian countries or identify resources to turn to when necessary.

- Be familiar with culture-bound syndromes and how East Asian clients manifest their psychological problems.
- Understand how East Asian clients' racial/ethnic identity may change as they gain experiences in the United States.
- Gain knowledge on issues (e.g., visa regulations, Student and Exchange Visitor Information System [SEVIS] of U.S. Immigration and Customs Enforcement) faced by international students in general and on the acculturation process that East Asian students may experience in particular.

Skills

- Help East Asian international students deal with stigma associated with seeking mental health services.
- Develop culturally sensitive counseling techniques that fit East Asian cultural values.
- Address possible differences on cultural values and communication styles between the counselor and East Asian client in a therapeutic way.
- Help East Asian international students identify their strengths and develop local social support systems.
- Make connections with community resources (e.g., interpreters, indigenous healers).
- Work effectively with faculty and staff members to offer assistance on different aspects of East Asian international students' adjustment difficulties.
- Develop and promote outreach programs (e.g., a conference on new visa regulations, job search interviews, and support group for international students' spouses).

Recommendations for Faculty

As mentioned previously, faculty members in U.S. higher education are generally open to ideas for individual initiative but are not typically directive or structured in ways that are helpful for East Asian international students. We suggest that a culture clash may exist when a faculty member expects students to take the initiative while students want direction. The following recommendations are directed toward counselor educators but are applicable to other disciplines as well. We recommend the following for faculty:

- Provide structured guidance initially to help East Asian international students feel "successful."
- Reward achievements (such as with financial aid/scholarship incentives).
- Clarify communications with students.
- Show an interest in the home culture of international students (e.g., learning common greetings and how to say "thank you" in East Asian students' languages).

- Begin with a parental role (authority, guidance) and then make a transition into a more equal or collaborative role.
- Develop system-oriented programs, such as sponsoring an International Forum to invite input of East Asian international students and organizing social activities to help students become familiar with U.S. culture.

Summary

This chapter focused on cultural values that influence East Asian international students' willingness to seek out counseling and their ability to benefit from such service. We discussed various factors associated with the adjustment and well-being of students from this population and their implications for assessment and counseling. Additionally, suggestions were provided for counselors to improve their awareness, knowledge, and skills in effectively working with East Asian international students, and recommendations were made for faculty interventions. In conclusion, counselors are encouraged to introduce these strategies as "working hypotheses" to avoid making overgeneralizations of these materials to the uniqueness that is presented with each client.

References

American Psychiatric Association. (1994). *Diagnostic and statistical manual of mental disorders* (4th ed.). Washington, DC: Author.

Arthur, N. (1997). Counselling issues with international students. *Canadian Journal of Counselling, 31,* 259-274.

Atkinson, D. R., & Gim, R. H. (1989). Asian-American cultural identity and attitudes toward mental health services. *Journal of Counseling Psychology, 36,* 209-212.

Brickman, P., Rabinowitz, V. C., Karuza, J., Coates, D., Cohn, E., & Kidder, L. (1982). Models of helping and coping. *American Psychologist, 37,* 368-384.

Brinson, J. A., & Kottler, J. (1995). International students in counseling: Some alternative models. *Journal of College Student Psychotherapy, 9,* 57-70.

Bullard, M. R. (2000, October). *Undiscussed linkages: Implications of Taiwan Straits security activity on global arms control and nonproliferation.* Monterey, CA: Center for Nonproliferation Studies, Monterey Institute of International Studies.

Cadieux, R. A., & Wehrly, B. (1986, Winter). Advising and counseling the international student. *New Directions for Student Services, 36,* 51-63.

Chen, Y. R., Brockner, J., & Chen, X. P. (2002). Individual–collective primacy and ingroup favoritism: Enhancement and protection effects. *Journal of Experimental Social Psychology, 38,* 482-491.

Chung, D. K. (1992). Asian cultural commonalities: A comparison with mainstream American culture. In D. K. Chung, K. Murase, & F. Ross-Sheriff (Eds.), *Social work practice with Asian Americans* (pp. 27-44). Newbury Park, CA: Sage.

Collins, T. M., Simons, M., Bamford, S., & Blazes, J. (1994, April). *A multicultural counseling practicum on a majority White campus*. Paper presented at the American Counseling Association Annual Convention, Minneapolis, MN.

Corey, G., Corey, M. S., & Callanan, P. (1997). *Issues and ethics in the helping professions* (5th ed.). Pacific Grove, CA: Brooks/Cole.

Dillard, J. M., & Chisolm, G. B. (1983). Counseling the international student in a multicultural context. *Journal of College Student Personnel, 24,* 101-105.

Diller, J. V. (1999). *Cultural diversity: A primer for the human services*. Belmont, CA: Wadsworth.

Hayes, R. L., & Lin, H. (1994). Coming to America: Developing social support systems for international students. *Journal of Multicultural Counseling and Development, 22,* 7-16.

Ho, M. K. (1976). Social work with Asian Americans. *Social Casework, 57,* 195-201.

Hong, G. K., & Ham, M. D. (2001). *Psychotherapy and counseling with Asian American clients: A practical guide*. Thousand Oaks, CA: Sage.

Hwang, K. K. (1987). Face and favor: The Chinese power game. *American Journal of Sociology, 92,* 944-974.

Hwang, K. K. (1997). Guanxi and mientze: Conflict resolution in Chinese society. *International Communication Studies VII: 1,* 17–42.

Jacobson, J. (2003, November 7). Foreign-student enrollment stagnates: New security measures lead to declines among Muslim countries. *Chronicle of Higher Education, Section: International, 50*(11), A1. Retrieved June 19, 2006, from http://www.admin.colostate.edu/caucus/documents/enrollmentstagnates. pdf#search='Foreign%20student%20enrollment%20stagnates'

Kaczmarek, P. G., Matlock, G., Merta, R., Ames, M. H., & Ross, M. (1994). An assessment of international college students adjustment. *International Journal for the Advancement of Counselling, 17,* 241-247.

Kim, B. S. K., Atkinson, D. R., & Yang, P. H. (1999). The Asian Values Scale: Development, factor analysis, validation, and reliability. *Journal of Counseling Psychology, 46,* 342-352.

Kim, J. (1981). Process of Asian American identity development: A study of Japanese American women's perceptions of their struggle to achieve personal identities as Americans of Asian ancestry (Doctoral dissertation, University of Massachusetts, 1981). *Dissertation Abstracts International, 42,* 1551.

Kim, U., Triandis, H. C., Kâğitçibaşi, Ç., Choi, S. C., & Yoon, G. (Eds.). (1994). *Individualism and collectivism: Theory, method, and applications*. Thousand Oaks, CA: Sage.

Lefley, H. P. (1989). Empirical support for credibility and giving in cross-cultural psychotherapy. *American Psychologist, 44,* 1163.

Lewthwaite, M. (1996). A study of international students' perspectives on cross-cultural adaptation. *International Journal for the Advancement of Counselling, 19,* 167-185.

Lopez, S. J., Snyder, C. R., & Rasmussen, H. N. (2003). Striking a vital balance: Developing a complementary focus on human weakness and strength through positive psychological assessment. In S. J. Lopez & C. R. Snyder (Eds.), *Positive psychological assessment: A handbook of models and measures* (pp. 3-20). Washington, DC: American Psychological Association.

Mori, S. (2000). Addressing the mental health concerns of international students. *Journal of Counseling & Development, 78,* 137-144.

Myers, D. G. (1996). *Social psychology* (5th ed.). New York: McGraw Hill.

National Center for Education Statistics. (2001). *Digest of education statistics, 2001.* Washington, DC: Institute of Education Sciences, U.S. Department of Education.

Niksch, L. A. (2005). North Korea's nuclear weapons program. In *CRS Issue Brief for Congress* (No. IB91141). Washington, DC: Congressional Research Service, The Library of Congress.

Paniagua, F. A. (1994). *Assessing and treating culturally diverse clients: A practical guide.* Thousand Oaks, CA: Sage.

Pedersen, P. B. (1991). Counseling international students. *The Counseling Psychologist, 19,* 10-58.

Root, M. P. (1985). Guidelines for facilitating therapy with Asian American clients. *Psychotherapy, 22,* 349-356.

Roysircar, G., Arredondo, P., Fuertes, J. N., Ponterotto, J. G., & Toporek, R. L. (2003). *Multicultural counseling competencies 2003.* Alexandria, VA: Association for Multicultural Counseling and Development.

Sandhu, D. S. (1997). Psychocultural profiles of Asian and Pacific Islander Americans: Implications for counseling and psychotherapy. *Journal of Multicultural Counseling and Development, 25,* 7-22.

Sedlacek, W. E. (2004). *Beyond the big test: Noncognitive assessment in higher education.* San Francisco: Jossey-Bass.

Sheu, H. B., & Lent, R. W. (in press). Development and initial validation of the Multicultural Counseling Self-Efficacy Scale-Racial Diversity Form. *Psychotherapy Theory, Research, Practice, Training.*

Sheu, H. B., & Sedlacek, W. E. (2004). An exploratory study of help-seeking attitudes and coping strategies among college students by race and gender. *Measurement and Evaluation in Counseling and Development, 37,* 130-143.

Sheu, H. B., & Sedlacek, W. E. (2005, April). *Effects of socioeconomic status and diversity orientation on social adjustment and life satisfaction by race.* Paper presented at the Annual Convention of the American Educational Research Association, Montréal, Quebec, Canada.

Snyder, C. R., Michael, S. T., & Cheavens, J. S. (1999). Hope as a psychotherapeutic foundation of common factors, placebo, and expectancies. In M. A. Hubble, B. L. Duncan, & S. D. Miller (Eds.), *The heart and soul of change: What works in therapy* (pp. 179-200). Washington, DC: American Psychological Association.

Sodowsky, G. R., Kwan, K. K., & Pannu, R. (1995). Ethnic identity of Asians in the United States. In J. G. Ponterotto, J. M. Casas, L. A. Suzuki, & C. M. Alexander

(Eds.), *Handbook of multicultural counseling* (pp. 123-154). Thousand Oaks, CA: Sage.

Sodowsky, G. R., Maguire, K., Johnson, P., Ngumba, W., & Kohles, R. (1994). World views of White American, mainland Chinese, Taiwanese, and African students: An investigation into between-group differences. *Journal of Cross-Cultural Psychology, 29,* 309-324.

Sue, D. W., & Sue, D. (2003). *Counseling the culturally diverse: Theory and practice* (4th ed.). New York: Wiley.

Sue, S. (1996). Measurement, testing, and ethnic bias: Can solutions be found? In G. R. Sodowsky & J. C. Impara (Eds.), *Multicultural assessment in counseling and clinical psychology* (pp. 7-36). Lincoln, NE: Buros Institute of Mental Measurements.

Sue, S., & Zane, N. (1987). The role of culture and cultural techniques in psychotherapy: A critique and reformulation. *American Psychologist, 42,* 37-45.

Surdam, J. C., & Collins, J. R. (1984). Adaptation of international students: A cause for concern. *Journal of College Student Personnel, 25,* 240-245.

Tracey, T. J., Leong, F. T. L., & Glidden, C. (1986). Help seeking and problem perception among Asian Americans. *Journal of Counseling Psychology, 33,* 331-336.

Uba, L. (1994). *Asian Americans: Personality patterns, identity, and mental health.* New York: Guilford Press.

Yeh, C. J., & Inose, M. (2002). Difficulties and coping strategies of Chinese, Japanese, and Korean immigrant students. *Adolescence, 37,* 69-82.

Yeh, C. J., & Inose, M. (2003). International students' reported English fluency, social support satisfaction, and social connectedness as predictors of acculturative stress. *Counselling Psychology Quarterly, 16,* 15-28.

Zhang, W. (1994). American counseling in the mind of a Chinese counselor. *Journal of Multicultural Counseling and Development, 22,* 79-85.

Zhang, N., & Dixon, D. N. (2003). Acculturation and attitudes of Asian international students toward seeking psychological help. *Journal of Multicultural Counseling and Development, 31,* 205-222.

Chapter 10

Counseling South Asian International Students

Farah A. Ibrahim and Michael Anthony Ingram

One international Asian population that has received increasing attention in the counseling literature is South Asians (Inman, Constantine, & Ladany, 1999; Inman, Ladany, Constantine, & Morano, 2001; Tewari, Inman, & Sandhu, 2003). This is a recent development, since in 1997 Das and Kemp reported that hardly any literature existed that addressed this population. This chapter describes various issues counselors and psychologists need to consider when counseling South Asian international students. The chapter focuses on the geography, history, and cultures of South Asia; examines the commonalities between South Asian and other international students; compares South Asian culture with U.S. culture; presents the unique issues South Asian international students may face while studying in the United States; addresses process and relationship issues in counseling South Asian international students; and provides a case scenario. This chapter does not address general information on international students because that information is addressed in several other chapters in this book.

Geographical Boundaries, History, and Cultures of South Asia

South Asia, originally called the Indian subcontinent, includes Bangladesh, Bhutan, India, Maldives, Nepal, Pakistan, Myanmar (Burma), Nepal, Sri Lanka (Ceylon), and Tibet (Ibrahim, Ohnishi, & Sandhu, 1997; Sinha, 1995). The cultures, languages, religions, belief systems, and economic structures are varied in these countries. The countries of South Asian have some of the oldest civilizations, and beliefs and values inherent in these cultures cannot be attributed to one religion or cultural base (Ibrahim et al., 1997). To put it in a historical perspective, many of these countries have some of the most famous historical and cultural backgrounds, such as the Indus Valley civilization that occurred 6000–7000 BC (Bharati, 1985). Additionally, Buddhism, Hinduism, Jainism, and Sikhism emerged in India (Das & Kemp, 1997). The Indian subcontinent was overrun by armies from Asia, the Caucasus Mountains, Greece, Arab Muslims, Mughals, and the British. All these influences are visible in modified forms as acculturation occurred over the centuries. Most of the South Asian countries have a legacy of British colonialism and have an administrative structure similar to the British system. All of these countries are poor, although India is now gaining prominence as an upcoming world economic power (Elliott, 2006; Sinha, 1995). The literacy rates are 20%–30%, except in Sri Lanka, where it is 85%. Life expectancy is between 40 and 50 years, except in Pakistan, where it is 52 years, and Sri Lanka, where it is 66 years (Mishra, 1986). South Asian identity is complex and complicated, given the range of countries, sociopolitical histories, religions, and other cultural influences. These nations remain mostly agrarian, except for the sudden explosion of high-tech industry in India (Bhanot, 1999; Elliott, 2006).

All over Asia, including South Asia, hard work and stoicism are revered and respected (Ibrahim et al., 1997). In addition, the societal and familial structure is lineal–hierarchical. Elders are very important in the lives of South Asians. They provide advice and guidance to all the generations; they are the counselors and mentors for the young. Teachers are another group that is highly respected and revered. Recently, since the Islamic fundamentalism movement began in Iran, many South Asian Muslim countries place religious leaders also in a highly revered position (Mohammad Arif, 2002). Religious leaders help settle family, marital, and community disputes according to religious laws. Most South Asian nations share a history of Hinduism or Buddhism. However, in Pakistan and Bangladesh, originally parts of India, while the original religions were Hinduism and Buddhism, Islam is now practiced, and although the cultural traditions reflect Hindu practices, the religious practices are Islamic (Moghni, 1987).

In Islamic South Asian countries, the relational system is patriarchal and follows the Judeo-Christian-Muslim belief that man (not in the generic sense) was made in the image of God and that women were created from Adam's rib and therefore secondary. Also the belief prevails that women, similar to the myth of Eve, can and do mislead men. Therefore, women must be supervised and protected. Virginity for women is very important if they hope to get married and have a family in these cultural systems. The overarching assumption underlying the status of women in South Asia is Confucian; that is, a woman belongs to a man, first to her father, then to her husband or brother, and finally to her son, although in Hinduism women were given equal power, as reported in historical events. However, as the subcontinent was repeatedly invaded by patriarchal outsiders, the culture has undergone change and the status of women is no longer equal (Bumiller, 1991; Ibrahim, 1994). Theoretically, the mother is accorded great respect, and children are told to revere her since "heaven lies under her feet." Gender roles in South Asia are clearly demarcated, with men talking care of matters outside the home and women in control of the home front, with regional and national variations according to the local culture, religion, and sociopolitical history. Children in these societies are welcomed and celebrated with the hope of bringing future honor and wealth to a family. Male children are highly valued as they are the income providers and caretakers of the parents and of unmarried sisters, aunts, and other female members of the family (Bumiller, 1991; Ibrahim et al., 1997). Males even when young enjoy a privileged position in South Asian families.

Shame and honor are the main socializing agents used in most South Asian and Asian cultures (Ibrahim et al., 1997). In South Asian culture, as in all Asian cultures, a dishonorable act of one family member creates shame for the whole family. In arranging marriages or accepting a marriage proposal, several generations of the family are scrutinized for shame, dishonor, mental and physical illness, and the income potential of originally the groom, and in the current economic atmosphere, of both the bride and the groom. Gender roles are also very clearly defined, and dishonor and shame can result from acting in culturally inconsistent gender behavior. Most South Asian societies accept three genders: male, female, and transsexual. Acceptance of homosexuality varies according to the specific culture, and even by region within the same country. Overtly accepted lifestyle is heterosexual, although a "don't ask, don't tell" philosophy prevails in South Asia, primarily because of dishonor and shame issues. Another characteristic of South Asia that significantly influences behavior is fatalism. Most events in a person's life are considered ordained and therefore accepted as fate (*kismet* in the Indian subcontinent). This perspective helps people cope with adversities and difficulties without blame. However, harmful acts are not accepted as part of *kismet,* and shame and dishonor follow these actions along with social or judicial retribution. Social class, similar to the caste system, is considered sacrosanct, and people do not generally navigate in social circles that are above or below them in terms of social class (Sachau, 1993). Of course, in Hinduism the caste system is quite hidebound and has been the source of significant oppression (Elliott & Dowson, 1996; Mistry, 1996; Sachau, 1993). Education and material wealth do, however, tend to create a break in rigid class rules. Thus, hard work and education are revered in South Asia.

Several unique languages are spoken in each country, and each culture has its own cultural traditions. However, underlying all the cultures, beliefs, and assumptions are Hindu culture and elements of Confucianism. The rituals of everyday life reflect these assumptions regardless of the religion practiced (Ibrahim et al., 1997). The ultimate goal of self-development in this cultural system is to be one with the cosmos. Denial of lower order needs is encouraged; lack of such denial is tolerated at earlier developmental stages. Bharati (1985) noted people who identify the self as the senses are either aesthetes at their best, or psychopaths at their worst. People who consider the intellect as the self are scholars, thinkers, or scientists at their best, and paranoid schizophrenics at their worst. The underlying message in South Asian philosophy is to lead a life free of material needs, because these needs trap people in unacceptable behavior and take them off their course of inner development. The ultimate goal of life is to overcome challenges or tests and to remain a compassionate person to ultimately achieve oneness with the divine.

Similarities and Differences Between South Asian and U.S. Culture

Takaki (1989) contended that Asian and Western cultures are so different that Asians and European Americans will never be able to come together in terms of cultural understanding and acceptance, similar to Kipling's (Kipling & Cornell, 1999) famous verse "the East is East, the West is West, and never the twain shall meet." It is helpful to consider this perspective from a worldview or beliefs, values, and assumptions perspective (Ibrahim, 1999). Table 10.1 outlines the generic worldviews of both cultures using Ibrahim and Owen's (1994) empirical research on worldview and Ibrahim's (1999) existential worldview and cultural identity theory, along with information from literature on U.S. mainstream and South Asian beliefs and worldviews. Given the limited research and information on counseling South Asians international students, this chapter presents a model for working with South Asians based on information gleaned from available literature on South Asian culture and issues international students face when they go abroad to study.

Commonalities Among South Asians and Other International Students

During the 2000–2001 academic year, the top 10 countries of origin for international students included China, India, Japan, Korea, Taiwan, Canada, Indonesia, and Mexico (Princeton Review, n.d.). Although, the presence of international students is essential for understanding global diversity as a part of the college experience, it takes a toll on international students if appropriate services are not available to address their adjustment needs. The United States has been the primary destination for international students and scholars for almost 50 years (American Immigration Law Foundation, 2003). These students come with definitive goals for achieving educational success; however, they may not have carefully considered the challenges the adjustment process entails (Trice, 2004).

To illustrate, research data suggest that South Asian international students, along with other international students, experience a significant number of ac-

Table 10.1

Similarities and Differences in South Asian and
U.S. Worldviews: Beliefs, Values, and Assumptions

Category	South Asian Culture	U.S. Culture
Human nature	A combination of good and bad	A combination of good and bad
Nature	Living in harmony with nature	Nature can be subjugated and controlled
	Accept the power of nature	Living in harmony with nature
Social	Lineal–hierarchical	Individualistic
	Collateral–mutual	Collateral–mutual
Time	Past and future	Present and future
Activity	Being-in-becoming	Doing
	Being	Being
	Doing	Being-in-becoming

Note. Developed from Ibrahim (1999), Ibrahim and Owen (1994), and a review of the literature on South Asian values. The value categories are derived from Kluckhohn's (1951) research on universal values.

ademic, social, and psychological stressors as they attempt to adjust and pursue their educational pursuits (Poyrazli, 2005). Although many of these stressors are in response to the same issues and concerns that their U.S. counterparts experience (i.e., feelings of sadness, loneliness, anxiety, fear, and confusion), South Asian international students also face additional adjustment challenges of living in a foreign country and speaking English as a second language. South Asian international students and other international students face significant adjustment problems. These can range from homesickness, loneliness, culture shock, language problems, adaptation to the United States, and acculturating to the academic system, as well as all the other stressors that students are prey to in the United States (Leong & Chou, 2002). Given the cultural differences between the East and the West (Takaki, 1989), South Asian international students, along with students from the East and cultures that are not Western, specifically face the following:

- Learning to live and exist in a culture that is quite different (Khoo & Abu-Rasain, 1994; Leong & Chou, 2002)
- Learning new customs for daily life in the United States and trying to adapt (Komiya & Eells, 2001; Nilsson & Anderson, 2004)
- Learning new university procedures and regulations and being far from friends and family (Khoo & Abu-Rasain, 1994; Nilsson & Anderson, 2004)
- Dealing with financial issues and difficulty in social interactions with U.S. students (Leong & Chou, 2002; Jacob, 2001; Ragin & Lennon, 2004; Trice, 2004).

These adjustment issues may affect academic success, psychological well-being, and the educational institutions' ability to retain these students (Barratt & Huba, 1994; Poyrazli, Arbona, Nora, McPherson, & Pisecco, 2002). Al-Mubarak's (2000) study showed that adjustment problems experienced by students from different cultures or regions of the world varied, specifically for African and Asian international students. The study revealed the most troublesome adjustment problems encountered by the international students were, in order of importance, financial aid first, then placement services, followed by social–personal. In addition, African international students encountered more difficulties in total adjustment and in more concern areas than the other participant groups in the study. Conversely, the Asian international students in the study expressed the greatest difficulties in the English language area. Students who were self-supported had more concerns than students who were financially supported by their families. The findings also showed that students who were supported by their families experienced more difficulties.

The adjustment process affects the long-term psychological well-being of all international students, including South Asians (Poyrazli, 2005). We agree with Arthur (2004) that given the global economy and the shrinking of the globe, there will be increasing numbers of people traveling abroad to study. Given the stress of sojourning and trying to be successful in another culture, it is critical that host cultures are prepared with the appropriate psychological assistance to reduce stress for international students. Although South Asian international students have much in common with students from other countries, they are also quite dissimilar in their cultural beliefs, daily life activities, and rituals from both U.S. and other international students. To understand these cultural dimensions, it is critical to understand the home cultures of South Asians.

Interventions With South Asian International Students

As noted earlier, the South Asian cultures are diverse and historically date back to 6000–7000 BC (Elliott & Dowson, 1996; Ibrahim et al., 1997). In many instances, the primary task that confronts the counselor is the ability to understand the cultural identity and the worldview of the client and to do an appropriate assessment prior to an intervention (Ibrahim, 1999). When working with international students, it is essential for counselors to recognize and understand all the variables recommended for transcultural clients. Although the literature on counseling international students repeatedly encourages counselors to understand the stressors faced by them (Leong & Chou, 2002), specific models for assessment and intervention that may be helpful in serving specific populations do not exist. Dana (2005) presented a detailed assessment model for cross-cultural counseling that we adapt and incorporate into the previous models presented by Ibrahim, Ohnishi, and Wilson (1994) and Lonner and Ibrahim (2002, in press).

Assessment Strategy for Effective Cross-Cultural Counseling With South Asian International Students

Given the cultural differences between South Asia and the United States, it is imperative that an appropriate assessment be conducted to understand the South Asian client. First, the assessment needs to establish where the client is from in South Asia. As noted earlier, South Asia is very diverse, with many cultural traditions, sociopolitical histories, religions, and languages. This will provide the background needed to assist the counselor in understanding the client (Ibrahim, 1999). The second step is to identify the client's beliefs, values, assumptions (worldview), and the cultural assumptions of the client's primary cultural group and the national cultural assumptions (Ibrahim, 1999). The third step is to understand the client's cultural identity, which includes gender, sexual orientation, ethnicity, religion, languages spoken, social class or caste (if the client is from India), educational level of the family and the client, region of the country the client grew up in, significant relationships in the family and social group, and, finally, the client's ability or disability status. A significant aspect of this assessment must address dominant or nondominant group identification in the home culture, because this variable is significant in addressing stress. The identified cultural identity and worldview must be considered against the backdrop of the client's larger culture to identify how closely the client aligns him- or herself with his or her primary culture (Ibrahim et al., 1994; Lonner & Ibrahim, 2002, in press). It is also significant to understand if the client is from a religious group that the dominant group identifies with in his or her home culture (e.g., a Zoroastrian from Pakistan). Once this part has been clarified, it is important to look at Table 10.1 to understand how close or distant the client's assumptions are from mainstream U.S. beliefs, values, and assumptions (Johnson, Wall, Guanipa, Terry-Guyer, & Velasquez, 2002; Oetting & Beauvais, 1990–1991). This will provide an index of acculturation to U.S. culture. This is the fourth step in the assessment process.

International students from South Asia may be highly acculturated or may be completely unacculturated to mainstream U.S. culture. As a result of European and British occupation and control, most of the countries of South Asia were exposed to Western culture. South Asians understand European cultures, especially Anglo Saxon assumptions. Also, in the last 40 years, some international students may have been exposed to U.S. culture through the American schools that flourished in several South Asian countries to educate U.S. diplomats, sojourners, U.N. workers, and business persons' and professionals' children. These schools usually admit local children who can afford the tuition and are preparing for higher education in the United States. In addition, several students may have lived in the United States as children when their parents were students at U.S. universities or when their parents were employed as diplomats or professionals. The fifth step is to become aware of the generational exposure to U.S. culture and understanding of the system (i.e., acculturation level).

Some students may be the first generation making it to higher education, with no exposure to U.S. culture except Hollywood productions and American television shows. Each level of acculturation requires a different intervention. Researchers and theorists consider acculturation to be a major moderator variable in adaptation and perceived stress (Leong & Chou, 2002; Sue & Morishima, 1982). It is evident that the more distant the international student's culture from U.S. culture, the more stressful the adaptation (Kagan & Cohen, 1990). It is also critical to recognize that most international students are planning to return home, so the goal of counseling should be to create a bicultural acculturation adaptive model that will help the student negotiate American culture, attain his or her goals, and be able to return home. Counseling can be a great help in this process and in helping international students to attain their goals and prepare to reenter their culture at the completion of their studies (Pedersen, 1991).

Recommendations for Counseling South Asian International Students

It is generally accepted that most international students, and especially students from collectivistic cultures, do not use traditional counseling services (i.e., individual and group counseling; Leong & Chou, 2002). It is important for counselors to understand that, coming from South Asia with shame as the major socializing force that guides and shapes behavior, the South Asian international student's lack of ability to handle intense stress is seen as shameful, and in most cases counseling is perceived by the unacculturated South Asian sojourner as needed by people with mental illness. Therefore, when attempting to counsel international students from South Asia, it would be useful for counselors to focus on the (a) strategies for coping on a college campus and (b) ways to provide relevant survival and success information, such as pointing out cultural differences and how to negotiate these differences (Furnham & Bochner, 1982; Jacob, 2001). Focusing on these may assist in the process of introducing the international students to the many help-providing resources on campus and aid in the development of trust with service providers.

It is also accepted that most traditional South Asian societies tend to be collectivistic, patriarchal, and agrarian (Bhanot, 1999). Given these background variables, and the South Asian international student's specific cultural identity and worldview, erroneous assumptions are often drawn. One of the assumptions about collectivistic systems is international students from these cultures need a "directive" process (Sodowsky, 1991; Yau, Sue, & Hayden, 1992). This assumption has usually been misunderstood to imply the value of "telling" the client what solutions to choose or advising the client (Sodowsky, 1991; Yau et al., 1992). South Asians prefer dialogue without judgment or specific direction. Using metaphor, myth, and poetry, examples from the current literature, media, and stories of empowerment and survival from the international student's cultural context to make a point are much more effective than advising or "telling." Directive in the sense of being "active" and "fully engaged" with the client is helpful for South Asian clients. In addition, international students from this cultural system have great respect for teachers and helpers; therefore, it is important to recognize that they will not be able to directly confront the counselor when the counselor makes erroneous assumptions. The client will simply not return; because South Asian clients are extremely polite, confrontation as understood in U.S. culture would be impossible for them. Empathic responding (Ingram & Nakazawa, 2003) and advanced accurate empathy (Ivey & Ivey, 2002) in the earlier stages of relationship building are critical to developing trust with clients from this population (Ibrahim et al., 1997).

The focus on self-development (Bharati, 1985; Ibrahim et al., 1997; Kakar, 1991) contributes to independent thinking; however, behavior still remains within cultural bounds. In working with South Asian international students, counselors need to understand their fiercely independent style of thinking in a very controlled and controlling society (Bharati, 1985; Ibrahim et al., 1997; Kakar, 1991; Sinha, 1995). This presents an interesting paradox that confronts a naïve counselor working with South Asian clients. The most ethical and professionally valid emphasis would be to help the clients in clarifying their worldview (beliefs, values, and assumptions) and cultural identity, to help clients identify which values are negotiable and which are not, and then to confront the problem or issue at hand to resolve the concerns brought to counseling. The counselor will have to take responsibility to remain vigilant regarding client cultural needs and be careful not to impose his or her own assumptions or rush the process along without fully exploring how different goals and solutions would affect the clients' lives in terms of peace of mind and comfort with their own culture while negotiating U.S. mainstream culture.

In understanding worldview and cultural identity of South Asian international students, counselors need to know the following basic beliefs and values:

1. Self-respect, dignity, and self-control: these three variables are a part of socialization for all South Asians;
2. Respect for family/filial piety;
3. Awareness and respect for community;
4. Fatalism;
5. Humility;
6. Along with respect for hierarchy, a high need for egalitarian and respectful relations between and among all age groups;
7. Individualism (i.e., individual control of one's destiny);
8. Success, which is seen as important but not at the cost of one's spirituality; most South Asians are very spiritual beings and will not jeopardize their spiritual journey in this material world (Ibrahim et al., 1997).

Implications for counseling are very specific given this value system. Primarily, South Asian international students will not own any goal or outcome that was not generated by them. They require a mutually respectful relationship; even though there is respect for older people, teachers, and helpers, this does not preclude the premise for respect among communicators. Knowledge of the student's acculturation level to U.S. culture and strength of connection to his or her own culture are important in establishing a therapeutic relationship, appropriate goals, and process (Nilsson & Anderson, 2004; Sandhu & Asrabadi, 1998). It is important to understand the client's spiritual identity before goals and outcome are established. Recognition of the client's age and stage of life in planning goals and outcome for counseling is also important. In addition, it is essential to recognize that the client comes from a high-context cultural setting and is very skilled at reading nonverbal cues (Hall, 1976). Because the counselor is experiencing difficulty understanding the client does not imply that the client is not reading nonverbal cues to understand the counselor; as communication is mostly nonverbal in South Asian culture, the client is adept at reading judgment, rejection, lack of respect, and so on.

Counselors must recognize and understand the role of humility in South Asian cultural identity, which is sometimes misunderstood as low self-concept in the West. Using a relational style, the counselor and client can explore and understand each other's worldview; this will increase trust and can help South Asian international students explore their worldview, cultural identity, or acculturation level to their own and U.S mainstream culture (Ibrahim, 1991, 1999; Ibrahim et al., 1994). Humility emerges in a behavioral context as never talking about personal accomplishments or assets. The counselor will have to recognize this and check the validity of the assumptions being made with South Asian clients during the narratives that clients engage in as they talk about their lives, challenges, and significant events. In general, in South Asia people cannot boast about their achievements or assets; others, such as family members and friends, are supposed to present these credentials. Because individual counseling does not allow for this premise, it is important to listen very carefully to the dialogue and confirm strengths and assets as they emerge.

Another significant issue that has been identified is national, racial, or psychological identity (Cross, 1995; Helms, 1995). This can be a component of worldview and may have a much greater significance for the client as it actually defines his or her worldview. Phinney (1990) addressed the issue of ethnic identity as being central for most people. Most cultures of the world separate themselves on the basis of ethnic identity, and this is a key aspect of identity for South Asians. However, when South Asians come to the United States, it is the first time in their lives that they are asked to define themselves racially. South Asian international students suffer from these ascribed definitions and as being seen as less than White Americans. The politics of race appears to have a deleterious effect on most international students who are not classified as White (Leong & Chou, 2002; Sodowsky & Plake, 1992). Students from Africa, Asia, and South America tend to report more prejudice directed at them than European international students (Sodowsky & Plake, 1992). One of the tasks facing the counselor is to help the international students reintegrate their identity as they perceive themselves, and empower them to not allow U.S. culture to redefine their identity. Whether the client's conception is a racial, ethnic, or national identity, it must be solidified, and the client needs to learn to keep his or her self-definition secure by setting boundaries on their self-definition, that is, not allowing others to define him or her, except as "international sojourners/students."

Case Scenario

A young South Asian male, Rahul, comes to the university counseling center with a number of somatic and psychological symptoms, stomach distress, and lack of sleep. Rahul is a high achiever and has been sent by his government to earn graduate degrees in computer science. Rahul is a Christian in a country that is predominantly Buddhist or Hindu. He identifies with the West through his religious beliefs and has been looking forward to studying in a society in which his religion will not automatically classify him as a "second-class citizen," but he has been disappointed and angry at his treatment by his American Christian peers.

The counselor adopts relationship-building strategies, along with a focus on cultural sensitivity to Rahul's culture (mutual respect, empathic responding, and advanced accurate empathy). A worldview and cultural identity assessment is conducted in which the counselor and the client both participate, making their values, beliefs, and assumptions transparent. In identifying the client's primary culture, the counselor learns that, as a Christian, Rahul is a religious minority in his country. The counselor establishes Rahul's acculturation level to U.S. culture.

The counselor learns that Rahul does not identify with the larger culture of his country, since he has always belonged to a nondominant group and is marginalized. Rahul's religious beliefs govern his value system; however, culturally, he behaves in a manner consistent with his culture of origin, although he does not feel he identifies with it. After all the issues are explored, the primary concern that emerges as a focus in counseling is Rahul's treatment as a person of color by his faculty and peers.

Coming from an ethnically monolithic culture, Rahul has never perceived himself as a "person of color." In addition, he has become very conscious of the color hierarchies that govern U.S. society and the stereotypes that are ascribed to ethnic and racial nondominant groups in this society. He feels immense shame as being seen as less than White people and the ascriptions that may be assigned to him in U.S. society as a "person of color." He is also enraged by such characterizations and feels denigrated by his Christian peers in the United States. Unfortunately, he was not aware of the politics of race in the United States and its implications for him as a South Asian.

After goal-setting, the counselor uses cognitive–behavioral strategies to help Rahul identify his thoughts about racism, the racial ascriptions he is assigning to himself, and strategies to help him clarify his own identity and to choose his identity as a national of a South Asian country rather than accepting a new definition imposed on him by others. Strategies on how to define himself and educate his peers and faculty about his identity are also explored. Rahul's conceptions of race and ethnicity are identified as egalitarian, and he is asked to apply his own beliefs to his identity and not let others define him.

The most difficult task for the counselor is to help Rahul come to terms with his distress over his Christian brethren in the United States and their inability to see him as one of them. This distress had been a part of his identity since early childhood because of his marginalized status as a religious minority, and his dream to come to a Christian country and finally feel okay about himself is crushed. The counselor encourages Rahul to explore churches of different denominations and find one that focuses on fraternity and brotherhood. He is encouraged to take charge of the situation by creating a community for himself during his sojourn that will support and reinforce him as a human being and as a follower of Jesus Christ. He is also empowered to focus on his strengths, his intellect, his character, and his spirituality to help him cope with the challenges of color hierarchies in the United States. As the counseling process comes to a close, Rahul has once again found his equilibrium and is functioning well as an advanced graduate student.

Summary

This chapter presented an overview of concerns that international students face in general and issues that confront South Asian international students in particular. We discussed an assessment strategy to help clarify the South Asian international student's identity, worldview, and acculturation level to his or her own culture and the host culture. Recommendations for counseling South Asian international students were presented, along with a case study.

References

Al-Mubarak, A. H. (2000). Adjustment problems, coping methods, and choice of helpers of international students attending a large Pennsylvania university. *Dissertation Abstracts International, 61*(1-A), 94.

American Immigration Law Foundation. (2003). Foreign students on campus: An asset to our nation. *Immigration Policy and Focus, 2.* Retrieved August 23, 2005, from http://www.ailf.org/ipc/ipf0203.asp

Arthur, N. M. (2004). *Counseling international students: Clients from around the world.* New York: Kluwer Academic/Plenum.

Barratt, M. F., & Huba, M. E. (1994). Factors related to international undergraduate student adjustment in an American community. *College Student Journal, 28,* 422-435.

Bhanot, M. (1999, August). Challenges to regional cooperation in South Asia: A new perspective. *OJPCR: The Online Journal of Peace and Conflict Resolution, 2.3.* Retrieved September 12, 2005, from http://www.trinstitute.org/ojpcr

Bharati, A. (1985). The self in Hindu thought and action. In A. J. Marsella, G. Devos, & F. L. K. Hsu (Eds.), *Culture and self: Asian and Western perspectives* (pp. 185-230). New York: Tavistock.

Bumiller, E. (1991). *May you be the mother of a hundred sons: A journey among the women of India.* New York: Knopf.

Cross, W. E., Jr. (1995). The psychology of nigrescence. In J. G. Ponterotto. J. M. Casas, L. A. Suzuki, & C. M. Alexander (Eds.), *Handbook of multicultural counseling* (pp. 93-122). Thousand Oaks, CA: Sage.

Dana, R. H. (2005). *Multicultural assessment: Principles, applications and examples.* Mahwah, NJ: Erlbaum.

Das, A. J., & Kemp, S. E. (1997). Between two worlds: Counseling South Asian Americans. *Journal of Multicultural Counseling and Development, 25,* 23-34.

Elliot, M. (2006, June 26). India awakens. *Time,* pp. 36-49.

Elliot, M., & Dowson, J. (1996). *The history of India as told by its own historians* (Vol. II). New Delhi: Low Price Publications.

Furnham, A., & Bochner, S. (1982). Social difficulty in a foreign culture: An empirical analysis of culture shock. In S. Bochner (Ed.), *Cultures in contact* (pp. 161-198). New York: Pergamon.

Hall, E. T. (1976). *Beyond culture.* New York: Doubleday.

Helms, J. E. (1995). An update of Helms's White and people of color racial identity models. In J. G. Ponterotto, J. M. Casas, L. A. Suzuki, & C. M. Alexander (Eds.), *Handbook of multicultural counseling* (pp. 181-198). Thousand Oaks, CA: Sage.

Ibrahim, F. A. (1991). Contribution of cultural worldview to generic counseling and development. *Journal of Counseling & Development, 70,* 13-19.

Ibrahim, F. A. (1994). Suicidal behavior in Asian-American women. In S. S. Canetto & D. Lester (Eds.), *Women and suicide* (pp. 144-156). New York: Springer/Verlag.

Ibrahim, F. A. (1999). Transcultural counseling: Existential world view theory and cultural identity: Transcultural applications. In J. McFadden (Ed.), *Transcultural counseling* (2nd ed., pp. 23-57). Alexandria, VA: American Counseling Association.

Ibrahim, F. A., Ohnishi, H., & Sandhu, D. (1997). Asian-American identity development: South Asian Americans. *Journal of Multicultural Counseling and Development, 25,* 34-50.

Ibrahim, F. A., Ohnishi, H., & Wilson, R. (1994). Career counseling in a pluralistic society. *Journal of Career Assessment, 2,* 276-288.

Ibrahim, F. A., & Owen, S. V. (1994). Factor analytic structure of the Scale to Assess World View©. *Current Psychology, 13,* 201-209.

Ingram, M., & Nakazawa, M. (2003). Community college counselors: Developing empathy through sociocultural poetry. *Community College Journal of Research and Practice, 27,* 485-493.

Inman, A. G., Constantine, M. G., & Ladany, N. (1999). Cultural value conflict: An examination of Asian Indian women's bicultural experience. In D. S. Sandhu (Ed.), *Asian and Pacific Islander Americans: Issues and concerns for counseling and psychotherapy* (pp. 31-41). Commack, NY: Nova Science.

Inman A. G., Ladany, N., Constantine, M. G., & Morano, C. K. (2001). Development and preliminary validation of the cultural values conflict scale for South Asian women. *Journal of Counseling Psychology, 48,* 17-27.

Ivey, A. E., & Ivey, M. B. (2002). *Intentional interviewing and counseling.* Pacific Grove, CA: Brooks/Cole

Jacob, E. J. (2001). Using counseling training and collaborative programming strategies in working with international students. *Journal of Multicultural Counseling and Development, 29,* 30-42.

Johnson, M. L., Wall, T. L., Guanipa, C., Terry-Guyer, L., & Velasquez, R. J. (2002). The psychometric qualities of the Orthogonal Cultural Identification Scale in Asian Americans. *Journal of Multicultural Counseling and Development, 30,* 181-191.

Kagan, H., & Cohen, J. (1990). Cultural adjustment of international students. *Psychological Science, 1,* 133-137.

Kakar, S. (1991, Winter). Western science, Eastern minds. *Wilson Quarterly, 15,* 109-116.

Khoo, P. L. S., & Abu-Rasain, M. H. (1994). Counseling foreign students: A review of strategies. *The Counselling Psychology Quarterly, 7,* 117-134.

Kipling, R., & Cornell, L. L. (1999). *The man who would be king and other stories.* New York: Oxford University Press.

Kluckhohn, C. (1951). Values and value orientations in the theory of action. In T. Parsons & E. A. Shields (Eds.), *Toward a general theory of action* (pp. 388-433). Cambridge, MA: Harvard University Press.

Komiya, N., & Eells, G. T. (2001). Predictors of attitudes toward seeking counseling among international students. *Journal of College Counseling, 4,* 153-161.

Leong, T. L., & Chou, E. L. (2002). Counseling international students and sojourners. In P. B. Pedersen, J. G. Draguns, W. J. Lonner, & J. E. Trimble (Eds.), *Counseling across cultures* (5th ed., pp. 185-207). Thousand Oaks, CA: Sage.

Lonner, W. J., & Ibrahim, F. A. (2002). Appraisal and assessment in cross-cultural counseling. In P. B. Pedersen, J. G. Draguns, W. J. Lonner, & J. E. Trimble (Eds.), *Counseling across cultures* (5th ed., pp. 355-380). Thousand Oaks, CA: Sage.

Lonner, W. J., & Ibrahim, F. A. (in press). Assessment and appraisal in cross-cultural counseling. In P. B. Pedersen, J. G. Draguns, W. J. Lonner, & J. E. Trimble (Eds.), *Counseling across cultures* (6th ed.). Thousand Oaks, CA: Sage.

Mishra, P. K. (1986). *Dhaka summit and SARK: A broad overview.* Calcutta: Neetaji Institute of Asian Studies; New Delhi: K. P. Bagchi.

Mistry, R. (1996). *A fine balance.* New York: Vintage Books.

Moghni, S. M. (1987). Development of modern psychology in Pakistan. In G. H. Blowers & A. M. Turtle (Eds.), *Psychology moving East: The status of Western psychology in Asia and Oceania* (pp. 23-37). Boulder, CO: Westview Press.

Mohammad Arif, A. (2002). *South Asian Muslims in New York.* New York: Anthem Press.

Nilsson, J. E., & Anderson, M. Z. (2004). Supervising international students: The role of acculturation, role ambiguity, and multicultural discussions. *Professional Psychology: Research and Practice, 35,* 306-313.

Oetting, E. B., & Beavais, F. (1990-1991). Orthogonal cultural, identification theory: The cultural identification of minority adolescents. *International Journal of Addictions, 25,* 655-685.

Pedersen, P. B. (1991). Counseling international students. *The Counseling Psychologist, 19,* 10-58.

Phinney, J. (1990). Ethnic identity in adolescents and adults: Review of the literature. *Psychological Bulletin, 108,* 499-514.

Princeton Review. (n.d.). *Foreign exchange student programs.* Retrieved August 23, 2005, from http://www.princetonreview.com/college/research/articles/international/intstudents.asp

Poyrazli, S. (2005). International students at U.S. universities. *Eye on Psi Chi, 9,* 2, 18-19.

Poyrazli, S., Arbona, C., Nora, A., McPherson, B., & Pisecco, S. (2002). Relation between assertiveness, academic self-efficacy, and psychosocial adjustment among international students. *Journal of College Student Development, 43,* 632-642.

Ragin, J., & Lennon, N. (2004). *We're here for international students.* Retrieved August 9, 2005, from http://www.utexas.edu/student/cmhc/booklets/Internatl/internat.html

Sachau, E. C. (1993). *Alberuni's India.* New Delhi: Low Price Publications.

Sandhu, D. S., & Asrabadi, B. R. (1998). An acculturative stress scale for international students: A practical approach to stress measurement. In C. P. Zalaquett & R. J. Wood (Eds.), *Evaluating stress: A book of resources* (Vol. 2, pp. 1-33). Lanham, MD: Scarecrow Press.

Sinha, J. B. P. (1995). Factors facilitating and impeding growth of psychology in South Asia with special reference to India. *International Journal of Psychology, 30,* 741-753.

Sodowsky, G. R. (1991). Effect of culturally consistent counseling tasks on American and international student observers' perceptions of counselor credibility: A preliminary investigation. *Journal of Counseling & Development, 69,* 253-256.

Sodowsky, G. R., & Plake, B. S. (1992). A study of acculturation differences among international people and suggestions for sensitivity to within-group differences. *Journal of Counseling & Development, 71,* 53-59.

Sue, S., & Morishima, J. K. (1982). *The mental health of Asian Americans.* San Francisco: Jossey-Bass.

Takaki, R. (1989). *Strangers from different shores: A history of Asian Americans.* Boston: Little Brown.

Tewari, N., Inman, A. G., & Sandhu, D. S., (2003). South Asian Americans: Culture, concerns and therapeutic strategies. In J. Mio & G. Iwamasa (Eds.), *Culturally diverse mental health: The challenges of research and resistance* (pp. 191-209). New York: Brunner-Routledge.

Trice, A.G. (2004). Mixing it up: International graduate students' social interactions with American students. *Journal of College Student Development, 45,* 671-687.

Yau, T. Y., Sue, D., & Hayden, D. (1992). Counseling style preference of international students. *Journal of Counseling Psychology, 39,* 101-104.

Chapter 11

Counseling African International Students

Anika K. Warren and Madonna G. Constantine

Although the percentages of African international students attending institutions of higher education in the United States have increased substantially over the past 50 years (Institute of International Education, 2004, 2005; Mtebe, 1985), African international students still remain a relatively small population in many U.S. colleges and universities. For instance, during the 2004–2005 academic year, African international students consisted of only 6.4% (38,100) of the total international student population enrolled in U.S. colleges and universities (Institute of International Education, 2005). Over the past several years, Asian international students constituted the largest percentage of international student enrollment in the United States, followed by European, Latin American, African, and Middle Eastern students (Constantine, Okazaki, & Utsey, 2004; Institute of International Education, 2005). Table 11.1 provides data on the countries of origin of African students enrolled in U.S. colleges and universities during the 2004–2005 academic year (Institute of International Education, 2005).

African international college students represent an elite group of individuals by virtue of having been selected to attend schools by their parents or their government (Phinney & Onwughalu, 1996). Nonetheless, many researchers have reported that some African international students experience adjustment problems when they sojourn to the United States and that interpersonal, psychological, and medical problems such as social isolation, anxiety, depression, fatigue, and impairment of the immune system may stem from cultural adjustment difficulties (Bradley, Parr, Lan, Bingi, & Gould, 1995; Komiya & Eells, 2001; Mtebe, 1985; Yoon & Portman, 2004). Some cultural adjustment concerns that African international students experience can be alleviated through culturally sensitive and appropriate counseling interventions. Reducing the adjustment problems of African international students requires that college and university employees (e.g., mental health counselors, student personnel staff, and faculty members) better understand their cultural backgrounds, presenting concerns, and counseling needs.

Table 11.1

Total African International Students Matriculating at U.S. Institutions of
Higher Education by Country of Origin for the 2004–2005 Academic Year

Place of Origin	No. of Students	Place of Origin	No. of Students
Africa	36,100	North Africa	3,898
Africa, unspecified	0	Algeria	143
East Africa	13,675	Egypt	1,574
Burundi	82	Libya	39
Comoros	23	Morocco	1,571
Djibouti	5	Sudan	290
Eritrea	194	Tunisia	268
Ethiopia	1,129	Western Sahara	13
Kenya	6,728	North Africa, unspecified	0
Madagascar	127	Southern Africa	2,240
Malawi	375	Botswana	338
Mauritius	188	Lesotho	41
Mozambique	106	Namibia	66
Reunion	8	South Africa	1,699
Rwanda	191	Swaziland	96
Seychelles	10	Southern Africa, unspecified	0
Somalia	55	West Africa	13,782
Tanzania	1,332	Benin	180
Uganda	632	Burkina Faso	277
Zambia	794	Cape Verde	40
Zimbabwe	1,695	Côte d'Ivoire	622
East Africa, unspecified	1	Gambia	445
Central Africa	2,505	Ghana	3,114
Angola	431	Guinea	225
Cameroon	1,364	Guinea-Bissau	11
Central African Republic	32	Liberia	343
Chad	75	Mali	345
Congo	23	Mauritania	58
Equatorial Guinea	104	Niger	234
Gabon	145	Nigeria	6,335
São Tomé & Príncipe	8	Senegal	725
Congo/Former Zaire	323	Sierra Leone	308
Central Africa, unspecified	0	St. Helena	1
		Togo	514
		West Africa, unspecified	5

Note. From Open Doors 2004 (Institute of International Education, 2005).

The primary objective of this chapter is to call attention to the cultural adjustment issues and counseling needs of many African international students enrolled in U.S. institutions of higher education. Specifically, we discuss salient background information regarding African international students both in their home continent and in the United States, identify some cultural adjustment issues of African students who sojourn to U.S. colleges and universities, and delineate important mental health and therapeutic considerations for counselors working with African international college students. We also provide a case example that illustrates potential presenting concerns of African international students, along with practical guidelines for counseling these students.

The Continent of Africa

The continent of Africa covers one seventh of the inhabited world and has been described as the birthplace of humanity (Manyika, 2001). Africa is the second largest continent in the world, with over 50 nations, 700 million people, 800 ethnic groups, 1,000 languages, and a plethora of religions, beliefs, customs, and traditions (Essandoh, 1995; Manyika, 2001; Nwadiora, 1996; *The World Factbook,* 2006b). Africans speak one third of all languages in the world (Essandoh, 1995). In contrast, the United States is approximately three tenths the size of Africa and has been described as the world's most powerful nation having one primary language and a total population of 298 million people (*The World Factbook,* 2006a).

Writing about the demographic and cultural backgrounds of African international students as if they are one collective group does not fully capture the complexity of the African continent or its people. However, because of their shared history and geographical proximity, many commonalties exist among African people (Constantine, Anderson, Berkel, Caldwell, & Utsey, 2005; Essandoh, 1995; Mtebe, 1985; Nwadiora, 1995). For example, most African countries (except Ethiopia) have experienced trauma related to centuries of European colonization and social changes enforced through outside domination (Manyika, 2001; Okeke, Draguns, Sheku, & Allen, 1999). In recent years, modern technology and rapid worldwide transformation have challenged the political liberation of many African countries (Okeke et al., 1999).

Many of the cultural norms practiced by African international students date back to their challenging experiences stemming from European colonization and political domination. As such, some African cultural norms have been used as coping strategies to keep African people connected to one another while surviving centuries of European colonization and dominance. The family has been characterized as the cornerstone of most African countries, tribes, and cultures (Nwadiora, 1996). "Family" in African cultures refers to all persons who are biologically related as well as those who are related through marriage. Many African cultures also have been characterized as (a) valuing interpersonal relationships and social interactions; (b) maintaining close bonds with family and community; (c) having values that reflect cooperation, social harmony, collective responsibility, integration, oral tradition, group survival, and social time perspective; and (d) perceiving mind, body, and spirit as interconnected (Constantine, Myers, Kindaichi, & Moore, 2004; Okeke et al., 1999; Pratt, 1993).

In accordance with African cultural norms, researchers have found that (a) Nigerian children spend more time interacting with people than with physical objects, (b) Ghanaian adults interact socially at higher rates than adults from the United States and England, and (c) Nigerian and Zimbabwean managers possess more social or group-oriented goals than they do self-oriented and material goals (Okeke et al., 1999). Thus, many Africans tend to perceive cultural norms such as social interaction, group survival, and collective responsibility as more important than U.S. cultural norms such as individualism, materialism, and competition.

Because many African international students possess some awareness of the advantages and may be less aware of social problems associated with living in the United States, adjusting to the United States may be particularly challenging for these individuals. For example, some African international students may assume that U.S. cultural norms such as presumed racial equality, economic opportunity, freedom, and justice exist for all people residing in the United States (Lewis, 2000; Phinney & Onwughalu, 1996). Several researchers, however, have found that unexpected encounters of racial discrimination have made the cultural adjustment process particularly difficult for Black African international students attending U.S. colleges and universities (Bagley & Copeland, 1994; Constantine et al., 2005; Manyika, 2001; Phelps, Taylor, & Gerard, 2001). Therefore, African international students may experience marked cultural adjustment difficulties upon realizing that the "American dream" is not obtainable for *all* people.

Cultural Adjustment Issues

During their tenure in the United States, a fundamental cultural adjustment issue for many African international students is determining which U.S. cultural norms are most important or appropriate for them to adopt. Mainstream cultural norms in the United States have been defined primarily by the beliefs and practices of the White American majority group and have been characterized by the following: (a) individualism (i.e., the individual is the most important societal unit); (b) social assertiveness (i.e., an individual speaks on behalf of him- or herself); (c) the nuclear family (i.e., the ideal family is described as having a mother, a father, and children); (d) rationalism (i.e., mind, body, and spirit are separate entities); (e) time (i.e., time is perceived as quantity); (f) European aesthetics (i.e., beauty is defined by European standards); (g) an action orientation (i.e., a person is responsible for what happens to her or him); (h) universalism (i.e., the normative and best characteristics are defined by European culture and include independence and self-reliance in relationships); (i) competition (i.e., society's resources presumably belong to the "best" person or people); (j) historical accounts (i.e., the "most important" history in the United States has been written and defined by Whites); (k) racism (i.e., being a member of the White racial group makes one superior to members of other racial groups); and (l) sexism (i.e., being a member of the male sex makes one superior to members of the female sex; Constantine, Myers, et al., 2004; Helms, 1992).

Balancing African and U.S. cultural norms may be particularly challenging for African international students in light of the fact that many mainstream U.S. cultural norms (e.g., social assertiveness, individualism, and competition) are considered essential to success in many U.S. educational and professional systems, yet are antithetical to some African cultural norms. For example, the African normative belief that each human being is continuously connected to cosmos, other living creatures, and natural phenomena is inconsistent with U.S. beliefs such as individualism and independence (Sodowsky, Maguire, Johnson, Ngumba, & Kohles, 1994). However, this African belief could have either positive or negative effects on African international students' adjustment experiences, which makes balancing competing cultural norms particularly challenging. For example, although beliefs regarding the interconnectedness with all life forms might drive some African international students' desire to engage with others, such beliefs also may create negative emotional reactions and heighten cultural adjustment issues in incidents in which African international students are expected to compete with others, engage in self-assertive behaviors, or thrive in isolation from other human beings (Constantine et al., 2005).

Determining what behaviors are most appropriate to adopt may be further complicated by the fact that some demographic groups in the United States have cultural norms that differ from the mainstream U.S. culture. For example, some Black ethnic groups in the United States (e.g., African Americans) have cultural norms that are consistent with both U.S. culture (e.g., social assertiveness) and African culture (e.g., communalistic attitudes). Therefore, it is not surprising that some African international students struggle as they attempt to determine which cultural norms and behaviors are culturally appropriate and acceptable in different contexts and settings and with different populations. This is complicated further by the fact that most African international students living in the United States retain the cultural norms and beliefs of their homeland, which may result in longer adjustment periods, especially when the size of the cultural gaps between the cultures of origin and the new culture are significant (Essandoh, 1995). However, some African international students will assimilate more quickly to U.S. cultural norms, even if their norms differ from more traditional African cultures (Sodowsky et al., 1994). Thus, an awareness of the extent to which a client identifies with the cultural norms of her or his homeland is a vital step when assessing the unique cultural adjustment problems and counseling needs of an African international student.

Cultural adjustment concerns for African international students also might result from some individuals' misconceptions about Africa, Africans, and Black people. For instance, research indicates that a common misperception by people living in the United States is that Africa is a jungle and that Africans are uncivilized individuals (e.g., "savages"; Constantine et al., 2005; Traoré, 2004). These misconceptions and misperceptions can have a profoundly negative impact on how individuals from the United States and around the globe relate to African international students, and such fallacies may contribute to feelings of depression, confusion, anxiety, and self-doubt for African students and could result in isolation from others who could potentially provide them with support to ease their cultural adjustment concerns.

Research specifically examining African international college students' adjustment issues is limited. However, two studies published over 20 years ago indicated that adjustment issues of African students are not entirely parallel to those of their international counterparts. For example, Adelegan and Parks (1985) reported that getting the food, clothing, and music of their homeland, adjusting to a new climate, and coping with troublesome news from their homeland about loved ones or traumatic events were the most difficult adjustment issues for African international students. In another study, Mtebe (1985) identified and ranked the 10 most and least severe adjustment problems experienced by African international students attending U.S. colleges and universities (see Table 11.2).

In more recent studies, researchers have found that the most salient cultural adjustment problems for Kenyan, Nigerian, and Ghanaian international students (Constantine et al., 2005) and African immigrant women (Lewis, 2000) were related to (a) prejudice and discriminatory treatment, (b) social isolation (e.g., loneliness), (c) separation from family and friends, and (d) financial concerns. Findings from some of the aforementioned studies indicate that unlike their Asian international counterparts, many African international students do not perceive English proficiency, immigration status, parental-imposed academic pressures, and change in social roles as significantly affecting their adjustment to the United States (Essandoh, 1995; Swagler & Ellis, 2003). More important, results from the above-mentioned investigations suggest that, in the context of counseling African international students, counselors should consider the unique adjustment issues of each client and not assume that all international students or all African students experience similar cultural adjustment issues.

Counseling African International College Students

Although data indicate that the percentages of African international students attending U.S. colleges and universities have increased substantially, literature on the unique counseling needs of African international students is sparse. The extant literature on counseling African international students has suggested that university counseling centers are one of their least used campus resources and

Table 11.2

Ranking of Adjustment Issues of African International Students (Mtebe, 1985)

Most Severe	Least Severe
1. Getting a work permit for an off-campus job	1. English proficiency
2. Finding a part-time job at the university related to degree program	2. Understanding lectures
	3. Adjusting to housing
3. Getting work experience in field of study before returning home	4. Academic achievement
	5. Participating in class discussion
4. Cultural differences	6. Obtaining housing
5. Adjusting to climate	7. Academic course work
6. Homesickness	8. Giving oral reports in class
7. Having enough money for basic living expenses	9. Examination system
	10. Getting used to American food
8. Sponsorship	
9. Receiving money from spouses without delay	
10. Being accepted by U.S. social groups	

that offices for international student services are one of the most frequently used resources. Hence, international student advisors may function as counselors for many African international students (Yoon & Portman, 2004). Rather than using Western-based university counseling centers, some African international students may initially prefer to use social support systems and problem-solving techniques consistent with African cultural norms (e.g., speaking with family members, friends, and the clergy; accessing indigenous healers; taking herbal remedies; Constantine, Myers, et al., 2004). However, research has indicated that the longer international students live in the United States, the more likely they are to seek Western-based counseling services (Komiya & Eells, 2001). Thus, it is vital that all counselors develop culturally appropriate counseling skills, especially those who might work with African international students at some level.

In general, counselors should be aware of the cultural-bound nature of many Western mental health theories and services (Constantine, Myers, et al., 2004). In particular, counselors should be cautious when using counseling techniques focused on differentiation, individualism, and enmeshment and should not over-pathologize behaviors or notions of illness that differ from Western-based as-sumptions of mental health (Constantine, Myers, et al., 2004; Essandoh, 1995). For example, if an African international student seeks counseling for academic and/or vocational issues, it is important that the counselor conceptualize the student's possible need to consult with her or his family members as a healthy cultural practice or norm. That is, the counselor should be able to develop cul-turally appropriate counseling interventions based on his or her knowledge of normative African behaviors and not assume that the student has "enmeshment" issues related to the student's family.

Previous literature in the area of coping has suggested that Black individuals in general tend to use diverse and flexible responses to deal with stressful or dif-ficult situations, including social support networks, spirituality, prayer, and humor (e.g., Broman, 1995; Ellison & Taylor, 1996; Nebedum-Ezeh, 1997). Attempting to deal with the multitude of stressors associated with being an African international student may call for the use of varied coping practices that may not focus prima-rily on mastery of the environment, as found in many Eurocentric conceptualiza-tions of coping (Azibo, 1996), but instead on daily survival in sometimes challenging situations and environments (Constantine et al., 2005). In the context of seeking individual counseling, some African international students may prefer to work with active and directive counselors who come across as credible ex-perts (i.e., authority figures) and trustworthy healers with professional bound-aries (Essandoh, 1995).

In addition, some African international students may wish to seek indigenous forms of healing to help them develop the skills necessary to cope with per-sonal distress (Constantine et al., 2005). Examples of indigenous healing re-sources include meditation, yoga, astrology, fortune telling, burning incense, aromatherapy, music, song, dance, and poetry (Constantine, Myers, et al., 2004; Essandoh, 1995). Counselors should be aware that the use of indigenous African healing methods may vary among African students by gender, age, degree of acculturation, English language proficiency, symptoms, and cultural backgrounds (Moletsane, 1995). Therefore, it is important that counselors recognize when African international students may be in need of such healing resources and provide culturally appropriate indigenous healing referrals to clients when warranted.

Counselors working with African international students also should consider how etiological differences about mental illness and psychological disorders as well as therapeutic similarities between U.S. and African norms may influence their clinical work (Constantine, Myers, et al., 2004). In most African countries, mental illness and psychological disorders are rooted in sociocultural, spiritual, or cosmic factors that have not been subjected to theory development or research and may not be consistent with research and theory based notions of mental illness and psychological disorders in the United States (Essandoh, 1995). However, culturally appropriate counseling interventions may include accepting African students' etiology of their mental health issues and establishing clinical strategies that integrate U.S. and African cultural norms and therapeutic strategies.

Case Scenario

The following case was developed on the basis of themes from several African international college students who sought assistance at a university counseling center. The case is not intended to represent the broad range of African students' presenting concerns. Rather, it is intended to further illustrate therapeutic issues that some African international students present in counseling and to discuss interventions that may be culturally appropriate.

Chinwé, a 19-year-old Nigerian first-year college student at a large northeastern university in the United States, was referred to the university counseling center by an advisor in the international student office on campus. Chinwé's academic advisor became concerned after Chinwé reported crying in her dorm room daily and feeling sick to her stomach at night and in class.

During her intake session at the counseling center, Chinwé indicates that she is having difficulty sleeping at night, participating in class discussions, grocery shopping, commuting on mass transit, and managing her own expenses. She attributes some of her difficulties to interactions with others. For example, Chinwé has received some negative reactions to her accent and her questions about U.S. culture. These experiences often leave her feeling "inadequate, unintelligent, and useless."

Chinwé also expresses feelings of loneliness and sadness. She states, "I feel I'm smart and capable of doing my schoolwork on my own, but I really want to make friends I can study with. I'm all by myself here. I miss my family and friends and the beauty of Nigeria too. I didn't do well on my test yesterday because all I can think about is going home. I'm not sure I want to be here."

With regard to her family background, Chinwé is the youngest of four children. She and her siblings were raised by their parents, grandparents, and other family members. Chinwé describes her family as very close, supportive, and protective. While speaking about her family and friends in Nigeria, Chinwé reports, "They try to understand what I'm going through [in school], but they don't really get it [entirely]. They are not familiar with how things work here. Coming here is much more difficult than I ever thought it would be."

When asked what she wants to gain from counseling, Chinwé replies, "I just want somebody to talk to about all of this. Sometimes I think people [on campus] aren't too happy having African students studying here. They just assume that I come from a different world and that [the United States] is better."

Counseling strategies with Chinwé may include addressing her cultural adjustment problems via interpersonal and psychoeducational interventions focusing on (a) alleviating her depressive symptoms; (b) developing a local support system; (c) encouraging her bicultural competence; and (d) incorporating music, dance, drawing, poetry, or other nontraditional interventions in counseling sessions to help her express her feelings (Constantine, Myers, et al., 2004; Essandoh, 1995). Chinwé also may benefit from joining an international students' support group on campus to interact with students who may have similar cultural adjustment concerns. In addition, counselors can help her to identify local African or Nigerian conclaves, families, and organizations in which she can talk about her cultural experiences, interact socially, and receive support and advice from other Africans.

Practical Guidelines for Counseling African International College Students

Constantine and colleagues (Constantine et al., 2005; Constantine, Myers, et al., 2004) identified several ways in which counselors might work more effectively with people of color and immigrants in maximizing their mental health treatment and effectiveness, and Essandoh (1995) delineated five issues that counselors face when working with African international college students. In this chapter, we culled literature on counseling people of color, immigrants, and African international college students to summarize five practical guidelines for counselors to use when addressing the cultural adjustment concerns of African college students should they present for counseling.

1. Explore your worldviews, assumptions, and biases to determine if or how they might be interfering with your ability to work competently with African international college students.
2. Encourage African international college students to share their beliefs about the etiology of their adjustment concerns and the best ways to alleviate them. In addition, involve these students in the selection of preferred and appropriate treatment strategies and plans.
3. Identify culturally based values (e.g., having a strong communal orientation) that might encourage these students' use of therapeutic resources (e.g., support groups) to alleviate their cultural adjustment problems or concerns. For example, conducting treatment in a group format could (a) emphasize social interaction among African international

students, (b) encourage African international students to learn from each other's experiences, and (c) create an atmosphere of relatedness and connectiveness among students who might be experiencing similar cultural adjustment concerns.

4. Consider providing postmigratory information to African international students regarding U.S. social customs and norms.

5. Incorporate close friends and family members to assist with treatment goals when possible or warranted.

Summary

Counselors who are interested in working with international college students from Africa must familiarize themselves with local African communities and communitywide resources, and with the cultural, social, familial, and political backgrounds of their individual clients. We hope that the issues and interventions outlined in this chapter will increase counselors' awareness about counseling African international students, as well as about some of the unique cultural backgrounds and experiences of this population. More broadly, we hope this chapter will improve the likelihood that African international students will receive and benefit from culturally appropriate counseling interventions.

References

Adelegan, F. O., & Parks, D. J. (1985). Problems of transition for African students in an American university. *Journal of College Student Personnel, 26,* 504-508.

Azibo, D. (1996). *African psychology in historical perspective and related commentary.* Trenton, NJ: Africa World Press.

Bagley, C. A., & Copeland, E. J. (1994). African and African American graduate students' racial identity and personal problem-solving strategies. *Journal of Counseling & Development, 73,* 167-171.

Bradley, L., Parr, G., Lan, W. Y., Bingi, R., & Gould L. J. (1995). Counselling expectations of international students. *International Journal for the Advancement of Counselling, 18,* 121-131.

Broman, C. L. (1995). Coping with personal problems. In H. W. Neighbors & J. S. Jackson (Eds.), *Mental health in Black America* (pp. 117-129). Thousand Oaks, CA: Sage.

Constantine, M. G., Anderson, G. M., Berkel, L. A., Caldwell, L. D., & Utsey, S. O. (2005). Examining the cultural adjustment experiences of African international college students: A qualitative analysis. *Journal of Counseling Psychology, 52,* 57-66.

Constantine, M. G., Myers, L. J., Kindaichi, M., & Moore, J. L. (2004). Exploring indigenous mental health practices: The role of healers and helpers in promoting well-being in people of color. *Counseling and Values, 48,* 110-125.

Constantine, M. G., Okazaki, S., & Utsey, S. O. (2004). Self-concealment, social self-efficacy, acculturative stress, and depression in African, Asian, and Latin

American international college students. *American Journal of Ortho-psychiatry, 74,* 230-241.

Ellison, C. G., & Taylor, R. J. (1996). Turning to prayer: Social and situational antecedents of religious coping among African Americans. *Review of Religious Research, 38,* 111-131.

Essandoh, P. K. (1995). Counseling issues with African college students in U.S. colleges and universities. *The Counseling Psychologist, 23,* 348-360.

Helms, J. E. (1992). *A race is a nice thing to have: A guide to being a White person or understanding the White persons in your life.* Topeka, KS: Content Communications.

Institute of International Education. (2004, November). *International students in the U.S.: International student enrollments declined by 2.4% in 2003/2004.* Retrieved January 6, 2005, from http://opendoors.iienetwork.org

Institute of International Education. (2005, November). *International students in the U.S.: Data tables from Open Doors 2004.* Retrieved June 20, 2006, from http://opendoors.iienetwork.org

Komiya, N., & Eells, G. T. (2001). Predictors of attitudes toward seeking counseling among international students. *Journal of College Counseling, 4,* 153-160.

Lewis, J. V. (2000). Black immigrant women: Psychological adjustment to United States culture. *Dissertation Abstracts International, 61*(5-B), 2768.

Manyika, S. (2001). Negotiating identities: African students in British and American universities. *Dissertation Abstracts International, 62*(1-A), 97.

Moletsane, R. (1995). Black South African students in predominantly White United States universities. *Dissertation Abstracts International, 57,* 1003.

Mtebe, W. L. (1985). Hierarchy of adjustment problems as perceived by African students and international student advisors. *Dissertation Abstracts International, 45*(7-A), 2007.

Nebedum-Ezeh, G. C. (1997). An examination of the experiences and coping strategies of African students at predominantly White institutions of higher education in the United States. *Dissertation Abstracts International, 58*(6-A), 2106.

Nwadiora, E. (1995). Alienation and stress among Black immigrants: An exploratory study. *Western Journal of Black Studies, 19,* 58-71.

Nwadiora, E. (1996). Nigerian families. In M. McGoldrick & J. Giordano (Eds.), *Ethnicity and family therapy* (pp. 129-138). New York: Guilford Press.

Okeke, B. I., Draguns, J. G., Sheku, B., & Allen, W. (1999). Culture, self, and personality in Africa. In Y. T. Lee, C. R. McCauley, & J. G. Draguns (Eds.), *Personality and person perception across cultures* (pp. 139-162). Mahwah, NJ: Erlbaum.

Phelps, R. E., Taylor, J. D., & Gerard, P. A. (2001). Cultural mistrust, ethnic identity, racial identity and self-esteem among ethnically diverse Black university students. *Journal of Counseling & Development, 79,* 209-216.

Phinney, J. S., & Onwughalu, M. (1996). Racial identity and perception of American ideals among African American and African students in the United States. *International Journal of Intercultural Relations, 20,* 127-140.

Pratt, C. B. (1993). A cross-cultural study of news media preferences: African versus White U.S. students. *Journal of Black Studies, 23,* 314-331.

Sodowsky, G. R., Maquire, K., Johnson, P., Ngumba, W., & Kohles, R. (1994). World views of White American, Mainland Chinese, Taiwanese, and African students. *Journal of Cross-Cultural Psychology, 25,* 309-324.

Swagler, M. A., & Ellis, M. V. (2003). Crossing the distance: Adjustment of Taiwanese graduate students in the United States. *Journal of Counseling Psychology, 50,* 420-437.

The World Factbook. (2006a). *The world factbook 2006: US.* Retrieved November 10, 2006, from http://www.cia.gov/cia/publications/factbook/geos/us.html

The World Factbook. (2006b). *The world factbook 2006: World.* Retrieved November 10, 2006, from http://www.cia.gov/cia/publications/factbook/geos/xx.html

Traoré, R. L. (2004). Colonialism continued: African students in an urban high school in America. *Journal of Black Studies, 34,* 348-369.

Yoon, E., & Portman, T. A. A. (2004). Critical issues of literature on counseling international students. *Journal of Multicultural Counseling and Development, 32,* 33-44.

Chapter 12

Counseling International Students From the Middle East

Caroline G. Henry and Nadya A. Fouad

A Midwest Airlines flight from Milwaukee to San Francisco was canceled Sunday night after a passenger discovered Arabic-type handwriting inside an in-flight magazine. The 7:25 p.m. flight carrying 118 passengers and five crew members had already pulled away from the gate at Mitchell International Airport when a passenger flipping through the Midwest Airlines magazine tucked in the seat pocket saw the writing and told a flight crew member. The writing, which was scribbled on a page of the magazine, turned out to be Farsi, the Iranian language. . . . The plane returned to the gate, and passengers were taken off the plane.

—*Milwaukee Journal Sentinel,* September 21, 2004

The above scenario is part of the environment that international students from the Middle East face when coming to study in the United States. This reaction may be a factor in the gradual decrease in the number of international students from the Middle East studying in the United States (U.S. Department of Education, 2003). During the 2000–2001 academic year, the total number was down 10% from the previous year, with decreases of 25% each from Saudi Arabia (4,175) and Kuwait (2,212) and 15% from the United Arab Emirates (1,792). The combined total number of students coming from all countries in the Middle East was just 34,803, down from 38,545 in the previous year, and representing only 6% of the total number of international students studying in the United States. An especially steep decline has been reported in the number of new students from Islamic countries, including Saudi Arabia, Pakistan, and the United Arab Emirates. In 1983, Iran was the leading country of origin, with 26,760 students studying in the United States. Today, with only 2,258 students, it is not even in the top 20 sending countries. Assuming the continuation of the current volatile social and political relationships shared between the United States and many Middle Eastern countries and the societal reactions to Middle Eastern students in the United States, these decreasing trends are expected to continue.

Many counselors who work with international students are left with unanswered questions. What factors have led to this sharp and ongoing decline? What impact are those issues having on students from the Middle East who are currently studying in the United States? What can we, as counselors, do to improve the conditions these students are living under, and how can we help them overcome the challenges they face and effectively cope with the problems they encounter? What factors do we need to include to be effective counselors? In keeping with multicultural guidelines (American Psychological Association, 2003) and multicultural counseling competencies (Sue, Arredondo, & McDavis, 1992), we need to have sufficient knowledge of these students' cultural backgrounds to help them cope with the issues they face as Middle Eastern international students studying in the United States. This chapter focuses first on a perspective of cultural influences on those from the Middle East (including the impact of the September 11, 2001 terrorist attacks) and how those cultural influences affect the view of mental health for international students from the Middle East. We provide a case scenario to discuss these issues in context, and we finish the chapter with a discussion on counseling Middle Eastern international students.

Diversity

Like many other ethnic groups, Middle Easterners include a diversity of ethnic origins. They are one of the most widely misunderstood and frequently misrepresented groups of people in the world. One of the most common misconceptions is the interchangeable usage of the terms *Arab, Muslim,* and *Middle Eastern.* Arab pertains to an ethnic group of individuals who share the same culture and language but are not necessarily of the same race (Abudabbeh, 1996). Arabic is the language spoken throughout the Arab countries, although Arabic dialects can differ greatly. Muslims are followers of the Islam religion and are found throughout the world. Although 80% of all Arabs are Muslim (Nassar-McMillan, 2003a), Arabs make up only 15%-20% of the world's Islamic population (Council on Islamic Education, 2000). The Middle East refers to a diverse group of countries, including 22 nations that are predominantly Arab such as Jordan and Syria, as well as several non-Arab Muslim countries such as Turkey. Israel and Iran are also part of the Middle East. Most people from the United States believe that Iranians are Arab, when in fact they are more likely to be Persian and to speak Farsi (Erickson & Al-Timmi, 2001).

9/11

The vast sociopolitical effects resulting from the terrorist attacks of 9/11 have had a huge impact on everyone living in the United States. However, as the newspaper account at the beginning of this chapter notes, those individuals who are originally from Middle Eastern countries, or who even just appear to be of Arab descent, have faced some of the most drastic changes. Many of these people have lost their sense of individual freedom and personal security. Overall, the United States has experienced an increase in anti-Arab biases, covert and overt discrimination, degradation of civil liberties, and even hate crimes against Arab Americans

(Joseph, 2002). As a result, many Arabs living in the United States are experiencing a sense of marginalization and alienation from mainstream society. During the week following September 11, 2001, calls to eight U.S. universities with many international students from the Middle East confirmed that 25 to 60 students enrolled at each institution had withdrawn by that time (McMurtie et al., 2001). Countries such as Kuwait and Saudi Arabia, which had thousands of students studying in the United States on government scholarships, provided free airfare home for those students who chose not to stay. Throughout the 1980s, students from Asia and the Middle East occupied first and second place among international students coming to the United States. Since then, the flow from the Middle East has been superceded by that from Europe and Latin America. The virtual absence of a focus on the Middle East is a particularly troubling aspect of U.S. international education because of the considerable importance of this region for the U.S. economy and international affairs (Cummings, 2001). For example, the U.S. economy's dependence on Middle Eastern oil and concern about the instability of that region have been important aspects of governmental policy for many years, and as of this writing, the 2,000th U.S. soldier has just died in the U.S. war in Iraq.

Middle Eastern Culture

To date, very little information is available on Middle Eastern international students as a population, although a recent body of literature has emerged that describes Arab Americans as an ethnic group living in the United States. This body of knowledge is pertinent to counselors who work with international students from the Middle East because it is highly likely that these students will share the same cultural values and customs as Arab Americans. Furthermore, international students can benefit greatly by connecting with members of an ethnic group in their community who will provide support and help them maintain a strong ethnic identity.

According to research conducted by the Center for Immigration Studies, Middle Easterners are one of the fastest growing immigrant groups in the United States (Camarota, 2002). Currently, there are an estimated 2 to 3 million Arab Americans living in the United States. Arab Americans tend to have more education than other U.S. ethnic groups, in part because educational achievement and economic advancement are encouraged within Arab cultures (Erickson & Al-Timmi, 2001). California has the highest Middle Eastern population of any state, and Virginia has the fastest growing population of Middle Eastern immigrants, followed by Michigan, New York, and Texas. Some of the major populations of Arab Americans can be found in large urban cities, such as Washington, DC, Chicago, Detroit, and Cleveland (Zogby, 2001).

Religion

A large portion of Arab culture stems from the religious teachings of Islam. For many Arabs, religion is a central component of their identity and plays an integral part in their daily lives. Most Arab Americans are Muslims or Christians. For Muslims, or followers of Islam, the Quran (Koran) is the actual word of God (Allah). Under the direction of Muhammed, the verses and chapters of the Quran were organized in the order in which they are used today. The Quran is considered the primary guide for Muslim life. It emphasizes the significance of knowledge and encourages Muslims to learn about God's laws and the world of nature. Nydell (1987) outlined some basic Islamic values and religious attitudes commonly found among Arabic-speaking people: (a) One must always uphold his or her dignity, honor, and reputation; (b) loyalty to family takes precedence over personal needs; (c) it is important to always behave in ways that reflect well on others; (d) everyone believes in one God and acknowledges His power; (e) piety is one of the most admirable characteristics a person can possess; and (f) humans cannot control all events because much depends on God. The last leads to a cultural emphasis on the role of fate in determining events. For example, two typical expressions about some future event or action are "*In Sha Allah*" ("If God is willing") and "*Ma Sha Allah*" ("This is what God wished"). Some common Muslim religious practices include dietary restrictions (e.g., abstinence from pork and alcohol); prayer five times a day, turned toward Mecca; worship services held at a mosque on Friday, which is the Sabbath; and fasting from sunrise to sunset during the holy month of Ramadan (Jackson, 1997).

Family

The family is the foundation of Islamic society and Arab culture. The security and stability offered by one's family is highly valued and important for spiritual growth. Islam promotes a collectivist view of family and community, as opposed to the independent or individualist thinking, needs, feelings, and thoughts of Western culture (Zogby, 2001). As the central structure of Arab culture, family plays an important role in the individual and collective identities of most Arabs (Erickson & Al-Timmi, 2001). Arab families encourage their members to remain interdependent and may discourage self-reliance, differentiation, and individual aspirations. Most Arabs belong to an extended family system, on which they depend for both emotional and financial support. Family intimacy is achieved indirectly. Members rely primarily on unspoken expectations and are not accustomed to confronting each other (Nobles, 2000). It is common for family members to keep information from each other that may be troubling or disturbing.

In most Arab families, men are considered the head of the household. Grown sons are responsible for the welfare of their parents and their unmarried sisters. Although women typically adopt a more a passive role in public, they exert a great deal of influence within the home and participate in decision-making processes regarding important family issues. The less overt style of exerting interpersonal influence than is common in Western cultures contributes to the common perception of Arab women as submissive and oppressed (Jackson, 1997). Most Arab families adopt a hierarchical style of communication. Children are expected to honor and obey their parents. In terms of the extended family, older men typically demand the most respect. Arranged marriages are fairly common in Arab cultures. Dating and social mixing of the opposite sexes is sometimes restricted because of the importance placed on an individual's character and reputation within the community (Jackson, 1997). In terms of gender role expectations, men are expected to exhibit religiosity, hospitality, and courage, whereas for women, chastity is greatly valued (Zogby, 2001).

Cultural Values

The foundation of Arab culture is based on loyalty and family cohesion. Because of the collectivistic nature of the culture, conformity is valued and expected. The enhancement of family honor and status is an important goal for each family member and often leads to hard work, conservatism, educational attainment, and economic advancement (Erickson & Al-Timmi, 2001). Other characteristics highly valued by Arabs include magnanimity, generosity, and hospitality. Social formalities, rules of etiquette, and good manners are extremely important in Arab culture (Nobles, 2000). In contrast to American stereotypes of Arabs as angry, violent, and dangerous, Muslims are expected to exert kindness toward others and help those who are less fortunate (Erickson & Al-Timmi, 2001). Typically, Arab culture has a less structured time orientation than Western cultures, with a greater concern for what is currently taking place and a lesser regard for what is scheduled for that day (Abudabbeh, 1996). Customs include standing and sitting closer to each other than Westerners normally would and having more physical contact between members of the same gender (e.g., kissing on both cheeks is customary in greeting someone of the same sex; Nobles, 2000).

Sociopolitical Factors

Immigration to the United States from the Arab regions of the Middle East has occurred in four waves (Nassar-McMillan, 2003a, 2003b). The first wave, immigrants who arrived between 1875 and 1925, consisted primarily of Christians from Syria, Lebanon, Palestine, and Jordan who were trying to escape the Ottoman Empire. The second group came to the United States after World War II. This group consisted mainly of educated Muslims from countries including Palestine, Egypt, Syria, Jordan, and Iraq. The third wave of immigrants was also primarily educated Muslims, who came to the United States seeking better economic opportunities in the 1960s. Included in this group were many Palestinians who immigrated as a means for escaping Israeli occupation of Palestinian lands.

The most recent immigrants have been Iraqi refugees who fled the Middle East during or after the Persian Gulf War in the early 1990s. Many of them were seeking asylum after having fought on the U.S. side in the war. The new refugee population has presented some additional challenges to mental health professionals treating this subgroup. These individuals may be dealing with specific issues such as broken family ties, economic plight, posttraumatic stress disorder, depression, substance abuse, or pathological gambling (Nassar-McMillan & Hakim-Larson,

2003). Furthermore, this group may have mixed feelings about U.S. policies toward the Middle East. For example, the United States has a history of strong political and economic alliances with Israel. Some Arab Americans perceive this relationship as taking sides in the Arab–Israeli conflict, and therefore denigrating to the Arab cultural heritage. In addition, many Arab American immigrants have previously endured decades of political instability in their home countries, which may have contributed to a worldview that is cautious and untrusting of Western society.

Acculturation and Ethnic Identity

Arab Americans are one of the most diverse ethnic groups in the United States. Defining Arab Americans in terms of country of origin, race, ethnicity, and religion is a daunting task that contributes to the intraethnic confusion among individuals and communities (Nassar-McMillan, 2003a, 2003b). Arab Americans originate from many different countries with tremendous regional and national differences in language, politics, religion, and family values. For example, individuals from Saudi Arabia are more likely to be Muslim, hold more conservative values, and have a higher standard of living than individuals from Lebanon or Syria, who are more likely to be Christian, hold liberal or "Westernized" values, and have a lower standard of living (Erickson & Al-Timmi, 2001). As with all immigrant groups, levels of acculturation differ among Arab Americans. The longer they have resided in the United States, the more likely they are to have had opportunities to learn the language, laws, and systems of the dominant culture. Historically, Muslim Arabs have had a more difficult time assimilating into mainstream U.S. society than have their Christian counterparts (Jackson & Nassar-McMillan, 2006).

Compared with the United States, where skin color is the primary means of social identification and distinction, Arab classifications may be based on any or all of the following: racial, religious, and ethnic factors. Examples of Arab classifications include White Christian, White Muslim, Black Christian, and Black Muslim (Nydell, 1987). While residing in the United States, a number of issues may inhibit the development of a positive Arab ethnic identity, including experiences of racism, social stigma, and religious discrimination, as well as distress over U.S. foreign policy in the Middle East and negative Arab images and stereotypes in the U.S. media (Erickson & Al-Timmi, 2001). Frequently misrepresented in the press, Arab Americans are routinely negatively portrayed in the media and are often the victims of the resulting stereotypes, as shown in the news item at the beginning of this chapter. These stereotypes present serious challenges to Arab Americans' development of a positive ethnic identity.

Discrimination and the Media

Negative images and misperceptions of Arabs in the media have resulted in a cultural marginalization and have had profoundly negative effects on Arab Americans' self-image (Suleiman, 1988). Since the U.S.-Iraq war in January 1991, a dramatic increase in the number of attacks involving physical violence, such as arson, bombings, and physical assaults against Arab Americans, has taken place (Joseph, 2002). Anyone who may be identified as an Arab, Muslim, or Middle Easterner living in the United States may be targeted as a terrorist-enemy. Forty percent of Arab Americans polled reported having experienced ethnic discrimination (Abudabbeh & Aseel, 1999). Moreover, the average American does not realize that he or she holds any prejudice toward Arab Americans (Abudabbeh, 1996).

Especially during a political crisis between the U.S. and Arab world, the U.S. media (including newspapers, TV shows, TV news, and films) tend to portray Arab men as terrorist enemies and Arab women as being pathologically oppressed by their men, their society, their religion, and their culture. Naber (2000) investigated the manner in which the media conflates the categories of Arabs, Middle Easterners, and Muslims. On the basis of the findings, she concluded that the media images (a) erase differences among Arabs, Middle Easterners, and Muslims; (b) create a fixed boundary of difference between the "Arab–Middle Eastern–Muslim" and the "White American"; (c) portray an imaginary hierarchical relationship between the superior "White American" and the inferior "Arab–Middle Eastern–Muslim"; and (d) serve to justify U.S. intervention in Middle East affairs. Anti-Arab imaging removes all trace of the diverse composition of the Arab American community. The resulting attacks against individuals and community organizations have instilled fear in Arab Americans and have led many to conceal their ethnic identity and avoid participation in Arab American community organizations (Naber, 2000).

Views of Mental Health

Many Arabs subscribe to the Islamic concept of predeterminism, or fatalism, and therefore may resist the notion of proactive change that is often used in counseling (Nobles, 2000). When dealing with psychological problems, Arab Americans are most likely to first confer with a family member. A man will provide guidance for another man; a woman will consult with another woman (Nydell, 1987). Many Arab Americans do not feel comfortable disclosing personal matters and family issues with strangers, including counselors. Attitudes toward mental health issues and help-seeking behaviors may be related to country of origin and perhaps also to educational level. For example, Lebanese culture is more supportive and accepting of emotional and psychological problems, whereas other cultures, such as Yemeni culture, advocate "holding problems in," which results in more physical manifestations of mental health problems that often become the presenting issues (Nassar-McMillan & Hakim-Larson, 2003).

While Arabs tend to be highly emotional and full of zest for life, they are also bound by stringent rules and expectations. Discussions of illness, death, or other painful events tend to be uncomfortable for Arab clients (Nobles, 2000). Additionally, many Arab Americans are more concerned for the well-being of their families than for their own individual happiness or personal fulfillment. In fact, placing one's personal needs before those of the family may lead to confusion and feelings of guilt at having betrayed their family (Erickson & Al-Timmi, 2001). Typically, Arab Americans seek mental health services only as a last resort. Somatization of symptoms is common, and they often describe emotional pain in physical terms or through physical complaints (Abudabbeh, 1996). This phenomenon may be attributed to a heightened mind–body connection, the stigma and shame associated with mental illness, or a lack of terminology in Arab language to describe mental states and disturbances. In the case of Middle Eastern international students, like many other international students, their mental health may be greatly affected by the acculturation experiences they encounter during their stay in the United States.

Issues Facing Middle Eastern International Students

A number of factors may affect the acculturation experiences of international students from the Middle East who are studying in the United States. Examples of these factors are country of origin, length of time in the United States, separation from family, ability to speak English, and long-term plans to stay in the United States. Students from developing countries (e.g., Turkey) studying in the United States often do not return home immediately following the completion of their studies but stay and work. Sometimes they participate in a year of job training, which may be extended if students are able to find employer sponsorship (Tansel & Gungor, 2003). Some students may wish to uphold their Arab cultural identity but are unsure how to adhere to traditional customs and beliefs without a sense of community with which to identify. Many experience ambivalence as they try to become familiar with and integrated into American culture while still maintaining their cultural roots. The result can be a feeling of belonging to neither culture (Nobles, 2000). Because of the interdependent nature of Arab families, a transition away from an extended family support system is likely to result in feelings of isolation and disengagement.

During a crisis, Middle Eastern individuals tend to depend heavily on their family for support and help in coping and may become distraught if family members are unavailable for help (Jackson, 1997). In some Middle Eastern countries, mental illness carries a stigma. Middle Eastern international students may hold negative attitudes about mental illness and strongly resist seeking treatment for emotional concerns (Abudabbeh, 1996). Furthermore, Arabs tend to mistrust individuals outside of their own culture and religion, which may make it especially difficult for counselors to develop a strong rapport with international students from the Middle East. Because of the collectivistic nature of Arab society, community involvement is extremely important. The influence of community leaders is so profound that an endorsement of mental health services may encourage Arab international students to seek counseling when they would otherwise be unwilling to do so (Nassar-McMillan & Hakim-Larson, 2003). In Arab cultures, one's sense of worth and self-esteem often depends on whether one is valued and appreciated as a member of their family or community.

Counseling Middle Eastern International Students

Discussions about counseling international students from the Middle East invariably begin with encouraging counselors to examine their own perceptions and biases. Erickson and Al-Timmi (2001) identified five common stereotypes held about Arabs and Muslims: (a) Most Arabs are terrorists, angry, and irrational; (b) Islam is a religion of oppression; (c) Arab families are oppressive, particularly to women; (d) Arabs are rich oil sheiks; and (e) Arab culture has nothing to offer, so all Arabs should become Westernized. They recommended that counselors of Middle Eastern international students examine their own beliefs, and they encouraged the counselors to find ways to learn more about Arab culture and examine ways that the current political climate affects their perceptions of the Middle East and people from the Middle East.

The importance of fate in Middle Eastern cultures may make a proactive, insight-oriented or intrapersonal-focused therapeutic approach less effective than more problem-solving or cognitive–behavioral approaches (Nassar-McMillan, in press). Erickson and Al-Timmi (2001) recommended more psychoeducational or cognitive–behavioral approaches, noting that insight-oriented approaches may cause anxiety or distress for clients unaccustomed to a self-focused approach.

Culturally appropriate counseling with Middle Eastern international students may also include dispensing with Western notions of traditional therapy modalities. For example, clients may not be used to self-disclosure in a 50-minute period, and counselors may want to consider lengthening the therapy time. Given the importance of family in the Arab culture, counselors may also want to consider bringing in family members, if they live in the United States (Nassar-McMillan, in press). Typically, gift-giving is a common Middle Eastern cultural practice, and counselors may need to become comfortable accepting small gifts or tokens of appreciation. More critically, counselors may need to serve as an advocate for the client with departments or faculty, particularly if they suspect that a student is a victim of discrimination.

Nassar-McMillan (2003a, 2003b), Erickson and Al-Timmi (2001), and Jackson (1997) had additional suggestions for counselors of Arab Americans, and by extension, Middle Eastern international students. These include finding ways to establish relationships and credibility with potential clients before they attend counseling. Thus, the counselor may want to attend various campus events frequented by Middle Eastern students. Recommendations also include noting that the presence of physical symptoms may underlie emotional concerns, attending to the role of religion and collaborating with religious leaders when appropriate, and approaching counseling from a holistic perspective, including mind, body, and spirit in determining outcomes. Jackson and Nassar-McMillan (in press) recommended becoming comfortable using the expressions of *"In Sha Allah," "Ma Sha Allah,"* and *"Assalamu Alakum"* (hello). They suggested, for example, that a client who asks if the counselor can solve his or her problem may be answered with "In sha Allah (if God is willing), I will do my best." The term *Assalamu Alakum* is a formal greeting, and the response is *"Wa Lakum Salam"* ("And may peace be unto you").

Case Scenario

Hussein is a sophomore at a large private, religiously affiliated university. He has come to the United States from Egypt to study engineering, and he attends the university because he has been told it has a good engineering school. Hussein seeks counseling from the university counseling center because he is severely depressed and struggling with his classes. His grades are falling; he reports that he is in danger of flunking out of school. The concerns he raises with his counselor are intense feelings of isolation, depression, lack of problem-solving ability, conflict about being a Muslim in a Christian environment, and feelings of discrimination from others on campus.

He cannot talk to his friends about his struggles with the course work because he is ashamed of not doing well. He cannot talk to his parents back home because they have made significant sacrifices to send him to the United States to study. Each time he talks to his mother, she tells him how proud she is of him and how his entire family is counting on him to return to be an important engineer. He feels he would be letting her and the entire family down, feels that he is not acting as a man should, and describes himself as in deep physical pain.

We focus our discussion about ways to provide counseling for Hussein by embedding our comments in the framework developed by Sue et al. (1992) of awareness, knowledge, and skills. Specifically, we first discuss the counselor's need to be aware of his or her own cultural assumptions and biases. Second, we focus on the knowledge we recommend Hussein's counselor should have or seek out. And finally, we discuss the skills a counselor will need to appropriately provide counseling to Hussein.

Awareness

The first step for Hussein's counselor is to be aware of his or her own assumptions and biases about Arab men. As we have discussed at length, the Arab–Israeli conflict, the 9/11 terrorist attacks, and the longstanding portrayal of Middle Eastern men as angry and aggressive may have had a deep and unconscious impact on the perceptions of counselors. Counselors who may pride themselves on openness and awareness of cultural diversity may have a negative perception of Middle Eastern clients because of the pervasive climate of fear around terrorism in the United States in the early 21st century. Hussein is seeking counseling, in part, because of his perceptions of discrimination on campus. It is critical that the counselor not do more harm by unconsciously perpetuating that discrimination.

A counselor working with Hussein must also realize how difficult it may have been for him to seek counseling. As noted above, for Middle Eastern students, seeking counseling services is often seen as a last resort. Hussein notes that he is feeling isolated, that he cannot speak of his struggles to either his family or his friends. It is imperative for the counselor to assess the severity of Hussein's depression and to perhaps refer him for medication to augment therapy.

Hussein describes himself as being in deep physical pain. Erickson and Al-Timmi (2001) suggested that emotional pain is often displayed in somatic symptoms and cautioned therapists not to view this as a symptom of pathology but rather as a cultural expression of psychological pain. The counselor needs to be aware of the role of religion for Muslims on that campus and any recent conflicts or events that have occurred that may have affected Hussein's perception of a conflict between his religion and the predominant Christian religion on campus. Finally, the counselor should be aware of gender role expectations for men in Egypt.

Knowledge

The counselor needs to have an understanding of the importance of the family in Middle Eastern cultures and how central it is for Hussein to be loyal to his family. It is important for the counselor to have knowledge of differences between Egypt and other Middle Eastern cultures, along with how those differences may be affecting Hussein while he is in the United States. Are his friends also from Middle Eastern cultures, and how is he viewed by them? Hussein's family made financial sacrifices to send him to the United States to study; this may indicate his family's socioeconomic status is middle class, while his friends may be from more affluent families. Are these factors possibly contributing to his feelings of inadequacy and isolation?

It is important that the counselor also have knowledge of processes of acculturation and the effects of stigma on clients. Hussein is in the midst of adjusting to the U.S. culture and his place in that culture. He feels the effects of being a member of a stigmatized group (Crocker, Major, & Steele, 1998; Major, Quinton, & McCoy, 2002), which may include experiencing prejudice and discrimination, becoming aware of the negative value of his cultural group, worrying about acting in a way consistent with the stereotypes about Arabs, and not knowing how to interpret comments made by others.

Skills

Hussein may have never sought counseling before, and thus the counselor may want to begin with an orientation to the counseling process, the expectations that they each may have of the outcomes of therapy, and a clarification of his or her role, as well as Hussein's role, in the counseling process. The counselor can talk about what is expected in counseling (e.g., in talk therapy) and also what the process of counseling may include (such as homework or time commitments).

Hussein has presented with two major problem areas, those of depression and failing classes. Culturally appropriate counseling with Hussein will need to take into account his cultural focus on fate, and the counselor may want to use cognitive–behavioral therapy to treat his depression while addressing his shame about his academic work. As noted earlier, assessment of the depression should also include consideration of a referral for medication. The counselor may want to address Hussein's perception of his control over his feelings, or whether he is feeling that his depression is his fate to endure. Traditional cognitive–behavioral techniques may need to be modified if Hussein perceives his depression as located outside his control. The counselor may also validate Hussein's religious and spiritual beliefs and perhaps discuss times when his faith has been of help to him in the past.

It is also important for the counselor to get much more information about Hussein's academic performance. Is he, indeed, failing every course, or does he feel like a failure because he is not doing well but is in reality not failing? If Hussein is doing so poorly, are there academic reasons? Is engineering too difficult for him? Or is it a field in which he is not interested? Who is teaching his classes, and is language a barrier? Was he well prepared to study in the U.S. system, and how different is it from the system used in Egypt? Does he understand the expectations of amount of study needed outside of class, and does he possess time management skills? Understanding the causes of Hussein's academic problems will help the counselor to see how she or he could serve as an advocate with the College of Engineering or his professors and to identify ways that other resources within the university can help him.

Summary

International students from the Middle East are faced with many of the same concerns that other international students face but have additional barriers resulting from societal perceptions of Arabs after the 9/11 attacks and the negative portrayals of Arabs in the media. To be most effective as counselors and advocates for their clients, counselors working with Middle Eastern international students are encouraged, most critically, to examine their own assumptions and attitudes and to understand the great differences among Middle Eastern cultures.

References

Abudabbeh, N. (1996). Arab families. In M. McGoldrick, J. Giordano, & J. K. Pearce (Eds.), *Ethnicity and family therapy* (2nd ed., pp. 333-346). New York: Guilford Press.

Abudabbeh, N., & Aseel, H. A. (1999). Transcultural counseling and Arab Americans. In J. McFadden (Ed.), *Transcultural counseling* (pp. 283-296). Alexandria, VA: American Counseling Association.

American Psychological Association. (2003). Guidelines on multicultural education, training, research, practice, and organizational change for psychologists. *American Psychologist, 58,* 377-402.

Camarota, S. A. (2002). *Immigrants from the Middle East: A profile of the foreign-born population from Pakistan to Morocco.* Washington, DC: Center for Immigration Studies.

Council on Islamic Education. (2000). *Teaching about religion in national and state social studies standards.* Fountain Valley, CA: Freedom Forum First Amendment Center.

Crocker, J., Major, B., & Steele, C. (1998). Social stigma. In D. T. Gilbert & S. T. Fiske, (Eds.), *The handbook of social psychology* (Vol. 2, 4th ed., pp. 504-553). New York: McGraw-Hill.

Cummings, W. (2001). Current challenges of international education. *ERIC Digest.* (ERIC Document Reproduction Service No. ED464523)

Erickson, C. D., & Al-Timmi, J. (2001). Providing mental health services to Arab Americans: Recommendations and considerations. *Cultural Diversity and Ethnic Minority Psychology, 7,* 308-327.

Jackson, M. (1997). Counseling Arab Americans. In C. Lee (Ed.), *Multicultural issues in counseling: New approaches to diversity* (2nd ed., pp. 333-349). Alexandria, VA: American Counseling Association.

Jackson, M., & Nassar-McMillan, S. C. (2006). Counseling Arab Americans. In C. C. Lee (Ed.), *Multicultural issues in counseling: New approaches to diversity* (3rd ed., pp. 235-247). Alexandria, VA: American Counseling Association.

Joseph, S. (2002). Against the grain of the nation: The Arab. In M. Suleiman (Ed.), *Issues in Arab America* (pp. 257-271). Philadelphia: Temple University Press.

Major, B., Quinton, W. J., & McCoy, S. K. (2002). Antecedents and consequences of attributions to discrimination: Theoretical and empirical advances. In M. P. Zanna (Ed.), *Advances in experimental social psychology* (Vol. 34, pp. 251-330). New York: Academic Press.

McMurtie, B., Bollag, B., Brender, A., del Castillo, D., Cheng, M., & Overland, M. A. (2001). Arab students in U.S. head home, citing growing hostility. *The Chronicle of Higher Education, 48,* 42-45.

Naber, N. (2000). Ambiguous insiders: An investigation of Arab American invisibility. *Ethnic and Racial Studies, 23,* 37-61.

Nassar-McMillan, S. C. (in press). Applying the multicultural guidelines to Arab American populations. In D. W. Sue & M. G. Constantine (Eds.), *Multicultural competencies for working with people of color: Clinical practice implications.* New York: Teachers College Press.

Nassar-McMillan, S. C. (2003a). Counseling Arab Americans. In N. A. Vacc, S. B. DeVaney, & J. M. Brendel (Eds.), *Counseling multicultural and diverse populations* (4th ed., pp. 117-139). New York: Brunner-Routledge.

Nassar-McMillan, S. C. (2003b). *Counseling Arab Americans: Counselors' call for advocacy and social justice.* Denver, CO: Love.

Nassar-McMillan, S. C., & Hakim-Larson, J. (2003). Counseling considerations among Arab Americans. *Journal of Counseling & Development, 81,* 150-159.

Nobles, A. Y. (2000). Cultural determinants in the treatment of Arab Americans: A primer for mainstream therapists. *American Journal of Orthopsychiatry, 70,* 182-191.

Nydell, M. (1987). *Understanding Arabs: A guide for Westerners.* Yarmouth, ME: Intercultural Press.

Sue, D. W., Arredondo, P., & McDavis, R. J. (1992). Multicultural counseling competencies and standards: A call to the profession. *Journal of Counseling & Development, 70,* 477-486.

Suleiman, W. (1988). *Arabs in the mind of America.* Brattleboro, VT: Amana Books.

Tansel, A., & Gungor, N. D. (2003). "Brain drain" from Turkey: Survey evidence of student non-return. *Career Development International, 8,* 52-69.

U.S. Department of Education, National Center for Education Statistics. (2003). *The condition of education 2003* (NCES 2003-067). Washington, DC: U.S. Government Printing Office.

Zogby, J. (2001). *What ethnic Americans really think: The Zogby culture polls.* Washington, DC: Zogby International.

Chapter 13

Counseling International Students From Europe

Johanna E. Nilsson, Margaretha S. Lucas,
Supavan Khamphakdy-Brown, and Maria Sveinsdottir

Although much has been written about international students and their unique experiences, little attention has been given to those who come from Europe, even though they represent 14% of the almost 600,000 international students in the United States (Chin, 2002). Because the amount of difficulties experienced by international students is usually associated with the degree of cultural difference between the students' and the U.S. culture (Sheehan & Pearson, 1995), researchers and counselors have assumed that European international students, especially those from Western Europe, do not face noteworthy difficulties while studying in the United States given the cultural similarities (Williams, 2001). In our literature review for this chapter, we were not able to find any articles or books that directly focused on European international students and counseling issues. Therefore, this chapter is based on literature describing international students' issues in general, European culture and attitudes, and some of our own experiences as European international students in the not-so-distant past. Specifically, we first address Europe and its cultural diversity. Second, we discuss how Europeans may view the United States and how European international students may experience the United States and its people while living here. Third, we address concerns that international students from Europe may face while studying in the United States and issues to consider when counseling these students. A case scenario concludes the chapter.

Europe

Even though Europe is only a little larger than the United States, it hosts more than 40 nations and over 30 languages (Slomp, 2000). Barzini (1983) described the European countries as "grab bags" of kingdoms, duchies, and principalities that never really got along and became united through the centuries, sometimes by force, other times by decree, into nation states. The 1648 Peace Treaty of Westphalia, Germany, was the beginning of the European system of sovereign nations, declaring the independence of small nations, such as Switzerland, and recognizing the right of nations to determine their religion (Slomp, 2000). For centuries, Europeans have been able to travel freely over each other's land, oftentimes mixing their culture with that of others. For instance, the German culture contributed significantly to the Czech and Polish cultures, and the French culture is strongly marked by influences from Italy and Spain (Kumar, 2003). Although many of the European nations share similarities in the parliament system (spread across the continent by the Scandinavians), in religion (as a result of Irish holy men who brought Christianity and built monasteries all over Europe), and in art, science, and poetry (through Greek influences), each country has strived to retain its own homogeneous culture (Barzini, 1983). To illustrate the diversity within Europe and make it understandable to people from the United States, Slomp (2000) noted the following:

> Consider the United States. Imagine that everything West of the Mississippi is one country, whose population speaks Russian. All other states are fully independent and speak their own language, with a few exceptions. Massachusettsian is also spoken in Connecticut; two languages are spoken in both Georgia and Tennessee; and in Maryland three languages exist—Pennsylvanish, Virginian, and New Jersic. To make things a bit more complicated, New York has three regional languages in addition to New Yorkish: Big Applish, Hudsonian, and Upstateic. Moreover, in the Russian-speaking region there are a number of smaller peoples who strive for independence. They are concentrated around the San Francisco Bay area and speak languages like Bayish, Gayish, and Siliconian. (p. 1)

In the last decades, Europe has undergone profound political, social, and institutional changes toward uniformity. An example of this uniformity is the surge of institutional unification that resulted in the Maastricht Treaty on the European Union (EU). EU is an attempt to unite a large part of Europe on a voluntary basis for the purpose of strengthening Europe's social, political, and economic progress and security while leaving intact variations in nationalities, such as national languages. EU unifying effort has had an impact on all societal sectors, from farming to higher education. The 1999 Bologna Declaration is the result of 29 European countries' pledge to reform and make the quite diverse higher education system in Europe more compatible across countries (European Commission, 2006).

Citizens in EU member countries are now also EU citizens who are afforded the right to live, work, and vote in local elections in their EU country of choice (Berezin, 2003; Feldblum, 1997; Hansen & Schröder, 2001). Presently EU consists of 25 member countries and 454 million citizens; more countries are likely to join the union in the future (Europa, n.d.). Because of the unification of Europe, scholars have discussed whether the European culture can be referred to as single and unique (e.g., Berezin, 2003; Kumar, 2003; Pells, 1997; Wintle, 1996). Whereas Pells argued that referring to Europe as a unified whole is a matter of verbal convenience, Wintle concluded that a European cultural identity exists, founded on a partially shared history and cultural heritage. Although one should not minimize the cultural differences among the European nations, what holds Europe together is an acceptance of these differences and understanding of each other's historical and cultural legacies (Kumar, 2003). This understanding is also emphasized in the EU's official dictum, "Unity in diversity."

European Nations in Historical, Geographical, and Cultural Contexts

In this section, we provide specific information about differences among some European nations and their temperaments, within their respective historical and geographical contexts. When reading the descriptions, it is important to keep in mind that the distinctions provided are generalizations, intended to isolate, magnify, and emphasize only those characteristics that set the nations apart. The reality is more complex than such distinctions can provide; the people in the unique European nations are more like one another, and like people in the United States, than different. Regardless, we believe it is important for mental health professionals in the United States working with European international students to have a sense of the diversity in Europe and how Europeans distinguish themselves from each other. Owing to space limitations, we only focus on a few countries.

The Scandinavians

Even though the early Scandinavians, the Vikings, residing in the north of Europe, are best known for their ferociousness and hostilities toward other European countries, archaeological evidence also shows a culture advanced in the manufacturing of arms and jewelry, as well as in shipbuilding and commerce. The Vikings succeeded in mobilizing economic resources and in dominating hostile landscapes. Scandinavians' sagas and literature show pride not only in a past that included voyages as far as North America but also in the creation and introduction to the rest of Europe of Iceland's Althing, the earliest form of parliamentary government. The jury of English common law was a direct outgrowth of Viking ideas about community obligations and sworn investigations, both vital steps in building a civil society (Rosenthal, 1993–1998).

Currently, the Scandinavian countries are prosperous welfare states and models for other European countries, although they have lost some glamour because of increased unemployment rates in the last decade (Slomp, 2000). Modern Scandinavians, which include Norwegians, Danes, Swedes, Fins (who do not always identify as Scandinavians; Swallow, 2001), and Icelanders, tend to be a reserved group of people, of whom the Danes are the most outgoing. Being humble, responsible, and hardworking are common virtues (Svensson, 2003; Swallow, 2001).

The English and the Irish

The Brits are considered as the most class conscious in Europe (Kramer, 1988; Slomp, 2000). Barzini (1983) called them "The Imperturbable British" and portrayed them as stoics, meeting the challenges of life with a stern and tranquil mind together with a sense of duty and moral worth. Barzini conferred that these characteristics, combined with British austerity and their ancient prestige, may cause others to perceive them as tenacious, stubborn, and arrogant. However, regardless of their shining past, more than anyone the British nowadays have come to accept that "all predominant power seems for a time invincible, but, in fact, it is transient" as stated by prime minister Tony Blair when he addressed a joint session of the U.S. Congress on July 18, 2003 (Kinsley, 2003, p. A.25).

The Irish celebrate their Celtic heroes while lamenting their suffering and hardships endured in historical struggles of political, economical, and cultural independence from Britain. "England's difficulty is Ireland's opportunity" (Microsoft Encarta Encyclopedia, 1993-1998) expressed Ireland's old principle of rebellion against the British. Religion colors social and political life, as the Catholic Church played an uncontested role in the struggle of liberation from Great Britain (Slomp, 2000). Despite their hardships, wit and humor (often in the form of satire) characterize the Irish (Microsoft Encarta Encyclopedia, 1993-1998).

The Germans and the Swiss

Germany and Switzerland are both located in Central Europe. The Germans have been described as orderly and productive and their country as the richest and most technologically advanced of the European nations (Barzini, 1983). Kramer (1988) suggested that Germans' need for order is a reaction to a history of devastating wars and defeats. Another reaction to this history is contemporary Germans' marked skepticism of military power and use (Lord, 2003). The Swiss are described as industrious, self-protective, prudent, and keeping, at all cost, a climate of neutrality, despite the incessant threat of its neighbors (Kramer, 1988; Slomp, 2000). Even today the Swiss have sealed storage tanks of food, fuel, and medicine, intended to help them survive other nations' nuclear catastrophe. Their lack of confidence in other nations' common sense may also explain their willingness to finance other nations' foolish endeavors, allowing them to survive themselves (Kramer, 1988).

The Dutch and the Belgians

Both the Dutch—"The Careful Dutch" (Barzini, 1983)—and the Belgians' characters have been tempered by historical battles and the encroaching North Sea; they are viewed as willful, stolid, hardworking, parsimonious, earnest, and methodical. They respect law and fear war, having been for centuries geographically convenient battlegrounds for powerful foreign armies vying for European supremacy. Dutch paintings lack the pomp, grandeur, and glory of Venetians, and instead show the lives of ordinary people in an understated way (Barzini, 1983). The Dutch pride themselves with being an egalitarian society with low unemployment rates and few citizens living below the poverty level (Janin & Van Eil, 2003).

Belgians, whose country was created by diplomats in the 19th century, are imbued with Dutch and French culture. Part of the population, the Flemish, speak Dutch with an accent the Dutch find humorous, and the Walloons speak French with an accent the French find equally amusing. While people in many European nations have vacillated in their support of the EU and the euro (the new European currency), fearing a loss of their nationality and culture, the Belgians have been strong supporters of both ideas (Elliott, 2003).

The French and the Italians

French culture is still regarded as the polestar by many intellectuals everywhere; its language allows the expression of precise thoughts and nebulous concepts with clarity and elegance. According to Barzini (1983), however, "The Quarrelsome French" too loudly and firmly pronounce themselves as number one in Europe, as if they doubted this themselves. The French are known for their contempt of foreigners, their efforts to protect their language from "barbaric infiltrations," and their adoration of intelligence (Kramer, 1988). According to Kramer, intellectualism, controversy, contrasts, rivalry, and a certain amount of confusion provide the French with their own special niche in a global theatre.

Throughout history, Italy has been ruled by Byzantines, Germans, Arabs, Normans, French, Spanish, and Austrians, and only recently its different regions and city states have been united, based on foreign models. According to Barzini (1983), who called his compatriots "The Flexible Italians," these experiences, combined with a justified pride in their glorious past when they were the teachers of the world, render Italians skeptical, resigned, pessimistic, and suspicious of all government laws and regulations. They tend to glorify ancient, often obsolete, manners and rituals and to obey only those laws they themselves privately decide are just and useful. Like people in other Mediterranean countries, Italians strongly identify with family, at times to the exclusion of relationships with friends and acquaintances.

Eastern Europeans

The industrial revolution divided Europe into an advanced, more developed Western part and a less developed Eastern part (Slomp, 2000). Following World War II, communism and the cold war further strengthened this divide (Kumar, 2003). When communism deteriorated in the 1980s, the Soviet Union, Czechoslovakia, and Yugoslavia fell apart, Germany was reunited, and countries such as Poland, the Czech Republic, Estonia, and Hungary started to move toward democracy and free enterprise (Slomp, 2000). At times, these Central and Eastern European countries are described as emerging countries, but Eastern European history is rich and the countries proud of their glorious pasts (Slomp, 2000). For example, at the end of the 15th century, the Jagiellonian University in Poland was famous for mathematics and astronomy and boasted graduates such as Copernicus

(Tanner, 1989). The cultural heritage of these countries is captured in movements such as the Renaissance and the Protestant Revolution, which reached as far as the western part of the Ukraine, bringing with them the spirit of free inquiry and individualism found across Europe (Dalton, 2003; Slomp, 2000) to Mongol autocracies, which stressed responsibility and service to the state (Dalton, 2003). Nations' characteristics in this part of Europe often include a sense of fatalism, especially in Russia (Dalton, 2003). The Hungarians, known for "nursing the blues," suffer from one of the world's highest suicide rates (Ardó, 2003). Ukrainians are known as defiant (Dalton, 2003), and the Czechs, who, like many Eastern and Central Europeans, value culture and education, are described as reserved and quiet (Nollen, 2001).

The European View of the United States

The Europeans' view of the United States is complex and embedded in a historical context. Some have described it as a struggle between resisting and embracing the Americanization of Europe (Bischof, 2006). Many (maybe especially young) Europeans are drawn to the youth-oriented U.S. culture and its friendly people (Bulthuis, 1986; Laski, 1948; Sørensen & Petersen, 2006), and Europeans of all ages enjoy the cultural products that have crossed the Atlantic Ocean (McNeill, 2004). Yet, the spread and impact of the U.S. culture in Europe and throughout the world, as a "major vehicle of economic globalization," driven by commercial interests rather than by tradition, cause strong reactions in Europeans (Stephan, 2006; Winders, 2001, p. 253). Many fear a loss of the cultural diversity that has long characterized Europe (McNeill, 2004). In the following discussion, it is important to keep in mind that even though differences between Europeans and people in the United States clearly exist, Europeans tend to exaggerate "deficiencies" of people in the United States, emphasizing and magnifying the traits that separate them from the United States (Barzini, 1983).

Although most Europeans respect U.S. wealth and military strength and are grateful for its role in liberating Western Europe after World War II, European postwar economic and military dependency on the United States brought about mixed emotions among Europeans, ranging from appreciation to resentment or anti-Americanism (Pells, 1997; Stephan, 2006). In stark contrast to the United States' vitality and power, the aftermath of World War II left Germany overpowered and divided. Italy, also defeated, had lost its former grandeur, and Britain, France, the Netherlands, and Belgium no longer possessed their colonial empires. The United States assumed the role and the importance that Europe previously enjoyed. For many Europeans, the realization that their countries no longer mattered on the international arena was distressing, especially when they perceived the global leadership rested in the hands of a supremely confident country that lacked the awareness and sensibility that is developed from experience, failure, and suffering (Pells, 1997).

The tendency by the United States to see itself as the world's best hope, mentor, and example, coupled with a penchant to intervene where they deem necessary and having the means to do so, tends to frighten Europeans (Barzini, 1983). In their view, lack of involvement by the United States in the crises in Hungary in 1956 and in Czechoslovakia in 1968, juxtaposed with actions taken by the United States in Vietnam in the 1960s and 1970s, evidence inconsistencies between declared principles and actions (Pells, 1997). Many Europeans believe that living without concrete threats against their country until recently allowed the United States to develop an abstract philosophy of human rights that is not linked to survival but to entitlements. The wish to pursue happiness developed into a right to be happy (Frum, 2000). Europeans can also wonder about the U.S. political party system. For them, Democrats and Republicans are close to one another philosophically, and on the conservative side of the political spectrum. In contrast, almost all European countries have large social democratic parties, supported by the working and middle classes (Slomp, 2000).

However, in the 1990s, after the fall of the Berlin Wall and the end of the cold war, anti-Americanism had almost diminished in Europe just to resurge owing to the events that followed September 11, 2001. Although there was initially an unprecedented effort to support people in the United States and cooperate with the U.S. government, many Europeans began to question the U.S. approach to fight terrorism in 2002 (Body-Gendrot, 2004; Gallis, 2004). Political and cultural terms used to unify the people of the United States, such as "enduring freedom" and "axis of evil," were interpreted very differently by Europeans (Stephan, 2006). For Europeans, terrorism was nothing new but something that had plagued countries such as Spain, Italy, England, and Germany for decades (Gallis, 2004; Wallace, 2004). Similarly, in this time period, the U.S. rejection of the Kyoto environmental treaty and the lack of support for the International Criminal Court further added to many Europeans' view of the U.S. government as self-serving and above international cooperation (Wallace, 2004). To be noted is that many Europeans distinguish between their view of the U.S. government and its foreign policy and that of its citizens.

European International Students

Observations of European Students Visiting the United States

European international students in the United States are a diverse group of students, representing more than 45 different European nations (Chin, 2002). Table 13.1 presents the 20 most representative European countries at U.S. universities. Although European international students' experiences in the United States will vary, this section discusses common reactions and observations that they may have.

European international students at U.S. universities, especially if they come from one of the smaller European countries, decide that people from the United States know very little about their home country. This is surprising to them, because in their own country they are inundated with American cultural trends. U.S. politics make their news daily, whereas news programs like "World News Tonight"

Table 13.1

Number of International Students
From the Top 20 European Countries, 2001–2002

Country	No. of Students	Country	No. of Students
1. Germany	9,613	11. Greece	2,599
2. United Kingdom	8,414	12. Norway	2,323
3. France	7,401	13. Ukraine	2,195
4. Russia	6,643	14. Yugoslavia, former	2,027
5. Spain	4,048	15. Netherlands	1,791
6. Sweden	4,041	16. Switzerland	1,680
7. Italy	3,333	17. Hungary	1,242
8. Bulgaria	3,584	18. Czech Republic	1,152
9. Romania	3,325	19. Albania	1,129
10. Poland	2,606	20. Ireland	1,053

Note. Data from 2001 to 2002 (Institute of International Education, 2002).

on U.S. television involves almost exclusively news about the United States. The World Series includes only the United States and Canada.

Many European students may be taken by the United States' seemingly unlimited space. The vast spaciousness of the United States has created both a culture and society quite different from the European, with a focus on individualism, self-motivation, and geographic mobility. In contrast, many European countries are densely populated. Spatial restrictions have shaped a view of limited possibilities, political prudence, the importance of conservation, and social and communal bonds (Gorer, 1964; Laski, 1948; Wallace, 2004).

Reserved Europeans, especially those from Northern, Central, and Eastern Europe, but even those from Mediterranean countries who tend to be intimate mostly with family members and close friends, may be pleasantly surprised by and possibly suspicious of the affable people in the United States—their casual demeanor, amiableness, easy self-disclosure, and willingness to open their doors to strangers (Bulthuis, 1986; Laski, 1948). In Europe, friendships are developed more slowly; they typically are based on common experiences and mutual appreciation of personalities and interests, and they tend to be enduring. European students who may be lonely and homesick will experience such openness and hospitality as welcoming and healing, even though their passing nature may eventually disappoint some of them (Baudrillard & Turner, 1989; Bulthuis, 1986).

People from the United States work harder and longer hours than Europeans. In Europe, work, especially physical work, is viewed as befitting for mostly the lower class. In the United States, however, people find dignity in work of all forms. Even blue-collar workers see themselves as mostly middle class, and they believe that success and advancement are possible for all (McElroy, 1999; Story, 1982). Even though Europeans respect the U.S. drive and desire to succeed, they may not fully understand it. In their mind, leisure time, idleness, and relaxation are not sufficiently valued in the United States (Gorer, 1964; Laski, 1948; Maritain, 1958).

Ironically and surprisingly to many European international students, the United States with its high standard of living, its space and national resources, its openness and generosity, and its view of itself as the world's mentor and example, has a strong appetite for self-criticism (Pells, 1997). While criticism of their country from international students is not easily accepted, people in the United States easily pass judgment on themselves. Statistics on crime, reports on juvenile delinquency, and full accounts of dishonest and immoral acts are exposed and analyzed in U.S. newspapers, magazines, and television talk shows. People in the United States do not hesitate to express their disapproval of government actions and are willing to challenge them up to the highest court (Cunliffe, 1992).

Challenges European International Students Face at U.S. Universities

The literature on international students has indicated that living abroad and facing cultural and language barriers may negatively affect students' social and academic adjustment as well as emotional well-being (e.g., Charles & Stewart, 1991; Hamboyan & Bryan, 1995; Hechanova-Alampay, Beehr, Christiansen, & Van Horn, 2002; Meyer, 1995; Mori, 2000; Parr, Bradley, & Bingi, 1992; Poyrazli, Arbona, Nora, McPherson, & Pisecco, 2002; Rajapaksa & Dundes, 2002–2003). Fouad (1991) stated that social and environmental factors rather than individual intrapersonal factors predict international students' success. The following discussions on culture shock and language barriers address these factors with their concomitant difficulties.

Culture Shock
Culture shock is a multifaceted experience resulting from numerous stressors a person faces while adapting to a different culture (Winkelman, 1994). According to Winkelman, culture shock is normal in a foreign environment and is caused in part by cognitive overload and behavioral inadequacies. He described four sequential and cyclical phases of culture shock. In the honeymoon or tourist phase, people experience excitement, euphoria, positive expectations, and idealizations, primarily because they have not yet had to deal with differences in any substantial way. In the crises or cultural shock phase, things start to go wrong. Problems escalate, cultural differences become irritating, and the international students become increasingly disappointed, frustrated, and tense. In the adjustment and reorientation phase, these students learn how to adjust effectively. Even though some will return home during the crises or seek isolation by living in an ethnic enclave, many will adjust and adapt by resolving problems and differences and will begin to appreciate the new culture. Typically, adjustment is slow and cyclical, involving recurrent crises and readjustments. Finally, during the adaptation, resolution, or acculturation stage, there is a stable adaptation to and management of the new culture.

International students' struggles to adjust become apparent in the cultural shock phase when they encounter behaviors that seem familiar. The students are likely to interpret such behaviors not within the U.S. cultural context, but within that of their own culture. For example, the European student may interpret statements by U.S. students such as "How are you?" "I'll call you," and "Let's have lunch" literally, as evidence of interest in their lives and not as a greeting or as a way to end the conversation, as U.S. people might (Bulthuis, 1986; Mori, 2000). When the person who asked the question or extended the invitation continues to walk or does not call to arrange a time to meet for lunch, European students will likely feel hurt, confused, and disappointed and may retreat back into the safety of the international student community (Bulthuis, 1986). It also becomes tempting to ascribe such behavior to American "superficiality," a stereotype international students may have brought with them.

Language Barriers

Language barriers can also impede European students' academic performance and social adjustment during the culture shock phase. Although English is the native language for British and Irish international students, and in spite of the fact that many non-English-speaking European students are familiar with the English language, having had to learn it as early as in elementary school, many European students will struggle with language barriers. For example, unlike the English language, many European languages distinguish between formal and informal address, as in German *Sie* and *du*, and in French *vous* and *tu*. Using one or the other gives the speaker and the listener cues regarding distance versus proximity in social contact. Not having these signals in the English language can add to the confusion and misunderstanding European international students feel. For instance, a European student who has been introduced to others by a U.S. student as a friend probably expects a closeness and loyalty that the U.S. student may be unwilling or unable to give.

Having an accent can also distort effective communication (Lacina, 2002) and may be a source of discrimination. Compared with students from other continents, European international students may not experience the same amount of discrimination due to the fact that many can blend in with the majority U.S. student population on campus; however, being European does not necessarily mean that one is Caucasian. Because a good number of international students experience discrimination in the United States, often resulting in adjustment difficulties (Surdam & Collins, 1984), this may be another area of concern for European international students.

Language barriers and adjusting to a different educational system can result in students receiving lower grades than expected, leading to a loss of academic self-efficacy, which in turn predicts lower general adjustment (Poyrazli et al., 2002). International students, including those from Europe, may not fully understand the U.S. educational system. They may have to adapt to differences regarding grading system, expectations about class attendance, student–faculty interactions, selecting courses, and learning relevant study skills. They may not be familiar with terms or concepts like *graduate, undergraduate, major, major professor,* or *transcript,* as was true for one of the authors of this chapter. Understanding lectures, deciphering instructor expectations, expressing opinions in class discussions, answering essay questions, writing research papers, and finding a supportive advisor require a cultural and language know-how and sophistication that many international students do not possess (e.g., Charles & Stewart, 1991; Meyer, 1995; Mori, 2000; Parr et al., 1992; Thomas & Althen, 1989).

Likewise, career-related problems can arise for international students who must select majors that are relevant both to their own personal interests and to those of their family or community. Additionally, because international students may wish to return to their own home countries following graduation, many must make choices based on available job markets back home. Some may find themselves overqualified or graduating with training not specific enough to their own culture (Fouad, 1991).

Adaptation to a new culture involves learning to compromise between role identities students brought from home and new roles they are attempting in the United States (Williams, 2001). They must suspend at least some culturally based reactions and become more tolerant of the local culture, which may manifest internally at times as a conflict of loyalties. Research shows, however, that for most international students, adjustment improves over time (Hechanova-Alampay et al., 2002). Counseling can provide management and resolution from culture shock by providing support and insight into the cross-cultural adaptation process and by helping the students to manage stress, anxiety, and ambiguity (Walton, 1990).

To compensate for language difficulties and to make good grades, many international students may spend a great amount of time studying, which consequently leads to less time for social activities (Wan, Chapman, & Biggs, 1992). This is regrettable because through contact with people from the United States, international students enter U.S. society. They learn the ins and outs of a culture through observation, imitation, and trial and error when socializing. Unfortunately, during the time when many international students experience culture shock and have feelings of confusion, loss, and helplessness in dealing with an unfamiliar environment (Winkelman, 1994), they may have little social support and feel the least able and prepared to counteract negative feelings by active learning and adapting.

Counseling European International Students

Several studies have been conducted on international students' preference about counselor characteristics and help-seeking attitudes. Unfortunately, European international students tend to constitute only a minority in the samples surveyed, so one has to be careful when generalizing the findings to this group. Research has shown that international students prefer counselors who present as interpersonally skilled, trustworthy, honest, genuine, empathic, warm, and accepting (Bradley, Parr, Lan, Bingi, & Gould, 1995). In addition, emotional openness toward one's own emotional experience, being a woman, and previous experience in counseling positively predicted international students' attitudes toward seeking counseling (Komiya & Eells, 2001). Dadfar and Friedlander (1982) found that international students who had not experienced counseling viewed it as a nontrustworthy and inappropriate manner to solve personal problems, which could partly explain the underutilization of counseling services and high dropout rates among international students (Anderson & Myer, 1985; Nilsson, Berkel, Flores, & Lucas, 2004).

Because international students tend to have more problems and have fewer resources of support (Pedersen, 1991), they may be more hesitant to seek help than U.S. students; many are experiencing significant distress when they do present for counseling (Lin, 1996, cited in Lin, 2000). They most likely are in the culture shock phase as this episode emerges usually within a few weeks or a month after arrival (Winkelman, 1994). During this time, differences in culture such as U.S. people's strong individualism (Deen, 2002) and the fact that many people in the United States know very little about European countries and may assume, often erroneously, that the international student hopes to live in the United States permanently, adds to students' feelings of invisibility, isolation, homesickness, loneliness, stress, anxiety, anger, mistrust, and ethnocentrism (Chen, 1999; Mori, 2000; Rajapaksa & Dundes, 2002–2003; Thomas & Althen, 1989). Thomas and Althen (1989) listed culture shock, academic difficulties, home country concerns, social isolation, depression, financial concerns, and political, religious, and social conflicts as possible presenting issues in counseling. In a study of international students who sought counseling at a university counseling center, feeling down, difficulties standing up for one's rights, shyness or being uncomfortable around people, worry/nervousness, and difficulties selecting a major or career because of lack of knowledge about self were the most common concerns (Nilsson et al., 2004).

Recommendations

On the basis of what we have discussed in this chapter, and in light of the multicultural counseling competencies, we have developed the following specific recommendations, addressing attitudes, knowledge, and skills needed for counselors when working with European international students (Sue, Arredondo, & McDavis, 1992).

Several of the counseling theories used in contemporary counseling centers in the United States originated in Europe or were created by European Americans, making these approaches appropriate for European students. Yet there are subtle differences between the approaches used in the United States and those used in Europe. It is important to keep in mind that behaviorism gained more attention in the United States (Bankart, 1997) and psychodynamic theory developed into a more optimistic and self-focused theory in the United States than proposed originally, which could have an influence on the counseling process (Frum, 2000).

Because of the underutilization of counseling services among international students, innovative methods have been suggested to serve this population (Arthur, 1997; Fouad, 1991; Lin, 2000; Siegel, 1991). For example, college counselors may need to adopt multiple helping roles, including advocate and resource person, just to name a few, to meet the needs of international students (Lin, 2000). Outreach and groups held outside of the counseling center may be additional ways to reach European international students (Jacob & Greggo, 2001; Nilsson et al., 2004; Smith, Chin, Inman, & Findling, 1999).

When working with European international students, counselors need to keep in mind the multifacetedness of European identity, including country of origin (history, culture, ethnicity), socioeconomic status, gender, religious affiliation, as well as personal values, beliefs, and goals (O'Leary, Page, & Kaczmarek, 2000). Having knowledge or at least some understanding of European students' country of origin, its history and culture, allowing students to discuss the differences between their culture and the U.S. culture, and giving them opportunities to express their possible frustration and disappointment with the United States will help validate their experiences and will facilitate rapport and alliance building. Because students may not raise such concerns themselves for fear of being impolite, ungrateful, or rejected, counselors need to be open to such concerns and help verbalize them.

To be able to respond appropriately to European international students, counselors must be aware of their own values, biases, and assumptions regarding international students and clients who are not fluent in English. Also, they must assess their feelings and biases toward Europeans and European cultures. Furthermore, counselors must have some understanding of their own culture, the U.S. mainstream culture, and how U.S. culture can be perceived by Europeans as well as how European international students may be perceived by U.S.-born individuals.

In addition, having knowledge about issues and experiences common to international students is important, as well as knowledge about factors that may ease the adjustment process for these students. Some of these factors have been documented as spending time with U.S. students (Hechanova-Alampay et al., 2002), feeling adequate in English (Surdam & Collins, 1984), and having support from families and faculty (Mallinckrodt & Leong, 1992; Wan et al., 1992). Although many international students do not have any friends from the United States (Rajapaksa & Dundes, 2002–2003), Pedersen (1991) hypothesized that European international students may socialize more with U.S. students than with international students from other continents. Regardless, some European international students may need guidance in how to reach out to U.S. students, faculty, and other university personnel to secure the social support system necessary for social and academic adjustment. Hayes and Lin (1994) cautioned counselors not to interpret international students' lack of a social network as a personal attribute and thus as diagnostic material, but rather view it as a natural characteristic of the international students' environment.

Case Scenario

The purpose of this case study is to illustrate possible concerns raised by European international students and how to address these issues in counseling. Below follows a description of a German student's presenting concerns along with conceptualization and treatment recommendations.

Ingeborg, a 21-year-old international student from Frankfurt, Germany, sought counseling for difficulties concentrating on her studies. She states that academic success is very important to her and that she is not doing as well as she knows she can. Ingeborg received a scholarship from a German foundation to study finance for a year at a small university in Georgia, where she has been for 2 months. Her scholarship covers tuition but not room and board. Ingeborg is also a student at Johann Wolfgang Goethe University in Frankfurt, where she is studying for her bachelor's degree in economics. She has taken a year off from her studies to study in the United States to gain proficiency in English and make herself more marketable for employment and advanced degree, as well as to experience firsthand much of what she had read about and seen on television regarding U.S. culture. Her parents, who are also university-educated, were very supportive of this opportunity, as were several of her friends who were also studying abroad in other European countries. Initially, Ingeborg was excited about the opportunity to study in the United States, and she was proud of receiving the scholarship.

At the time of her intake interview, however, Ingeborg tells the counselor that she would like to return home because "nothing is working out for me." She feels that she should not go home, however, because of the money invested in her to study abroad and because she worries about disappointing her parents. Ingeborg reports that she feels lonely, longs to be home with her friends and family, and has difficulty falling asleep at night. Although she e-mails her family and friends back home several times a day, she reports minimal contact with others and having few friends on campus.

Ingeborg lives in university housing and rooms with an 18-year-old female student from the United States. Because of their age difference, Ingeborg and her roommate, although polite to each other, do not engage in much conversation or share any extracurricular activities. Ingeborg discloses to the counselor that she spends her day going to classes and working a few hours in the university library; the remainder of the day and evening she spends in her room alone. Although the university has a few hundred international students, most of them are from Asia, and Ingeborg reports that she feels they are quite different from her. There are, however, a few male students from Germany, whom Ingeborg knows, but they are all on the tennis team and travel extensively during the tennis season. Ingeborg knows of some other international students from Europe, including a group of French and Norwegian students on campus, but she feels uncertain about how to approach them, stating that "they are already so close."

After a couple of sessions, Ingeborg further reveals that she is frustrated with U.S. university students. She is especially upset at her roommate and her roommate's friends, whom she describes as shallow, apathetic, and politically uninformed. "All they talk about is makeup, boys, and partying." Ingeborg, who was active in the Green party in Germany, is upset about the waste and the lack of care for the environment that she observes in this country. She is also upset that people from the United States know so little about Germany except for the Autobahn, Nazi Germany, and World War II. All these cultural differences appear to further isolate her from other students on campus.

The counselor approaches Ingeborg as an equal and encourages her to take part in a collaborative therapeutic relationship by discussing the nature of counseling and the role expectations for both the counselor and the client. In the first session, the counselor discusses confidentiality, emergency, and cancellation procedures, and the expected length of their counseling relationship, while gently encouraging Ingeborg to ask any questions. He asks Ingeborg to share her cultural background as well as the experiences that bring her to therapy. Although Ingeborg is tentative at first, once the counselor is able to create a safe and trusting relationship with her, with each subsequent session she begins to open up.

The counselor recognizes that Ingeborg is in the crisis phase of the four stages of culture shock (Winkelman, 1994). Although Ingeborg communicates well in English, she has not been able to form connections with others and thus lacks a support system that would make her adjustment easier. She appears confused about her relationships with people from the United States and insecure about the effort it takes to form deeper friendships, which came easily for her in Germany. She also seems to experience some cultural barriers in making friends with other international students. She is hurt by the lack of interest in her and knowledge about her country. Although the course material is not overly difficult for Ingeborg, she finds it hard to concentrate on her studies because of her sadness and worries.

Throughout the sessions the counselor validates Ingeborg's feelings of isolation and homesickness. He discusses openly and nondefensively the differences between the U.S. and German culture, as well as the stereotypes Ingeborg expresses about U.S. culture. He shows an interest in her culture by asking questions about Germany that Ingeborg gladly answers. He also expresses awareness of the experiences European international students can have while studying in the United States, such as adjusting to a different educational system and having to rebuild social support networks in the United States that might have been solid back home.

The counselor also helps Ingeborg explore social situations in which she was uncomfortable in order to identify what could be changed. They discuss how her accent and being an international student may result in U.S. students feeling awkward around her and not knowing how to approach her. They explore her responses to this awkwardness and her own tendency to isolate and protect herself. The counselor acknowledges Ingeborg's strengths of building good relationships in Germany and encourages her to understand her current struggles as a component of the adjustment process and not as a personal weakness. Ingeborg is asked to explore what kind of friendships she would like to have with Americans and what she would like to experience while being in the United States. With the help of her counselor, Ingeborg develops some strategies to make connections with U.S. students and other international students on campus. Her counselor links her to an international student organization to broaden her network of support, and they discuss in what classes and campus activities Ingeborg could get involved to increase her chances of meeting students who share similar values and interests. It becomes clear to Ingeborg and her counselor that Ingeborg's difficulties concentrating on her studies result from acculturation challenges rather than from problems with the course work itself.

By the end of the fall semester, Ingeborg has developed several significant friendships. She has joined the campus paper, where she has found a friend who also is interested in environmental issues. As Ingeborg grew comfortable with the differences between the German and U.S. cultures, she learned to express her feelings about these differences to her friends in sensitive ways. Although Ingeborg continues to face cultural barriers, she is increasingly able to manage these without rejecting the surrounding environment and isolating herself. She is actually able to more readily identify the positive attributes of her temporary home. When counseling is terminated, the counselor feels that Ingeborg has moved into the adjustment stage where she has the energy to resolve problems and appreciate new experiences (Winkelman, 1994). Ingeborg reports that she is enjoying her studies and campus life and is taking the difficulties she encounters in stride.

Summary

This chapter provided an overview of the cultural backgrounds and possible experiences and difficulties European international students may undergo while studying in the United States. While European international students share a cultural heritage, they also bring with them a unique cultural worldview based on their country of origin. The material presented on the different European cultures and European views of the United States could be used as a broad but limited framework for understanding these students. The European students who present for counseling may be experiencing culture shock because of differences in the educational system, in values and worldviews, and in understanding and formulating social relationships. They may feel confused with the U.S. educational system, frustrated with Americans' lack of knowledge or interest in their country, and hurt by misunderstandings and disappointments while trying to form deeper friendships with U.S. students. Furthermore, because of these experiences, they may feel isolated and unsupported, withdrawing into the international student community on campus, or worse yet, into themselves. Thus, counselors who work with European international students need to be prepared to deal not only with academic and social problems but also with those specifically related to acculturation and adaptation. To provide culturally sensitive treatment, counselors need to have some knowledge of the student's culture, along with how identification with the home country influences the student's values and beliefs and perception of the United States. These values need to be recognized and validated by the counselor. By creating a safe counseling environment, the counselors can encourage students to honestly share their frustrations and disappointments. While traditional counseling therapies appear to be appropriate with European students, innovative methods of reaching out to this group may access students who need the support but may be unfamiliar or fearful of the counseling process.

References

Anderson, T. R., & Myer, T. E. (1985). Presenting problems, counselor contacts, and "no shows": International and American college students. *Journal of College Student Personnel, 26,* 500–503.

Ardó, Z. (2003). *Culture shock! A guide to customs and etiquette: Hungary* (Rev. ed.). Portland, OR: Graphic Arts Center.

Arthur, N. (1997). Counselling issues with international students. *Canadian Journal of Counselling, 31,* 259–274

Bankart, C. P. (1997). *Talking cures: A history of Western and Eastern psychotherapies.* New York: Brooks.

Barzini, L. (1983). *The Europeans.* New York: Simon & Schuster.

Baudrillard, J., & Turner, C. (1989). *America.* New York: Verso Books.

Berezin, M. (2003). Territory, emotion, and identity: Spatial recalibration in a new Europe. In M. Berezin & M. Schain (Eds.), *Europe without borders: Remapping territory, citizenship, and identity in a transnational age* (pp. 1–30). Baltimore: Johns Hopkins University Press.

Bischof, G. (2006). Two sides of the coin: The Americanization of Austria and Austrian anti-Americanism. In A. Stephan (Ed.), *The Americanization of Europe: Culture, diplomacy, and anti-Americanism after 1945* (pp. 147–181). New York: Berghahn Books.

Body-Gendrot, S. (2004). America needs Europe. In A. Curtis (Eds.), *Patriotism, democracy, and common sense* (pp. 131–140). New York: Rowman & Littlefield.

Bradley, L., Parr, G., Lan, W. Y., Bingi, R., & Gould, L. J. (1995). Counselling expectations of international students. *International Journal for the Advancement of Counselling, 18,* 21–31.

Bulthuis, J. D. (1986). The foreign student today: A profile. *New Directions for Student Services, 36,* 19–27.

Charles, H., & Stewart, M. A. (1991). Academic advising of international students. *Journal of Multicultural Counseling and Development, 19,* 173–181.

Chen, C. P. (1999). Common stressors among international college students: Research and counseling implications. *Journal of College Counseling, 2,* 49–65.

Chin, H. -K. K. (2002). *Open Doors 2002.* New York: Institute of International Education.

Cunliffe, M. (1992). *European images of America—In search of America: Transatlantic essays, 1951-1990.* New York: Penguin.

Dadfar, S., & Friedlander, M. L. (1982). Differential attitudes of international students toward seeking professional psychological help. *Journal of Counseling Psychology, 29,* 335–338.

Dalton, M. (2003). *Culture shock! A guide to customs and etiquette: Ukraine* (Rev. ed.). Portland, OR: Graphic Arts Center.

Deen, N. (2002). Newcomers in European societies: Implications for educational and counseling. *International Journal for the Advancement of Counselling, 24,* 3–17.

Elliott, M. (2003). *Culture shock! A guide to customs and etiquette: Belgium* (Rev. ed.). Portland, OR: Graphic Arts Center.

Europa: Gateway to the European Union. (n.d.). Retrieved June 26, 2006, from http://europa.eu.int/abc/index_en.htm.

European Commission. (2006). *Higher education in Europe*. Retrieved June 23, 2006, from http://ec.europa.eu/education/policies/educ/higher/higher_en.html

Feldblum, M. (1997). "Citizenship matters": Contemporary trends in Europe and the United States. *Stanford Humanities Review, 5,* 96-113.

Fouad, N. A. (1991). Training counselors to counsel international students: Are we ready? *The Counseling Psychologist, 19,* 66-71.

Frum, D. (2000). *How we got here—The 1970s: The decade that brought you modern life (for better or worse)*. Cambridge MA: Basic Books.

Gallis, P. (2004). Introduction. In P. Gallis (Coordinator), *European counterterrorist efforts: Political will and diverse responses* (pp. 1-4). New York: Nova Science.

Gorer, G. (1964). *The American people: A study in national character*. New York: Norton.

Hamboyan, H., & Bryan, A. K. (1995). International students: Culture shock can affect the health of students from abroad. *Canadian Family Physician, 41,* 1713-1716.

Hansen, J. D., & Schröder, P. H. J. (2001). Economic integration in Europe: Setting the stage. In J. D. Hansen (Ed.), *European integration: An economic perspective* (pp. 1-16). New York: Oxford University Press

Hayes, R. L., & Lin, H. (1994). Coming to America: Developing social support systems for international students. *Journal of Multicultural Counseling and Development, 22,* 7-16.

Hechanova-Alampay, R., Beehr, T. A., Christiansen, N. D., & Van Horn, R. K. (2002). Adjustment and strain among domestic and international student sojourners. *School Psychology International, 23,* 458-474.

Jacob, E. J., & Greggo, J. W. (2001). Using counselor training and collaborative program strategies in working with international clients. *Journal of Multicultural Counseling and Development, 29,* 73-88.

Janin, H., & Van Eil, R. (2003). *Culture shock! A guide to customs and etiquette: Netherlands* (Rev. ed.). Portland, OR: Graphic Arts Center.

Kinsley, M. (2003, July 25). Blair dares to be interesting. *The Washington Post,* p. A25.

Komiya, N., & Eells, G. T. (2001). Predictors of attitudes toward seeking counseling among international students. *Journal of College Counseling, 4,* 153-160.

Kramer, J. (1988). *Europeans*. New York: Farrar, Straus & Giroux

Kumar, K. (2003). The idea of Europe: Cultural legacies, transnational imaginings, and the nation-state. In M. Berezin & M. Schain (Eds.), *Europe without borders* (pp. 33-50). Baltimore: Johns Hopkins University Press.

Lacina, J. G. (2002). Preparing international students for a successful social experience in higher education. *New Directions for Higher Education, 117,* 21-27.

Laski, H. J. (1948). *The American democracy: A commentary and interpretation*. New York: Viking Press.

Lin, J. G. (2000). College counseling and international students. In D. C. Davis & K. M. Humphrey (Eds.), *College counseling: Issues and strategies for a new millennium* (pp. 169-183). Alexandria, VA: American Counseling Association.

Lord, R. (2003). *Culture shock! A guide to customs and etiquette: Germany* (Rev. ed.). Portland, OR: Graphic Arts Center

Mallinckrodt, B., & Leong, F. T. L. (1992). International graduate students, stress and social support. *Journal of College Student Development, 33,* 71-78.

Maritain, J. (1958). *Reflections on America.* New York: Scribner's.

McElroy, J. H. (1999). *American beliefs: What keeps a big country and a diverse people united.* Chicago: Ivan R. Dee.

McNeill, D. (2004). *New Europe: Imagined spaces.* New York: Oxford University Press.

Meyer, L. (1995). Academic acculturation for foreign graduate students: Meeting new concepts of research and writing. *College ESL, 5,* 83-91.

Mori, S. (2000). Addressing the mental health concerns of international students. *Journal of Counseling & Development, 78,* 137-144.

Nilsson, J. E., Berkel, L. A., Flores, L. Y., & Lucas, M. (2004). Utilization rate and presenting concerns of international students at a university counseling center: Implications for outreach programming. *Journal of College Student Psychotherapy, 19*(2), 49-59.

Nollen, T. (2001). *Culture shock! A guide to customs and etiquette: Czech Republic* (Rev. ed.). Portland, OR: Graphic Arts Center.

O'Leary, E., Page, R. C., & Kaczmarek, C. (2000). A comparison of perceptions of self among university students in Ireland and the U.S.: Implications for counseling. *International Journal for the Advancement of Counselling, 22,* 189-196.

Parr, G., Bradley, L., & Bingi, R. (1992). Concerns and feelings of international students. *Journal of College Student Development, 33,* 20-25.

Pedersen, P. B. (1991). Counseling international students. *The Counseling Psychologist, 19,* 10-58.

Pells, R. H. (1997). *Not like us: How Europeans have loved, hated, and transformed American culture since World War II.* New York: Basic Books.

Poyrazil, S., Arbona, C., Nora, A., McPherson, R., & Pisecco, S. (2002). Relation between assertiveness, academic self-efficacy, and social adjustment among international graduate students. *Journal of College Student Development, 43,* 632-641.

Rajapaksa, S., & Dundes, L. (2002-2003). It's a long way home: International student adjustment to living in the United States. *College Student Retention, 4,* 15-28.

Rosenthal, J. T. (1993-1998). *Microsoft Encarta Encyclopedia 99.* Redmond, WA: Microsoft.

Sheehan, O. T. O., & Pearson, F. (1995). Asian international and American students' psychosocial development. *Journal of College Student Development, 36,* 522-530.

Siegel, C. (1991). Counseling international students: A clinician's comments. *The Counseling Psychologist, 19,* 72-75.

Slomp, H. (2000). *European politics into the twenty-first century: Integration and division.* Westport, CT: Praeger.

Smith, T. B., Chin, L., Inman, A. G., & Findling, J. H. (1999). An outreach support group for international students. *Journal of College Counseling, 2,* 188-190.

Sørensen, N. A., & Petersen, K. (2006). Ameri-Danes and pro-American anti-Americans: Cultural Americanization in Denmark after 1945. In A. Stephan (Ed.), *The Americanization of Europe: Culture, diplomacy, and anti-Americanism after 1945* (pp. 115-146). New York: Berghahn Books

Stephan, A. (2006). Cold war alliances and the emergence of transatlantic competition: An introduction. In A. Stephan (Ed.), *The Americanization of Europe: Culture, diplomacy, and anti-Americanism after 1945* (pp. 1-20). New York: Berghahn Books.

Story, K. E. (1982). The student development professional and the foreign student: A conflict of values. *Journal of College Student Personnel, 23,* 66-70.

Sue, D. W., Arredondo, P., & McDavis, R. J. (1992). Multicultural counseling competencies and standards: A call to the profession. *Journal of Counseling & Development, 70,* 477-486.

Surdam, J. C., & Collins, J. R. (1984). Adaptation of international students: A cause for concern. *Journal of College Student Personnel, 25,* 240-245.

Svensson, C. R. (2003). *Culture shock! A guide to customs and etiquette: Sweden* (Rev. ed.). Portland, OR: Graphic Arts Center.

Swallow, D. (2001). *Culture shock! A guide to customs and etiquette: Finland.* Portland, OR: Graphic Arts Center.

Tanner, M. (1989). *Ticket to Latvia: A journey from Berlin to the Baltic.* New York: Henry Holt.

Thomas, K., & Althen, G. (1989). Counseling foreign students. In P. B. Pedersen, J. C. Draguns, W. J. Lonner, & J. E. Trimble (Eds.), *Counseling across cultures* (3rd ed, pp. 205-241). Honolulu: University of Hawaii Press.

Wallace, W. (2004). The European mistrust of American leadership. In A. Curtis (Ed.), *Patriotism, democracy, and common sense: Restoring America's promise at home and abroad* (pp. 125-130). New York: The Milton S. Eisenhower Foundation and Rowman & Littlefield.

Walton, S. (1990). Stress management training for overseas effectiveness. *International Journal of Intercultural Relations, 14,* 507-527.

Wan, T. -Y., Chapman, D. W., & Biggs, D. A. (1992). Academic stress of international students attending U.S. universities. *Research in Higher Education, 33,* 607-623.

Williams, P. (2001, Spring). Liminality among European exchange students. *International Education,* 19-40.

Winders, J. A. (2001). *European culture since 1848: From modern to postmodern and beyond.* New York: Palgrave.

Winkelman, M. (1994). Culture shock and adaptation. *Journal of Counseling & Development, 73,* 121-126.

Wintle, M. (1996). Cultural identity in Europe: Shared experience. In M. Wintle (Ed.), *Culture and identity in Europe* (pp. 9-32). Aldershot, England: Ashgate Press.

Chapter 14

Counseling International Students From Australia and New Zealand

Dale S. Furbish

The body of cross-cultural counseling literature about Australians and New Zealanders is not large when compared with what exists about issues for Asians, Hispanics, African Americans, and American Indians. Counselors in the United States who work with international students from Australia or New Zealand are therefore not likely to have many resources that address cross-cultural issues for Australians or New Zealanders. Moreover, because many Australians and New Zealanders have a historic European heritage, some U.S. counselors may assume that Australians and New Zealanders do not differ from European Americans. While it is true that Australians and New Zealanders probably have more points of similarity than differences to native European American students, U.S. counselors should be aware that international students from Australia and New Zealand are culturally different from students in the United States and that potential issues can arise during counseling as a result. Just as when counseling students from any other country or culture, U.S. counselors should undertake to use multicultural counseling competencies when counseling students from Australia or New Zealand. The development of multicultural counseling competencies begins with knowledge about the other culture (Sue et al., 1982). The goal of this chapter is therefore to present information about Australians and New Zealanders that could be helpful for U.S. counselors who are counseling international students from these countries.

Background

Australia and New Zealand are located in the Oceania region of the South Pacific. Geologically once part of the ancient super-continent Gondwanaland, Australia and New Zealand are now separate land masses and also separate countries. Although Australia and New Zealand are connected by historical, cultural, and economic elements, each must be recognized as a separate entity. Just as Americans and Canadians share much but can take exception when mistaken for one another, so Australians and New Zealanders should not be viewed as the same.

Indeed, both Australians ("Aussies") and New Zealanders ("Kiwis") possess a fierce sense of national identity. National loyalty and national pride have created intense but usually good-natured rivalry between the two nations, especially in sporting competition. Both Australian and New Zealand athletes have reputations as world-class competitors in a number of sports, and sports form an aspect of Australian and New Zealand national identities (Spoonley, Pearson, & Shirley, 1994). For example, rugby matches between the Wallabies (Australia) and the All Blacks (New Zealand) are events of national significance.

Together Australia and New Zealand are sometimes labeled the *antipodes*, which reflects that they are on the "other side of the world" from Europe. Both Australia and New Zealand were settled relatively recently when compared with other nations. Australia was first settled by the British in 1788 as a penal colony but did not achieve nationhood until 1901. New Zealand's first European settlers arrived in the 1790s with the establishment of whaling and sealing stations. New Zealand nationhood was established in 1840. Being far away from home and neighboring countries, these early settlers in Australia and New Zealand had little choice but to develop the ingenuity and resilience required to survive in isolation. Individualism, resourcefulness, and adaptability continue to be hallmarks of the Australian and New Zealand national characters.

As colonies of the British Empire, Australia and New Zealand were politically, socially, and economically tied to the "mother country." Colonists viewed Britain as the "center of the world" and the seat of legitimate culture. Travel to Britain and Europe was the means to learn and develop for those colonists who had the resources to do so. Continuing even today, the desire to travel and to experience other cultures is still an essential quality for many Australians and New Zealanders. As a result, Australians and New Zealanders retain an outward-looking perspective from their own countries. They have great curiosity about other cultures in every part of the world and an attitude that other countries and cultures have much of value to teach Australians and New Zealanders, who can then use that knowledge in their own country.

Cultural Characteristics of Australians and New Zealanders

The number of Australians and New Zealanders attending university in the United States is relatively small. In 2003, the U.S. Government issued 3,616 education visas to Australians and 1,152 education visas to New Zealanders (Office of Immigration Statistics, 2003). Differences in secondary school preparation, unfavorable currency exchange rates, and the relatively high cost of U.S. universities for international students are among the disincentives for Australians and New Zealanders to select study in the United States. On the other hand, postgraduate-level study (especially in disciplines and specialties not available at Australian or New Zealand universities) and participation in intercollegiate athletics are attractions for Aussies and Kiwis to U.S. universities.

Merta, Stringham, and Ponterotto (1988) suggested that living in a culture different from one's own inevitably produces some degree of stress. Yet, the degree of similarity between one's own and the host culture is a factor that facilitates adaptation to the new host culture (Furnham & Blochner, 1986). Because the majority of Australians and New Zealanders share a Eurocentric heritage with European Americans, adjustment issues to life in the United States are likely to be minimal. However, it should not be assumed that all Australian and New Zealand students will find the adjustment to be easy in every case.

Diversity Among Australians and New Zealanders

Despite the strong influence of British culture resulting from the colonial era, Australia and New Zealand are not monocultural countries. There is the possibility that a student from Australia or New Zealand may have a cultural heritage that is distinct from the dominant Australian or New Zealand culture. Australia is considered to be a multicultural society (Robinson, Loughran, & Tranter, 2000). In addition to indigenous Aboriginal culture, significant immigration to Australia from Italy, the former Yugoslavia, Greece, Germany, the Netherlands, Vietnam, and China has created an Australian society formed by a large number of people from a small number of distinct ethnic groups, each of which lends aspects of their culture to an "Australian culture" (Jupp, 1997). New Zealand, on the other hand, is bicultural (Robinson et al., 2000), the result of the influence of two large ethnic groups: Maori (New Zealand indigenous people) and European (referred to as Pakeha in New Zealand). New Zealand is legally bicultural (English and Maori) and trilingual (English, Maori, and Manual Communication). Although Maori and European cultures dominate, New Zealand has also seen significant immigration from the Pacific Islands (Fiji, Western Samoa, Niue, the Cook Islands, and Tonga), Asia (especially China and India), South Africa, and specific European countries (the Netherlands and former Yugoslavia). Cultural elements brought by immigrants from these countries contribute to the overall cultural environment of New Zealand, but many of the cultural specifics from the country of origin are retained by immigrants once they settle in New Zealand.

Determining the predominant cultural influence for an individual may be complicated by the degree to which an individual identifies with a particular culture. For example, a New Zealander may be ethnically Maori but have had little experience or identification with traditional Maori culture. This may be particularly likely for urban Maori, since traditional Maori culture and values are strongest in rural regions of New Zealand. Such complications support the cautions issued by Sue and Sue (2003) that it is inappropriate to generalize about individuals from a particular cultural group and that ethnicity is not always synonymous with culture.

Specific cultural knowledge is useful for cross-cultural counseling. However, as suggested above, the number of cultures, each different from one another, represented in Australia and New Zealand makes it unlikely that any one counselor will possess knowledge about all possible cultural backgrounds. Reflecting the diversity of specific cultures in Australia and New Zealand, and the need for general cross-cultural counseling competencies, Culbertson (1997) offered the following basic "commandments" for intercultural work:

> Thou shalt not transgress thy neighbor's cultural boundaries, but treat them with respectful awe.
> Thou shalt not dominate or manipulate the other.
> Thou shalt not insist on your own way being the right or best.
> Thou shalt not hurry. Cross-cultural trust and insight take a long time.
> Thou shalt listen attentively, not only with thine ears but with thine eyes.
> Thou shalt let go of all assumptions about the other.
> Thou shalt let go of power, including definitions about appropriate gender behaviour.
> Thou shalt make the other more important than thee, not simply equal to thee.
> Thou shalt use stories, rituals and symbols, but not rules from thine own culture.
> Thou shalt seek to offer insight and to recast roles, but not to liberate those who are not even imprisoned. (Culbertson, 1997, p. 16)

These guidelines were developed for counseling Pacific Island (Pasifika) clients in New Zealand. They reflect that although Pasifika is a collective term, the cultural differences among people from each individual Pacific Islands can be significant. The commandments display the benefits of adopting cultural sensitivities, regardless of the specific cultural differences between counselor and client.

Australian or New Zealand students who are from non-European backgrounds may identify with the culture of their origin, exhibiting attitudes and behaviors consistent with their cultural heritage. For example, students whose ancestors are Pasifika, Maori, or Aboriginal (Indigenous Australian) may be more reticent in counseling situations. Seeking help from outsiders in these cultures can be a threat to *mana* (one's personal status and power). Family and community elders are usual sources of counsel and advice in these societies. For an international student from Pasifika, Maori, or Aboriginal cultures, the formal academic qualifications of a counselor from the United States are not likely to be as important as age and gender of the counselor. Older women play important "counseling" roles in Pasifika, Maori, and Aboriginal societies, and it follows that students from these cultural backgrounds are likely to better relate to mature female counselors at U.S. universities.

Some Pasifika, Maori, or Aboriginal student behaviors may also be different from Western students and therefore open to misinterpretation by U.S. counselors. For example, downward cast eyes are indicative of respect rather than unwillingness to engage in a dialogue. U.S. counselors may also find that Aussie and Kiwi students from Pasifika, Maori, or Aboriginal cultures, which are collective cultures, may be less comfortable in one-to-one counseling than in group counseling formats. Identity is derived from a collective culture, and group identity is more highly valued than individuality. Australian or New Zealand students from these cultures are unlikely to have familiar levels of societal group support when they are far away from family and community. It may be unlikely that there will be significant numbers of other students or community residents from the same cultural backgrounds at most U.S. universities to give Pasifika, Maori, or Aboriginal students the level of group support that they experience in their home country. However, U.S. counselors should recognize the importance and benefits of group relationships and support when counseling students from these collective cultures.

Language Differences

Although English is the first language of most Australians and New Zealanders, language may still pose some concerns for some Australian and New Zealand international students and for Americans who interact with them. George Bernard Shaw's observation that the United States and Britain are two countries separated by a common language is relevant for the differences among Australian, New Zealand, and American English. Some Aussie and Kiwi terms may not be familiar to Americans. Examples are *knackered* (tired), *peckish* (hungry), and *spat the dummy* (had a tantrum). Other Aussie and Kiwi usages may seem familiar but can have very different intended messages. For instance, a *mate* is a friend, not a spouse. Australians and Kiwis use *partner* to refer to a life partner whether the context is marriage or a de facto (same or opposite gender) relationship. *Tea* is a drink, but it is also used to indicate a full meal. *Supper* is a light snack later in the evening. *Colleges* are secondary schools in Australia and New Zealand. Postsecondary schooling is categorically referred to as tertiary education or *uni* (university). These are but a few examples of words having different contextual meanings. The recommendation that follows from these comments on language is that clarification may be necessary for all parties when Aussies, Kiwis, and Americans are communicating.

Literature About Australian and New Zealand Cultures

Cultural Values

Australia and New Zealand have historical and contemporary social, cultural, political, and economic ties to Great Britain. Both countries are properly considered developed Western societies. Research studies generally hypothesize that Australians and New Zealanders embody characteristics similar to those found in other developed Western counties such as the United Kingdom and the United States. Often, the observation is made that Australia tends to be more like the United States, whereas New Zealand tends to be more similar to the United Kingdom.

Researchers have used samples of Australian or New Zealand participants to represent Western culture and values in studies that compare Western and non-Western societies. For example, Niles (1994, 1999) based her study of cross-cultural work ethics on data from samples of Australians and Sri Lankans. The sample of Australians held attitudes toward work (Protestant work ethic) similar to samples from other developed Western countries, whereas the sample of Sri

Lankans were more similar to samples from non-Western countries. Ramburuth and McCormick (2001) used a sample of Australian students for comparing a Western-tradition educational system with Asian-tradition educational systems in their study of learning style preferences. Hamid (1994) drew from a sample of New Zealand students to represent a Western culture in his study of self-monitoring, locus of control, and social encounters between Western and Eastern students. Peterson and Devlin (1998) reported similar attitudes toward entry-level jobs in their comparison of graduating accounting students in the United States and New Zealand. These studies all support the notion that Australians and New Zealanders have more similarities than differences to the United States and other Western societies.

The Overseas Experience

There are distinctive Australian and New Zealand cultural events that are widely experienced by many Aussies and Kiwis. An iconic cultural phenomenon for Australians and New Zealanders is the "overseas experience." Often referred to as the "Big OE," the overseas experience is a period, usually lasting at least 1 year, of international travel, work, and sometimes formal study undertaken by young Aussies and Kiwis. Traditionally the destination for the OE has been London, but Hong Kong, Tokyo, Dubai, and Singapore are increasing in popularly for an OE. For Australians and New Zealanders, the OE is a rite of passage, a social norm, a source of pride, and an experience that provides common conversational currency among those who undertake it (McCarter, 2001). Characteristically, the OE is begun with only minimal planning, thus requiring the development of flexibility, adaptability, and improvisational decision-making skills. An underlying motivation for the OE is the adventure of travel on a limited budget as well as the experience of surviving in other cultures.

Although work performed during the OE is usually unskilled and undertaken mainly to support travel and minimal living expenses, personal and intellectual maturity are often acquired during this period of travel. Inkson and Myers (2003) identified improved self-confidence, better self-knowledge, independence, self-reliance, and better understandings of other cultures and peoples in young Aussies and Kiwis who have completed an OE. Although the OE is a distinctive Australian and New Zealand phenomenon, it is certainly not unique to these countries. Exploring the world is an increasingly common activity among young people from many countries. However, the OE holds a special significance for young Aussies and Kiwis who are discovering themselves and developing personal and career competencies by exploring the world.

Personality Factors

A commonly held stereotype is that Australians are talkative and outgoing whereas New Zealanders are more reticent. Myers–Briggs Type Indicator (MBTI) studies on Australian and New Zealand students tend to confirm these observed differences between the two cultures. Although the numbers of students in the samples were small and the authors warned about overgeneralizations, Macdaid, McCulley, and Kainz (as cited in Myers, McCaulley, Quenk, & Hammer, 1998) found a higher percentage of Australians preferring Extroversion to Introversion, whereas Bathurst (as cited in Myers et al., 1998) reported a greater percentage of New Zealand students preferring Introversion to Extroversion. Overall, ESTJ (Extroverted Sensing Thinking Judging; i.e., extroverted thinking with introverted sensing) accounted for the most frequent MBTI code for the Australian sample, whereas ISFJ (Introverted Sensing Feeling Judging; i.e., introverted sensing with extroverted feeling) was the most frequently occurring code for the New Zealand sample. However guarded these conclusions, they do tend to support the commonly held notion that Australians are often more interactive with others, whereas New Zealanders tend to be seen as more guarded and inwardly reflective.

Issues for Australian and New Zealand International Students in the United States

Educational Differences

Fewer Australians and New Zealanders attend university in comparison with people from the United States. Although a university degree is becoming more important for many occupations, 18% of Australians (Australian Bureau of Statistics, 2003) and 11% of New Zealanders (Statistics New Zealand, 2002) hold a bachelor's or higher qualification, compared with the 24% of the U.S. population holding at least a bachelor's degree (U.S. Census Bureau, 2000). Australian and New Zealand students are therefore more likely to be first-generation tertiary students. These students may not have role models or experience the family encouragement and support for attaining a university qualification that U.S. students may have. As a result, U.S. counselors working with Aussie and Kiwi international students may find that they are more easily discouraged about their studies. Support from a counselor could be a significant factor for those students without other sources of emotional support and encouragement.

Counselors working with Australian and New Zealand international students in U.S. colleges and universities should be aware of differences between the secondary education systems in Australia and New Zealand and the United States. Influenced by the British educational system, Australians may attend through 12 years of primary and secondary education, and New Zealand students may attend through 13 years (New Zealand requires children to begin school at age 5, a year earlier than Australia). Those students wishing to attend traditional university study usually complete through Year 12 (Australia) or Year 13 (New Zealand). However, there are qualifications awarded to students who do not wish to attend university and who complete 10 years of school. University-bound students are expected to select school subjects that will support their admission into a specific program during their last 3 years of secondary school. Therefore, these students may not take as many liberal studies subjects as their U.S. counterparts. Both Australia and New Zealand have national curricula that define the competencies and standards for secondary school subjects. Exams, usually essay style, are nationally administered at the end of the school year to assess a student's mastery of the subject and to award grades. Admission to university programs is based on the results from these end-of-year exams rather than standardized university admission examinations (SAT or ACT) in the United States. Most Australian and New Zealand bachelor's degrees are designed for 3 years of study. Professional qualifications such as medicine and law do not require an undergraduate degree for admission but are entered into at first-degree level.

Study Skills

Because of differences in secondary curricula and assessment techniques, Australian and New Zealand undergraduate students may find study in the United States quite different from their experience at home and therefore may require assistance to adjust. Because Aussie and Kiwi secondary students are generally assessed by the end of the year, the more frequent quizzes and tests used in U.S. schools may necessitate the acquisition of new study habits and strategies. More frequent assessments may also result in time management concerns for those students who have not experienced such assessment schedules. Further, Australian and New Zealand international students are likely to be less familiar with the assessment formats used in U.S. schools. Because essay and short answer formats are the most common assessment techniques used in Australian and New Zealand secondary schools, formats such as multiple choice, true-false, matching, and fill-in-the blank may be unfamiliar and problematic. Assistance may be required for the development of the revised study and test-taking strategies that are required to succeed in U.S. higher education environments.

Achievement

Counselors from the United States may also find differences in Aussie and Kiwi students' attitudes toward achievement. A characteristic often attributed to Australian and New Zealand students is the *tall poppy syndrome* (Boyes, 2004). Tall poppy syndrome occurs when students fear that achieving will distinguish them from their peers. Rather than having a positive sense of pride in their achievements, talented Aussie and Kiwi students can fear that high achievement will lead to social rejection by their peers. The result is that less than full effort to achieve is exerted. Beyond mere modesty, the tall poppy syndrome can lead to self-sabotage and purposeful lowering of goals. A complication of tall poppy syndrome is that it can lead to a paradox for Aussie and Kiwi students who fear both not succeeding and succeeding. Students suffering from tall poppy syndrome are likely to require encouragement to develop self-confidence and pride in their abilities.

Career Development

In comparison with secondary schools in the United States, career counseling and services are often not as widely available in the Australian and New Zealand educational environments. Career programs are being developed and expanded in Australian and New Zealand secondary schools, but the general opinion is that much more is required (Elkin & Sutton, 2000; McCowan & Hyndman, 1998; McCowan, McKenzie, Medford, & Smith, 2001). Aussie and Kiwi students may therefore be less knowledgeable about career planning and occupational options than their U.S. counterparts. As a result, career interventions at the tertiary level may be particularly useful and needed to assist Australian and New Zealand students with their career exploration and decision making.

Aussie and Kiwi students are less likely to have taken the standardized career assessments to measure interest, values, and aptitudes that are frequently used in U.S. secondary schools. Few career-related psychometric instruments have been developed or normed in Australia or New Zealand, and overall career counselors tend to not use standardized assessment in their work (Furbish, 2002). As a result, Aussie and Kiwi students are less likely to be familiar with their measured occupational interests, values, or aptitudes compared with their U.S. counterparts. Because of this, Aussie and Kiwi students may also be less accepting of psychometric assessment procedures during career counseling. Their reaction to career assessments may be fear that the assessments will "put them in a box." Therefore, U.S. counselors who consider using career assessments with Aussie or Kiwi students will need to ensure that the students are comfortable with assessment and understand the purpose and results.

Occupational descriptions and requirements in Australia and New Zealand may be quite different from those in the United States. This can be an especially important issue for Aussie and Kiwi students intending to return home after the completion of their studies in the United States. Because most occupational information available to U.S. counselors is likely to come from American sources and describe the American context, it would be helpful to be aware of resources developed in Australia and New Zealand. A useful Internet site for Australian occupational information is available at http://www.myfuture.edu.au, and good New Zealand occupational information is found at http://www.careers.govt.nz.

Personal Adjustment

Aussie and Kiwi students attending university in the United States may experience personal adjustment issues that require counseling. An obvious concern may be feelings of isolation and separation caused by separation from family and significant others. By geography alone, Aussie and Kiwi students attending university in the United States are far from home and far from familiar emotional support systems. Isolation from family may be particularly important for students who identify with Aboriginal, Maori, or Pacific Island (Pasifika) cultures. Extended families (*whanau/fono*) are significant sources of emotional support and affiliation. Affiliation with other Maori or Polynesian students, community members, or staff (if available) may be of particular importance. In any case, homesickness is not easily ameliorated by a quick trip home for these students because considerable time and money are required to fly to Australia or New Zealand, even from the U.S. West Coast. Orientation and integration activities to U.S. university life are likely to be important mechanisms for Aussie and Kiwi students to form new support systems and affiliations.

It may be useful for U.S. counselors working with Australian and New Zealand international students to be aware that the reversed seasons between the northern and southern hemispheres could create issues for antipodean students. In Australia and New Zealand, Christmas is the beginning of the 2- to 3-month summer holidays. Separation from family over the Christmas holiday and unfamiliar seasonal conditions may heighten feelings of loneliness during this period. The relatively short period away from classes at the North American Christmas may make travel back home unattractive or financially impossible, thus Australian and New Zealand students may be particularly vulnerable during the holiday season.

Reentry

Returning home after the completion of study may pose another issue for international students from Australia and New Zealand. There may very well be conflicting emotions about what to do after graduation. While family, safety and security, sense of identity, and friends are strong attractors for returning home after studying and living overseas, perceived lack of employment opportunities, salaries, and career advancement are disincentives for returning (Inkson & Carr, 2004). Such conflicts between personal and career desires may make postgraduation decisions difficult. New Zealanders may be especially susceptible to conflicts because its economy and employment market are perceived as not providing the opportunities available in other countries. Indeed, Dumont and Lemaitre (n.d.) reported that 24.2% of New Zealanders with university qualifications do not reside in New Zealand. Balancing lifestyle, career, and family considerations may therefore create significant issues after graduation.

Counseling Australian or New Zealand International Students

Counselors in the United States working with Australian or New Zealand international students should be especially aware of privacy and confidentiality issues for these students. Although standards of ethical counseling practice are assumed in the United States, students from Australia and New Zealand may not be aware of them. Both Australia and New Zealand have national legislation to protect the privacy of all citizens, and privacy is frequently an important concern for Aussies and Kiwis. Aussie and Kiwi students should therefore be reassured that counseling is confidential and private within the ethical standards of the profession.

Generally, Australians and New Zealanders tend to be informal in their relationships. It is not unusual for Aussies and Kiwis to address older adults, teachers, supervisors, and other authority figures by their first name even on initial meeting. Honorific titles, such as Doctor, are not always used. The intimate and relaxed style exhibited by Aussies and Kiwi does not denote a lack of respect or otherwise breach decorum but reflects casual social relationships typical in Australian and New Zealand societies. U.S. counselors working with Aussies and Kiwis may find them less differential to authority than U.S. students.

Counseling Models

Manthei and Miller's (2000) description of the models used by New Zealand counselors will be familiar to most U.S. counselors. While their list reflects a diversity of counselor training and theoretical foundations, constructivist models have particularly influenced counseling practice in Australia and New Zealand. Moreover, Australian and New Zealand authors have contributed greatly to the professional literature on constructivism. Singaravelu, White, and Bringaze (2005) suggested that counseling approaches that are based on principles of social construction and narrative therapy are utilitarian for working with cross-cultural clients. These approaches place the counselor in the role of a learner. Because a counselor cannot be expected to know about all cultures, constructivist approaches encourage international students to narrate personal stories in their own words, from which the counselor and client extract meaning. For these reasons, and because of the widespread use of constructivist counseling approaches in Australia and New Zealand, brief discussions of narrative therapy (White & Epston, 1990), solution-focused strategies (de Jong & Berg, 2002), and systems theory (Patton & McMahon, 1999) follow.

Narrative Theory

Narrative theory has been greatly influenced by the writings of Michael White in Australia and David Epston in New Zealand (see White & Epston, 1990). Narrative approaches draw out clients' ideas (often called stories) about their lives and seek to understand them using the clients' subjective points of view. Counselors assist clients to then reconsider the meanings that they attach to problematic or self-limiting aspects of their lives by identifying events in their lives that challenge clients' interpretation of the self-defeating story. Clients are assisted to reconstruct a story that is preferred, less restricting, but equally valid and takes advantage of skills, abilities, and resources available. This approach promotes clients as "agents," that is, active forces, in their lives rather than recipients of another's direction. Cochran (1997, 1998) applied the narrative philosophy to counseling on career issues. He suggested using narratives to create meaning for clients' careers. Narratives help create meaning by configuring characters and events into "a coherent plot [that] offers the potential for rich rather than impoverished implications" (Cochran, 1998, p. 13). Narratives also provide a temporal organization with the potential of movement to fulfillment, provide order to the chaos, and offer instruction in what leads to what.

Solution-Focused Counseling

Solution-focused counseling is another constructivist model used widely in Australia and New Zealand. It is an approach that requires a shift away from clients dwelling on problems to the creation of possibilities and hope (Manthei & Miller, 2000). The emphasis in solution-focused counseling is on generating solutions rather than analyzing the root of the problem. To accomplish the creation of solutions, counselors assist clients to identify aspects of their lives that are working well and the resources that are being used in these successful situations. These same resources are then applied to the current problematic situation. Solution-focused counseling strives to be short term and specific. In New Zealand, Miller (2004) extended solution-focused techniques to career counseling. She suggested that by using a three-stage process of clarifying the client's career issue, identifying client competencies that have been instrumental in achieving past success, and constructing homework tasks that will allow the successful application of client competencies to the current problem, career issues are quickly and capably addressed.

Systems Theory

Australians Patton and McMahon (1999) have developed a Systems Theory Framework (STF) for use in career counseling. Their model represents a metatheoretical account of career development that represents three interconnected systems: the individual system, the social system, and the environmental/societal system (McMahon, Patton, & Watson, 2004). Intrapersonal variables such as gender, values, sexual orientation, ability, disability, interests, skills, age, knowledge, physical attributes, aptitudes, ethnicity, self-concept, personality, beliefs, and health are relevant. Also relevant are contextual variables such as family, geographical location, political decisions, historical trends, globalization, socioeconomic status, and the employment market. An STF assists career clients to construct their career stories by taking into account a variety of relevant influences. Subjective meaning is authored in the career story by clients. Through the development of a collaborative relationship with clients, counselors assist clients to explore meaning and to coauthor with counselors new meaning. Through this process, the next chapters of clients' career stories are written through their actions (McMahon et al., 2004).

Case Scenario

Graham is a 23-year-old New Zealander completing his bachelor's degree in sports and recreation at a U.S. university. Two years ago, he met Anne, an American student, while both were participating in a mixed-league intramural volleyball program. They began to date casually, but over the past year their relationship has become more serious. With the completion of his qualification, Graham now intends to return home to New Zealand. He is close to his family, who owns a farm and lives in small rural community. Although he knew that his relationship with Anne would be affected by his return to New Zealand, he has not extensively discussed the topic with her. His belief was that somehow their relationship would work out. Only recently, Graham invited Anne to return to New Zealand with him. Anne responded that although she also wished to continue their relationship, she did not want to move to the other side of the world, especially to live in a small community where there would be limited opportunities to take advantage of her accounting degree. Graham is devastated by her decision. After a week of emotional upset, Graham makes an appointment at the university's counseling center.

An STF of career development (Patton & McMahon, 1999) provides a useful model for conceptualizing Graham's issues. As mentioned above, STF proposes career-influencing factors that originate from three levels: the individual system, the social system, and the environmental/societal system. Further, STF acknowledges the interaction (recursiveness) within and between these systems.

Graham's return home to New Zealand exemplifies the interactions among these systems. His relationship to his family (a social system influence), his own career plans (an individual system influence), his relationship with Anne (another social system influence), and the employment opportunities available to him and Anne in rural New Zealand (an environmental/societal system influence) are all important to Graham and define the contexts of his concerns.

Consistent with the constructivist underpinnings of STF, Graham's counselor can encourage Graham to begin developing his story and draw personal meaning from it. Following Peavy's (1992) suggestions for counseling from a constructivist perspective, Graham's counselor is concerned with developing a cooperative alliance (relationship factor), encouraging self-helpfulness (agency factor), assisting Graham to elaborate and evaluate the constructions and meanings associated with his decisions (meaning-making factor), and helping him reconstruct and negotiate personally meaningful and socially supportable realities (negotiation factor).

During counseling, Graham begins to see himself as the enactor of his story rather than a passive bystander. Graham is able to identify skills and competencies that he had previously used when making big decisions. For example, he did extensive research on the Internet before selecting his university in the United States. He begins to feel that he can use those same skills for investigating options for residence and work. After discussion with Anne, Graham and Anne agree to explore residing in Australia. Graham views Australia as a viable option because he can still frequently visit his family in New Zealand. Because the job market in Australia is larger than in New Zealand, both he and Anne can access interesting work. The flexibility and adaptability he demonstrated when he moved to the United States to attend university are similarly useful for relocating to Australia. Although he does not know anyone in Australia, he recognizes the skills he acquired through travel that would support him in learning and settling into a new environment. Graham's counselor is able to assist him to identify solutions to the issues of concern by coauthoring with Graham a desirable story and helping him recognize and use the resources he possesses to make the story a reality.

Summary

Fewer students from Australia or New Zealand are enrolled in U.S. universities when compared with international students from many other countries. Because of the relatively small number of Aussie and Kiwi students, U.S. counselors may not have as much experience with them as clients as they have with other international students. As a result, the counselors' knowledge of Australian and New Zealand cultures may not be as great as their knowledge of the more highly represented international students' cultures.

Moreover, U.S. counselors may not have as many resources for learning about Aussie and Kiwi cultures. The professional literature on international students is likely to provide information about students from the more highly represented countries and cultures of origin. Nonetheless, appropriate cultural knowledge is as important when interacting with Aussie and Kiwi clients as it is when assisting other international students. U.S. counselors may therefore need to make extra effort to locate background information about antipodean cultures.

Although individual students from Australia and New Zealand possess unique qualities and characteristics, some issues are probable for many Aussie and Kiwi international students. First and foremost is that these students are far from home. Concerns about isolation and homesickness may be frequent. Further, U.S. counselors should recognize that these students' educational experiences are probably different from the majority of U.S. students. Study skills and similar scholastic adjustments may be necessary.

English is the first language for most Australians and New Zealanders. Language, therefore, is not likely to be a severe concern for Aussie and Kiwi international students. Further, the European heritage shared by many U.S., Aussie, and Kiwi students is likely to result in many cultural overlaps. While language and aspects of cultural commonality with the United States are advantageous for Aussie and Kiwi international students, U.S. counselors should still be alert to cultural differences. Counselor acknowledgment and knowledge of Australian and New Zealand cultures will facilitate interaction between U.S. counselors and students from these countries in the same way that cultural sensitivity is useful when counseling any international student.

References

Australian Bureau of Statistics. (2003). *Measures of a knowledge-based economy and society, Australia, 2003.* Retrieved March 31, 2005, from http://www.abs.gov.au/Ausstats/abs@nsf

Boyes, K. (2004). The power of mistakes. *Education Today, 1,* 15.

Cochran, L. (1997). *Career counseling: A narrative approach.* Thousand Oaks, CA: Sage.

Cochran, L. (1998). A narrative approach to career education. *Australian Journal of Career Development,* 7(2), 12–16.

Culbertson, P. (1997). *Counseling issues and South Pacific communities.* Auckland, New Zealand: Accent.

de Jong, P., & Berg, I. (1998). *Interviewing for solutions.* Pacific Grove, CA: Brooks/Cole.

Dumont, J., & Lemaitre, G. (n.d.). *Counting immigrants and expatriates in OECD countries: A new perspective.* Retrieved March 31, 2005, from http://www.oecd.org/dataoecd/27/5/33868740.pdf

Elkin, G., & Sutton, Z. (2000). Career advisors in New Zealand secondary school: A challenging role for the 21st century. *Australian Journal of Career Development, 9*(3), 7–12.

Furbish, D. (2002). A snapshot of New Zealand career practitioners. *Australian Journal of Career Development, 11*(2), 13–17.

Furnham, A., & Blochner, S. (1986). *Culture shock.* London: Methuen.

Hamid, P. (1994). Self-monitoring, locus of control, and social encounters of Chinese and New Zealand students. *Journal of Cross Cultural Psychology, 25,* 353–368.

Inkson, K., & Carr, S. (2004). International talent flow and careers: An Australasian perspective. *Australian Journal of Career Development, 13*(3), 23–28.

Inkson, K., & Myers, B. (2003). "The Big OE": Self-directed travel and career development. *Career Development International, 8*(4), 170–182.

Jupp, J. (1997). Immigration and national identity: Multiculturalism. In G. Stoker (Ed.), *The politics of identity in Australia* (pp. 132–144). Melbourne, Australia: Cambridge University Press.

Manthei, R., & Miller, J. (2000). *Good counseling: A guide for clients.* Auckland, New Zealand: Pearson Education.

McCarter, N. (2001). *The Big OE: Tales from New Zealand travelers.* Auckland, New Zealand: Tandem Press.

McCowan, C., & Hyndman, K. (1998). A career advisory system for Australia?: Summary of a review. *Australian Journal of Career Development, 7*(1), 35–41.

McCowan, C., McKenzie, M., Medford, L., & Smith, N. (2001). Careering in the South Pacific: An overview of career guidance and counseling policy in Australia and New Zealand. *Australian Journal of Career Development, 10*(3), 28–34.

McMahon, M., Patton, W., & Watson, M. (2004). Creating career stories through reflection: An application of the Systems Theory Framework of career development. *Australian Journal of Career Development, 13*(3), 13–17.

Merta, R., Stringham, E., & Ponterotto, J. (1988). Stimulating culture shock in counselor trainees: An experiential exercise in cross-cultural training. *Journal of Counseling & Development, 66,* 242–245.

Miller, J. (2004). Extending the use of constructivist approaches in career guidance and counselling: Solution-focused strategies. *Australian Journal of Career Development, 13*(1), 50–59.

Myers, I., McCaulley, M., Quenk, N., & Hammer, A. (1998). *MBTI manual* (3rd ed.). Palo Alto, CA: Consulting Psychologists Press.

Niles, F. (1994). The work ethic in Australia and Sri Lanka. *Journal of Social Psychology, 134,* 55–59.

Niles, F. (1999). Toward a cross-cultural understanding of work-related beliefs. *Human Relations, 52,* 855–868.

Office of Immigration Statistics. (2003). *Temporary admissions.* Retrieved March 31, 2005, from http://uscis.gov/graphics/shared/aboutus/statistics/TEMP03yrbk/2003TEMP.pdf

Patton, W., & McMahon, M. (1999). *Career development and systems theory: A new relationship.* Pacific Grove, CA: Brooks/Cole.

Peavy, V. (1992). A constructivist model for training career counselors. *Journal of Career Development, 18,* 215–229.

Peterson, R., & Devlin, J. (1998). Attitudes of graduating accounting seniors on entry-level positions: An international comparison. *Journal of Education for Business, 74*(1), 54–59.

Ramburuth, P., & McCormick, J. (2001). Learning diversity in higher education: A comparative study of Asian international and Australian students. *Higher Education, 42,* 333–350.

Robinson, G., Loughran, R., & Tranter, P. (2000). *Australia and New Zealand: Economy, society and environment.* London: Arnold.

Singaravelu, H., White, L., & Bringaze, T. (2005). Factors influencing international students' career choice: A comparative study. *Journal of Career Development, 32,* 46–59.

Spoonley, P., Pearson, D., & Shirley, I. (1994). *New Zealand society.* Auckland, New Zealand: Dunmore Press.

Statistics New Zealand. (2002). *Highest qualification for the census.* Retrieved March 31, 2005, from http://www2.stats.govt.nz/

Sue, D., Bernier, J., Durran, A., Feinberg, L., Pederson, P., Smith, E., et al. (1982). Position paper: Cross-cultural counseling competencies. *The Counseling Psychologist, 10,* 45–52.

Sue, D., & Sue, D. (2003). *Counseling the culturally diverse: Theory and practice* (4th ed.). New York: Wiley.

U.S. Census Bureau. (2000). *Educational attainment by sex.* Retrieved March 31, 2005, from http://factfinder.census.gov

White, M., & Epston, D. (1990). *Narrative means to therapeutic ends.* New York: Norton.

Chapter 15

Counseling International Students From the Former USSR

Oksana Yakushko and Tanya I. Razzhavaikina

Since the fall of the "iron curtain" in the late 1980s to early 1990s, many more international students from the former Union of Soviet Socialist Republics (USSR) have enrolled in U.S. colleges and universities. The number of these students is typically low in comparison with international students from other countries and continents. According to recent statistics on international enrollment in U.S. universities, in 2003–2004, 572,509 international students attended U.S. institutions of higher education (Chin, 2004). Students from the former Soviet Union represented 2.1%, or 12,027, of all international students (Chin, 2004). The majority of individuals from the former USSR came from Russia (5,532 students) and Ukraine (2,004 students).

A review of the literature regarding cultural adjustment and counseling work with students from the former USSR revealed that little or no attention has been devoted to this topic. Virtually no publications focusing on counseling international students from the former USSR were found. However, the presence of international students from the former USSR on U.S. campuses requires mental health counselors to attend to the unique experiences and needs of this group of students. This chapter provides an overview of the possible issues that international students from the former USSR may face while studying in the United States. Special attention is given to historical and cultural background, attitudes toward mental health, and unique challenges to well-being of the international students from the former USSR. Lastly, a case example and suggestions for counseling this group of international students are shared.

Historical and Cultural Background

Before its breakup, the USSR was a vast country with one of the most diverse populations. It spanned 11 time zones and included individuals from over 130 nationalities who spoke in more than half of the known languages in the world. A typical misunderstanding and mistake that Americans make in speaking about the USSR is to equate it with Russia, the largest of the former Soviet Republics. Often

American media and individuals refer to people from the Soviet Union as "Russians," which is inaccurate and may even be perceived as offensive by those from the former Soviet Union who belong to other nationalities.

The late 1980s and early 1990s brought tremendous changes to this union of the republics, which was joined by the ideals of socialism and communism. *Perestroika*, or rebuilding, of the socialist system did not succeed. Instead it ended in the revolt of the people in many parts of the country and, later, a military coup. A majority of the republics broke away from Russia in more than just political or administrative ways. Many of the newly independent states experienced revivals of cultural and religious nationalism that demanded a clear dissolution of the bonds with Russia.

The former USSR included 15 republics, which became independent countries following the events of the late 1980s to early 1990s: Russia, Belarus, Ukraine, Moldova, Tajikistan, Kazakhstan, Turkmenistan, Uzbekistan, Kyrgyzstan, Azerbaijan, Armenia, Georgia, Latvia, Lithuania, and Estonia. Russia, Belarus, and Ukraine are countries with Slavic linguistic and historical heritage. The majority of people in these nations are Orthodox Christians, even if most are nominally religious. Moldova is also located on the western edge of the former USSR but is more closely related to the Roma culture, sharing linguistic and cultural similarities with Romania. Tajikistan, Kazakhstan, Turkmenistan, Uzbekistan, Kyrgyzstan, and Azerbaijan are located in the south central region of the former USSR. Most of these nations are culturally close to both Middle Eastern and Asian cultures and have recently experienced the revival of Islam. Individuals from these cultures, along with people from Georgia and Armenia, also share some physical characteristics with Middle Eastern and Asian cultures. However, Georgia and Armenia differ greatly from these other nations in that they have had a strong tradition of Orthodox Christianity rather than Islam. Lastly, Latvia, Lithuania, and Estonia, the Baltic states, have had a unique relationship to the USSR, in that these countries joined the union nearly 30 years after it was formed. These countries maintained more connections with Western Europe and are culturally and linguistically more similar to their Scandinavian neighbors. Roman Catholic Christian traditions have been historically influential in these nations.

It is imperative to note that former USSR republics and their cultures are far from being homogeneous. Russia, or more accurately, the Russian Federation, still contains a vast landmass and a great number of culturally diverse people. Although ethnic Russians are the cultural majority, the country also has, for example, individuals from indigenous Siberian people groups (e.g., Inuits) and ethnic Asians (e.g., Koreans). People's mobility within the former Soviet Union as well as the contacts with other prosocialist countries, especially in Africa, also contributed to ethnic and racial diversification of the former Soviet nations. Furthermore, within each of the former Soviet states, people differ in terms of their religious practices, socioeconomic class, and rural versus urban home environments.

Despite the remarkable diversity of its people and civilizations, the former USSR brought together these various cultures under one banner, that of communism. Thus, individuals from the former Soviet Union may share characteristics that uniquely distinguish them from all other groups of people around the world. The characteristics that may be especially noticeable for counselors are the cultural norms for mental health, expectations of the educational system, and unique mental health concerns. It is important that counselors working with international students from the former Soviet Union keep in mind both these similarities and differences.

Unique Issues Faced by International Students From the Former USSR

Many of the concerns that international students from the former Soviet Union may bring to counseling are similar to their international peers from other countries (Mori, 2000; Razzhavaikina, 2006a; Yakushko, Davidson, & Sanford, 2005). These students may feel homesick, culturally isolated, confused, or overwhelmed by the newness of their environment or may be dealing with stereotypes. They may also arrive in the United States with histories of mental health difficulties such as depression, anxiety, substance abuse, or poor body image. However, some of their concerns may be significantly different from those of other students, or the difference may lie in how their issues are presented in relation to a "typical" college student. Attitudes about mental health and unique psychological concerns, along with the marked differences between American and the former Soviet educational systems, are among these different concerns that international students from the former USSR may present with during counseling.

Attitudes Toward Mental Health Counseling

Students' attitudes toward mental health have been profoundly shaped by the history of counseling in the former USSR. Counseling and psychotherapy were not commonly available or sought in the days of the Soviet Union. During the Soviet era, information about mental health counseling concepts and practices was scarce; more focus was given to neuroscience and psychobiology rather than counseling practice (Havenaar, Meijler-Iljina, van den Bout, & Melnikov, 1998). In the past, individuals with mental illness were treated solely by psychiatrists within a medical setting. Mental illness was typically associated with prisonlike mental institutions that were especially infamous for their psychobiological treatments of political dissidents (Daw, 2002). The "paternalistic models of the State and of psychiatry" (Korinteli, 2003, p. 374) resulted in clients' viewing any mental health helpers as figures of authority. Psychiatrists were not trusted with less clinically severe issues (Mokhovikov, 1994), and these difficulties, if treated, were addressed often by regular physicians through a focus on psychosomatic concerns (Roth, 1994) as well as such techniques as convincing, explaining, distracting, and hypnosis (Havenaar et al., 1998). Mental health counseling, especially on college and university campuses, was nearly nonexistent during the Soviet era.

After the fall of the Soviet Union, all of the newly formed states and their people experienced tremendous political, social, and economic transitions

(Rubchak, 2000). Although people continued to distrust the medically controlled field of mental health (Roth, 1994), a general interest in psychology and counseling has developed (Havenaar et al., 1998). The nondirective approaches have become especially attractive, in part because of the move away from the authoritarian styles of Soviet medicine and psychiatry and in part because of Western influences (Havenaar et al., 1998). It is also important to note that this exposure may differ for individuals who arrive from such countries as Russia (especially Russian metropolitan areas), where psychological treatments are becoming more commonplace, versus those who arrive from rural areas or countries with less developed traditions of mental health practice (e.g., rural areas of Tajikistan). Given all the aforementioned historical and cultural influences, it is not surprising that many students from the former USSR have very negative stereotypes of mental health services and may not choose counseling as a valuable and appropriate option to deal with their emotional and relational concerns.

Unique Mental Health issues

The recent political upheavals in most of the former Soviet nations have undoubtedly contributed to the increase in mental health difficulties suffered by their peoples. The World Health Organization (2004) indicated that many of the former Soviet states were among the worst countries in terms of overall mortality, negative trends in population growth, and the prevalence of mental health disorders. Contributing to the high mortality and prevalence of mental illness are the increased AIDS cases associated with drug addictions, high suicide rates, and instances of physical health difficulties associated with poor economic conditions (World Health Organization, 2004). Among other areas that have demanded the attention of mental health professionals in the former USSR are high divorce rates; alcoholism and drug addictions, instances of which have doubled since the early 1990s; and unemployment and poverty (Cockerham, 2000; Daw, 2002; Pridemore, 2002). In addition, alcoholism has been traditionally viewed as a culturally sanctioned way to deal with individual emotional or relational concerns. These difficulties may be among the strongest influences on the mental health of the international students from the former USSR.

In addition to these concerns, many of which have been brought on by the unstable political and economic environments, mental health struggles typically faced by American and other international students may take on a different appearance for students from the former USSR. Students may be more likely to present with somatic rather than emotional concerns. They may also be unaware that they are having a difficulty that might be commonly experienced by others. For example, eating disorders and body image concerns have been invisible in the former USSR, and female students who develop these difficulties may have no language to describe them (i.e., no constructs such as anorexia and bulimia).

International students from the former Soviet Union may also develop unique difficulties while studying in the United States because of their experiences of being stereotyped and the associated stigma upon arrival. A typical person from the

United States (U.S. counselors among them) often carries unpleasant and sometimes inaccurate views of what former Soviet countries are like. Many continue to hold cold-war era images of the Soviet Union as dark, very cold, economically depressed, and generally "backward" and generalize these stereotypes to students from the former USSR. These misconceptions, even if unspoken, may contribute to students' feeling misunderstood and stigmatized. Additionally, a typical American refers to all people from the former Soviet Union as "Russians" and has difficulty with the geographic, let alone the cultural and historical location of the former Soviet states. Several examples that are contrary to common stereotypes are that countries in the south central region of the former USSR, such as Uzbekistan, have a very warm, sunny, desert climate; some individuals from the former Soviet Union have a great amount of wealth by Western standards; and much of the world's scientific and cultural richness has come from this country. Table 15.1 provides the correct ways of naming former USSR republics and their citizens. It also summarizes information on culture, religion, population, and geographical location of each republic.

Unique Educational Experiences

The authoritarian style of mental health treatment during the Soviet era was not dissimilar to the generally authoritarian system of education, especially at the higher education levels. The Soviet secondary and higher education school systems were and continue to be outstanding in terms of students' educational

Table 15.1

Former USSR Republics: People, Language, Population, Culture, Religion, and Location in the Former USSR

Country	People	Language	Population	Cultural Heritage	Major Religion	Location
Russia	Russians	Russian	145,546,000	Slavic	Orthodox	Central
Ukraine	Ukrainians	Ukrainian	47,793,000			Southern
Belarus	Balarussians	Belarussian	9,873,000			Western
Moldova	Moldovans	Moldovan	4,253,000	Romanian		
Georgia	Georgians	Georgian	4,660,000			Southern
Armenia	Armenians	Armenian	3,220,000			
Tajikistan	Tajiks	Tajik	6,574,000		Muslim	South Central
Kazakhstan	Kazakhs	Kazakh	14,787,000	Middle Eastern		
Turkmenistan	Turkmens	Turkmen	5,703,000	and Asian		
Uzbekistan	Uzbeks	Uzbek	25,672,000			
Kyrgyzstan	Kyrgyzs	Kyrgyz	5,033,000			
Azerbaijan	Azerbaijani	Azerbaijani	8,233,000			
Latvia	Latvians	Latvian	2,320,000	Scandinavian	Lutheran	Western
Estonia	Estonians	Estonian	1,353,000			
Lithuania	Lithuanians	Lithuanian	3,458,000		Catholic	

achievements (U.S. Department of Education, 2003). For instance, the USSR had one of the highest literacy rates among countries in the world (Human Development Reports, 2003; Seager, 2003). However, the pedagogical principles were mostly focused on the students' attainment of knowledge rather than on personal development.

Historically, teacher training in the former Soviet Union had followed the traditional Eastern European model of an instructor imparting information and the student learning, with very little student involvement and participation in the teaching process. Consequently, classrooms in the former Soviet Union, whether in elementary schools or universities, are typically not interactive. In particular, the college-level learning process usually consists of attending lectures over the course of the semester, which ends with 3–4 weeks of intense examinations. A professor, the authority on the subject, delivers lectures to audiences of hundreds of students; students are expected to gain knowledge through the memorization of the professor's notes on the subject matter. Furthermore, interactions between the teacher and the students are not encouraged. "Cheating" on the final exams often is expected by students; it generally takes on a form of a careful and elaborate system of students "taking care" of one another by sharing notes during the exams. Additionally, because of the difficult economic conditions and the underpaid status of teachers at all levels, favoritism and bribery are not uncommon.

College and university students in the former USSR are typically not viewed as independent adults. A majority of them study in local educational institutions and live with their parents. There is neither an expectation nor the financial ability for most of the students to become "independent" from their families. In fact, an image of a typical family in the former Soviet Union is one of which children, parents, and grandparents live together. Moving away to go to college may be both culturally atypical and personally as well as financially difficult if not impossible for many students from the former USSR.

Case Scenario

Lena is a 17-year-old student from Kazakhstan. Her mother is ethnically Kazakh and her father is ethnically Russian. Both parents are engineers, which was not a highly paid or respected occupation in the former USSR. Lena grew up in a working-class district of Alma-Ata, the capital of Kazakhstan. She excelled in science courses at her secondary school and, with the help of a relative who had connections with a university in the United States, came to pursue a degree in civil engineering at the university.

Upon arrival at her university, Lena learns that she is the only Kazakh student there. She also learns that the only other person who had attended her university from Kazakhstan was a young man who was dismissed from the university for cheating on his exams. Lena has met other students from the former Soviet Union with whom she could speak Russian, but because she neither looks White nor shares their cultural interests, she feels excluded from their groups. Lena also encounters difficulties with perceptions about women in sciences in her engineering program. Very few other women are pursuing degrees in engineering, and there are no female faculty members in her area of studies. In addition to cultural isolation and not fitting in predominantly male classes, Lena struggles financially. Her parents cannot support her, and her student visa allows her to only work on campus. Thus she works night shifts at the school cafeteria to have some spending money. Even though her job provides some money, Lena knows she will not be able to afford to return to Kazakhstan and visit her family for at least 2 more years. She misses her family greatly and is uncomfortable living in a residence hall.

Lena sought counseling after her resident assistant cited her for the possession of alcohol. During the assessment, Lena shares that she relies on alcohol during times when she feels especially lonely and down, which are becoming more frequent. She cries throughout her first counseling session about her fear that she is going to be seen as "crazy" if others learn about her attending counseling, even though she think she will enjoy talking to someone about how she feels.

Lena's case is a typical example of what students from the former USSR may experience and bring with them to counseling. Counselors working with Lena can begin with a careful assessment of what factors may be contributing to her difficult feelings and consequent use of alcohol. Lena may be unfamiliar with what the process of counseling may entail and may not understand or trust that what she shares will truly be confidential. She may understate her use of alcohol but be willing to share her feelings of cultural isolation and missing her family.

In addition to creating a safe space for Lena to share, counselors also need to provide her with tools for dealing with her situation. She may be offered information about adoptive families, about such organizations as Women in Science and Engineering on her campus or via the Internet, as well as about possible ways she can meet other Kazakh people in the larger community. If Lena experienced instances of racism, it would be important to help her integrate these and help her to understand the highly racially conflictual U.S. society. Lena may also benefit from learning about the influence of alcohol on her body and her emotions, challenging some of the myths regarding the comforts of alcohol that she may have learned growing up. Most important, Lena may benefit from finding someone who can openly and respectfully listen to her story and help her integrate her difficult experiences. This will then have the potential to make her educational progress and adjustment process in the United States much more positive.

Suggestions for Counseling

This case scenario, along with an overview of the historical, cultural, and educational experiences that may be common for international students from the former Soviet Union, can serve as a guide to counselors who work with individuals from this student group. Many of the issues faced by these students may be similar to their American and other international peers. Therefore, counselors can use their multicultural counseling competencies to develop rapport and helpful strategies in working with students from the former USSR. However, as was previously alluded to, unique approaches may also be important in the mental health treatment of these students.

In working with international students from the former USSR, counselors especially need to educate themselves about these students' unique cultural, historical, and personal heritage. Counselors also need to challenge their own assumptions of what they associate with "Soviet" or "Russian." With the exception of this chapter, few other resources are available for learning more about the mental health counseling and mental health needs of individuals from the former USSR (e.g., Yakushko, 2005). As with all international students, an attitude of respect and openness can facilitate a stronger and more productive counseling relationship (Navarro & Yakushko, 2005).

Mental health counselors in the United States may need to provide international students from the former USSR with information regarding their presenting concerns that helps them to both normalize and understand their experiences. As mentioned earlier, these students may have no culturally relevant constructs to describe their emotional struggles. For example, brochures describing depression, anxiety, or eating disorders that describe typical symptoms of these conditions may be helpful.

These students may also be reluctant to seek help out of fear of seeing themselves or being seen by their helpers as "crazy." Taking into consideration the stigma that former USSR students may have about counseling and psychotherapy, counselors might consider contacting these students through outreach (e.g., presentations in English Language Learners classes, student clubs) and group work (e.g., a discussion group). These alternatives to individual counseling could provide a safe, nonthreatening, and much less stigmatized environment for students to disclose and explore their personal experiences, issues, and concerns (Razzhavaikina, 2006b).

Particular attention must be paid to difficulties that are more culturally acceptable for many individuals from the former USSR. For example, the use of alcohol has had a long-standing tradition of being a cultural panacea for feeling down or worried. International students from the former Soviet Union may use alcohol privately rather than publicly, which is the opposite of the pattern for U.S. students. Moreover, the use of alcohol may be equally prevalent for female and male students.

Counselors should also keep in mind the differences in educational systems between the former Soviet Union and the United States, as described earlier. International students from the former Soviet Union may report feeling overwhelmed by the expectation to talk during their classes, to view their learning as interactive and democratic, and to keep up with a constant workload of readings and papers. These students may not understand that there is a strong legal and cultural prohibition against cheating on U.S. campuses. It also may not be an ethic of "cheating" per se that these students may miss; rather, they may wish for a stronger student community with an ethic of care and support for each other's learning.

Not unlike other international students, students from the former USSR will be homesick and culturally out of place when they arrive in the United States.

However, their homesickness may be especially severe, considering that in their culture they would not be expected to move out from their parents' homes for many more years. Helping these students find adoptive families (i.e., host families) on their campuses or in their communities may help relieve the sense of loss that comes with a sudden break of connections that are essential to their sense of belonging and well-being.

Moreover, students from the former Soviet Union may deal with racism, if they are non-White, and the stigma of coming from a "backward socialist" country. These students may have to cope with constant stereotyping and, at times, oppression. Lastly, these students may encounter cultural isolation, because only a small number of students from the former Soviet Union attend U.S. colleges or universities, and an even smaller number of students may be from their particular country of origin. Counselors can help students deal with their feelings of loneliness and isolation as well as help them find on- and off-campus resources for connecting with others culturally similar to them.

On the positive side, it is important to note that, similar to other international students, students from the former USSR see their process of cultural adjustment to the United States as both a positive and challenging experience (Razzhavaikina, 2006a). A number of positive psychology concepts were found to be incorporated in students' definitions of their adjustment experiences, including hope, optimism, and personal strengths (Razzhavaikina, 2006b). Therefore, strengths-oriented counseling may be an effective counseling approach that would seem to fit former USSR students' perceptions of their adjustment to the demands of the American culture.

Summary

This chapter presented an introduction to some of the challenges that international students from the former USSR face while studying in the United States, as well as suggestions for how U.S. counselors may approach therapeutic work with these students. The former USSR was a vast country with an extraordinary number of diverse cultures and peoples. Thus, this chapter can only be seen as a general introduction rather than a comprehensive guide. Those who work with students from the former USSR can enjoy an opportunity to gain more comprehensive knowledge about their clients and their cultures and be rewarded with learning about the unique and rich experiences these clients bring with them to U.S. campuses.

References

Chin, H. K. (2004). *Open Doors: Report on international educational exchange.* New York: Institute of International Education.

Cockerham, W. C. (2000). Health lifestyles in Russia. *Social Science and Medicine, 51,* 1313–1324.

Daw, J. (2002, June). Russian psychology fights to bring psychotherapy to a needy but wary public. *Monitor in Psychology, 33,* 23–25.

Havenaar, J. M., Meijler-Iljina, L., van den Bout, J., & Melnikov, A. V. (1998). Psychotherapy in Russia. *American Journal of Psychotherapy, 52,* 501–514.

Human Development Reports. (2003). *Adult literacy rate.* Retrieved September, 24, 2005, from http://www.undp.org/hdr2003/indicator/indic_2_2_1.html

Korinteli, R. (2003). On the psycho-social conditions of psychotherapy in post-Soviet Georgia. *Journal of Analytical Psychology, 48,* 371–380.

Mokhovikov, A. N. (1994). Suicide in the Ukraine. *Crisis,* 15, 137.

Mori, S. (2000). Addressing the mental health concerns of international students. *Journal of Counseling & Development, 78,* 137–144.

Navarro, R., & Yakushko, O. (2005). Attending to the career development needs of diverse students. In P. Gore (Ed.), *Facilitating the career development of students in transition* (pp. 103–122). Columbia, SC: National Resource Center for the First-Year Experience and Students in Transition.

Pridemore, W. A. (2003). Patterns of suicidal mortality in Russia. *Suicide and Life Threatening Behavior, 33,* 132–150.

Razzhavaikina, T. I. (2006a). *Cultural adjustment to the United Stated: A phenomenological study of international students' perspectives.* Manuscript submitted for publication.

Razzhavaikina, T. I. (2006b). *Discussion series for international students: A case study of effectiveness.* Manuscript in preparation.

Roth, L. H. (1994). Access to and utilization of mental health services in the former Soviet Union. *Journal of Russian and Eastern European Psychiatry, 27,* 6–18.

Rubchak, M. J. (2000). Engendering a feminist identity: Women's movement to feminism. *Journal of Women's History, 12,* 212–214.

Seager, J. (2003). Literacy. In J. Seager (Ed.), *The Penguin atlas of women in the world* (pp. 77–78). New York: Penguin Books.

U.S. Department of Education. (2003). *Average mathematics scale scores of fourth-grade students, by country: 2003.* Retrieved October, 1, 2005, from http://nces.ed.gov/timss/TIMSS03Tables.asp?Quest=1&Figure=1

World Health Organization. (2004). Prevalence, severity, and unmet needs for treatment of mental health disorders in the World Health Organization World Mental Health Survey. *Journal of the American Medical Association, 291,* 2581–2590.

Yakushko, O. (2005). Mental health counseling in Ukraine. *Journal of Mental Health Counseling, 27,* 161–167.

Yakushko, O., Davidson, M. M., & Sanford, T. C. (2005). *Seeking help in a foreign land: International students' counseling center utilization patterns.* Manuscript submitted for publication.

Part III

Counseling and Outreach Approaches

Chapter 16

Multinational Competencies of International Student Service Providers

Shu-Ping Lin and Paul B. Pedersen

This chapter takes an experiential approach to learning how to counsel international students. Reviews of the research literature are well covered in other chapters of this book and are not repeated here. Our hope is that the reader will capture the subjective feeling of what it is like for an international student to seek out counseling and also what it is like for a counselor working with an international student. We strongly encourage that the process of counseling international students be viewed as a journey of discovering the counselor's own culturally learned values and assumptions. It is a journey that should be embarked on like any physical journey: with an open mind, an appreciative attitude, and an eagerness to learn new ways of looking at the world. With this kind of humble attitude, a counselor will be in a better position to become not only a multiculturally competent counselor but also a multinationally competent counselor. A multinationally competent counselor is an individual who is aware of one's own cultural values, is open to and respects the complexity of different cultural value systems due to clients' national and ethnic background, and is willing to develop and provide culturally and nationally appropriate intervention. Given the complexity of the therapy work with international students, a light-hearted but caring attitude in reading this chapter is welcomed as a journey in becoming a multinationally competent counselor.

It has been suggested by scholars in the multicultural counseling and psychotherapy areas (Sue, Arredondo, & McDavis, 1992, p. 481) that "a culturally skilled counselor is one who is in the process of actively developing and practicing appropriate, relevant, and sensitive intervention strategies and skills in working with his or her culturally different clients." What does this statement mean for a client who is ethnoculturally and nationally different from the dominant/majority culture in the United States? One international student expressed this opinion:

I would like to have a counselor who is kind and attentive and very professional. When I describe the hardship that I have been experiencing to him or to her, I hope he or she can not only be a good listener (be empathetic) but also be able to guide me to see through the points of the problems. Also, he or she can suggest to me alternative ways to deal with the problems. I hope that he or she can understand where I come from and realize both racial and language barriers in my life here.

International students differ from most of the other minority groups and are in fact a "minority among minorities." Demographically, this group of people is not even counted as a minority in the United States. As the result of this circumstance, the problems and concerns that have been encountered by international students are similar to those of most minority groups, yet are at the same time uniquely different. How can competent counselors apply their multicultural awareness, knowledge, and skill in counseling this unique group of individuals? A whole set of new theoretical guidelines and practical techniques are required for further discussion.

Should a counselor need a wider perspective on psychotherapy theory and approaches in working with international students? To answer this question, a counselor first needs to ask him- or herself some critical questions to examine his or her theoretical orientation:

1. Is the concept of psychotherapy and counseling culturally originated from European middle-class culture?
2. Is my concept/training of psychotherapy and counseling culture-bound?
3. Is my treatment and intervention plan for psychotherapy and counseling individual-based?

By answering these three questions, counselors have the opportunity to examine their own theoretical biases. By appreciating each individual client's cultural uniqueness, counselors will understand that multicultural competencies are, indeed, needed in work with clients from different cultural backgrounds. To be successful in their work with international students, a competent counselor should first be a multiculturally competent counselor. Through developing multicultural competencies, a counselor increases his or her generic competency. Sue et al. (1998) introduced the standard of multicultural competencies to provide the basic framework and guidelines for reframing multinational competencies. A multinationally competent counselor will also be a multiculturally competent counselor. The list below is a summary of cultural competencies in three dimensions (Sue et al., 1998). Also, a list of guidelines and principles suggested by the American Psychological Association (APA) in enhancing multicultural competency is strongly suggested for counselors to enrich their therapy skills before their encounter with a client who comes from different ethnic and national backgrounds.

Dimension 1:
Counselor Awareness of Their Own Assumptions, Values, and Biases

-   Aware of cultural heritage and comfortable with differences but aware of limits

- Knows about oppression through racism and discrimination
- Skilled in self-improvement toward a nonracist identity

Dimension 2:
Understanding the Worldview of the Culturally Different Client

- Aware of emotional reactions toward other racial and ethnic groups
- Knows the culture of their client population and its influence on counseling and society
- Skilled in mental health issues of other cultures and actively involved with ethnic minority groups.

Dimension 3:
Developing Appropriate Intervention Strategies and Techniques

- Aware of religious and spiritual indigenous mental health service resources
- Knows how counseling fits with other cultures, institutions, and assessments
- Skilled in culturally appropriate counseling of indigenous people.

These guidelines were presented by a joint task force of APA Divisions 17 and 45 in the document "Guidelines on Multicultural Education, Training Research, Practice and Organizational Change for Psychologists" (American Psychological Association, 2003).

Even with the best skills and training, there may be times when the counselor and international student face unexpected misunderstandings as a result of cultural differences. We address some of these differences in the context of each of the three dimensions.

Dimension 1 differences. If the counselor has never met someone from the international student's country before, the likelihood of confronting a different client perspective is even higher than with other multicultural clients, both for the client and the counselor. It is also highly likely that the counselor will unintentionally offend the client by her or his ignorance. The geopolitical realities are that the counselor may well have been identified as being the enemy in that student's socialization. Finally, the familial support available to other minorities is typically thousands of miles away for the international student and far beyond help.

Dimension 2 differences. The counselor is often faced with a student who expresses (or conceals) emotion in unheard of ways so that the counselor will have an even more difficult time estimating emotion accurately. It would be impossible to know all the thousands of cultures from which international students come, so the counselor will often be "flying blind." The traditional ways of managing personal problems for international students would almost certainly not include counseling and are more likely to involve retreating inside oneself to mobilize intrapsychic resources without interference from any counselor.

Dimension 3 differences. Whereas the counselor is typically not trained to deal with before-birth or after-death issues, the non-Western international student often regard these as the only questions really worth discussing. The scientist-practitioner model of counselor training has neglected religious and spiritual issues. The first indigenous resource for the international student is within the self, looking inward for one's own strength. If that does not work, then family and relatives are consulted, and if that does not work, then trusted friends are consulted. Going to a counselor/stranger is a final resort after everything else has failed (Pedersen, 2000).

The difficulty of multinational counseling can be perceived as even greater than multicultural counseling for most counselors. The Michigan International Student Problem Inventory (Pedersen, 2004) describes 132 frequently occurring specific problems faced by international students. The resources for dealing with personal problems are also much fewer. This puts the multinational counselor in a difficult role. However, the multinational counselor is still held accountable for being competent and demonstrating that competence by following the established guidelines.

The American Psychological Association (2003) adopted the following six principles and six guidelines:

Principles

1. Enhance ethical conduct of psychologists by knowledge of differences in beliefs and practices.
2. Understand and recognize that the interface between an individual's socialization experiences is based on one's ethnic and racial heritage.
3. Recognize the ways in which the intersection of racial and ethnic group membership enhances understanding and treatment.
4. Have knowledge of historically biased approaches about cultural differences as deficits.
5. Be uniquely able to promote racial equity and social justice.
6. Know about the roles of organizations reflecting cultural differences.

Guidelines

1. Psychologists recognize their deficit thinking and biases about ethnic minority cultural groups.
2. Psychologists recognize the importance and pervasiveness of multiculturalism.
3. Psychologists use constructs of multiculturalism in education and training.
4. Psychologists recognize the importance of culture-centered and ethical research.
5. Psychologists apply culturally appropriate clinical approaches and skills.
6. Psychologists use a culturally informed organizational change processes.

The rest of this chapter offers theoretical guidelines and intervention approaches to enhance a counselor's multinational competence that will reflect on the framework provided by Sue et al. (1998) in their multicultural competency dimensions. The section on theoretical guidelines provides guiding principles and discussions in increasing the awareness at three different levels, which reflect primarily Dimensions 1 and 2 of the multicultural competency framework. The three levels of awareness are discussed in detail. The section on intervention provides intervention approaches through case studies of international students from different cultural and national backgrounds and primarily reflects Dimension 3.

Theoretical Guidelines for Multinational Competence

A multiculturally/multinationally competent counselor is expected, at minimum, to apply the competencies described by the multicultural guidelines in the counselor's work with an international student. Hence, the awareness of the cultural context for an international student's reporting concerns is essential for culturally attuned service delivered by a multinationally competent counselor. We introduce theoretical guidelines embedded in three layers for awareness in increasing the multinational competencies in work with international students. The three layers are (a) the individual level of awareness and appreciation of cultures in the process of psychotherapy, (b) the sociocultural and sociopolitical level of awareness for the life of international students, and (c) the universal level of awareness for individual uniqueness in a cultural context. The following sections deal with each level of multicultural awareness in turn.

Individual Level of Awareness in the Process of Psychotherapy

As suggested by Sue et al. (1998), a counselor's self-awareness of his or her own assumptions, values, and biases toward counseling work and toward lifestyles is the first step to delivering a culturally attuned service to their clients. We suggest that respect for each client's cultural values is highly recommended as a basic counseling skill, especially with international students who often share very different cultural values that, to some extent, might challenge a counselor's moral and ethical principles.

International students, unlike most minorities, enter the United States as adults with their own cultural values already fixed, and are therefore more set in their ways and vulnerable toward the majority's conflicting attitude toward their culture system. In some cases the international student leaves a high-status position back home and has to adjust to a "low-status" position as a mere undergraduate or graduate student in the United States, which also creates difficulty. A multinationally competent counselor will not only be aware of his or her own cultural values but also be an open-minded learner in understanding the influence of each client's culture on his or her thoughts and behavior.

Respecting the cultural values and treating clients as cultural teachers will not only convey the message of cultural acceptance to clients in releasing the distress from cultural encounters but also empower clients to gain their confidence in dealing with their concerns. Listed below are three major suggestions at the individual level.

1. *Be aware of the psychotherapy concept in different cultures.* It is essential for a counselor to understand the meaning and concept of psychotherapy in a client's cultural context and how the client perceives psychotherapy in his or her understanding before counseling begins. In most Asian cultures, psychotherapy is a Western concept that is still mostly a mystery. Seeing a counselor is highly stigmatized in most of these cultures and is almost equated to craziness. There is a folk saying in China, "Gee, you must be real crazy, if you see a counselor." Even living in the United States, most international students would still be involved with their fellow nationals back in their home country and their fellow nationals in the United States.

A collection of critical incidents (Pedersen, 1981, 1991, 1994) document some of the difficulties faced by international students. To reduce the cultural stigma, one male international student from Taiwan justified to his fellow nationals his visiting a counselor as "a chance to speak English with a native speaker" in seeing a counselor for his adjustment distress. This kind of justification is common among Asian international students given the negative meaning and stereotype about psychotherapy in their cultural systems. It would be beneficial for both counselor and client to discuss their perception of psychotherapy and counseling and to further address the concerns. By doing so, two functions of psychotherapy will be served in this exploration process. First, appreciation of the client's strength by taking the risk of being stigmatized by fellow nationals will empower the client to deal with his or her concerns and also release the client from the distress caused by the cultural stigma. Second, by displaying his or her acknowledgment toward, and interest in, understanding the client's cultural and national differences, the counselor will convey a higher quality of multinationally competent service to this client.

2. *Be aware of the cultural values of a "good client" in traditional psychotherapy.* The following is an example of a Korean international student's comment:

> Each time, I would wait for my counselor to say things first to guide me for the counseling. I always was polite to let her say something first. Yet, she said that I was too quiet and was resistant to therapy. I totally did not know where that came from. Also, one time, she asked me what the hidden message of my quietness is. I was just simply waiting for her to say things first and there was no trick I played in being quiet. And sometimes, it crept me off when she kept asking me to express my feelings. I just do not have a lot to say for feelings.

In such a manner, this undergraduate student from Korea expressed his frustration during our interview for the study of international students' cross-cultural experience.

As counselors, we all expect our clients, regardless of their cultural backgrounds, to be verbally and emotionally expressive, insightful, and open to therapy (Sue et al., 1998). When a client is quiet, we see her or him as playing some type of psychological game. But, this assumption is not always true for international student clients. Many international students just want their counselor to start first, as a gesture of courtesy. Showing respect for an authority figure and being polite is highly valued in most Asian and collectivistic cultures (Pedersen, 1994). Counselors need to be aware of one fact: International student clients must be highly motivated in dealing with their issues when seeking psychotherapy because seeing a counselor is the "final resort" for help.

3. *There is no counselor with magical multicultural knowledge, but a counselor who is multiculturally competent will keep an open mind.* Learning directly from your clients to expand your multicultural competence works better than just learning about your clients from textbooks and then stereotyping them into categories. Challenge your own cultural value systems as well as your clients'. A 26-year-old doctoral student expressed her mixed feelings about the arranged marriage back in her home country, India. She reported feeling anxious because she has never met her fiancé. She reported feeling excited about this marriage because she is going to marry someone from a higher caste level. Also, she reported that her family has exhausted their fortune to pay her dowry to the groom's family to lift their social class in the caste system.

As a counselor, you might be challenged by this cultural convention. However, there is no absolute right or wrong value in this complicated context and no need to be judgmental. Your client's attitude regarding this marriage is in her cultural context. You are entitled to make the client feel comfortable and learn about herself from this incident, but you have no right to impose your own cultural values on this client without the invitation from her to do so. The counselor will need sensitivity to the student's cultural context as being relevant in a psychotherapeutic setting for successful work with international students.

Be aware of your own cultural values and do not impose your cultural assumptions in judging others' behaviors and beliefs. Appreciate each client's cultural values and learn to understand how to make your own cultural value system more flexible. In doing so, a counselor will not only benefit himself or herself by developing an open-minded worldview but also provide a culturally balanced model for his or her clients to learn vicariously. In addition to the awareness at the individual level, it is very important for a counselor to be aware of the socio-cultural and sociopolitical context of international students.

Sociocultural and Sociopolitical Level of Awareness for the Life of International Students

In this section, both sociocultural and sociopolitical challenges are discussed in comprehending international students' concerns. As a multinationally competent counselor, one must be aware of the sociocultural challenges encountered by international students in cross-cultural experience in general. Without such awareness, a counselor faces a heightened risk of treating an individual out of the appropriate context, and thus pathologizing reactions as solely due to personality traits rather than recognizing the substantial influence of environmental circumstances. One international student reported going to a counselor and mentioning that he was from Africa. The counselor responded, "What country is that in?"

Sociocultural challenges faced by international students include the following:

1. *Sociocultural adjustment distress.* Most international students are from cultures that are significantly different from U.S. culture. Culture shocks in several areas, such as food, clothing, and leisure activities, are expected and encountered by them. All of these encounters can create stress when international students first encounter this culture. A student from Indonesia tells about meeting his advisor when first arriving at Ithaca airport. The president of Cornell University happened to be at the airport, and his advisor introduced the student to the 6-feet 3-inch towering president. The president stuck out his hand, smiling, and said "Glad to meet you!" The student looked up at him in shock and asked, "Why?"

Too much stress from daily life blended with academic stress can accelerate distress in the process of adjustment. Many international students experience adjustment syndromes, such as alienation, acculturation, identity conflict and confusion, and migration stress (Marsella & Pedersen, 2004).

2. *Friendliness is not equal to friendship in U.S. culture.* There is a common piece of advice offered to newly arriving international students by senior international students: "Americans are very friendly . . . but that doesn't mean they want to be your friends!" In casual interactions Americans often display interest and concern with people they have just met, primarily out of social politeness. However, to an international student, such behaviors would signify an interest in initiating a friendship, which may or may not be the intention of the American. Thus, such interactions can lead to misunderstandings, and frequently disappointment and frustration for international students. A Canadian international student commented, "It hurt me when I contacted an American after talking with her and she acted uncomfortable and expressed no interest in developing a friendship. But then why did she give me her phone number and invite me to call her?" Often times, this kind of culture difference can create a lot of frustration in the process of adjustment for international students, especially when they are new to this culture and need "American friends."

3. *Oppression, prejudice, and ignorance.* The reactions of a host country's residents can have a powerful effect on the well-being of international students. Ignorance of other cultures, expression of prejudiced attitudes, and deliberately oppressive actions can serve to dehumanize an international student. Other authors have thoroughly discussed the nature of such dynamics (see, e.g., Pedersen, 1991; Schmitt, Spears, & Branscombe, 2003), but the importance of recognizing these realities can not be overstated.

In addition to sociocultural challenges, international students also face myriad sociopolitical challenges, including the following:

1. *Awareness of the language/accent barriers.* English is the only language that capitalizes the first-person singular ("I"), which some international students

may regard as a symbol of the individualistic self-centeredness of English-language speakers. Whether they speak English as first language or second language, most international students are vulnerable to language barriers. Sometimes problems arise because of international students' accents. An international student teaching assistant from England reported her concern because of her English accent in teaching class. American students had complained to the department about not understanding "her funny accent," and she was asked to take a nonteaching position. A nonnative English speaker could have suffered from a similar experience. "People just listen to my language, rather than my ideas." A French accent is generally perceived as sexy by Americans, whereas Indian and other Asian accents are considered as an "ugly sounding" language.

2. *Awareness of the different nationalities/ethnicities among the category of international students.* What are counselors' assumptions about "international students"? How do counselors picture international students when they think of international students? A group of people who look East Asian? A group of people with darker color? Or a group of people scattered around the world with different colors? For example, an undergraduate student athlete from Germany, a Chinese middle-age married graduate student with two kids, and a single Turkish female student all identify themselves as international students, yet because of differing national and cultural origins, they all face problems and challenges unique to their own cultural groups.

Consider the following examples. A Taiwanese international student often will be annoyed by a counselor who wrongly assumes the student is a Chinese from mainland China. Students from South Korea will appreciate a counselor more if the counselor understands the difference between North and South Korea. Recently, after 9/11, international students from the Middle East and Asia have encountered more hostility than international students from other parts of the world. Thus, it is important to be aware of the within-group differences in the category of international students.

3. *Immigration stress.* Regardless of whether an international student is a sojourner or intends to remain in the United States, all international students must face specialized legal regulations. This includes working-limit regulations (20-hour work limit on campus, no off-campus working privileges), curriculum practical training, occupational practical training, varying levels of certification status regarding English proficiency, legal alien status checks, and a number of other practical requirements. The international "visitor" has none of the guaranteed rights that a U.S. national takes for granted and are governed under the "administrative rules" of the U.S. Citizenship and Immigration Services under the Homeland Security legislation. A student can be arrested, put in jail, and deported on the basis of an "anonymous tip" without ever finding out who accused them or even what they were accused of! All these factors are realities in the daily lives of international students that can affect their well-being. It is important for the multinationally competent counselor to be aware of such realities for international students.

4. *Power differential and the null environment in academia.* Because of differences in nationality, ethnicity, and language background, international

students are highly vulnerable to power struggles and, in the worst case, abuse. It is not uncommon for international students to be abused, mistreated, neglected, or ignored by their direct advisor or other power figures; this may not always be intentional. In one example, an advisor said that he expected the international student to schedule a visit if he had a problem, and because the student did not come to see him, the advisor believed everything was going well. In another example, international students may be easily pressured to far exceed the weekly hour work limit for an assistantship for fear of jeopardizing their funding. One student from Uganda described, "I work over 40 hours a week, often to 10 p.m. I am exhausted, but I cannot afford to protest to my advisor. I could lose my position, and I would not be able to send money back home to my family."

Another concern that international students have commonly encountered is the *null environment hypothesis*. A null environment, as defined by Freeman (1979), is an environment that neither encourages nor discourages individuals—it simply ignores them. The effect is to leave this group of individuals at the mercy of whatever environment or personal resources to which they have access (Betz, 1989). For most international students, the resources and support that they have access to are limited (Ying & Liese, 1994), which leave these students greatly vulnerable to prejudice and discrimination. However, most of the advisors and instructors at the college setting are either not aware of the limitation of international students' resources or are themselves the sources of prejudice. Because of this form of passive discrimination, by not being aware of the null environment effect from their advisors and others, as well as the frequent occurrence of negative messages regarding their ability, international students are often under great distress in coping with such environmental disadvantages.

Universal Level of Awareness for Individual Uniqueness in Cultural Context

An individual exists in a cultural context. When seeing a client for the first time, counselors need to strive to see the client as a person who carries her or his own unique life story and listen to it. Although it is important to be aware of cultural themes, it also important to be aware of the possible pain and depersonalization the student has experienced. Arthur (2004) suggested some cultural myths when counselors impose their limited understanding in their contact with their very first international student. Assuming, for example, that "international students are difficult to work with in counseling" or that "international students are the 'cream of the crop from their country'" can lead the counselor in a wrong direction.

Thus, it is important to see each individual as a fellow human being who shares the same basic set of emotions, struggles in relationships, family conflicts, losses, developmental concerns, and questions regarding spirituality. At the same time, all of these concerns must be understood in a cultural context. In other words, strive to balance these three levels as equally valid and important perspectives.

Psychotherapy Approaches for Counseling International Students

In this section, some suggested approaches are introduced for providing appropriate treatments and intervention plans for working with international students.

Hearing and Healing in Cultural and Individual Context

Go beyond language; listen to the meaning of language expressed by each international student rather than language itself. Listen comprehensively to each international student's concerns and stories, and respect the power of self-healing the student may implement during the process of listening. Learn to detect international students' emotional expression from their storytelling, and release emotional distress by commending them on their stories and challenges. Tell a student, for example, "It must be very stressful to face this situation, and I really admire your strength in hanging in there. I would cry a lot if I was in your situation." Listening provides a means to empower international students as well as a psychotherapy skill for decreasing their mental distress.

The Strength Approach in Seeing International Students

Often times, the numerous barriers and challenges from different levels that international students have encountered can easily discourage them. As a result, international students' well-being and self-esteem can suffer. In this regard, we suggest that counselors assume a coaching role in facilitating the healing process for international students. Identifying the existing strength of international students can be very therapeutic to international student clients as a counterbalance to their frustration from environmental stressors (Lin & Betz, 2004).

The International Student Survey of Strong Feelings (Pedersen, 2004) has proved useful in helping international students to articulate problems for which counseling might be appropriate. The assumption is that topics about which the international student has "strong feelings" might be areas in which counseling could be appropriate. A list of 90 items presents the topics of (a) meaning in life, (b) adventure achievement, (c) faults of Americans, (d) teachers and classmates, (e) academic problems, (f) self-confidence, (g) doubts and assurances, (h) the opposite sex, (i) family, and (j) community. The international student is asked to indicate on a 7-point scale the degree of positive or negative strong feelings he or she has about each item. The answer sheet is divided into nine columns of 10 items each for fast scoring. The degree of strong feelings (combining positive and negative scores) gives the counselor a place to start in counseling the international student.

Assisting clients to explore their inner strengths can act as an empowering process. In addition to appreciating international student clients' inner strengths, counselors can also encourage clients to use their cultural values as a resilience tool in the adjustment process. To empower international students, counselors should be mindful of the many other roles they can serve for a client, such as advocate, advisor, facilitator, and change agent (Atkinson, Thompson, & Grant, 1993). Most of all, the counselor needs to have a positive attitude toward international students. In her book *Counseling International Students,* Arthur (2004) devoted her beautiful and powerful words and thoughts to her children that demonstrate her most sincere appreciation in seeing international students' strengths: "To my daughter, Caitlin, 2 year old, and son, Travis, 1 year old . . . , as you grow up, I hope that you will explore the world as international students."

Adjustment as an Experimental/Experiential Adventure

A young student musician from Ukraine expressed, "Once I saw my life here as an adventure for exploring American cultures, I felt less stressed and started to enjoy my everyday life." Often times, international students can be frustrated by the numerous cultural challenges and differences in their daily life. As a result, there can be a lot of acculturative stress on international students besides their academic concerns. A multinationally competent counselor provides a different perspective in encouraging the international student to see the adjustment process as an experimental journey into American cultures. Help international student clients to appreciate the opportunities to explore a new world by studying abroad. By doing so, it will help clients manage the pressure to succeed and facilitate their adjustment. It also will create a lighter but caring attitude in adjusting to new cultures and in adapting new culture values for international students.

Action Oriented and Problem Solving

As the individual quoted at the beginning of this chapter stated, a counselor can "guide me to see through the points of the problems . . . [and] suggest to me alternative ways to deal with the problems." This thought, which was expressed by an international student, is in accord with the research findings (e.g., Exum & Lau, 1988; Pedersen, 1991) suggesting that most international students prefer a directive model of psychotherapy. In many cases, international students would see counselors as "expert and friend" (May & Jepsen, 1988) and expect counselors to provide practical guidelines in working through their problems much as a respected teacher might. Sometimes there is a stigma attached by international students to visiting a "head doctor," but the same functions when done by a "teacher" become status-enhancing education.

Because of the nature of concerns international students will encounter, a multinationally competent counselor should be able to implement problem solving. A counselor is encouraged to facilitate some concrete and feasible plans with international student clients in a cooperative manner. If necessary, a counselor can become a culture teacher in teaching and sharing some social skills to help clients better adjust to the new cultural environment.

Verbal and Nonverbal Language in Counseling

There is a language barrier in multinational counseling. We suggest when working with clients who speak English as a second language that counselors speak slowly, simply, and use clear expressions in a calm fashion. Avoid slang or idioms, and be sensitive to any confusion a client may experience because of language. Be ready to process many language-related concerns, whether in the first session or well into the therapeutic relationship.

Because of language barriers, some international students are more sensitive to the counselors' nonverbal expressions and tend to display gestures in expressing their concerns. The counselor is encouraged to pay more attention to both his or her own and the client's nonverbal expressions. It is also important to be aware of the differing cultural meanings that can be attributed to nonverbal behaviors.

Closing Thoughts

On one hand, being an international student can be a very painful and not so delightful experience because of distress coming from different areas, such as sociocultural adjustment, academic stress, cultural ignorance, and identity confusion. As counselors, we can inadvertently accelerate this distress if we are not multinationally competent. On the other hand, being an international student can be a very positive experience if counselors can guide international students to see their strengths and view their cross-cultural studying experience in an explorative and experiential fashion, like a journey. As counselors, regardless of our cultural background, we have the choice to decide our attitude in working with international students.

References

American Psychological Association. (2003). Guidelines on multicultural education, training, research, practice, and organizational change for psychologists. *American Psychologist, 58,* 377–402.

Arthur, N. (2004). *Counseling international students: Clients from around the world.* New York: Kluwer Academic/Plenum.

Atkinson, D. R., Thompson, C. E., & Grant, S. K. (1993). A three-dimensional model for counseling racial/ethnic minorities. *The Counseling Psychologist, 21,* 257–277.

Betz, E. N. (1989). Implications of the null environment hypothesis for women's career development and for counseling psychology. *The Counseling Psychologist, 17,* 136–144.

Exum, H. A., & Lau, E. Y. (1988). Counseling style preference of Chinese college students. *Journal of Multicultural Counseling and Development, 16,* 84–92.

Freeman, J. (1979). How to discriminate against women without really trying. In J. Freeman (Ed.), *Women: A feminist perspective* (2nd ed., pp. 194–209). Palo Alto, CA: Maryfield.

Lin, S. -P., & Betz, N. (2004, August). *The strengths and coping strategies among Chinese international students on their adjustment process: A shift towards a strength perspective.* Poster presented at the Annual Convention of the American Psychological Association, Honolulu, HI.

Marsella, A. J., & Pedersen, P. (2004). Internationalizing the counseling psychology curriculum: Toward new values, competencies, and directions. *Counseling Psychology Quarterly, 17,* 413-423.

May, W. C., & Jepsen, D. A. (1988). Attitude toward counselors and counseling process: A comparison of Chinese and American graduate students. *Journal of Counseling & Development, 67,* 189-192.

Pedersen, P. (1981, February). Personal problem solving resources for foreign students. In S. Dunnett (Ed.), *Factors affecting the adaptation of foreign students in cross-cultural settings* (Special Studies Series No. 134). Buffalo, NY: SUNY, Council on International Studies.

Pedersen, P. (1991). Counseling international students. *The Counseling Psychologist, 19,* 10-58.

Pedersen, P. (1994). International students and international student advisors. In R. Brislin & T. Yoshida (Eds.), *Improving intercultural interactions* (pp. 148-167). Beverly Hills, CA: Sage.

Pedersen, P. (2000). *Handbook for developing multicultural awareness* (3rd ed.). Alexandria, VA: American Counseling Association.

Pedersen, P. (2004). *One hundred and ten experiences for multicultural learning.* Washington, DC: American Psychological Association.

Schmitt, M., Spears, R., & Branscombe, N. (2003). Constructing a minority group identity out of shared rejection: The case of international students. *European Journal of Social Psychology, 33,* 1-12.

Sue, D. W., Arredondo, P., & McDavis, R. J. (1992). Multicultural counseling and competencies and standards: A call to the profession. *Journal of Counseling & Development, 70,* 477-486.

Sue, D. W., Carter, R. T., Casas, J. M., Fouad, N. A., Ivey, A. E., Jensen, M., et al. (1998). *Multicultural counseling competencies: Individual and organizational development.* Thousand Oaks, CA: Sage.

Ying, Y. W., & Liese, L. H. (1994). Initial adjustment of Taiwanese students to the United States: The impact of postarrival variables. *Journal of Cross-Cultural Psychology, 25,* 466-477.

Chapter 17

Group Work
With International Students

Laurie A. Walker and Robert K. Conyne

The United States continues to host more than half a million international students in its colleges and universities (Institute of International Education, 2005). Although this enrollment has now slowed owing to a number of factors, the large presence of international students provides a diverse population whose adjustment to a new culture presents concerns that are important to address. Therefore, service providers in higher education have a special responsibility to develop a more comprehensive understanding of how international students differ from their American counterparts and how they might assist in determining ways in which these students can feel more at home in their new environment. The purpose of this chapter is to describe how group work can be a useful method to assist in promoting positive experiences for international students on U.S. campuses and to encourage further development of this dynamic approach.

Interpersonal Needs of International Students
on Higher Education Campuses

International students who attend U.S. colleges and universities face many common concerns and difficulties: adjusting to a new university system, establishing an identity in an unfamiliar culture, communicating in a foreign language, dealing with financial worries, being uprooted from familiar social support systems, experiencing homesickness, and feeling lonely in general (Komiya & Eells, 2001). In addition, most international students are in a period of transition and eventually plan to return to their home countries after satisfying their educational objectives (Lacina, 2002). Many international students experience long periods of indecision as they process the advantages and disadvantages of residing in the United States either temporarily or permanently, which affects not only career and personal goals but also their sense of identity (Mori, 2000).

International students struggle to maintain a balance between acculturation and maintaining their own culture, which can often be stressful and sometimes reaches a crisis level (Lin & Yi, 1997). Cultural differences can produce significant interpersonal conflicts for these students. For instance, many foreign cultures tend to place a higher value on teamwork or collectivity, whereas U.S. culture tends to emphasize individualism (Lin & Yi, 1997). Cultural differences, then, may contribute to international students' misunderstanding amicable or sociable exchanges made by their American cohorts, which can lead to disappointment when attempting to form significant relationships with Americans (Mori, 2000).

Individual coping styles and social networks play significant roles in the social support systems of international students, contributing to their well-being (Hayes & Lin, 1994). Thus, it becomes important for institutions of higher education to provide international students with adequate support in the areas of counseling and other support services.

Underutilization of Mental Health Services by International Students

Despite the fact that international students tend to experience more problems than other students while adjusting to their unique circumstances, mental health services have been significantly underused by this population (Mori, 2000). Part of this underutilization may be because international students are more comfortable seeking out informal support networks consisting of friends or family rather than from counseling professionals (Smith, Chin, Inman, & Findling, 1999). Moreover, when international students do seek help, it is usually from medical rather than psychological services. Furthermore, there may be a stigma associated with the need for formal counseling by international students, which may result in feelings of shame or fear of being a failure (Boyer & Sedlacek, 1989).

Higher Education Environments in Relation to International Students

From the perspective of institutions of higher learning, recognizing the fact that international students underutilize counseling services reinforces the need for creating ways of linking students with alternative forms of support. Student well-being is in large part a function of the effort, frequency, and quality of the interactions between the student and various systems within the campus environment (Heggins & Jackson, 2003). Thus, it is important to examine whether faculty and student cultures promote or discourage student engagement in activities that enhance personal development.

Providing international students with an understanding of the process of adjusting to a new culture can help ease uncertainty and provide a smoother transition to an unfamiliar environment. Various campus services, such as the counseling center, Office of International Student Affairs, and Office of Student Affairs, along with collaborative interactions with academic departments such as counselor education programs, can assist in cultural adjustment (Jacob, 2001). Involvement and collaboration by these services can provide international students an opening to available support networks on campus, which may be in the form of individual or group support.

Group Work

Why Group Work Can Help

Group work is an interpersonal intervention that counselors can use to help group members to solve problems and to enhance their functioning. By definition, group work involves forming separately functioning individuals into a common collective (usually a small group size of 3-12) to accomplish desired goals, such as gaining information or learning how to navigate life challenges. Goal attainment in group work is attempted through generating interpersonal interaction, connection, and challenge/support among members and by members converting what is learned in the group to intentional action outside it.

It is the creation of a supportive structure and process that can be so helpful to members. All students in higher education face adaptation and adjustment challenges. In fact, meshing with the higher education experience in a way that is satisfying and meaningful is a chief developmental issue. However, as you have read throughout the pages of this book, international students are bombarded with a litany of demands that can exceed by far what most other students face. Taking those demands on all by oneself can be overwhelming, especially for "strangers in a strange land." Becoming a group member can dissolve feelings of isolation while developing and strengthening bonds of connection. Depending on the type of group (see below), involvement in group work can become a means through which international student members can get the following:

- Needed information about functional basics (e.g., What bus do you take downtown? Where do we wash our clothes? Where do we go for assistance with immigration issues?)
- Help with interpersonal issues (e.g., How do I adjust to being so far from my home and family? How can I meet other people from my home country?)
- Help with academic issues (e.g., How do I talk with my professors? Where can I get assistance with my English?)
- Help with psychological and emotional issues (e.g., therapy for anxiety or depression).

Types of Group Work

Group work is a broad multicultural method for counselor usage, spanning task, psychoeducational, counseling, and psychotherapy applications (Association for Specialists in Group Work [ASGW], 2000; Conyne, Wilson, & Ward, 1997). In addition, see Yau (2004) for a description of some ways that groups can be used with international students. Four basic types of group work exist (ASGW, 2000) that are appropriate for international students:

301

- *Task groups* are organized to help members accomplish concrete goals and to produce products. International student organizations provide a good illustration of task groups that are established to foster identity and social opportunities. International student discussion groups also can be helpful. Relevant topics for group discussions may include American styles of interaction and communication, American values and culture, and differences in instructional style and expectations for classroom performance.

- *Psychoeducation groups* are aimed at helping members gain knowledge and skill that will enable them to function more effectively with others. These groups often have a preventive goal at the outset. For example, international students can learn some unique American cultural nuances involved with how to initiate a conversation, how to listen to others speak, or how to interview more proficiently for a job interview. The specific skill training, practice, and feedback of skills characteristic of psychoeducation groups, couched within the ongoing group process, can concretely help international students become more confident and competent in negotiating everyday demands of campus life in the United States. See Conyne and Wilson (1999) for an example of a psychoeducation group video for international students that is accompanied by a training manual.

- *Counseling groups* can help international students with understanding and learning improved ways to relate to others and to manage their thoughts and feelings. These are interpersonal problem-solving groups (Trotzer, 1999) intended for members who are experiencing perplexing but "normative" life challenges, such as feeling lonely, being anxious about taking tests, or lacking confidence to say hello to someone from another ethnicity. The opportunity to work with and relate to others in the group can often generate ideas and models for action that otherwise would not be available to the members. The interpersonal focus of counseling groups can mesh well with the collective orientation of many international students, providing a supportive environment for interpersonal connection and solving of life problems.

- *Psychotherapy groups* can be instrumental for international students when they experience deeper emotional or psychological disturbance than what might ordinarily be anticipated. Depression, acute or chronic anxiety, and unmanageable feelings represent forms of distress for which a psychotherapy group might be appropriate.

Attention to Multicultural, Multinational Phenomena

All group work is multicultural (Bemak & Conyne, 2004). Even a group comprised of all White graduate students in counseling is multicultural, because of a range of differences in such dimensions as age, life experience, religious/spiritual orientation, socioeconomic status, political orientation, ethnicity, and so on.

When considering international students, the issue of multiculturalism is extended further to include dimensions of race and nationality. Therefore, any discussion of group work with international students must directly consider this issue, which we explore in the next section.

Best Practices Ideas in Group Work With International Students

Several important documents exist to guide practice in the area of group work (Conyne, Tang, & Watson, 2001). The ASGW has established "Best Practice Guidelines" in group work (ASGW, 1998a; Rapin & Conyne, 1999), "Professional Standards for the Training of Group Workers" (ASGW, 2000), and "Principles for Diversity-Competent Group Workers" (ASGW, 1998b). In 2003, the American Counseling Association approved "Multicultural Counseling Competencies" (Sue, Arredondo, & McDavis, 1992). In combination, these documents provide guidance about group types and leader skills, as well as how to effectively and appropriately deliver group services, while giving particular attention to issues of diversity. All of these considerations are valuable in relation to group work with multicultural diversity (Conyne et al., 2001).

Unfortunately, there is no existing document that specifically addresses working with international students in groups. Therefore, we are left with extrapolating ideas for best practice in group work planning, performing, and processing as these important steps apply to international students.

In brief, the best practices in group work are the following:

- *Planning*, which involves all activities prior to the first session/meeting of the group, such as setting general goals, designing the group plan, advertising the group, recruiting and selecting members, and many other important factors.
- *Performing*, which involves all within-session leadership activities, such as providing leadership functions and roles, developing a positive working climate, and helping members to apply learning.
- *Processing*, which occurs both within sessions (e.g., helping members to make sense of events and experiences that just occurred) and between sessions (e.g., when the leaders reflect on the preceding session and extract valuable insights and suggestions for future direction).

Below we highlight some particular aspects of best practices in group work that seem especially salient for application with international students.

Planning Issues of Particular Salience

Group Formation

When forming groups for international students, one important consideration is whether to combine students from similar cultures/ethnicities or to include a variety of students from different cultures/ethnicities in a group. According to Yau (2004), placing just one member of a culturally distinct group within a larger group may hinder that person's ability to successfully identify with other group members, thus subjecting him or her to being stereotyped by others in the group. Although homogeneous groups are perceived as having less conflict because it is culturally more cohesive and better attended, and as providing more support than are multiethnic heterogeneous groups, there are concerns that homogeneous groups may be more superficial and less creative and productive (Yalom, 1985). However, even when groups appear to be homogeneous at first glance, it is important to keep in mind that people are unique in many ways (gender, age, marital status, family of origin, occupation, beliefs/values). Once group members are able to acknowledge the similarities and differences among themselves, progress toward group and individual goals can begin.

Awareness of Self as Leader

Before beginning a group, it is important for leaders to reflect on their own thoughts and feelings about people who are different from them in a cultural or other respect. This type of reflection allows a leader to constructively approach prejudices, biases, and racist elements of his or her own life that may inadvertently influence group members in a negative way if not sufficiently addressed beforehand. A good place for a potential group leader to begin is with his or her own family background, in which most people acquire knowledge about their culture and relationships with others (Yau, 2004).

Assessment of Acculturation and Adjustment

To be an effective group leader with people of diverse culture, one must first understand the meaning of culture. According to Corey and Corey (2002), culture encompasses the values, beliefs, and behaviors shared by a group of people. Second, group theory and technique must be applicable to various cultures in ways that honor the beliefs and behaviors of those cultures. Third, group theories and techniques must be developed in ways that acknowledge, explore, and use group member differences to facilitate change and growth (Yau, 2004). Finally, differentiation of self among international students has been shown to predict greater psychosocial maturity, fewer problem behaviors, and better problem-solving skills and psychological adjustment in a college setting (Skowron, Wester, & Azen, 2004).

Performing Issues of Particular Salience

Leader Directness

The role of group leader/counselor is multifaceted and may include roles such as expert, educator, problem solver, information giver, analyzer, as well as one who provides suggestions and initiates alternatives (Yau, 2004). For instance, in a psychoeducational group in which the leader is in the role of information giver, he or she may be more directive and be viewed as the "expert" by group members. This tends to be the preferred group leader role for many international group members, such as those of Asian descent (Conyne, Wilson, Tang, & Shi, 1999). In the counseling group, the roles of both group leader and member may be more ambiguous. With international students, it is generally beneficial for group leaders to provide structure, taking on a directive rather than passive role. Above all, it is essential for the group leader to create a nonthreatening and safe group environment to assist members in gaining a sense of acceptance and security. This can be done by the group leader modeling the dynamics of group process, such as sharing of experience and receiving feedback. However, group leaders must be patient and not expect group members to openly share their feelings and concerns quickly in a group setting.

Relationship Between "Group Values" and Those of Each Member's Culture

As indicated above, international students tend to prefer a hierarchical relationship between group leader and member. Thus, it is important for the group leader to maintain this hierarchy, at least for the first few group sessions. Once group members become familiar with the group process behaviors and with each other in the group, they will become more comfortable in moving from a hierarchical to an egalitarian relationship. It is important to keep in mind that international students respond differently to egalitarian relationships, which is largely influenced by their level of acculturation to Western group process (Yau, 2004).

Distinguishing Personal and Cultural Variables

It is the task of the group leader to use ideas generated in the group to discuss underlying cultural differences and similarities (Conyne, Wilson, & Tang, 2000). The acknowledgment of cultural differences may help to increase cohesion among group members. Of course, this subject must be addressed in a sensitive manner. Helping group members tolerate and respect differences among individuals of other cultures and finding different ways of intercultural understanding will help bring these issues from a covert to an overt level and reduce the likelihood of presumptions.

Processing Issues of Particular Salience

Level of Personalization and Depth Within Sessions

International students may find that many Americans' style of direct confrontation, verbal assertiveness, and interrupting of others is counter to their preferred mode of communication. Thus, group leaders must be tolerant of an indirect way of interpersonal communication and be careful not to confront international students with regard to sharing emotions or disclosing problems of a sensitive nature (Yau, 2004). This will prevent shame or loss of face for the international student, which tends to be of high importance.

Application of In-Group Learning to Outside World

It is important to understand the worldviews of international students. In addition, group leaders must strive to understand the within-group differences among these students. By recognizing these differences and the cultures from which they originated, group leaders can then design appropriate interventions or strategies for maximizing the desired outcomes for the group in relation to real-world circumstances.

Drawing Meaning

Processing is all about creating meaning from group events and experiences. Commentaries among international student group members represent a unique opportunity to identify how culture and individual differences intersect and influence group behaviors and their future application (Conyne, 1998). Drawing out this rich information is challenging and exciting work for group leaders, and it can be especially helpful for group members.

Group Work Strategies to Consider Using With International Students

Outreach and Recruitment

Recruitment of international students to participate in group counseling or support groups within a college campus environment can be challenging. It is important to keep in mind that international students typically enter counseling in less formal ways than U.S. students. Outreach represents a potentially useful avenue for international students. Some suggestions for outreach to this group are through various student organizations, such as an International Students Association. This mode of outreach will help to first establish and build friendships with international students, because these students usually feel more comfortable when they see the helping professional as someone who is trustworthy and credible in an informal setting (Yau, 2004).

It also may be facilitative to refer to the group counseling program as a "workshop" or "discussion group," as the term *counseling* is often unfamiliar to this population. International students are more likely to attend workshops to learn skills that will enhance their social and academic adjustment in the host culture than they are to attend group counseling. Another way to successfully recruit international students is to work closely with campus networks of resource people who are culturally sensitive to the needs of such students, such as faculty members, administrators, residence advisors, and campus police.

Pregroup Meetings

Pregroup meetings are useful to potential group members who are interested in (a) understanding the U.S. academic system, (b) learning classroom behaviors, and (c) learning study skills for success (Yau, 2004). Pregroup meetings provide the group leader(s) the opportunity to assess, select, screen, and prepare international students for group work, taking into consideration acculturation levels and within-group differences of the students. Furthermore, they allow group leaders to assess the appropriateness of a group for students or if a one-to-one session may better suit their needs. This also may be a time to discuss membership, structure, duration of the group, expectations of group members, and group processes.

First Group Meeting

Typically, the purpose of the first group meeting is for the group leader to discuss the purpose of the group, the topics of discussion, techniques to be used, and group rules and confidentiality. This kind of orientation to persons, purpose, and methods is especially useful for international students, for whom group appreciation may be particularly unfamiliar. Therefore, it is useful to begin with an "icebreaker" activity to give the international students an opportunity to get to know each other and ease jitters or anxiety about the group. Personal introductions also are appropriate at this time, beginning with the leader, who serves as a model. Group and individual goals also should be discussed at this time to assist with orientation to the purpose and tasks of the group.

Group Structure and Process

Generally, a group of 3–12 students is optimal for effective group work. For international students, a maximum number of 10 group members helps to decrease inherent complexities that may arise. The format of the group should be both psychoeducational and process oriented, with the goal being to allow international students to share their problems in classroom settings and to receive support from the group members' problem-solving strategies. As mentioned earlier, group members expect the group leader to act as an expert or authority, especially at the beginning, and then gradually ease into a more collaborative culture over time.

Summary

The structure of group work with international students occupies a kind of "foreign" territory in existing professional literature. Few principles exist and research is scarce in this area. Furthermore, only limited examples of international student group work have been offered. This chapter extrapolated from existing group work and multicultural literature to connect with international student issues on U.S. campuses.

There remains much to be tried, much to be learned, and much potential surrounding international student group work. The general collective orientation of many international student cultures matches very well with the interpersonal and interdependent focus of group work. In sum, we hope the ideas and strategies suggested will encourage further development, application, and research in the area of group work with international students.

References

Association for Specialists in Group Work. (1998a). *Best practice guidelines.* Retrieved June 5, 2006, from http://www.asgw.org/best.htm

Association for Specialists in Group Work (1998b). *Principles for diversity-competent group workers.* Retrieved June 5, 2006, from http://www.asgw.org/diversity.htm

Association for Specialists in Group Work. (2000). *Professional standards for the training of group workers.* Retrieved June 5, 2006, from http://www.asgw.org/training_standards.htm

Bemak, F., & Conyne, R. (2004). Ecological group work. In R. Conyne & E. Cook (Eds.), *Ecological counseling: An innovative approach to conceptualizing person-environment interaction.* Alexandria, VA: American Counseling Association.

Boyer, S. P., & Sedlacek, W. E. (1989). Noncognitive predictors of counseling center use by international students. *Journal of Counseling & Development, 67,* 404-407.

Conyne, R. (1998). What to look for in groups: Helping trainees become more sensitive to multicultural influences. *Journal for Specialists in Group Work, 23,* 22-32.

Conyne, R., Tang, M., & Watson, A. (2001). Exploring diversity in therapeutic groups. In E. Welfel & R. E. Ingeysoll (Eds.), *The mental health desk reference* (pp. 358-364). New York: Wiley.

Conyne, R., & Wilson, F. R. (1999). *Psychoeducational group demonstration: A career development group for international students* [Video]. Alexandria, VA: Association for Specialists in Group Work, Insight Media, & Microtraining Associates.

Conyne, R., Wilson, F. R., & Tang, M. (2000). Evolving lessons from group work in China. *Journal for Specialists in Group Work, 25,* 252-268.

Conyne, R., Wilson, F. R., Tang, M., & Shi, K. (1999). Cultural similarities and differences in group work: Pilot study of a U.S.-Chinese task group comparison. *Group Dynamics: Theory, Research, and Practice, 3,* 40-50.

Conyne, R., Wilson, F. R., & Ward, D. (1997). *Comprehensive group work: What it means and how to teach it.* Alexandria, VA: American Counseling Association.

Corey, M., & Corey, G. (2002). *Groups: Process and practice* (6th ed.). Pacific Grove, CA: Brooks/Cole.

Hayes, R. L., & Lin, H. (1994). Coming to America: Developing social support systems for international students. *Journal of Multicultural Counseling and Development, 22,* 7-17.

Heggins, W. J., & Jackson, J. F. (2003). Understanding the collegiate experience for Asian international students at a midwestern research university. *College Student Journal, 37,* 379-392.

Institute of International Education. (2005). *U.S. sees slowing decline in international student enrollment in 2004/05.* Retrieved June 5, 2006, from http://opendoors.iienetwork.org

Jacob, E. J. (2001). Using counselor training and collaborative programming strategies in working with international students. *Journal of Multicultural Counseling and Development, 29,* 73-89.

Komiya, N., & Eells, G. T. (2001). Predictors of attitudes toward seeking counseling among international students. *Journal of College Counseling, 4,* 153-161.

Lacina, J. G. (2002). Preparing international students for a successful social experience in higher education. *New Directions for Higher Education, 117,* 21-27.

Lin, J. G., & Yi, J. K. (1997). Asian international students' adjustment: Issues and program suggestions. *College Student Journal, 31,* 473-480.

Mori, S. (2000). Addressing the mental health concerns of international students. *Journal of Counseling & Development, 78,* 137-145.

Rapin, L., & Conyne, R. (1999). Best practices in group counseling. In J. Trotzer (Ed.), *The counselor and the group: Integrating theory, training and practice* (pp. 253-276). Philadelphia: Taylor & Francis.

Skowron, E. A., Wester, S. R., & Azen, R. (2004). Differentiation of self mediates college stress and adjustment. *Journal of Counseling & Development, 82,* 69-78.

Smith, T. B., Chin, L. C., Inman, A. G., & Findling, J. H. (1999). An outreach support group for international students. *Journal of College Counseling, 2,* 188-190.

Sue, D. W., Arredondo, P., & McDavis, R. (1992). Multicultural counseling competencies: A call to the profession. *Journal of Counseling & Development, 70,* 477-486.

Trotzer, J. (1999). *The counselor and the group: Integrating theory, training, and practice* (3rd ed.). Philadelphia: Accelerated Development.

Yalom, I. (1985). *The theory and practice of group psychotherapy.* New York: Basic Books.

Yau, T. Y. (2004). Guidelines for facilitating groups with international college students. In J. Delucia-Waack, D. Gerrity, C. Kalodner, & M. Riva (Eds.), *Handbook of group counseling and psychotherapy* (pp. 253-264). Thousand Oaks, CA: Sage.

Chapter 18

Programs and Outreach for International Students

Mary Beth Engel, Gina Insalaco,
Hemla D. Singaravelu, and Kristi Kennon

International students arrive in the United States with educational aspirations and settle at colleges and universities across the nation. Along with the many positive experiences that these international students encounter, they may also experience anxiety, fear, adjustment issues, culture shock, social isolation, and loneliness (Lin, 2000). To reduce these stressors, universities in the United States have developed several successful programs, activities, and outreach services. These programs and services range from peer mentoring programs and nationality clubs to support for international spouses and their families. This chapter provides an overview of some of the successful programs that have been created for international students.

It must be noted that while we were conducting our research of various programs offered in universities across the United States, the constant message conveyed by most university officials was that their services have been downsized. This is due largely to the fact that they are learning and managing a new online database called Student and Exchange Visitor Information System (SEVIS). As discussed briefly in chapter 1, SEVIS is a networked computer system set up to track information on nonimmigrant international students and scholars attending educational institutions, such as universities, laboratories, nonprofit organizations, and secondary schools during their stay in the United States.

Mentoring Programs

Friendship and mentoring programs have been the most widely used and most successful programs created for international students. Mentors may be a source of information, a friend, or an advisor and are very helpful to new university students, whether they are freshman, transfers, or minority students. Purdue University offers a program called Flagship, which is an international friendship program that pairs international students with members of the lay community. Since its inception in 1995, Flagship has been very meaningful to students in terms of one-on-one support and levels of exchange with the community of Lafayette, Indiana (M. Brzezinski, personal communication, January 30, 2004).

The University of Wisconsin–Madison offers an International Friendship Program called BRIDGE (http://www.intstudents.wisc.edu/bridge/). BRIDGE was created as a peer mentoring program to help international students collaborate with students in the United States to gain support in their new surroundings. Peer mentors exemplify a commitment to one-on-one friendship by meeting with their partners 10 times throughout the year. These "new friends" act as valuable resources to international students, orienting them to a new language and a new culture.

The University of Wisconsin–Madison also connects international students to a community organization called Madison Friends of International Students (MFIS). MFIS relies on volunteers from the Madison area to create a variety of useful programs that accommodate the personal and social needs of the international student community. Providing a broad range of services, MFIS locates temporary housing, selects English conversation partners, and provides furniture and coat loans to those international students who are in need of assistance (Madison Friends of International Students, 2004).

The University of Texas at Austin offers another interesting peer mentoring program. Partnerships to Advance Language Study and Cultural Exchange (PALS) was founded in 1993 to bring together international students and American students "for the purpose of cultural exchange and to practice English conversation skills" (University of Texas at Austin, International Office, 2004). The matched pairs meet an hour per week throughout the semester to socialize in activities and conversation. Similar to other universities, PALS was created and developed "in response to a need repeatedly expressed by incoming international students for a medium to meet American students and to improve their English conversation skills."

Having such a wide range of outreach programs readily accessible to the international community can help reduce some of the initial stressors that these international students may encounter. Research findings suggest that good English conversation skills, a system of social support, and several contacts within the United States lead to more satisfaction in international students' study experiences in the country (Leong, 1984). The programs previously described support these research findings and provide models for universities throughout the United States to enhance the experiences of international students.

English as a Second Language (ESL)

In addition to facing social and cultural concerns, international students also have academic concerns that include understanding and comprehending grading systems, how to select course work, writing and speaking in English, and adjusting to the American classroom climate (Lin, 2000). Universities across the United States offer programs in support of helping international students make English their second language. As mentioned before, programs and social conversation hours facilitate international students' comfort in speaking the native language. Many universities also provide ESL classes to assist with any language barriers that these students may face.

One unique program offered by the University of Southern California (USC; 2006) is called the American Language Institute (ALI; http://www.usc.edu/dept/LAS/ALI/links.html). ALI was founded at USC in 1959 and bears the distinction of being one of the first programs to recognize that international students needed some sort of formal English instruction in order to complete their studies. ALI provides students with specific instruction based on their placement on the International Student English Examination, which was uniquely constructed at USC. Some students participate in ALI based on referral, recommendation, or requirement; others may participate for elective purposes to improve their skills.

Family Support

Other services and outreach that have become increasingly successful in involving the international student community are family support programs. Ohio State University sponsors international programs for men and women that offer support in English conversation and language classes. These programs are run mainly by volunteers, and there is no fee for those families who are interested in attending. This university also provides an online informational packet of materials on medical care and insurance for families, safety, child-care programs, schools, adult education on language, computer, business, childbirth, entertainment, recreation, shopping, household maintenance, and working in the United States (Office of International Education, 2002).

The University of Maryland offers a group program run by the advisors of the Office of International Education Services and the spouses of the international students who attend the University of Maryland. The International Spouses Organization (ISO) holds many social events such as potlucks and informational meetings to help the international community adjust to their new surroundings (University of Maryland International Programs, 2006).

Online Resources

Some international students may rely on the Internet as a primary resource when they enter into their new university. The Internet provides these students with a safe and secure way to access any information they need to help them adjust to their new surroundings. Many helpful handbooks and guides are posted on university Web pages to assist their international community. The Office of International Programs at the University of Pennsylvania offers the *International Student and Scholar Handbook: Coping With a New Culture* (http://www.upenn.edu/oip/iss/handbook/coping.html). This handbook offers phone numbers for services such as counseling and peer support. Frequently asked questions about campus life and getting involved in the local community are also addressed.

The Office for International Students and Scholars (OISS) Web site at New York University (http://www.nyu.edu/osl/oiss/index.html) provides international students with virtually all of the information they need in one convenient place. A variety of topics are addressed and include information about what to pack in a carry-on bag, how to complete essential tax forms, and what popular American slang expressions mean. A well-organized, comprehensive Web site such as this can be one of the most effective and efficient resources available for international students.

Career

Along with the resources provided on the Internet for peer and counseling support, international students also experience issues related to career decisions. These students come to the United States focusing on one career goal, yet upon arrival may feel the need to change majors to fit their abilities and interests (Singaravelu, White, & Bringaze, 2005). This change in career choice may become a problem if it fails to fulfill parental, government, or corporate expectations (Singaravelu et al., 2005).

To sort through career uncertainty, the University of Wisconsin–Madison offers a handbook titled *Career Planning for International Students* (2004). The handbook addresses many questions that international students may have about possible career opportunities after they finish their education at a particular university, such as career planning, résumé building, and working while in the United States. Furthermore, the Office of International Students and Scholars at many universities offers extensive information on their Web pages regarding regulations and employment overviews for J-1 students, visa and travel information, and practical training after graduation (e.g., http://www.hio.harvard.edu for Harvard University; http://www.slu.edu/centers/international for Saint Louis University; http://www.indiana.edu/~intlserv/Content/Students/Welcome/ for Indiana University Bloomington).

Counseling and Special Topics

Other online resources address sensitive topics such as answers to questions about counseling, cross-cultural adjustment, and sexual orientation issues for international students. Many international students tend to perceive counseling as an ineffective way to solve their personal problems. Discussing personal issues with strangers is often not an option because of certain cultural constraints (Hayes & Lin, 1994). In light of these cultural differences, common concerns, difficulties, and stressors that international students may encounter are addressed in online publications such as that on the University of Illinois at Urbana–Champaign Web site (http://www.couns.uiuc.edu/InternationalStudents/StudentConcerns.htm).

New York University's OISS Web site also provides information about the importance of developing a support network (http://www.nyu.edu/osl/oiss/beyond/cultural/develop.html). This Web site answers questions that international students may have about counseling. The following are some questions that may be asked: Why is counseling culturally acceptable in the United States? What counseling resources are available? Why should an international student see a counselor if he or she had a problem instead of seeking family or peers?

In terms of specific personal issues that international students may encounter (e.g., struggling with sexual identity), New York University provides a unique online resource titled *A Guide to Sexual Orientation for International Students* (http://www.nyu.edu/osl/oiss/beyond/life/dating/orientation.html). This resource provides facts and answers to questions about sexual orientation and gender identity in the United States. Some common questions that are asked include the following: What does "gay" mean? Will I have immigration problems because I am a gay or lesbian foreign student? Why do LGBT (lesbian, gay, bisexual, transgender) issues get so much attention in the U.S.? Can I get political asylum in the United States because I am gay or lesbian? With the help of New York University's Office of Lesbian, Gay, Bisexual, and Transgender Student Services, the international students in this community have access to answers that they may be seeking about sexual orientation and the United States.

Extracurricular Activities

Most universities provide a large range of international student organizations to accommodate a variety of cultures and nations. These clubs and organizations offer a unique support system to the international student population; students may seek out conationals with similar backgrounds and native languages. For example, the University of Michigan hosts several organizations, including the Arab Student Association, the Bangladesh Cultural Society, the Hindu Students Council, the Malaysian Students Association, and the Scandinavian Forum (http://www.umich.edu/~icenter/). Information about these clubs and other organizations are readily accessible online on university Web sites across the United States. Many universities also observe yearly cultural activities for the on-campus and off-campus communities. These events are typically sponsored by the international student office, student organizations, and other campus support services.

There are several more activities and services offered to international students that are not documented in this chapter. It would be advisable for a reader searching for programs for their international student population to conduct an online search of programs or services offered at different universities across the United States.

International students at universities across the United States have been given great opportunities to excel in their studies. Programs and outreach exist to facilitate a deeper understanding of American collegiate culture within international students. Not only do programs and outreach services encourage these students to overcome cross-cultural and language barriers, they also alleviate some of the stress that students may be feeling about entering into a new country. Finally, the aforementioned programs serve as a critical link, connecting international students to valuable academic, social, and government resources they will need to complete their studies in the United States.

References

Career planning for international students. (2004). Madison: University of Wisconsin. Retrieved August 31, 2006. from http://www.intstudents.wisc.edu/subcat1.asp?subcat_id=328

Hayes, R., & Lin, H. (1994). Coming to America: Developing support systems for international students. *Journal of Multicultural Counseling and Development, 22,* 7-16.

Leong, F. (1984). *Counseling international students: Resources in high interest areas.* Ann Arbor, MI: ERIC Clearinghouse Counseling and Personnel Services. (ERIC Document Reproduction Service No. ED 250 649)

Lin, J. (2000). College counseling and international students. In D. Davis & K. Humphrey (Eds.), *College counseling: Issues and strategies for a new millennium* (pp. 169-183). Alexandria, VA: American Counseling Association.

Madison Friends of International Students. (2004). *About us and our programs.* Madison: University of Wisconsin. Retrieved August, 31, 2006, from http://www.intstudents.wisc.edu/mfis

Office of International Education. (2002). *Information for international students.* Columbus: Ohio State University. Retrieved August 30, 2006, from http://www.oie.osu.edu/internationalstudents/lifeinus

Singaravelu, H., White, L., & Bringaze, T. (2005). Factors influencing international students' career choice: A comparative study. *Journal of Career Development, 32,* 46-59.

University of Maryland International Programs. (2006). *International spouses organization.* Retrieved August 31, 2006, from http://www.international.umd.edu/oip/330

University of Southern California. (2006). *Office of international services.* Retrieved August 30, 2006, http://www.usc.edu/dept/LAS/ALI/links.html

University of Texas at Austin, International Office. (2004). *PALS: Partnerships to Advance Language Study & Cultural Exchange.* Retrieved August 30, 2006, from http://studentorgs.utexas.edu/iopals/

Index

Tables are indicated by "t" following the page number.